FTB

THE RECORD OF A

FALLEN VAMPIRE

For the publication of the final volume, many revisions were incorporated and a special episode was added. Getting it all ready was hectic indeed! Anyway, here it is—the conclusion of the tale.

–Yuri Kimura

Artist Yuri Kimura debuted two short stories in Japan's *Gangan Powered* after winning the Enix Manga Award. Shortly thereafter, she began *The Record of a Fallen Vampire*, which was serialized in Japan's *Monthly Shonen Gangan* through March 2007.

Author Kyo Shirodaira is from Nara prefecture. In addition to *The Record of a Fallen Vampire*, Shirodaira has scripted the manga *Spiral: The Bonds of Reasoning*. Shirodaira's novel *Meitantei ni Hana wo* was nominated for the 8th Annual Ayukawa Tetsuya Award in 1997.

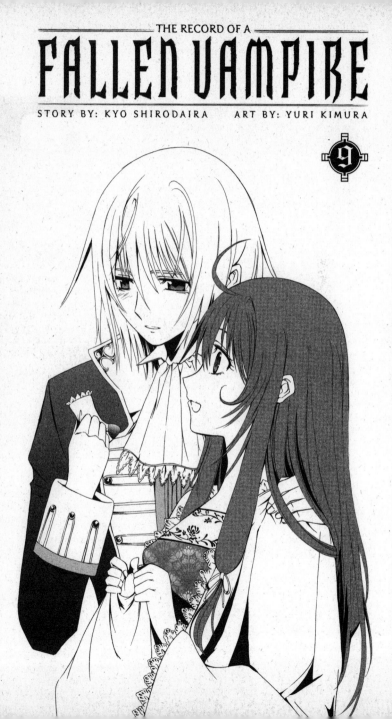

THE RECORD OF A

FALLEN VAMPIRE

STORY BY: KYO SHIRODAIRA ART BY: YURI KIMURA

9

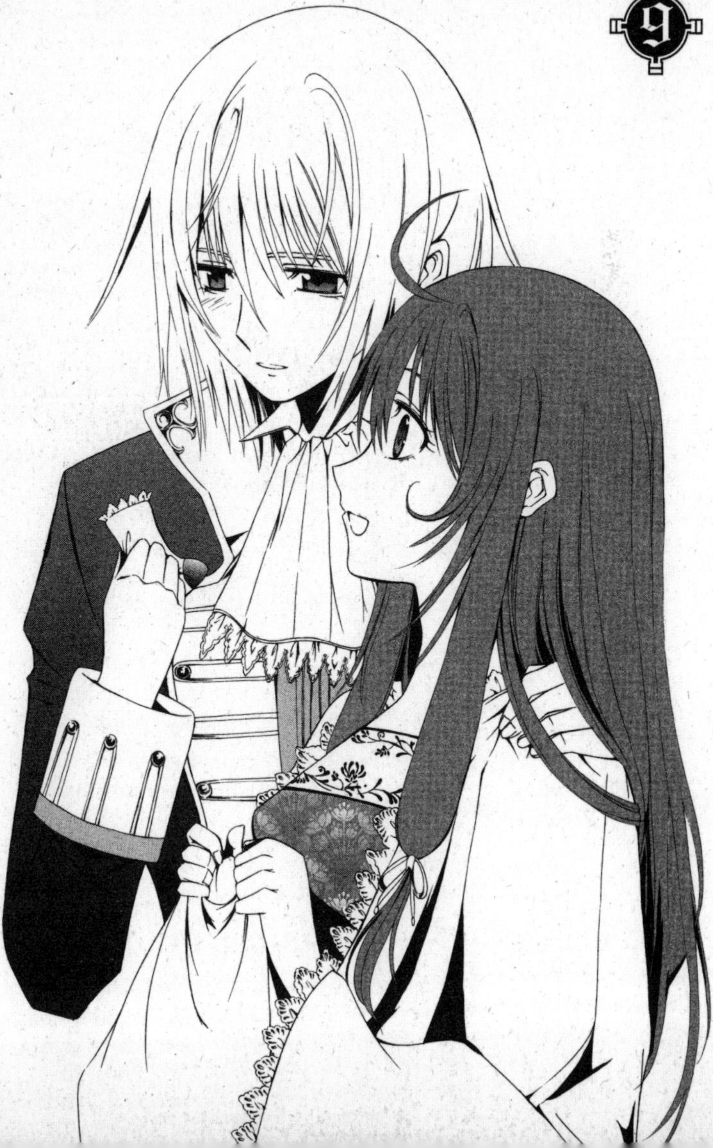

ONTENTS

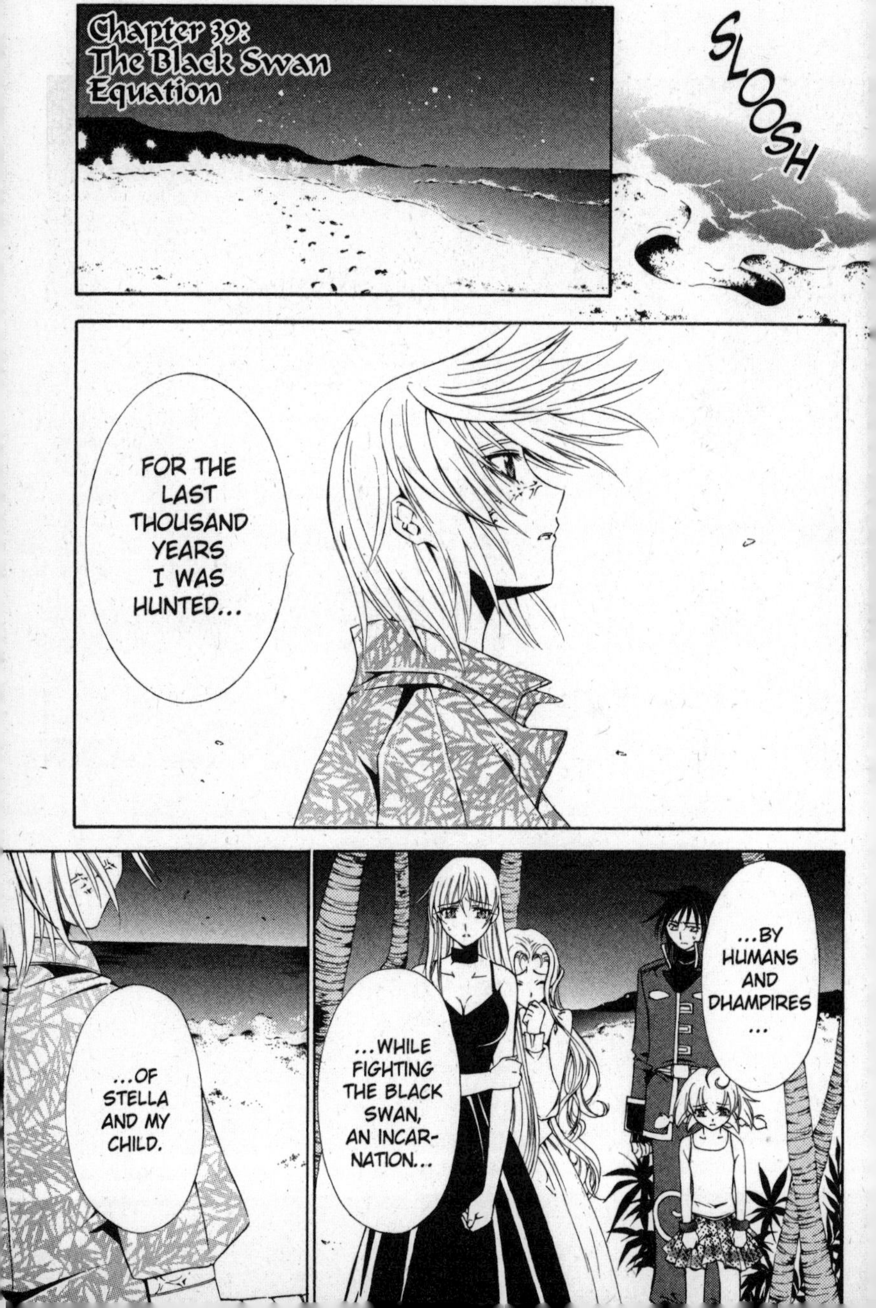
Chapter 39: The Black Swan Equation
SLOOSH
FOR THE LAST THOUSAND YEARS I WAS HUNTED...
...BY HUMANS AND DHAMPIRES...
...WHILE FIGHTING THE BLACK SWAN, AN INCARNATION...
...OF STELLA AND MY CHILD.

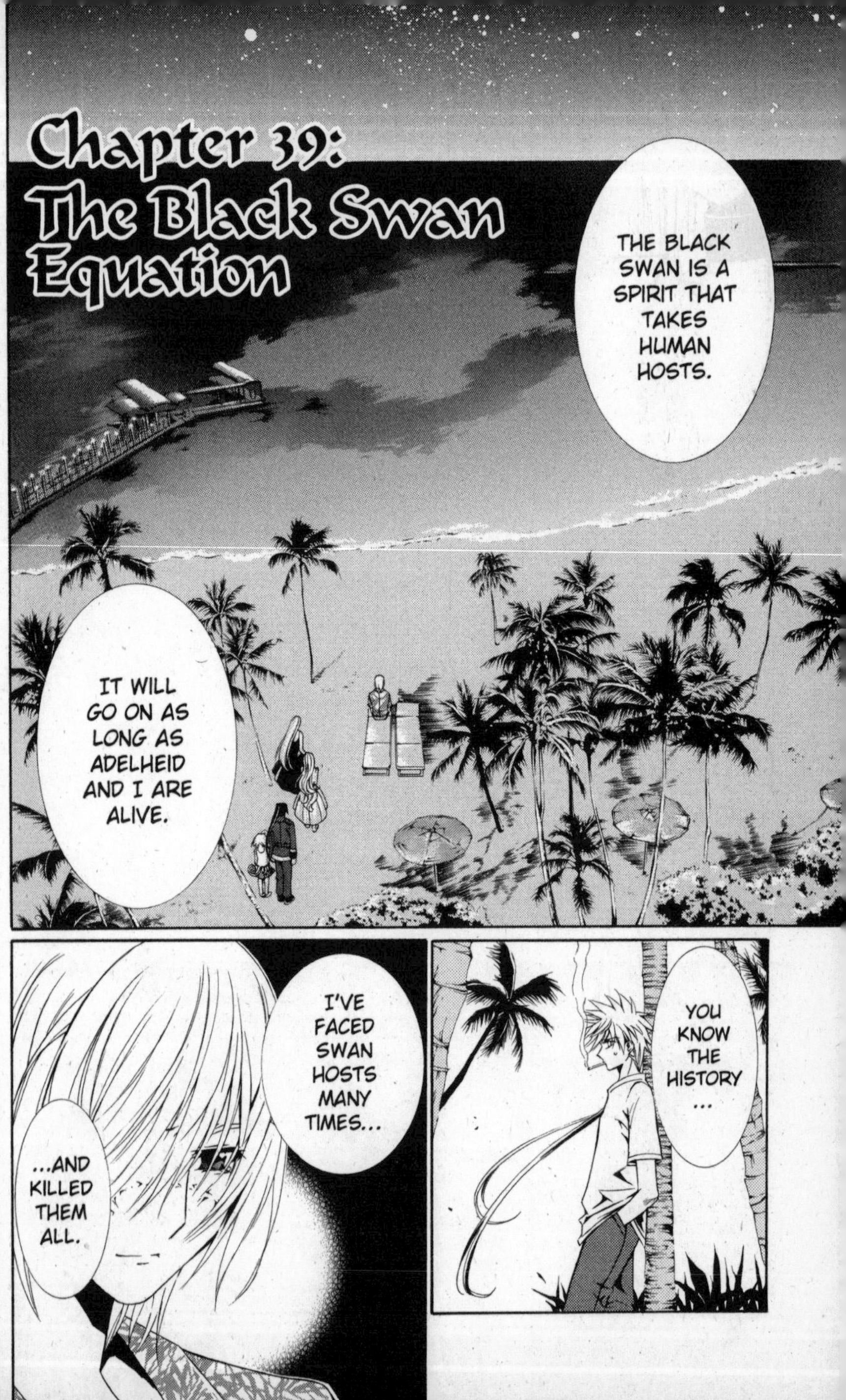
Chapter 39: The Black Swan Equation
THE BLACK SWAN IS A SPIRIT THAT TAKES HUMAN HOSTS.
IT WILL GO ON AS LONG AS ADELHEID AND I ARE ALIVE.
YOU KNOW THE HISTORY...
I'VE FACED SWAN HOSTS MANY TIMES...
...AND KILLED THEM ALL.

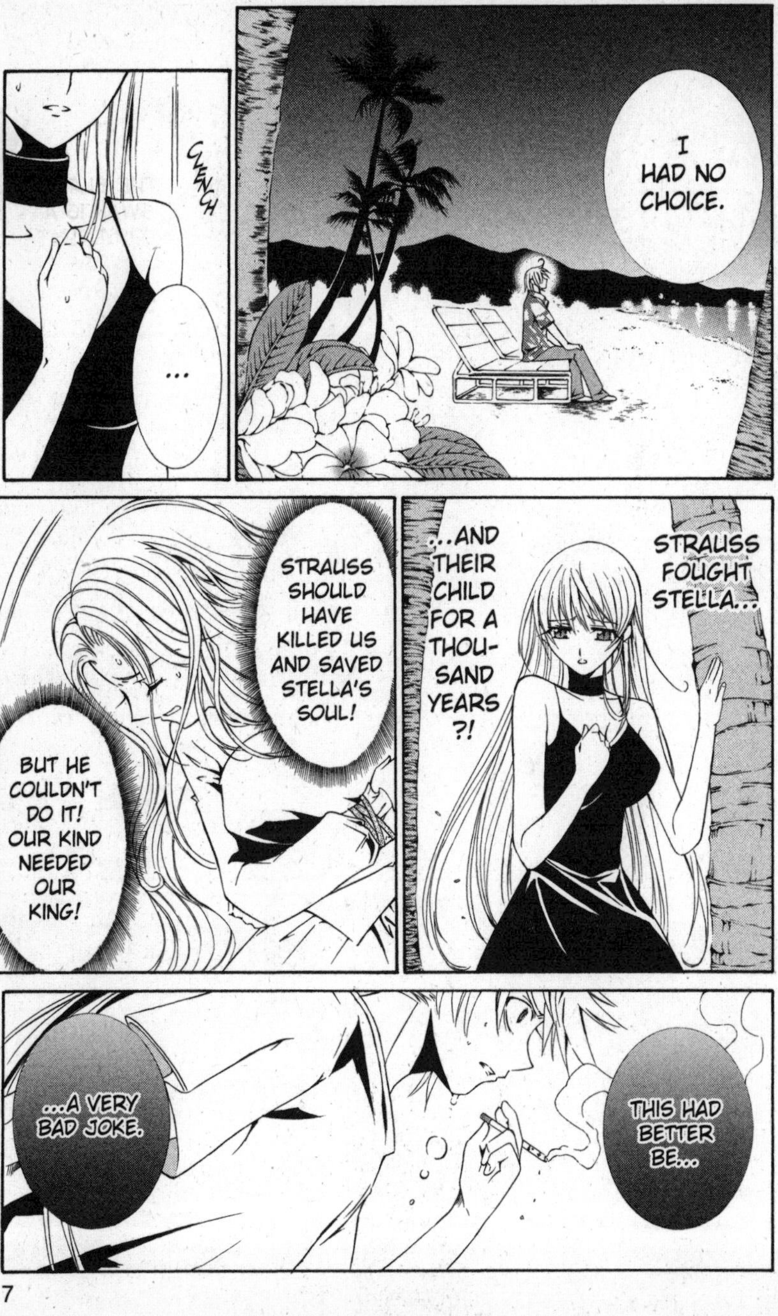
I HAD NO CHOICE.
CLENCH
...
STRAUSS FOUGHT STELLA...
...AND THEIR CHILD FOR A THOU-SAND YEARS?!
STRAUSS SHOULD HAVE KILLED US AND SAVED STELLA'S SOUL!
BUT HE COULDN'T DO IT! OUR KIND NEEDED OUR KING!
THIS HAD BETTER BE...
...A VERY BAD JOKE.

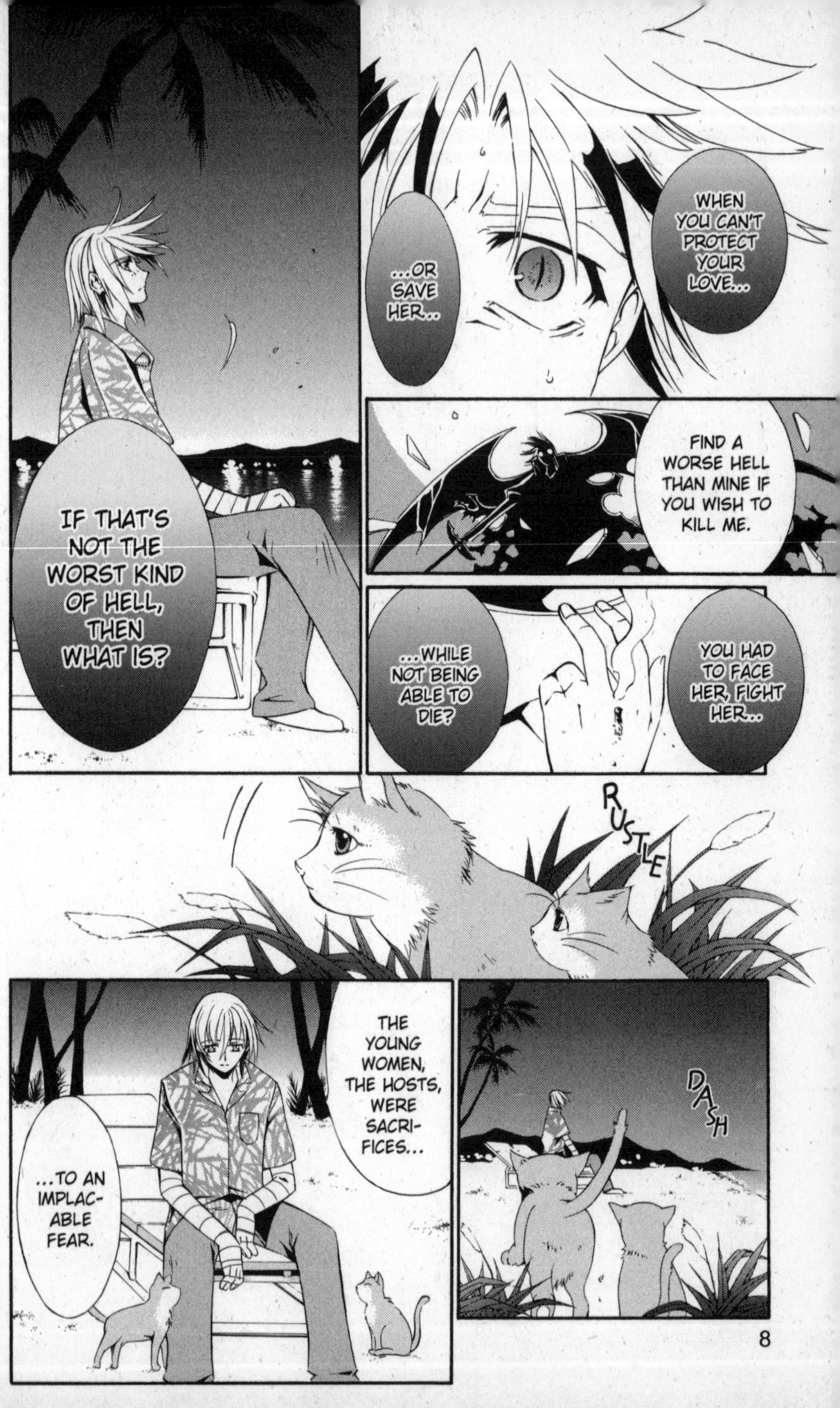
WHEN YOU CAN'T PROTECT YOUR LOVE...
...OR SAVE HER...
FIND A WORSE HELL THAN MINE IF YOU WISH TO KILL ME.
YOU HAD TO FACE HER, FIGHT HER...
...WHILE NOT BEING ABLE TO DIE?
IF THAT'S NOT THE WORST KIND OF HELL, THEN WHAT IS?
RUSTLE
DASH
THE YOUNG WOMEN, THE HOSTS, WERE SACRIFICES...
...TO AN IMPLACABLE FEAR.

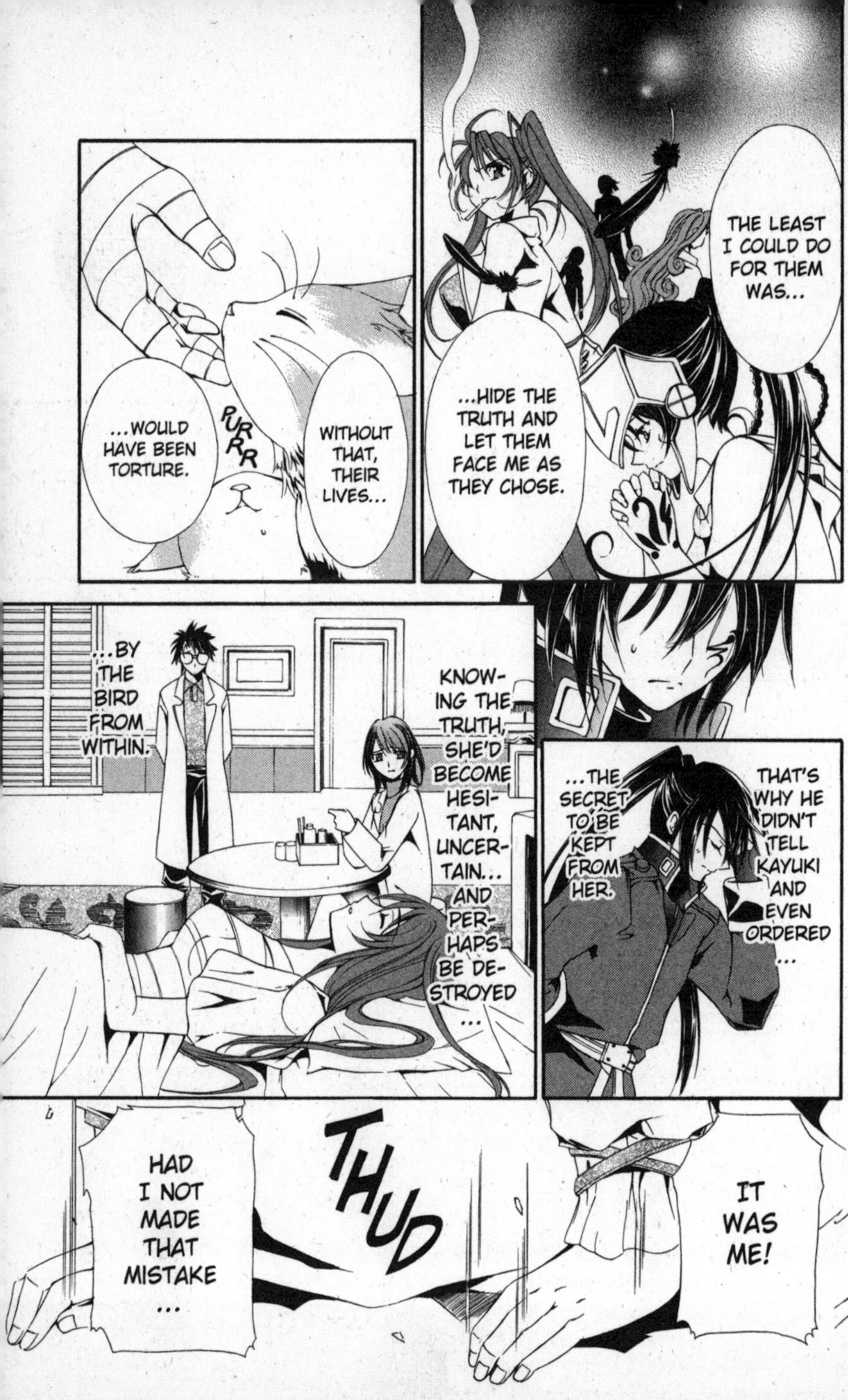
THE LEAST I COULD DO FOR THEM WAS...
...HIDE THE TRUTH AND LET THEM FACE ME AS THEY CHOSE.
WITHOUT THAT, THEIR LIVES...
PURR
...WOULD HAVE BEEN TORTURE.
THAT'S WHY HE DIDN'T TELL KAYUKI AND EVEN ORDERED...
...THE SECRET TO BE KEPT FROM HER.
KNOWING THE TRUTH, SHE'D BECOME HESITANT, UNCERTAIN... AND PERHAPS BE DESTROYED...
...BY THE BIRD FROM WITHIN.
IT WAS ME!
THUD
HAD I NOT MADE THAT MISTAKE...

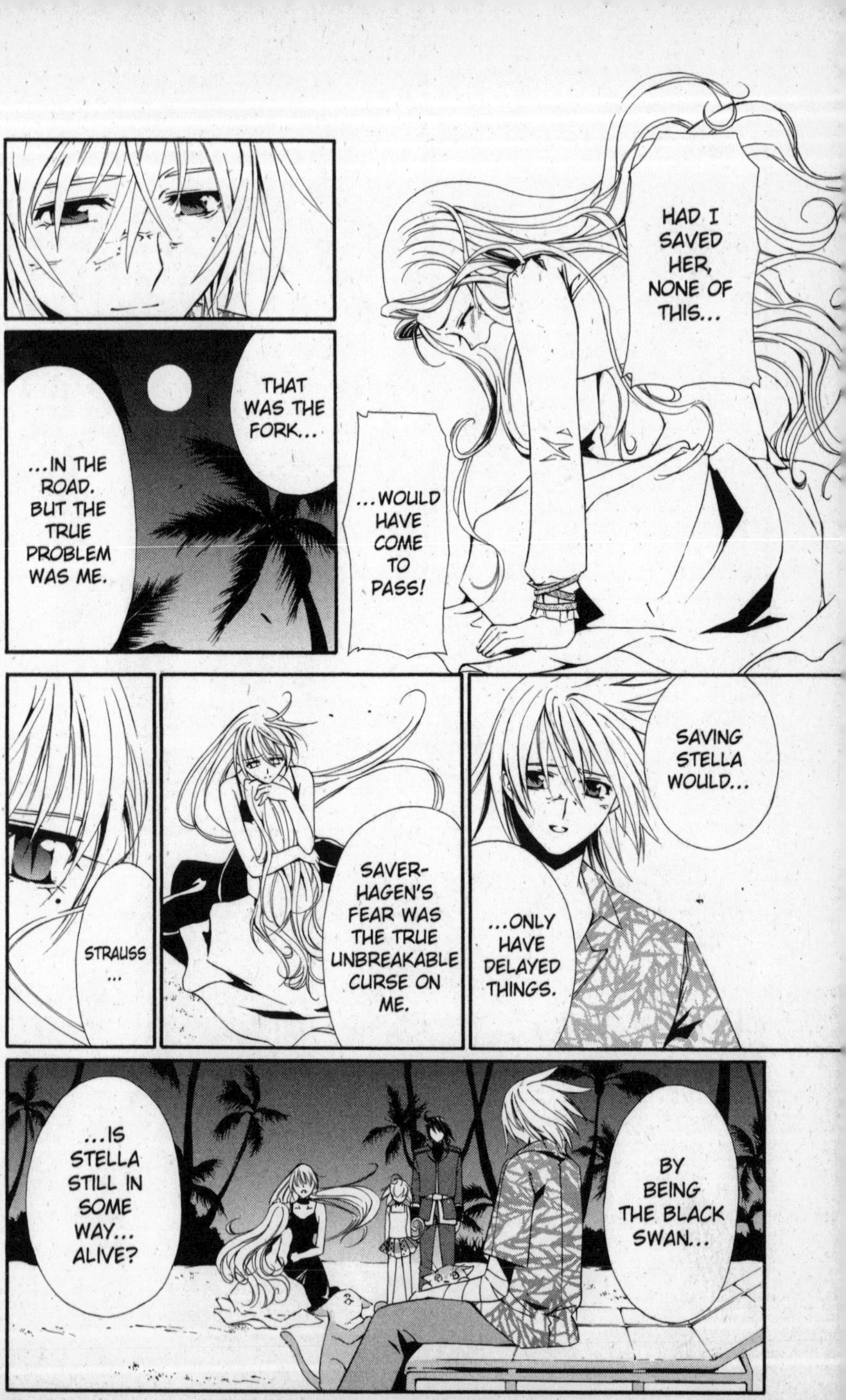
HAD I SAVED HER, NONE OF THIS...
...WOULD HAVE COME TO PASS!
THAT WAS THE FORK...
...IN THE ROAD. BUT THE TRUE PROBLEM WAS ME.
SAVING STELLA WOULD...
...ONLY HAVE DELAYED THINGS.
SAVER-HAGEN'S FEAR WAS THE TRUE UNBREAKABLE CURSE ON ME.
STRAUSS ...
BY BEING THE BLACK SWAN...
...IS STELLA STILL IN SOME WAY... ALIVE?

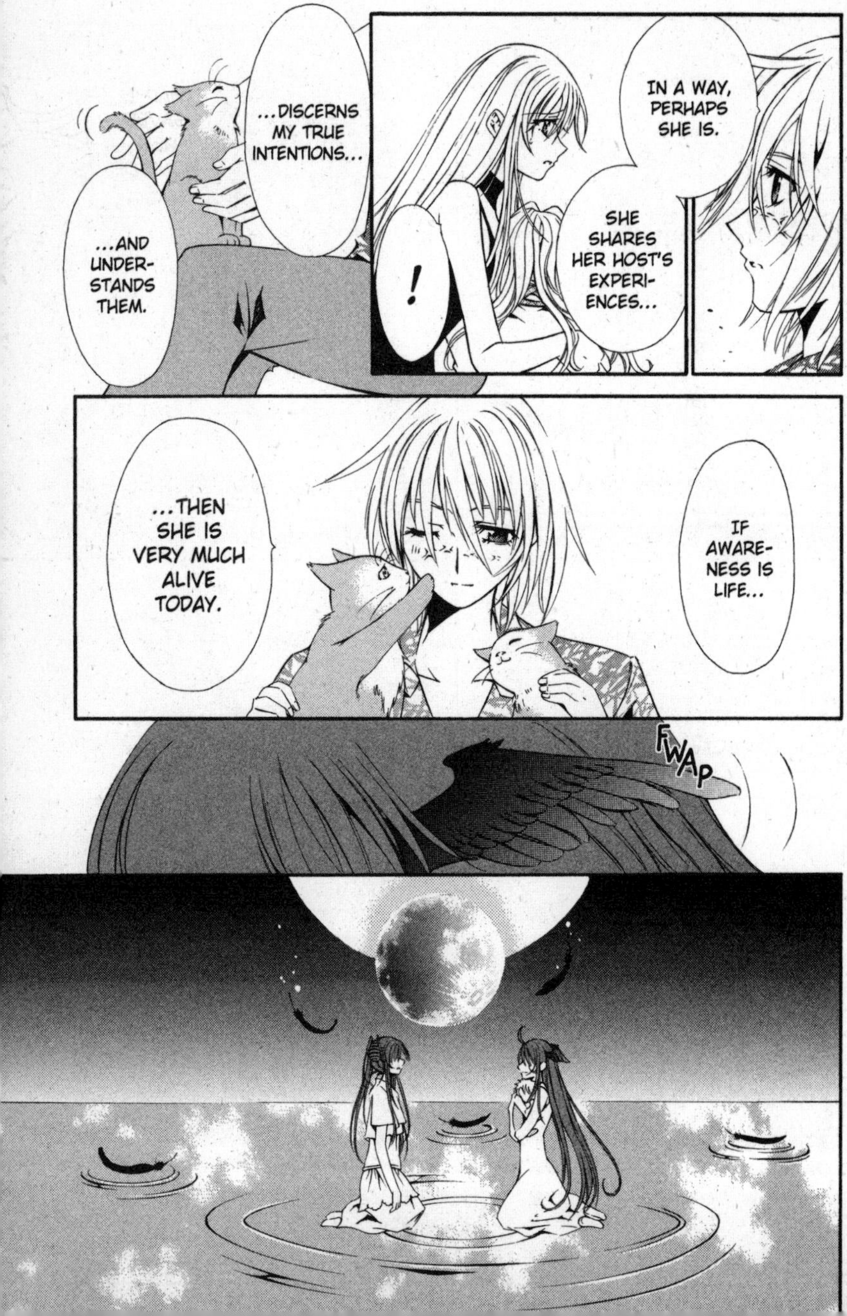
IN A WAY, PERHAPS SHE IS.
SHE SHARES HER HOST'S EXPERI- ENCES...
!
...DISCERNS MY TRUE INTENTIONS...
...AND UNDER- STANDS THEM.
IF AWARE- NESS IS LIFE...
...THEN SHE IS VERY MUCH ALIVE TODAY.
FWAP

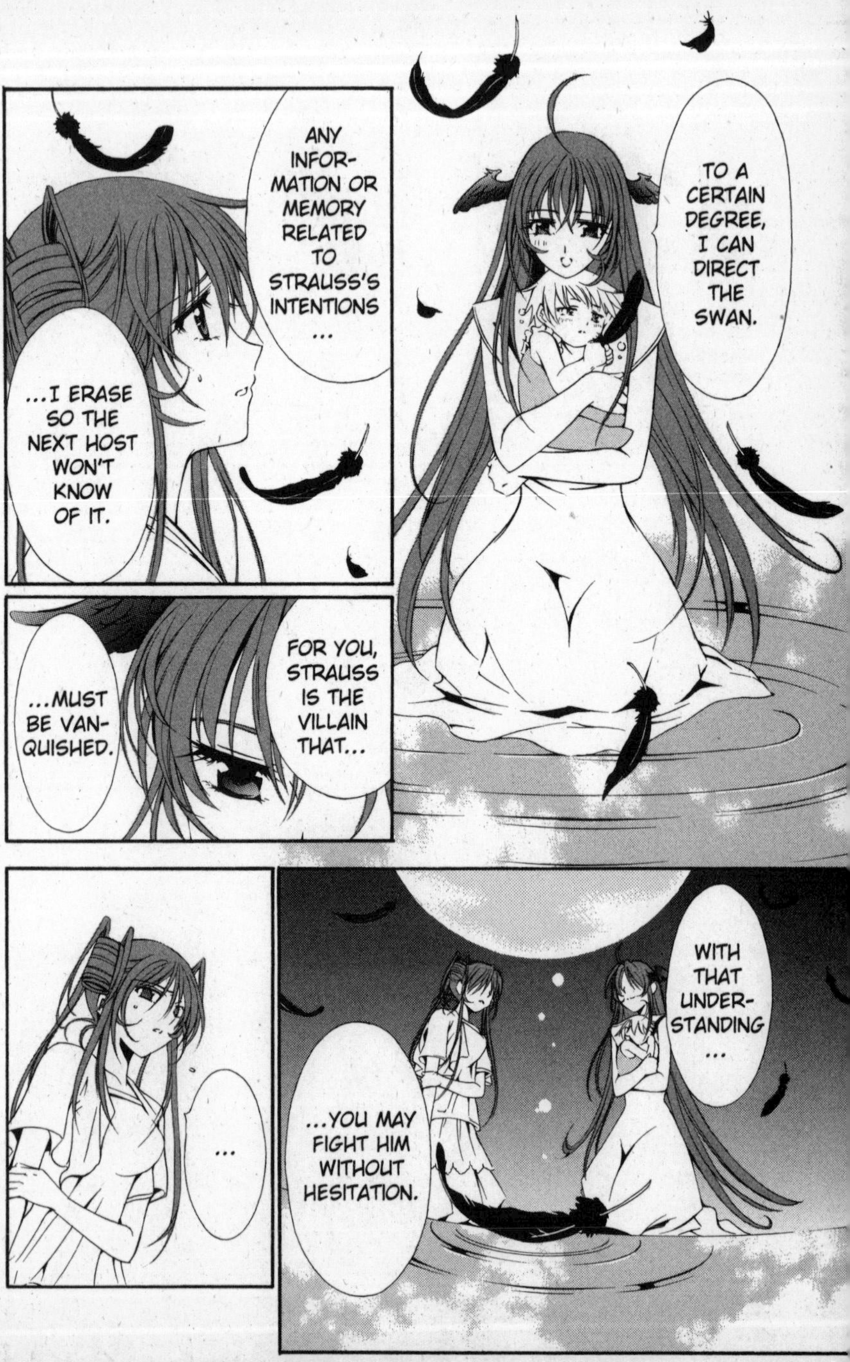
TO A CERTAIN DEGREE, I CAN DIRECT THE SWAN.
ANY INFORMATION OR MEMORY RELATED TO STRAUSS'S INTENTIONS...
...I ERASE SO THE NEXT HOST WON'T KNOW OF IT.
FOR YOU, STRAUSS IS THE VILLAIN THAT...
...MUST BE VANQUISHED.
WITH THAT UNDERSTANDING...
...YOU MAY FIGHT HIM WITHOUT HESITATION.
...

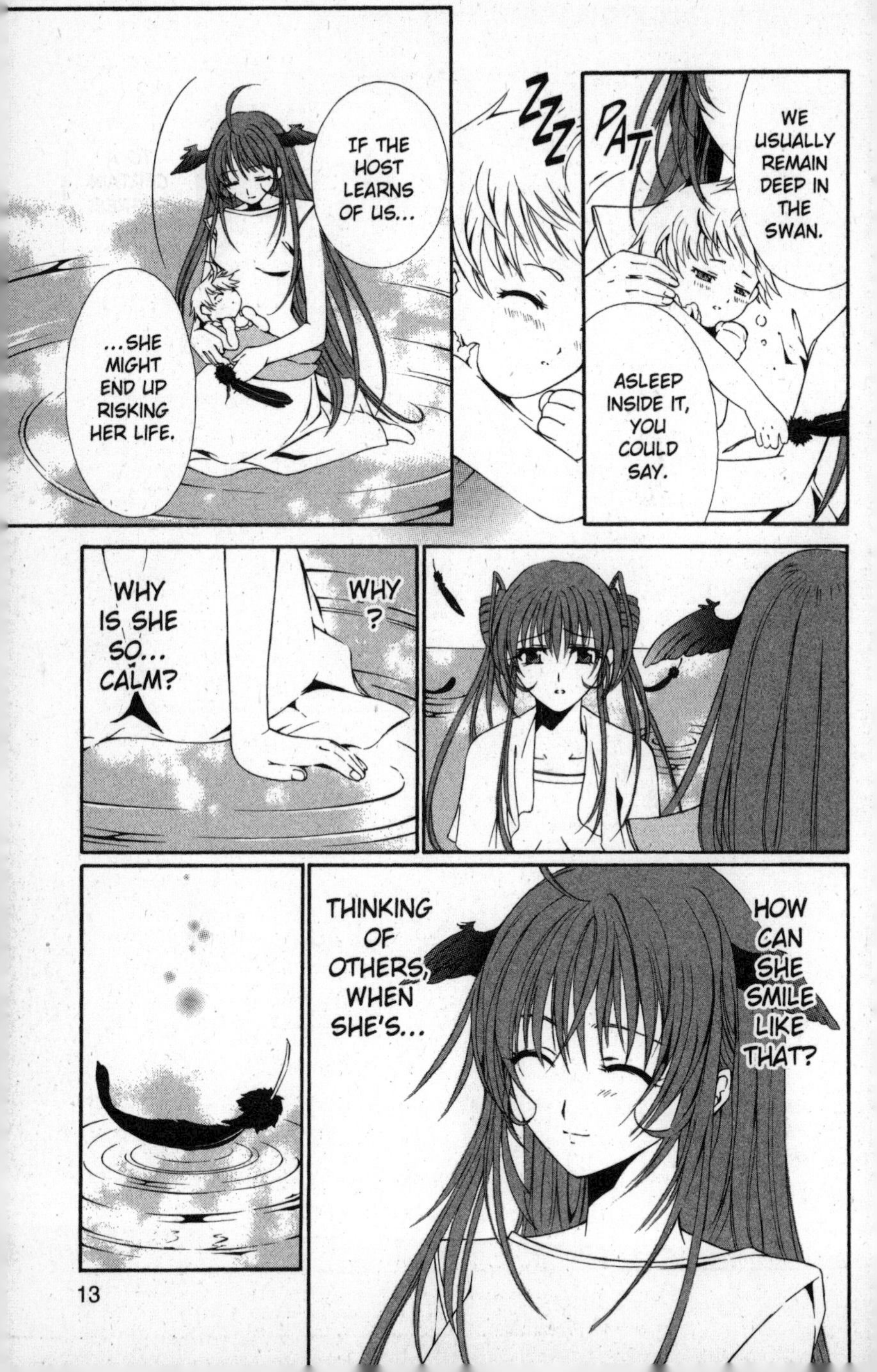
WE USUALLY REMAIN DEEP IN THE SWAN.
ZZZ
PAT
ASLEEP INSIDE IT, YOU COULD SAY.
IF THE HOST LEARNS OF US...
...SHE MIGHT END UP RISKING HER LIFE.
WHY?
WHY IS SHE SO... CALM?
HOW CAN SHE SMILE LIKE THAT?
THINKING OF OTHERS, WHEN SHE'S...

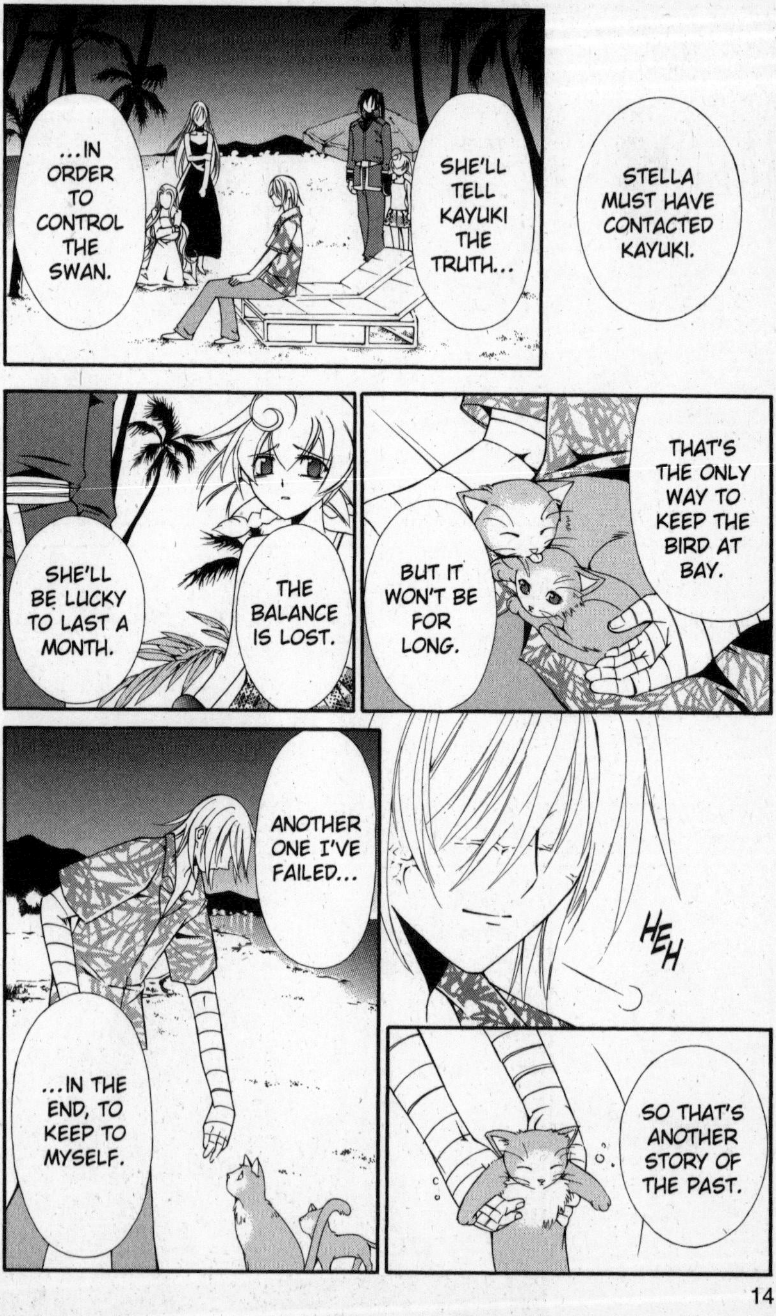
STELLA MUST HAVE CONTACTED KAYUKI.
SHE'LL TELL KAYUKI THE TRUTH...
...IN ORDER TO CONTROL THE SWAN.
THAT'S THE ONLY WAY TO KEEP THE BIRD AT BAY.
BUT IT WON'T BE FOR LONG.
THE BALANCE IS LOST.
SHE'LL BE LUCKY TO LAST A MONTH.
HEH
SO THAT'S ANOTHER STORY OF THE PAST.
ANOTHER ONE I'VE FAILED...
...IN THE END, TO KEEP TO MYSELF.

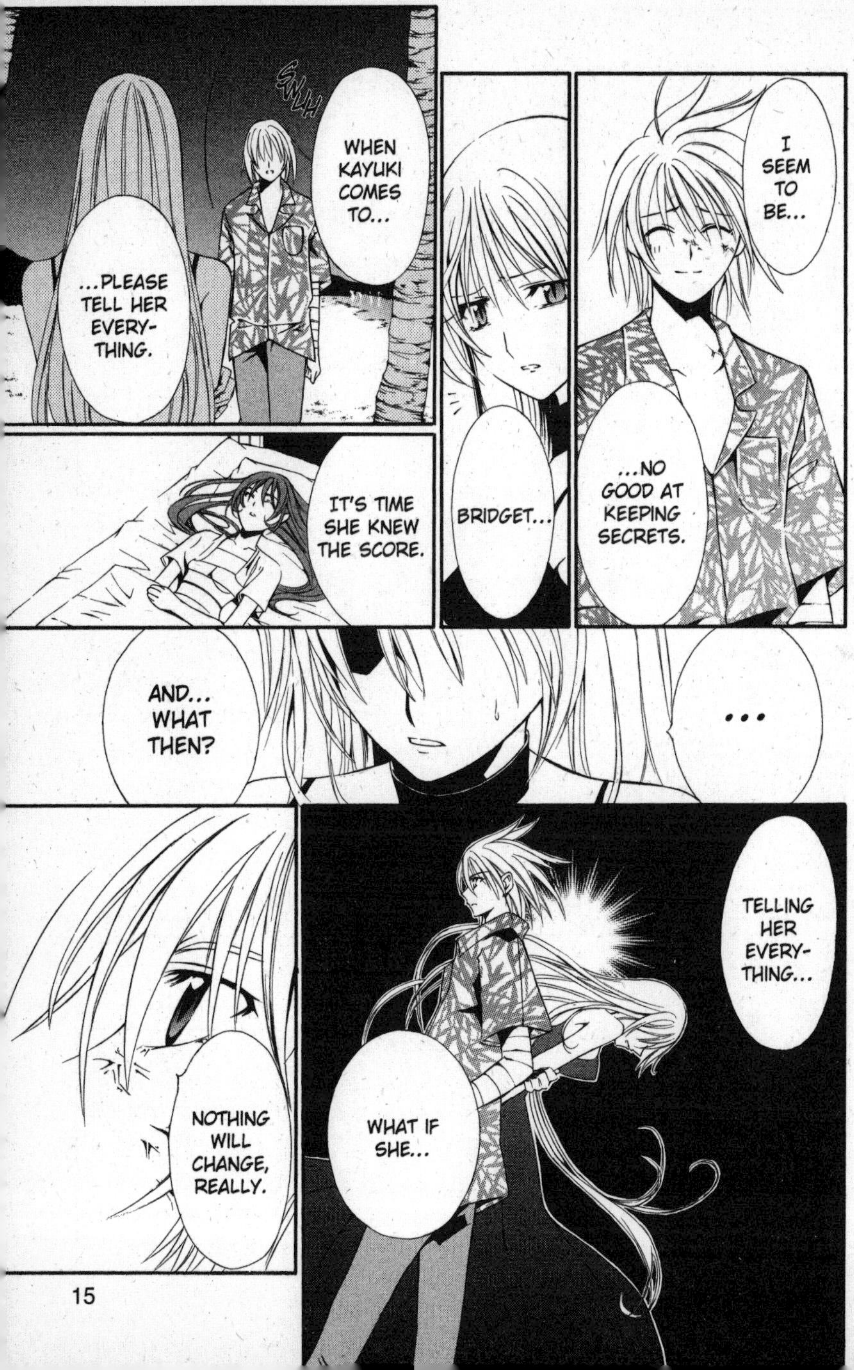
I SEEM TO BE...
...NO GOOD AT KEEPING SECRETS.
BRIDGET...
SWUH
WHEN KAYUKI COMES TO...
...PLEASE TELL HER EVERY-THING.
IT'S TIME SHE KNEW THE SCORE.
...
AND... WHAT THEN?
TELLING HER EVERY-THING...
WHAT IF SHE...
NOTHING WILL CHANGE, REALLY.

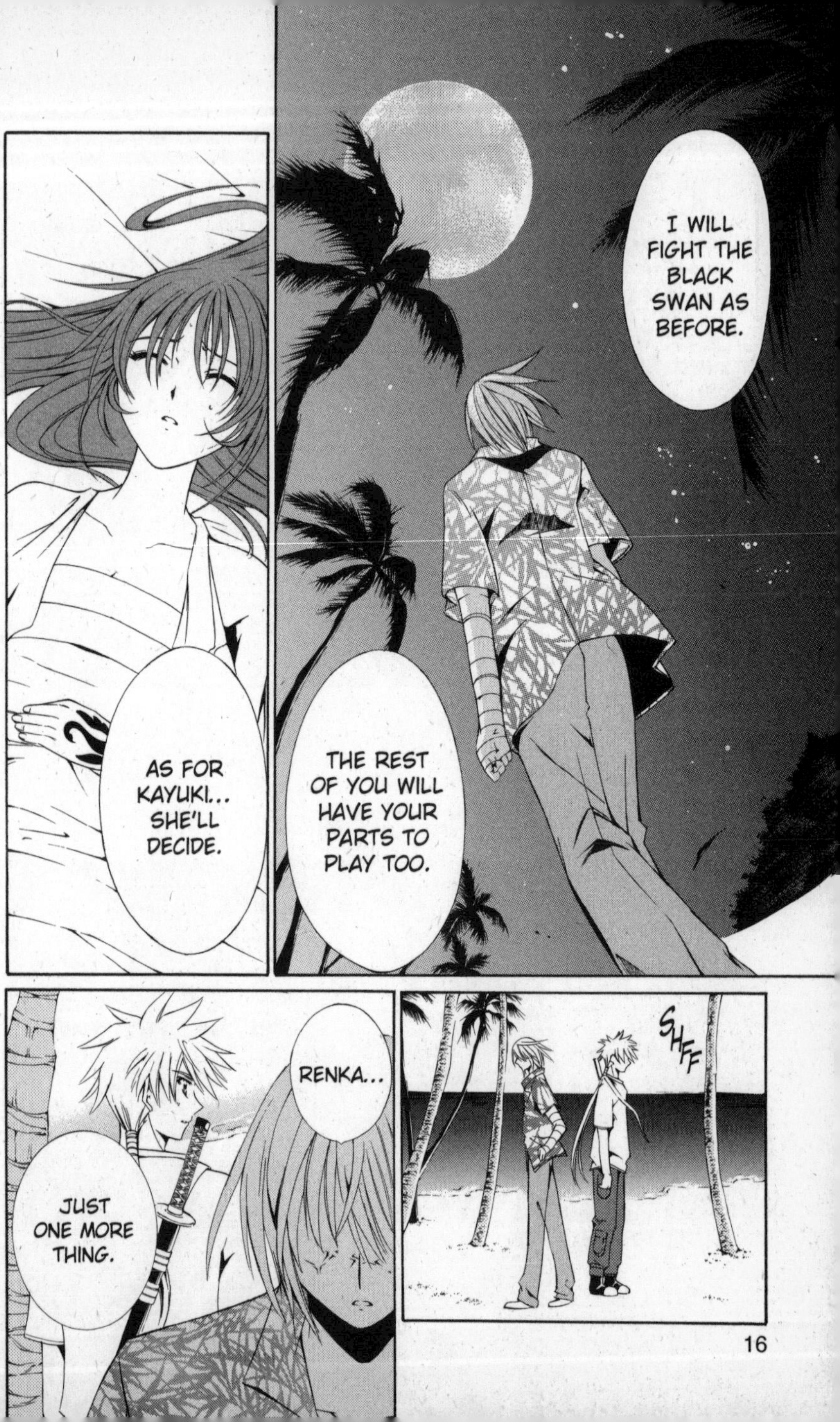
I WILL FIGHT THE BLACK SWAN AS BEFORE.
THE REST OF YOU WILL HAVE YOUR PARTS TO PLAY TOO.
AS FOR KAYUKI... SHE'LL DECIDE.
SHFF
RENKA...
JUST ONE MORE THING.

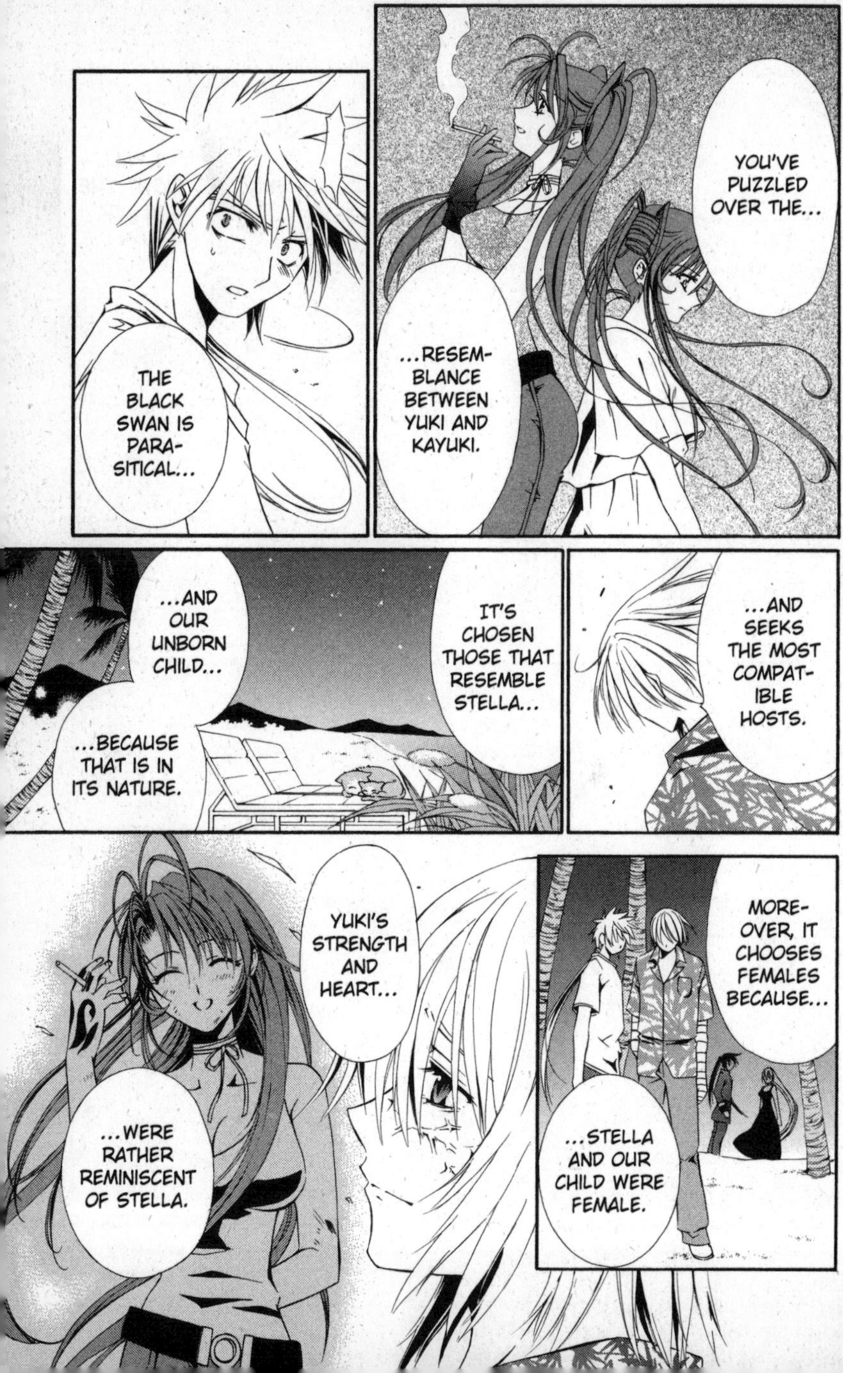
YOU'VE PUZZLED OVER THE...
...RESEMBLANCE BETWEEN YUKI AND KAYUKI.
THE BLACK SWAN IS PARASITICAL...
...AND SEEKS THE MOST COMPATIBLE HOSTS.
IT'S CHOSEN THOSE THAT RESEMBLE STELLA...
...AND OUR UNBORN CHILD...
...BECAUSE THAT IS IN ITS NATURE.
MOREOVER, IT CHOOSES FEMALES BECAUSE...
...STELLA AND OUR CHILD WERE FEMALE.
YUKI'S STRENGTH AND HEART...
...WERE RATHER REMINISCENT OF STELLA.

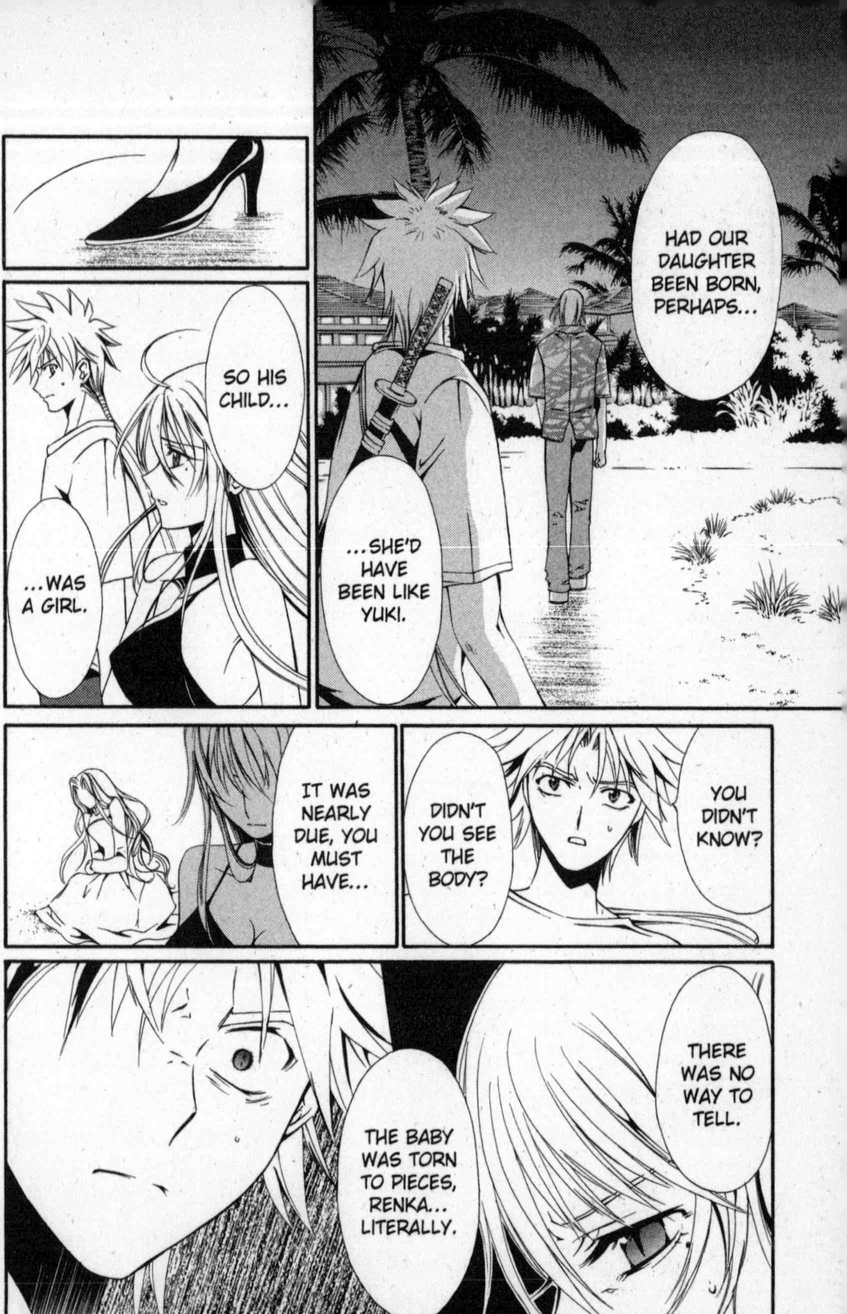
HAD OUR DAUGHTER BEEN BORN, PERHAPS...
...SHE'D HAVE BEEN LIKE YUKI.
SO HIS CHILD...
...WAS A GIRL.
YOU DIDN'T KNOW?
DIDN'T YOU SEE THE BODY?
IT WAS NEARLY DUE, YOU MUST HAVE...
THERE WAS NO WAY TO TELL.
THE BABY WAS TORN TO PIECES, RENKA... LITERALLY.

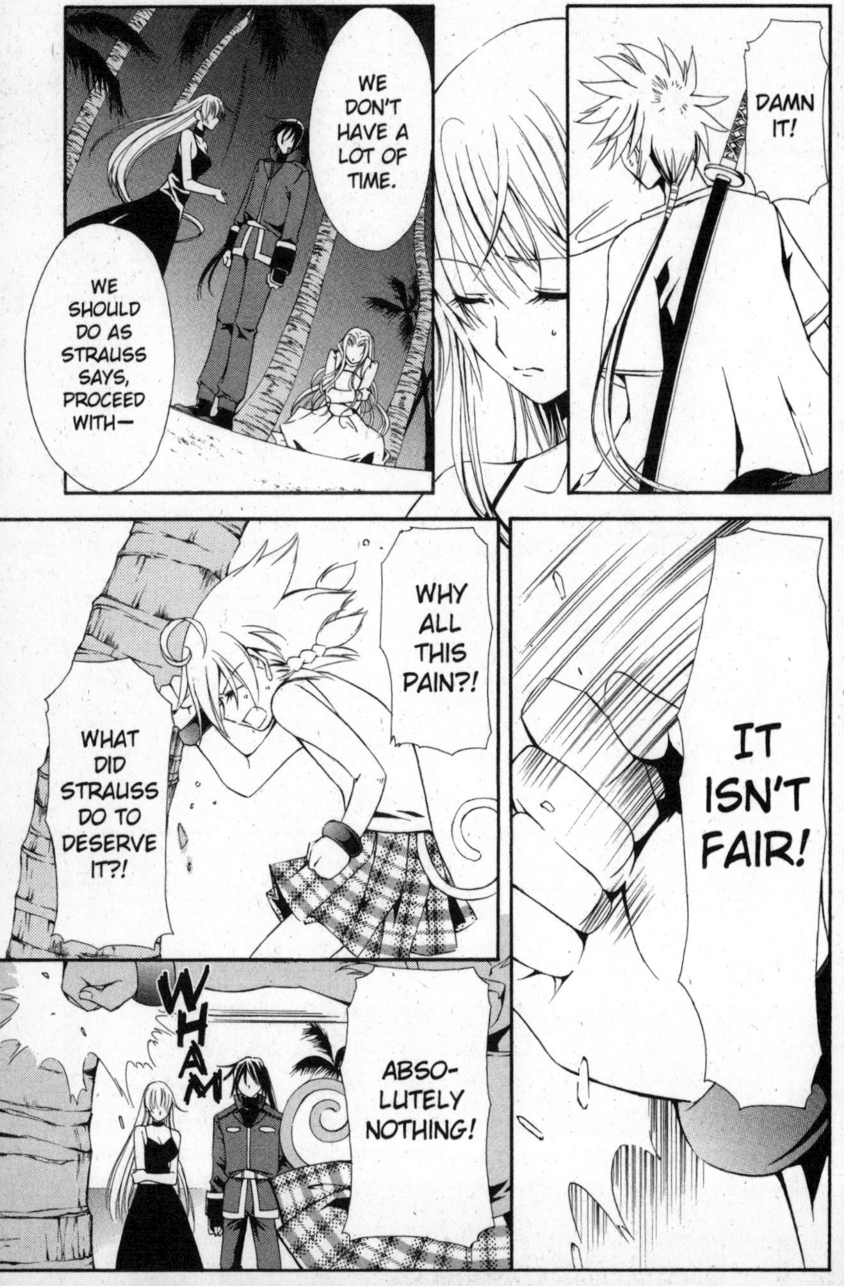
DAMN IT!
WE DON'T HAVE A LOT OF TIME.
WE SHOULD DO AS STRAUSS SAYS, PROCEED WITH—
IT ISN'T FAIR!
WHY ALL THIS PAIN?!
WHAT DID STRAUSS DO TO DESERVE IT?!
ABSO-LUTELY NOTHING!
WHAM

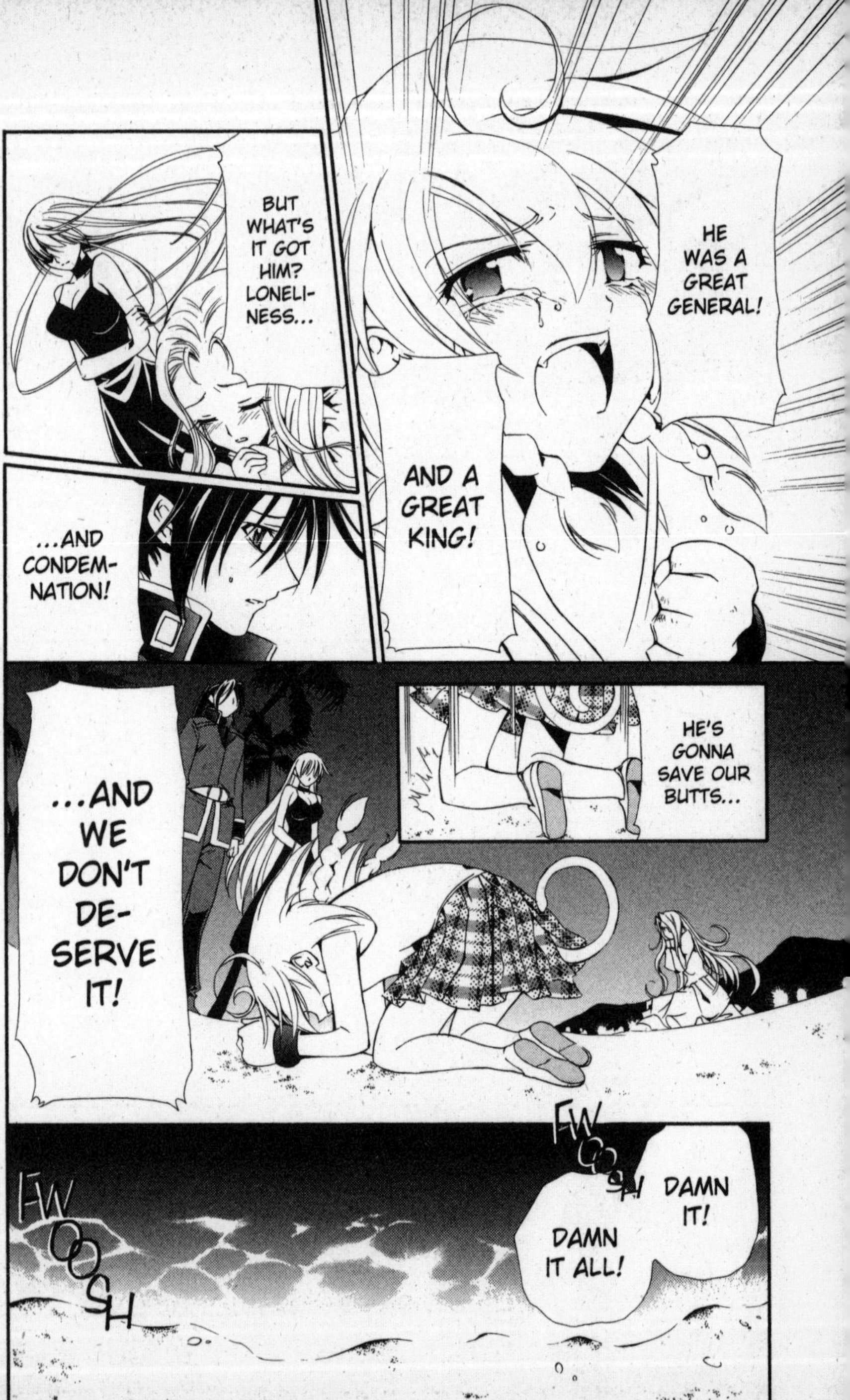
HE WAS A GREAT GENERAL!
AND A GREAT KING!
BUT WHAT'S IT GOT HIM? LONELI-NESS...
...AND CONDEM-NATION!
HE'S GONNA SAVE OUR BUTTS...
...AND WE DON'T DE-SERVE IT!
FWOOSH
DAMN IT!
DAMN IT ALL!
FWOOSH

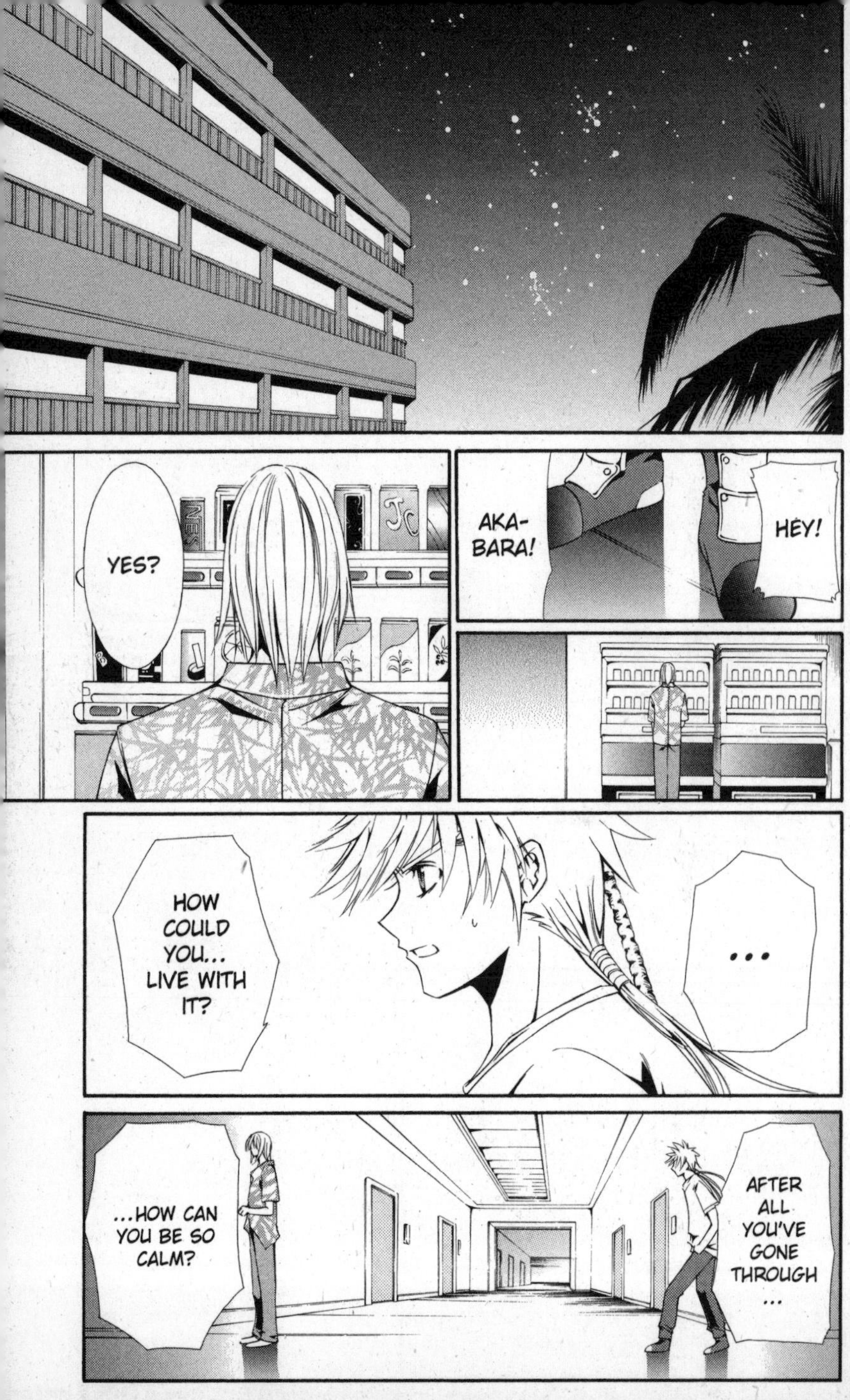
HEY!
AKA-BARA!
YES?
...
HOW COULD YOU... LIVE WITH IT?
AFTER ALL YOU'VE GONE THROUGH...
...HOW CAN YOU BE SO CALM?

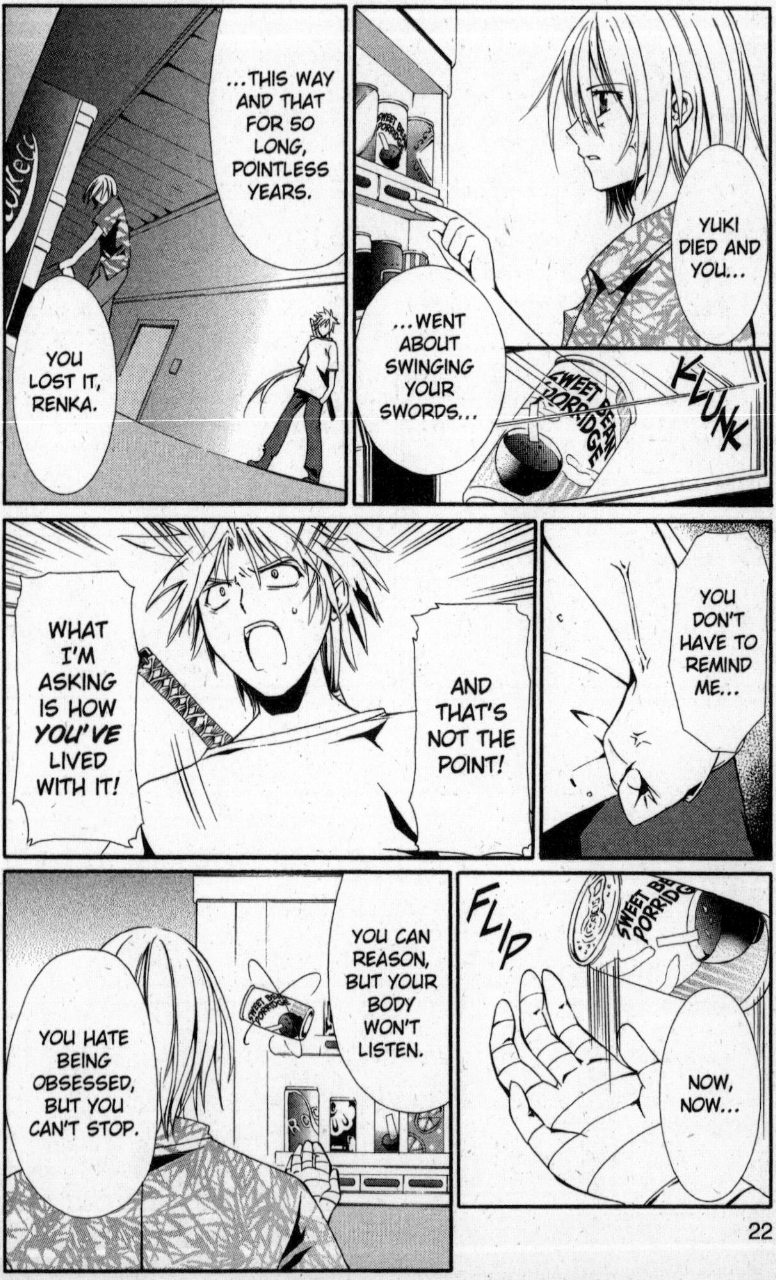
YUKI DIED AND YOU...
...WENT ABOUT SWINGING YOUR SWORDS...
SWEET BEAN PORRIDGE
KLUNK
...THIS WAY AND THAT FOR 50 LONG, POINTLESS YEARS.
YOU LOST IT, RENKA.
YOU DON'T HAVE TO REMIND ME...
AND THAT'S NOT THE POINT!
WHAT I'M ASKING IS HOW *YOU'VE* LIVED WITH IT!
FLIP
NOW, NOW...
YOU CAN REASON, BUT YOUR BODY WON'T LISTEN.
YOU HATE BEING OBSESSED, BUT YOU CAN'T STOP.

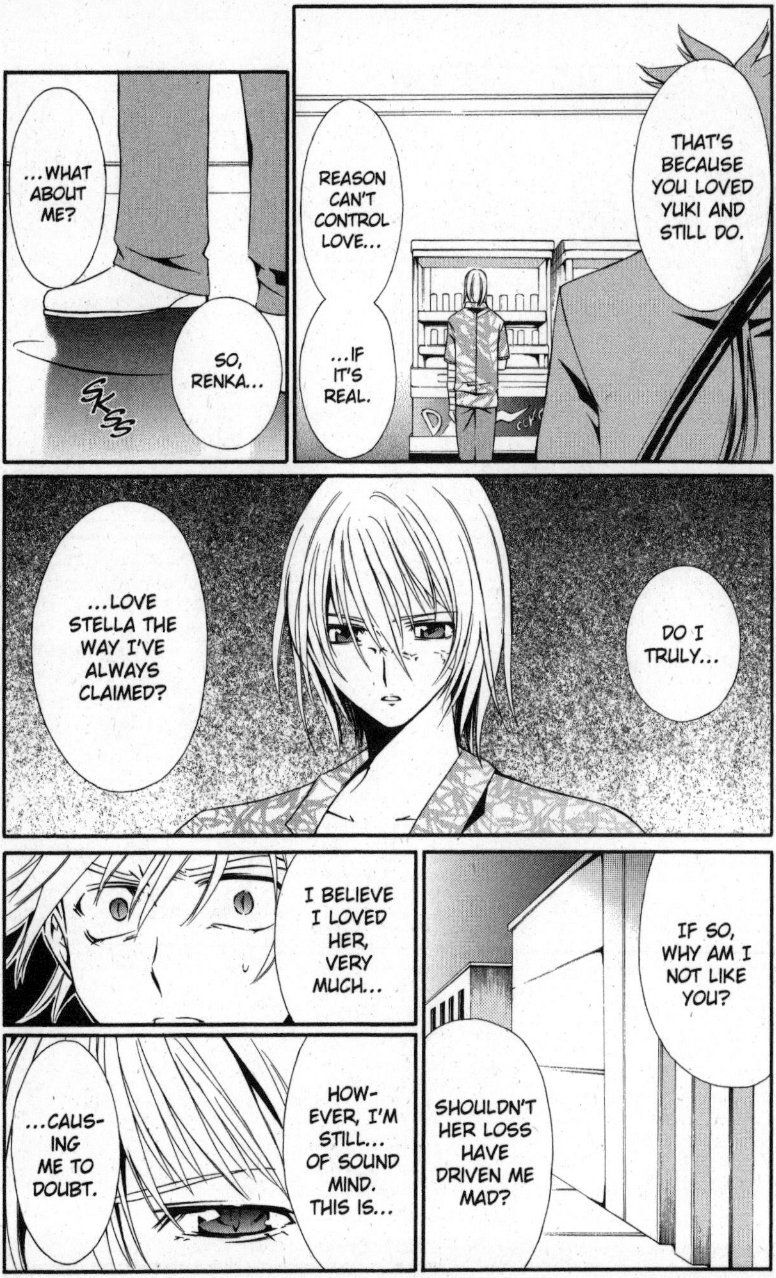
THAT'S BECAUSE YOU LOVED YUKI AND STILL DO.
REASON CAN'T CONTROL LOVE...
...IF IT'S REAL.
SO, RENKA...
...WHAT ABOUT ME?
SKSS
DO I TRULY...
...LOVE STELLA THE WAY I'VE ALWAYS CLAIMED?
IF SO, WHY AM I NOT LIKE YOU?
SHOULDN'T HER LOSS HAVE DRIVEN ME MAD?
I BELIEVE I LOVED HER, VERY MUCH...
HOW-EVER, I'M STILL... OF SOUND MIND. THIS IS...
...CAUS-ING ME TO DOUBT.

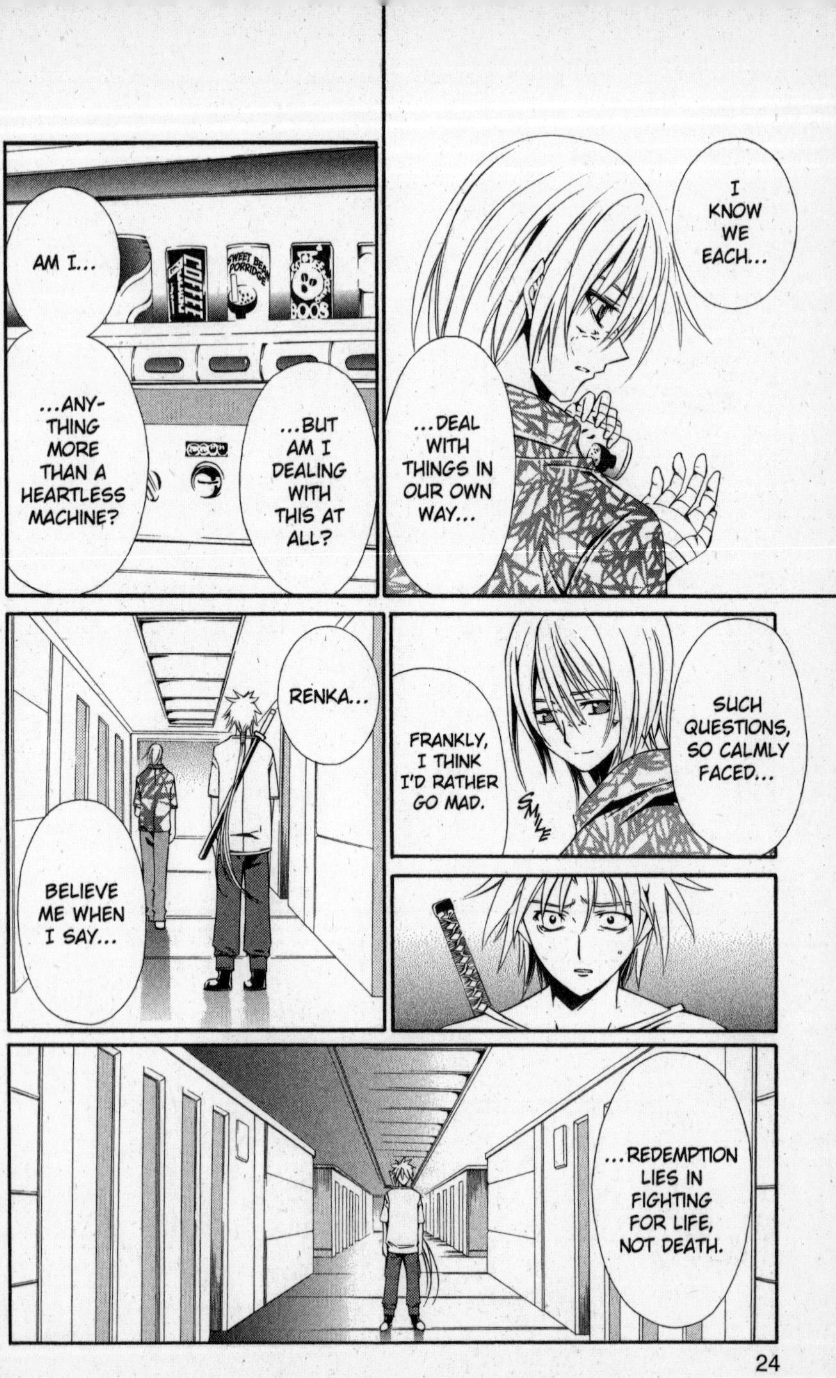
I KNOW WE EACH...
...DEAL WITH THINGS IN OUR OWN WAY...
...BUT AM I DEALING WITH THIS AT ALL?
AM I...
...ANY-THING MORE THAN A HEARTLESS MACHINE?
SUCH QUESTIONS, SO CALMLY FACED...
FRANKLY, I THINK I'D RATHER GO MAD.
SMILE
RENKA...
BELIEVE ME WHEN I SAY...
...REDEMPTION LIES IN FIGHTING FOR LIFE, NOT DEATH.

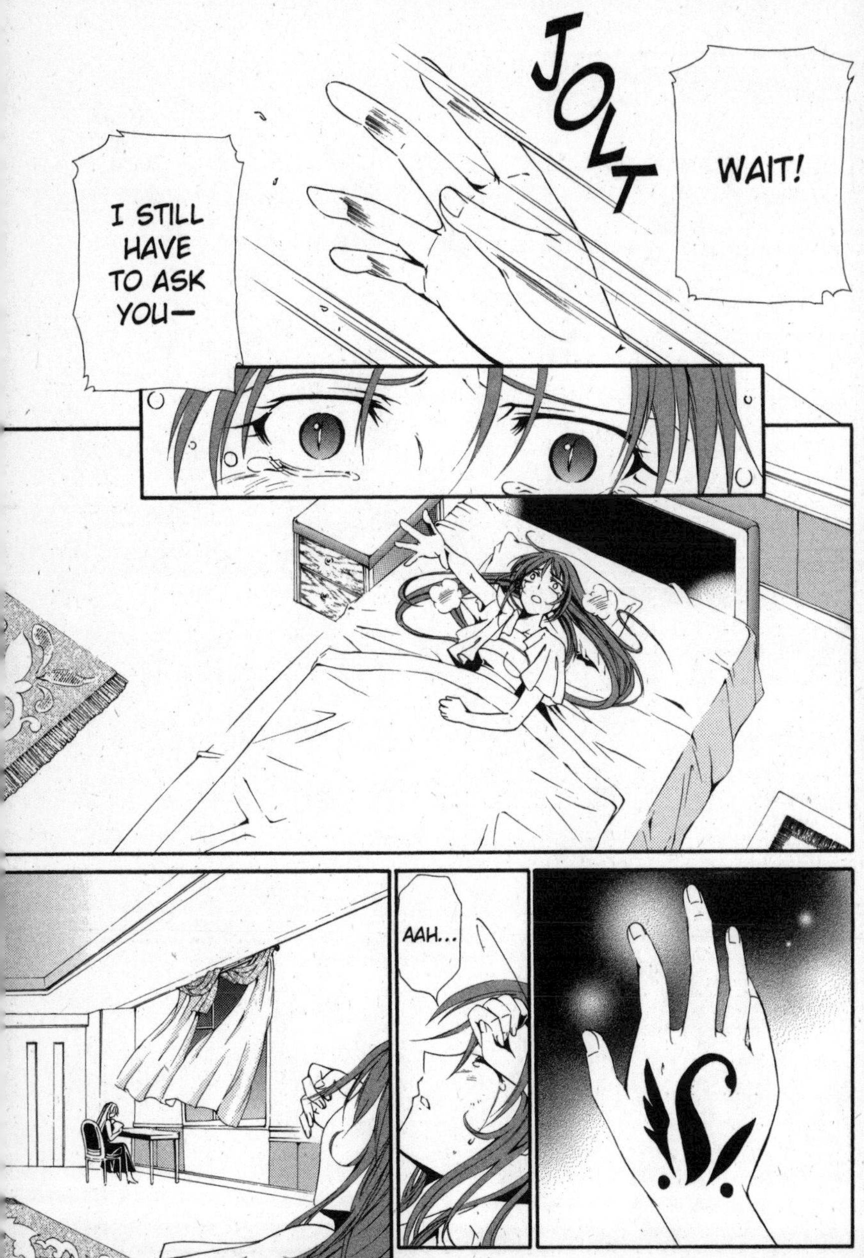
WAIT!
JOLT
I STILL HAVE TO ASK YOU—
AAH...

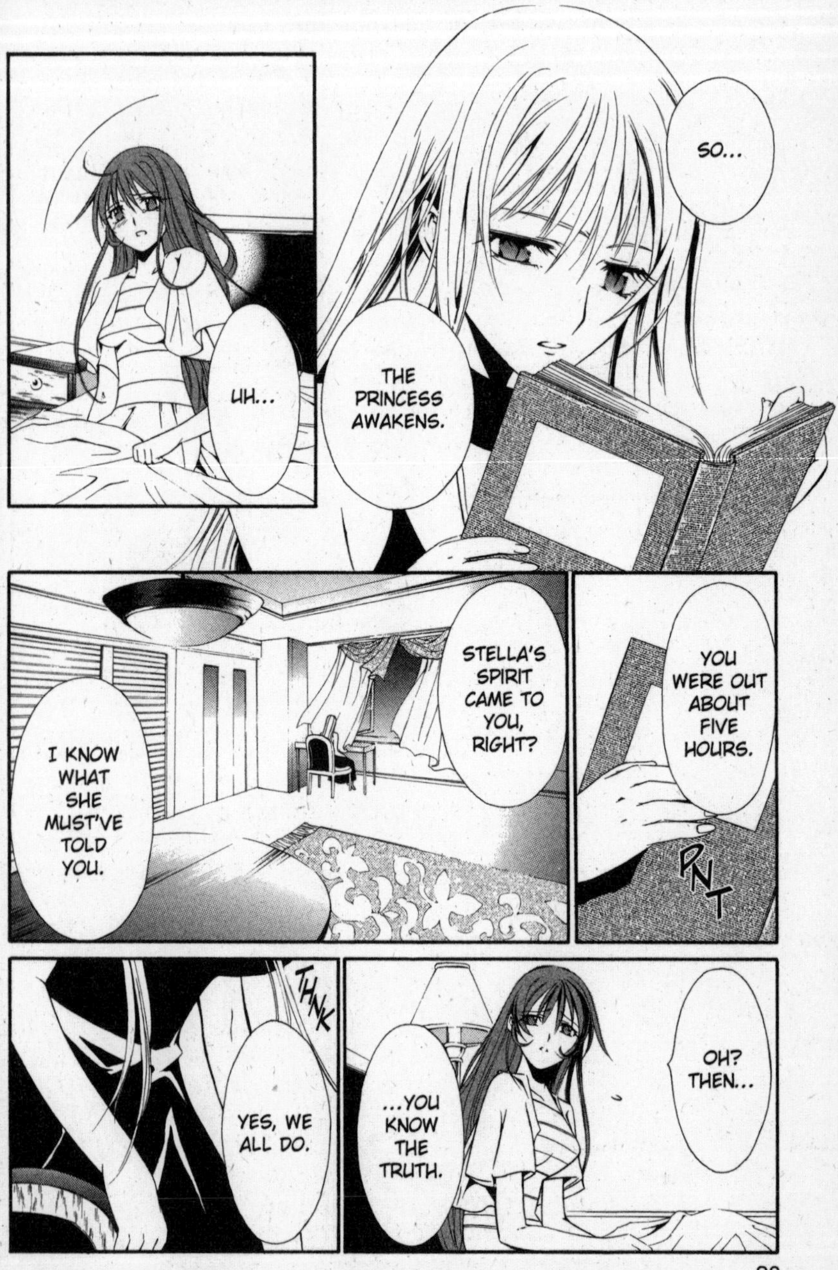
SO...
THE PRINCESS AWAKENS.
UH...
YOU WERE OUT ABOUT FIVE HOURS.
PNT
STELLA'S SPIRIT CAME TO YOU, RIGHT?
I KNOW WHAT SHE MUST'VE TOLD YOU.
OH? THEN...
...YOU KNOW THE TRUTH.
THNK
YES, WE ALL DO.

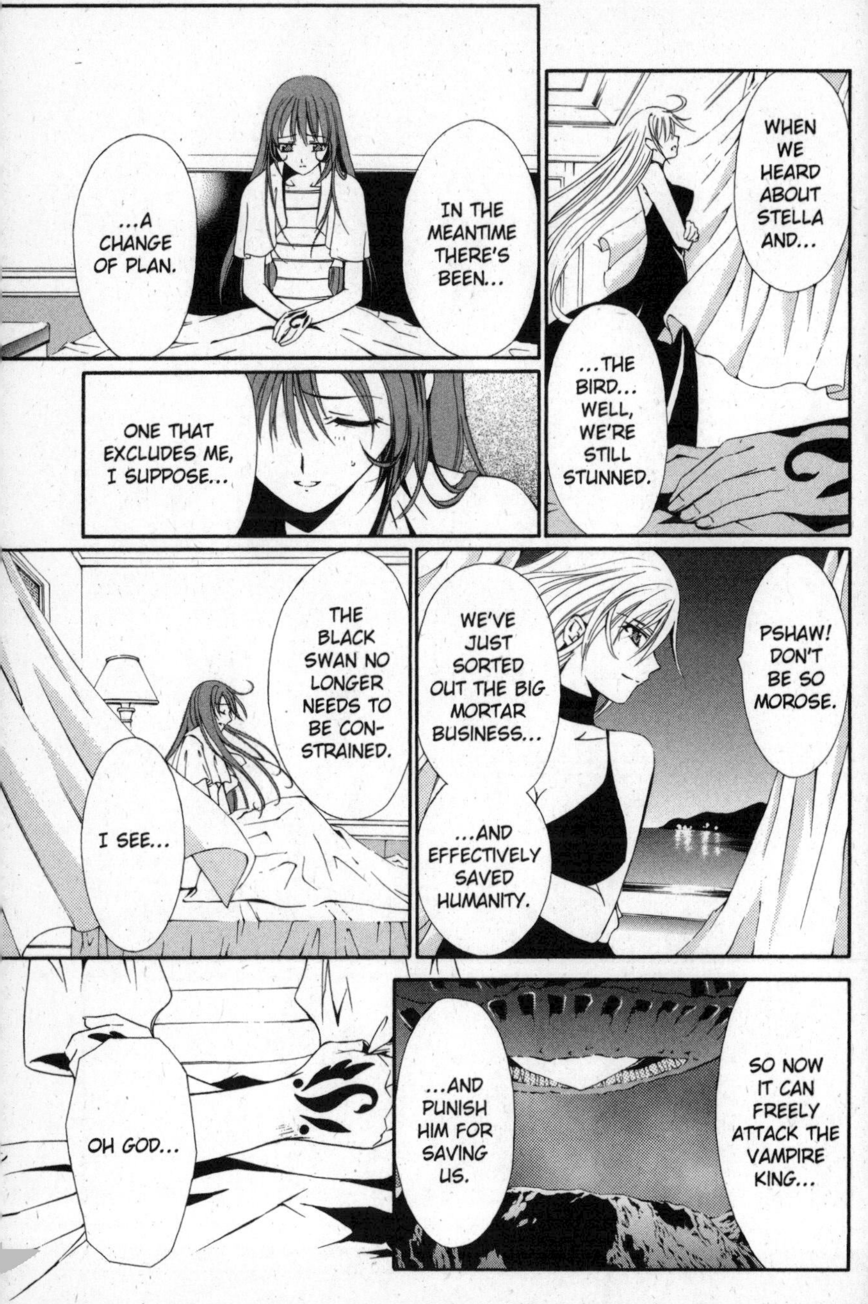
WHEN WE HEARD ABOUT STELLA AND...
...THE BIRD... WELL, WE'RE STILL STUNNED.
IN THE MEANTIME THERE'S BEEN...
...A CHANGE OF PLAN.
ONE THAT EXCLUDES ME, I SUPPOSE...
PSHAW! DON'T BE SO MOROSE.
WE'VE JUST SORTED OUT THE BIG MORTAR BUSINESS...
...AND EFFECTIVELY SAVED HUMANITY.
THE BLACK SWAN NO LONGER NEEDS TO BE CON-STRAINED.
I SEE...
SO NOW IT CAN FREELY ATTACK THE VAMPIRE KING...
...AND PUNISH HIM FOR SAVING US.
OH GOD...

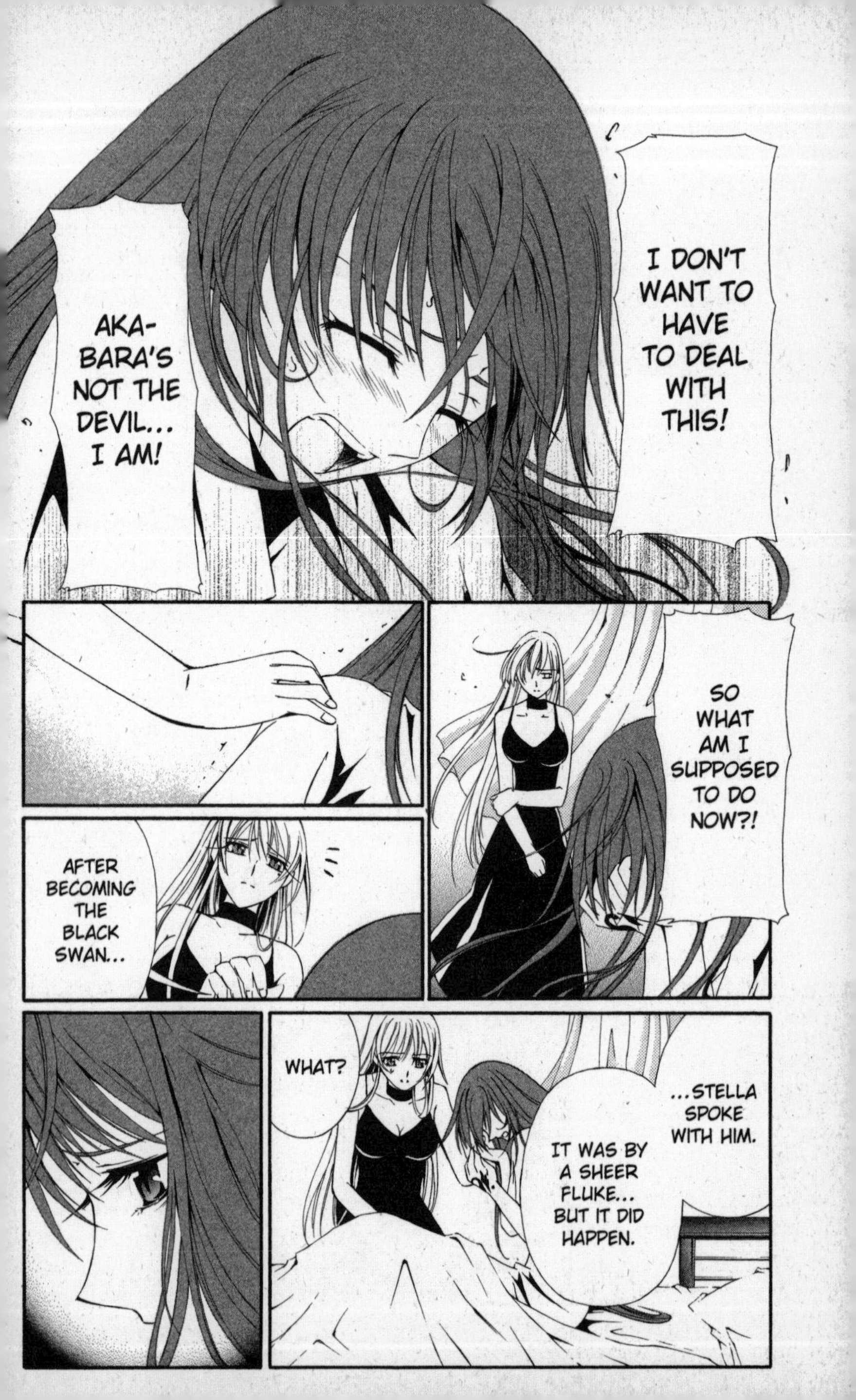
I DON'T WANT TO HAVE TO DEAL WITH THIS!
AKA-BARA'S NOT THE DEVIL... I AM!
SO WHAT AM I SUPPOSED TO DO NOW?!
AFTER BECOMING THE BLACK SWAN...
...STELLA SPOKE WITH HIM.
WHAT?
IT WAS BY A SHEER FLUKE... BUT IT DID HAPPEN.

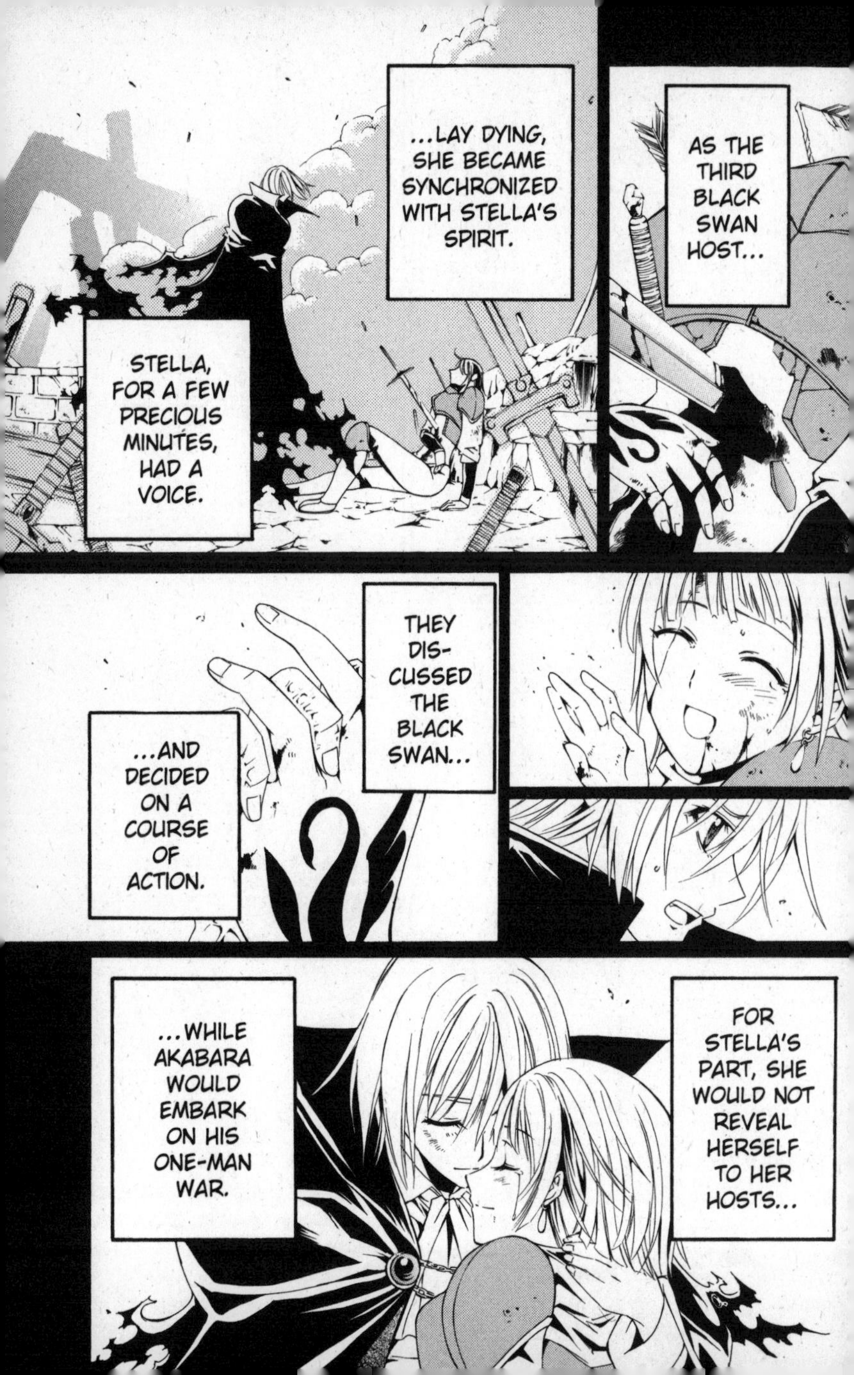
AS THE THIRD BLACK SWAN HOST...
...LAY DYING, SHE BECAME SYNCHRONIZED WITH STELLA'S SPIRIT.
STELLA, FOR A FEW PRECIOUS MINUTES, HAD A VOICE.
THEY DIS-CUSSED THE BLACK SWAN...
...AND DECIDED ON A COURSE OF ACTION.
FOR STELLA'S PART, SHE WOULD NOT REVEAL HERSELF TO HER HOSTS...
...WHILE AKABARA WOULD EMBARK ON HIS ONE-MAN WAR.

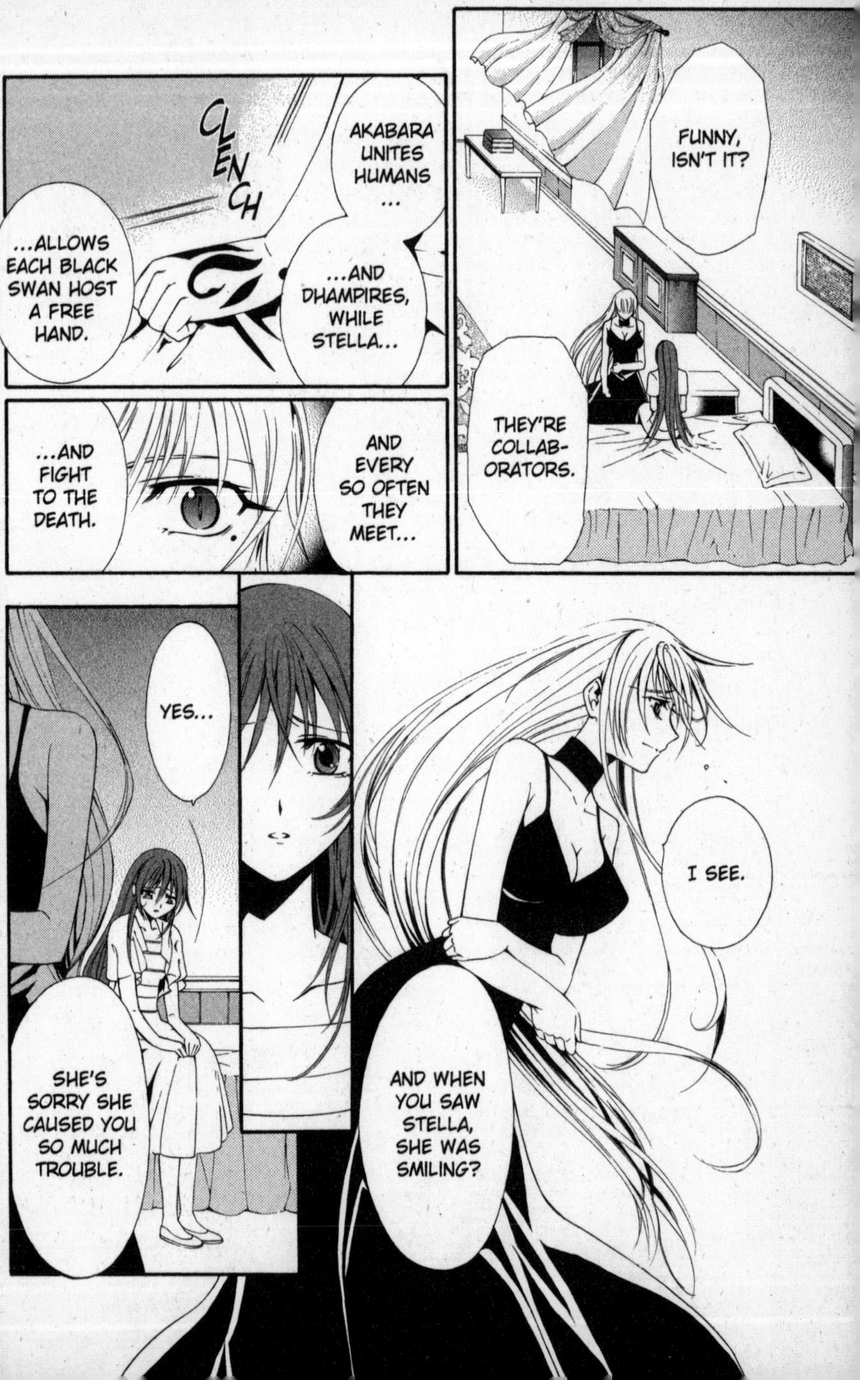
FUNNY, ISN'T IT?
THEY'RE COLLAB-ORATORS.
AKABARA UNITES HUMANS ...
...AND DHAMPIRES, WHILE STELLA...
CLENCH
...ALLOWS EACH BLACK SWAN HOST A FREE HAND.
AND EVERY SO OFTEN THEY MEET...
...AND FIGHT TO THE DEATH.
I SEE.
AND WHEN YOU SAW STELLA, SHE WAS SMILING?
YES...
SHE'S SORRY SHE CAUSED YOU SO MUCH TROUBLE.

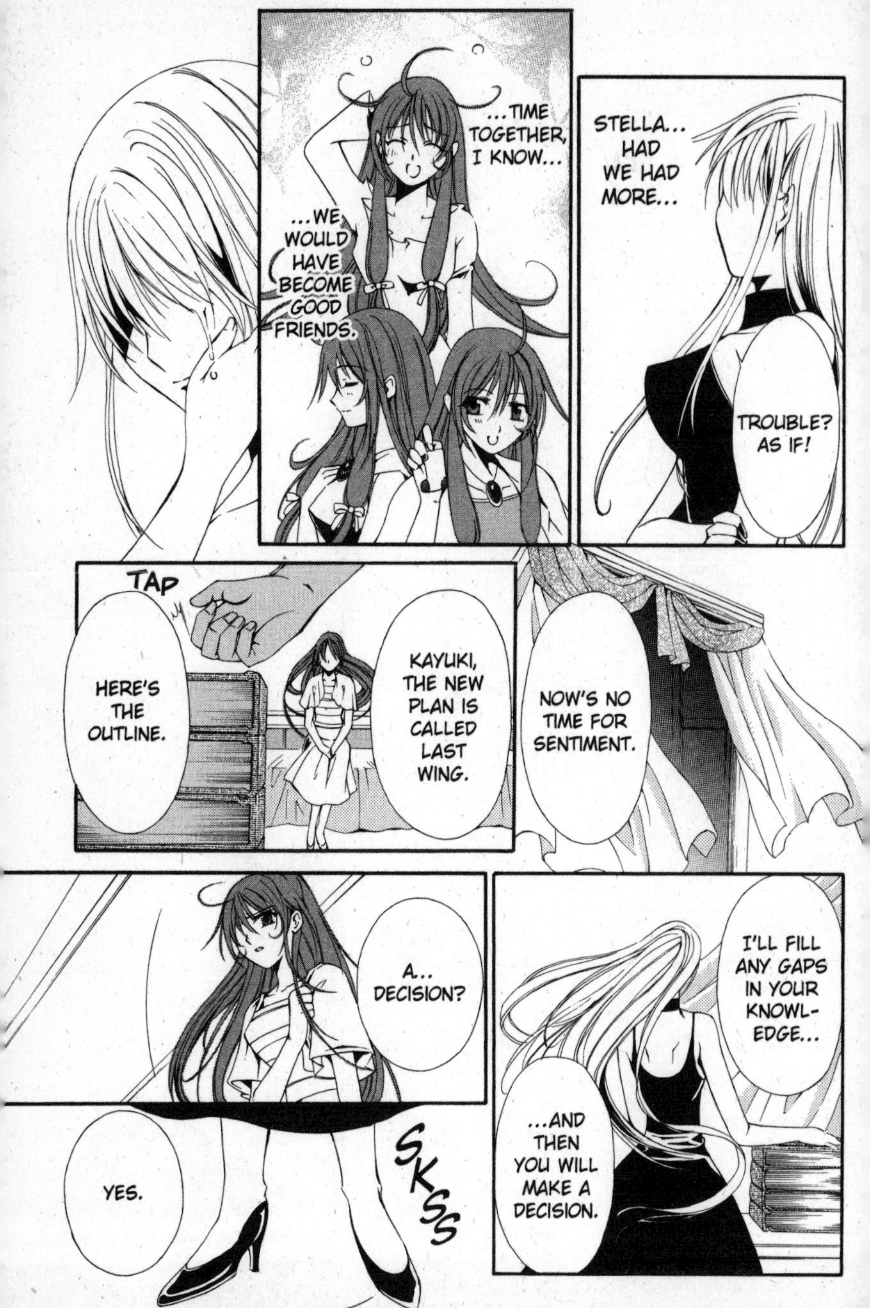
STELLA... HAD WE HAD MORE...
TROUBLE? AS IF!
...TIME TOGETHER, I KNOW...
...WE WOULD HAVE BECOME GOOD FRIENDS.
NOW'S NO TIME FOR SENTIMENT.
KAYUKI, THE NEW PLAN IS CALLED LAST WING.
TAP
HERE'S THE OUTLINE.
I'LL FILL ANY GAPS IN YOUR KNOWL-EDGE...
...AND THEN YOU WILL MAKE A DECISION.
A... DECISION?
SKSS
YES.

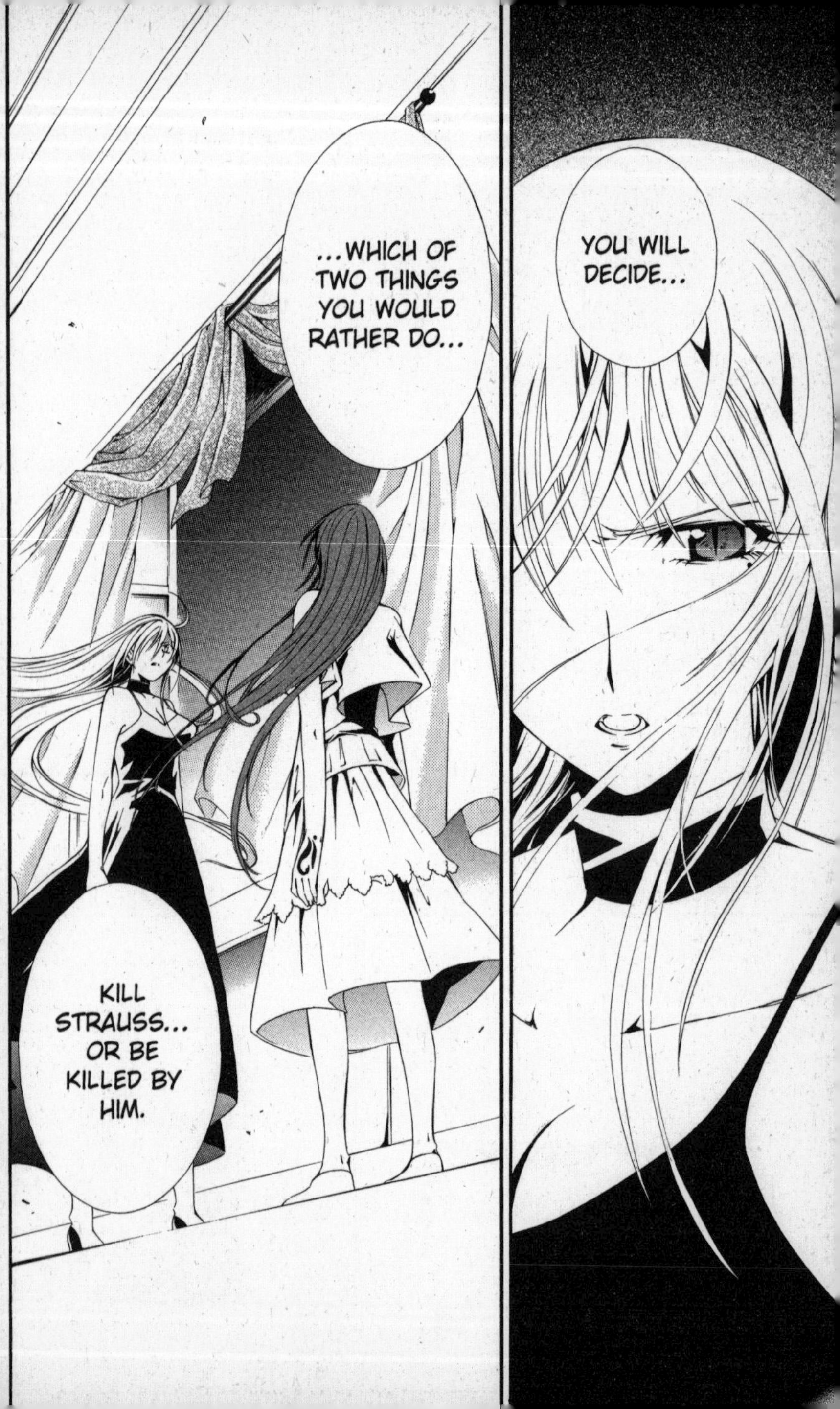
YOU WILL DECIDE...
...WHICH OF TWO THINGS YOU WOULD RATHER DO...
KILL STRAUSS... OR BE KILLED BY HIM.

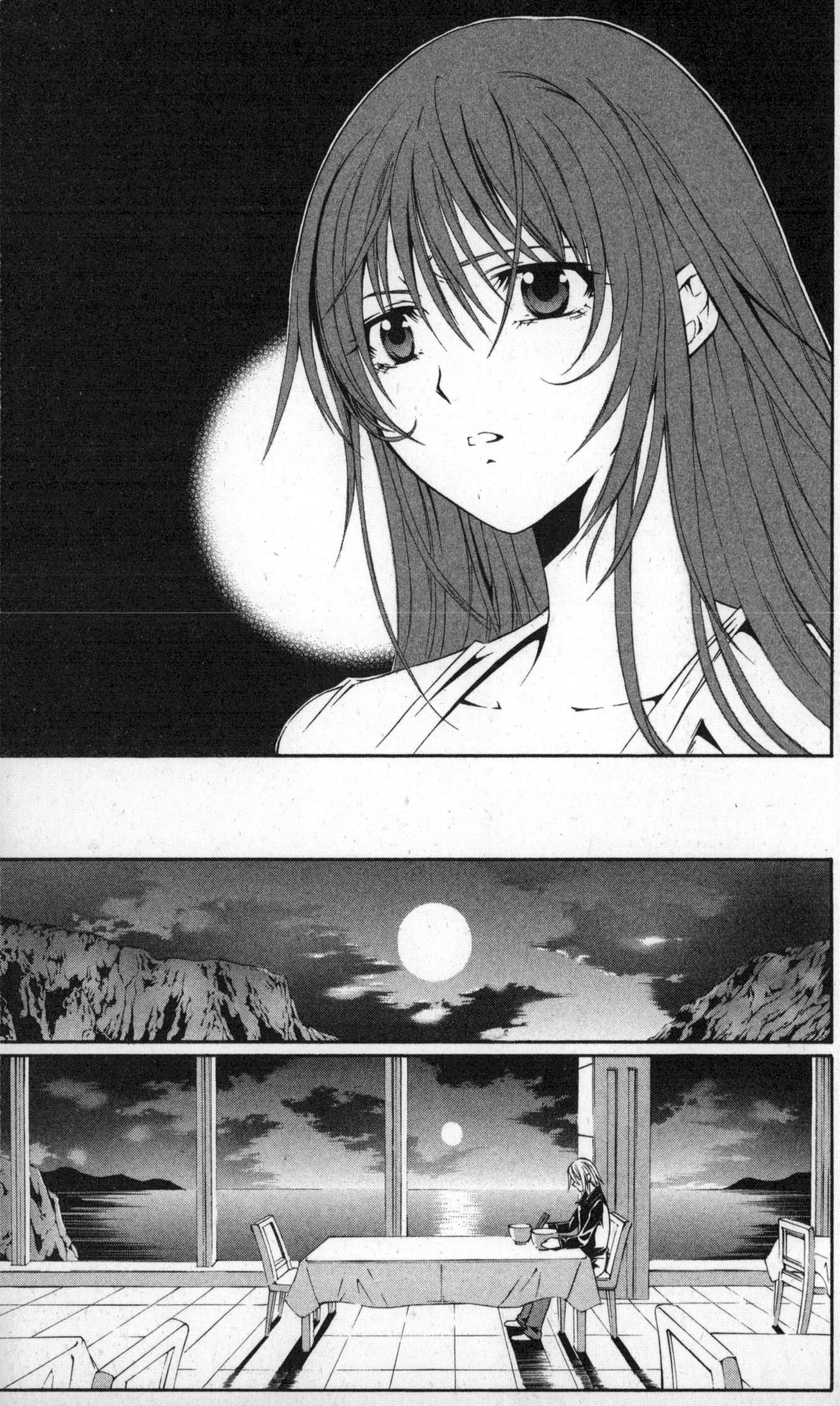

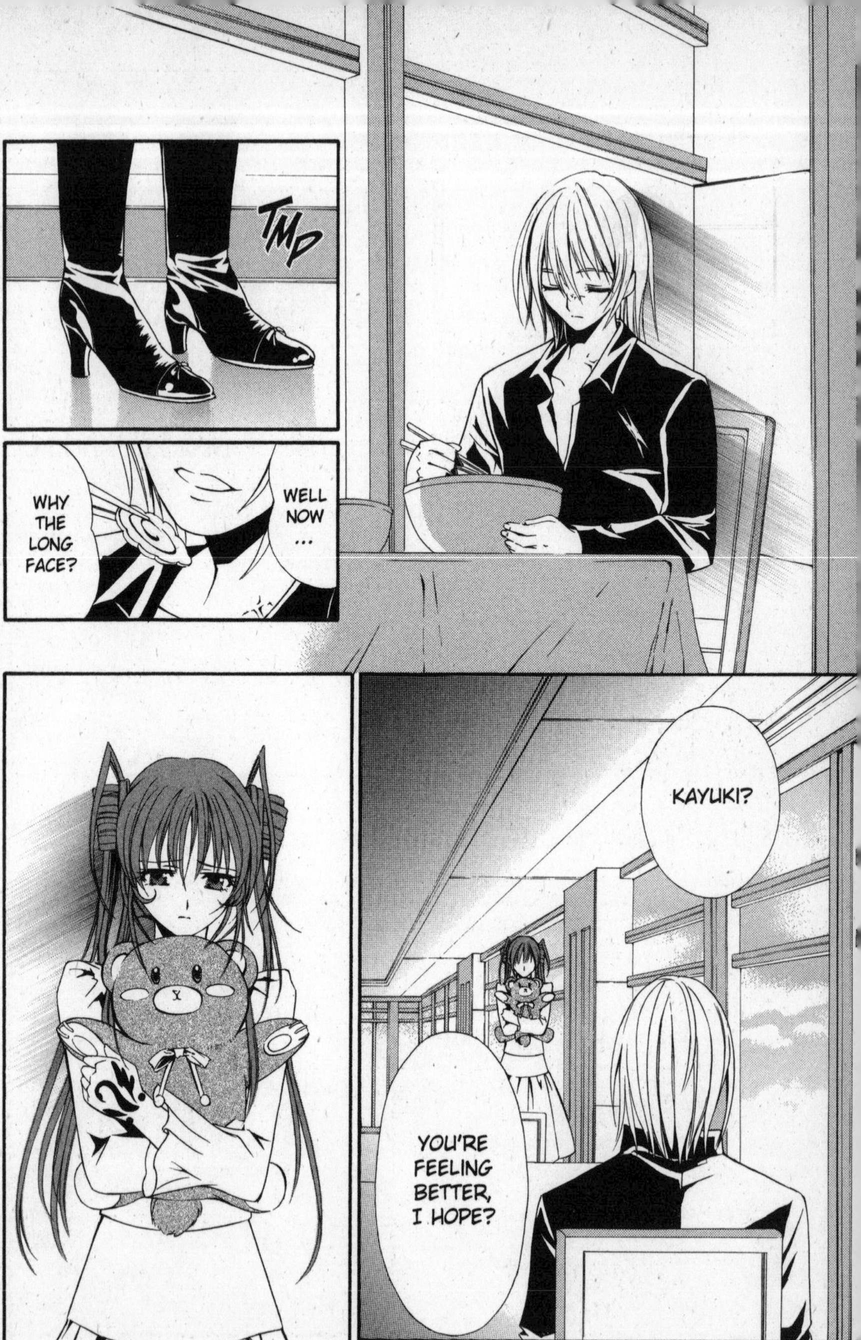
TMP
WELL NOW ...
WHY THE LONG FACE?
KAYUKI?
YOU'RE FEELING BETTER, I HOPE?

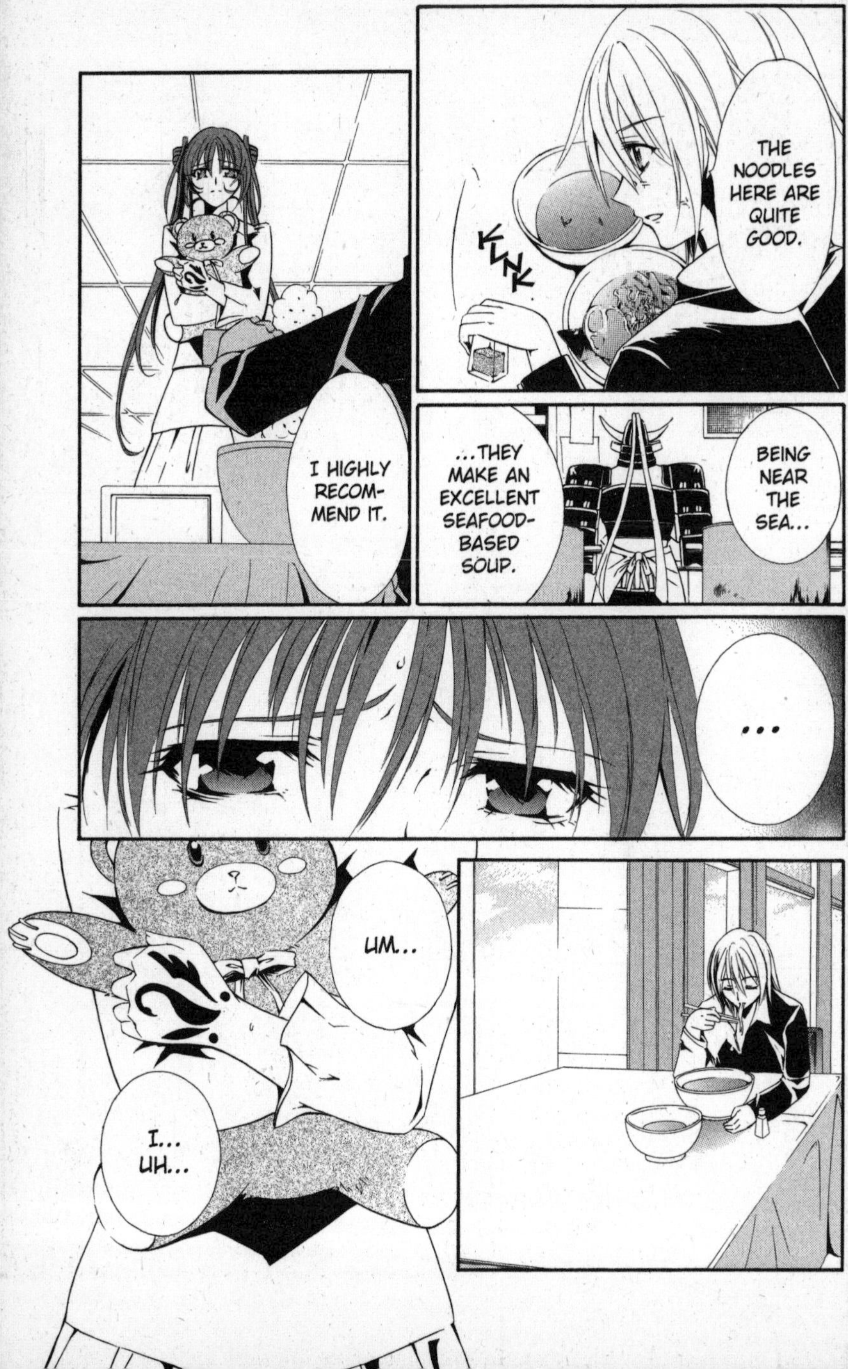
THE NOODLES HERE ARE QUITE GOOD.
KLUNK
BEING NEAR THE SEA...
...THEY MAKE AN EXCELLENT SEAFOOD-BASED SOUP.
I HIGHLY RECOMMEND IT.
...
UM...
I... UH...

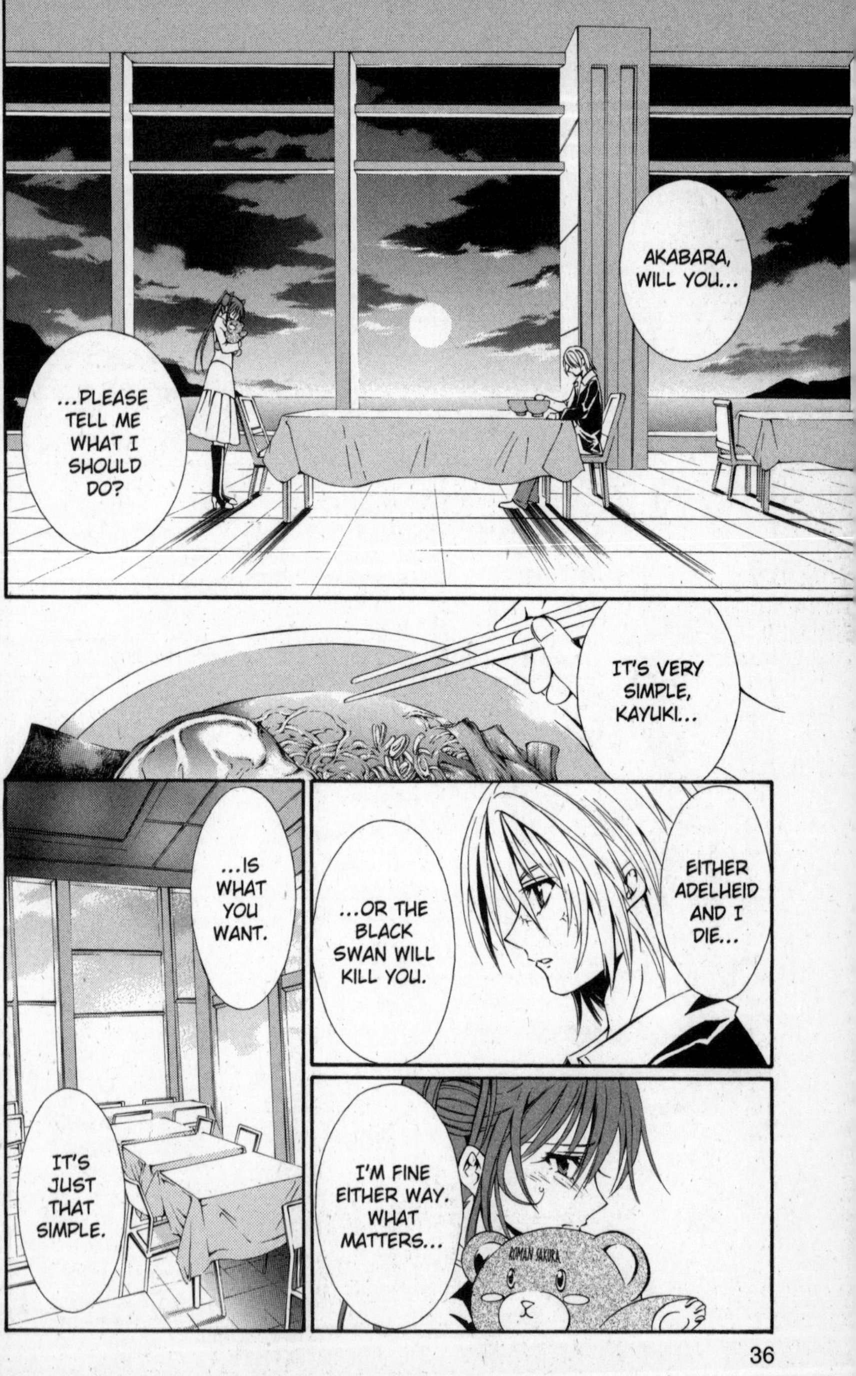
AKABARA, WILL YOU...
...PLEASE TELL ME WHAT I SHOULD DO?
IT'S VERY SIMPLE, KAYUKI...
EITHER ADELHEID AND I DIE...
...OR THE BLACK SWAN WILL KILL YOU.
I'M FINE EITHER WAY. WHAT MATTERS...
ROMAN SAKURA
...IS WHAT YOU WANT.
IT'S JUST THAT SIMPLE.

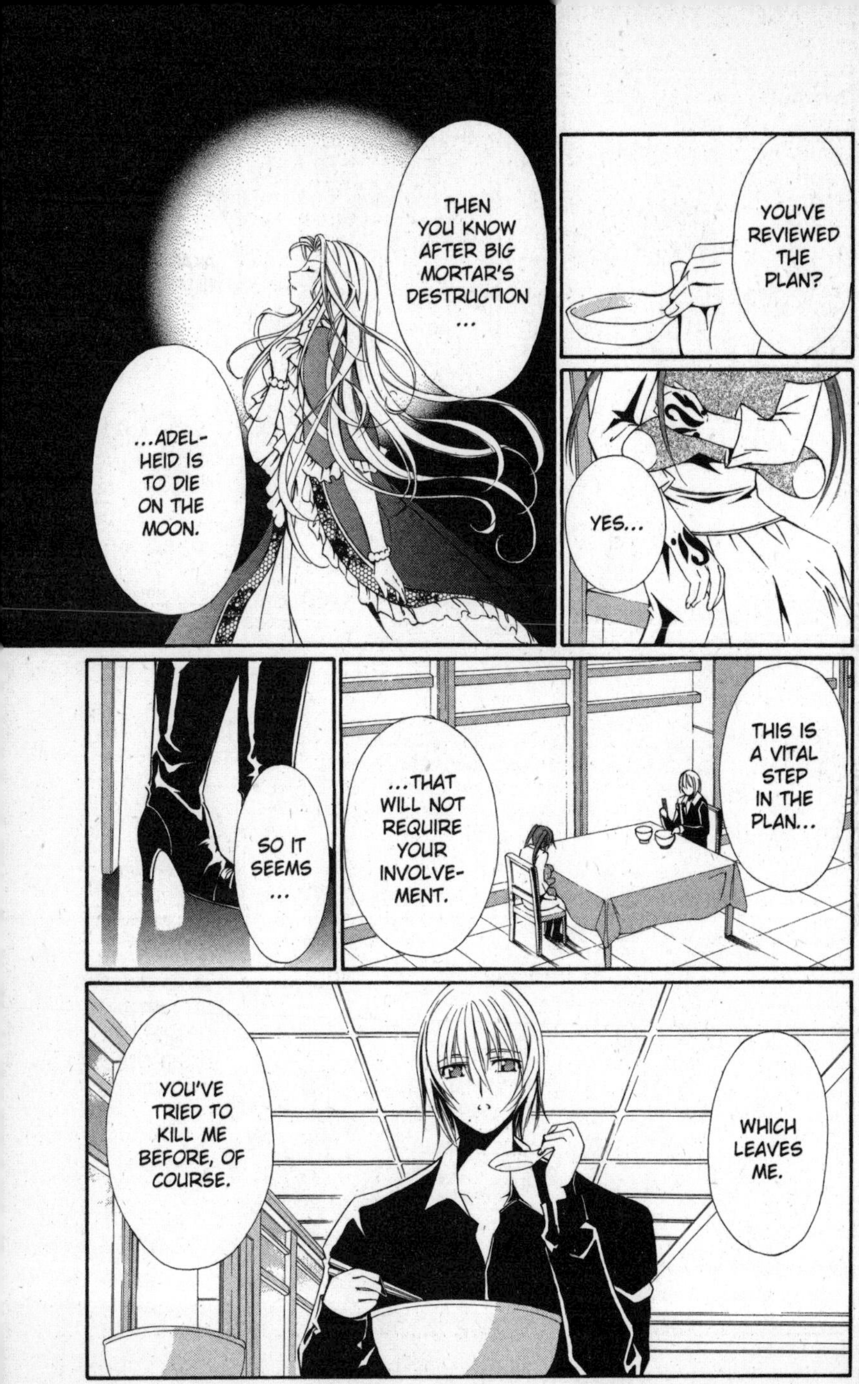
YOU'VE REVIEWED THE PLAN?
YES...
THEN YOU KNOW AFTER BIG MORTAR'S DESTRUCTION ...
...ADEL-HEID IS TO DIE ON THE MOON.
THIS IS A VITAL STEP IN THE PLAN...
...THAT WILL NOT REQUIRE YOUR INVOLVE-MENT.
SO IT SEEMS ...
WHICH LEAVES ME.
YOU'VE TRIED TO KILL ME BEFORE, OF COURSE.

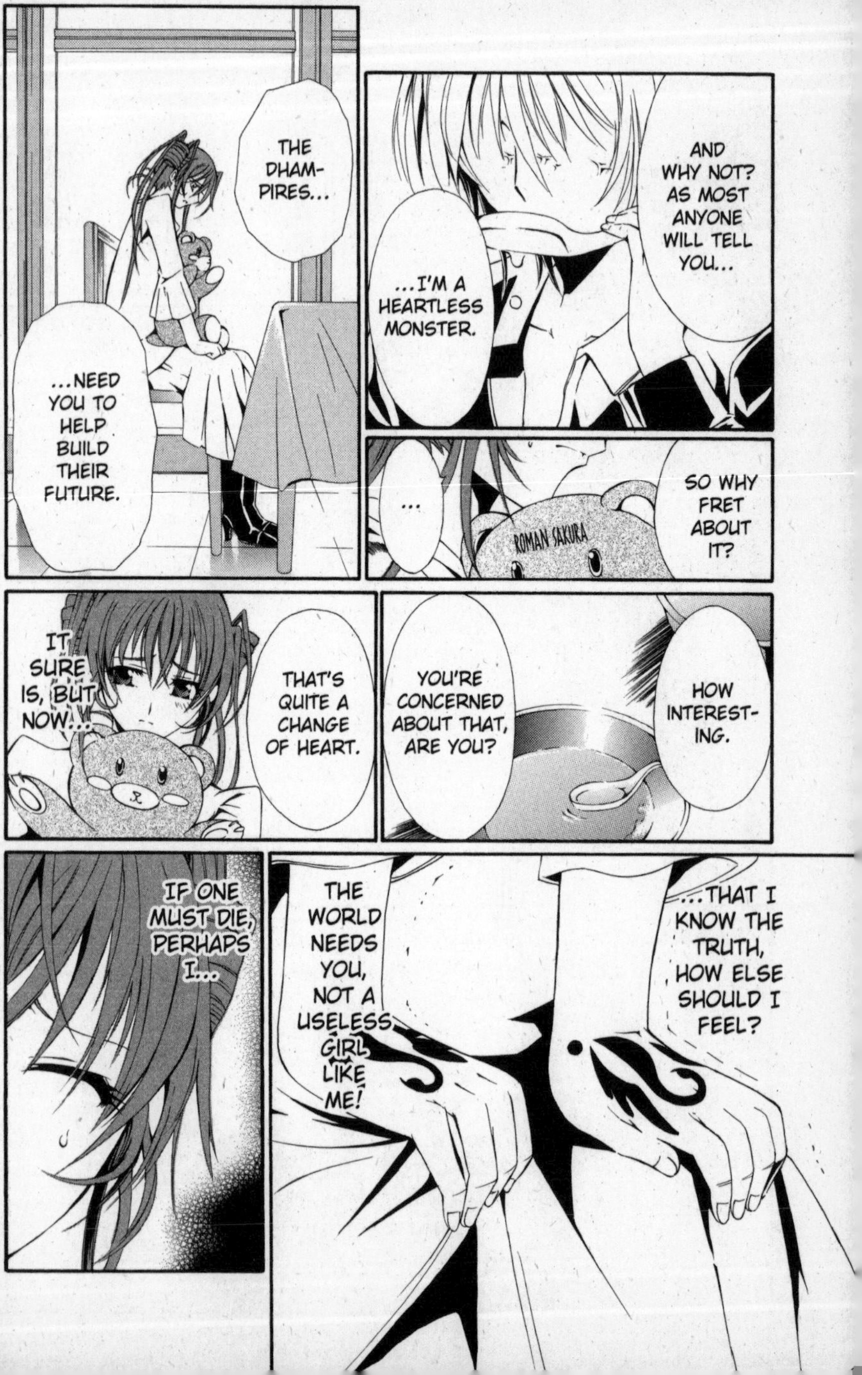
AND WHY NOT? AS MOST ANYONE WILL TELL YOU...
...I'M A HEARTLESS MONSTER.
SO WHY FRET ABOUT IT?
...
ROMAN SAKURA
THE DHAMPIRES...
...NEED YOU TO HELP BUILD THEIR FUTURE.
HOW INTERESTING.
YOU'RE CONCERNED ABOUT THAT, ARE YOU?
THAT'S QUITE A CHANGE OF HEART.
IT SURE IS, BUT NOW...
...THAT I KNOW THE TRUTH, HOW ELSE SHOULD I FEEL?
THE WORLD NEEDS YOU, NOT A USELESS GIRL LIKE ME!
IF ONE MUST DIE, PERHAPS I...

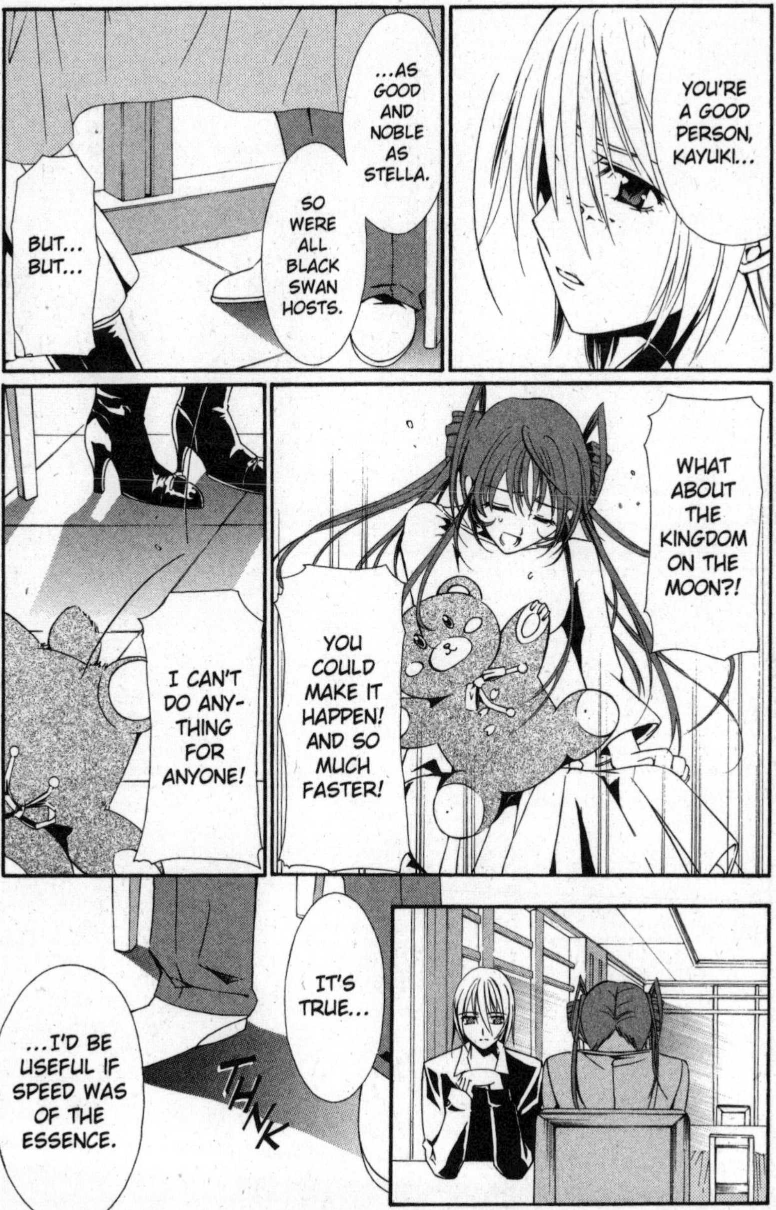
YOU'RE A GOOD PERSON, KAYUKI...
...AS GOOD AND NOBLE AS STELLA.
SO WERE ALL BLACK SWAN HOSTS.
BUT... BUT...
WHAT ABOUT THE KINGDOM ON THE MOON?!
YOU COULD MAKE IT HAPPEN! AND SO MUCH FASTER!
I CAN'T DO ANY-THING FOR ANYONE!
IT'S TRUE...
THNK
...I'D BE USEFUL IF SPEED WAS OF THE ESSENCE.

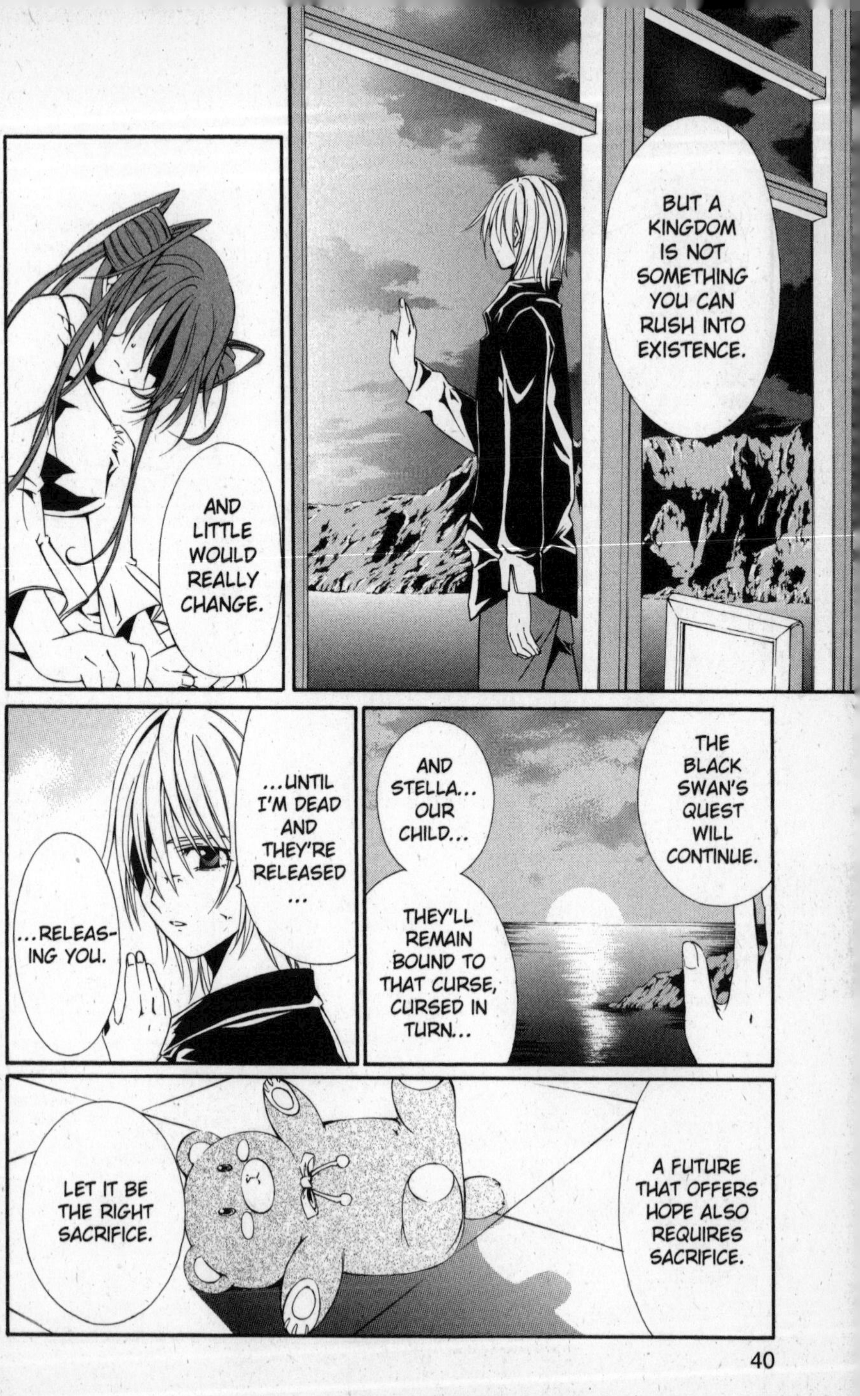
BUT A KINGDOM IS NOT SOMETHING YOU CAN RUSH INTO EXISTENCE.
AND LITTLE WOULD REALLY CHANGE.
THE BLACK SWAN'S QUEST WILL CONTINUE.
AND STELLA... OUR CHILD...
THEY'LL REMAIN BOUND TO THAT CURSE, CURSED IN TURN...
...UNTIL I'M DEAD AND THEY'RE RELEASED...
...RELEASING YOU.
A FUTURE THAT OFFERS HOPE ALSO REQUIRES SACRIFICE.
LET IT BE THE RIGHT SACRIFICE.

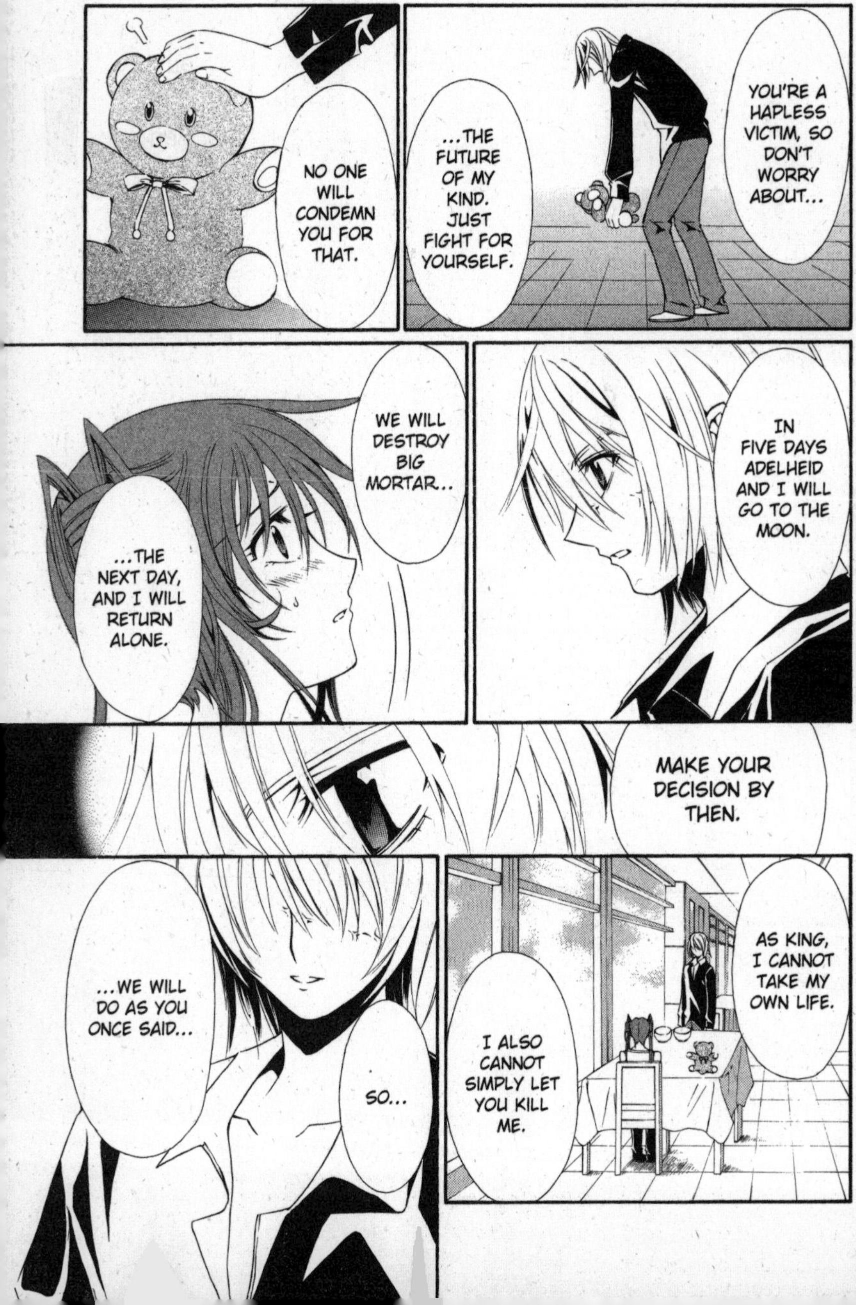
YOU'RE A HAPLESS VICTIM, SO DON'T WORRY ABOUT...
...THE FUTURE OF MY KIND. JUST FIGHT FOR YOURSELF.
NO ONE WILL CONDEMN YOU FOR THAT.
IN FIVE DAYS ADELHEID AND I WILL GO TO THE MOON.
WE WILL DESTROY BIG MORTAR...
...THE NEXT DAY, AND I WILL RETURN ALONE.
MAKE YOUR DECISION BY THEN.
AS KING, I CANNOT TAKE MY OWN LIFE.
I ALSO CANNOT SIMPLY LET YOU KILL ME.
...WE WILL DO AS YOU ONCE SAID...
SO...

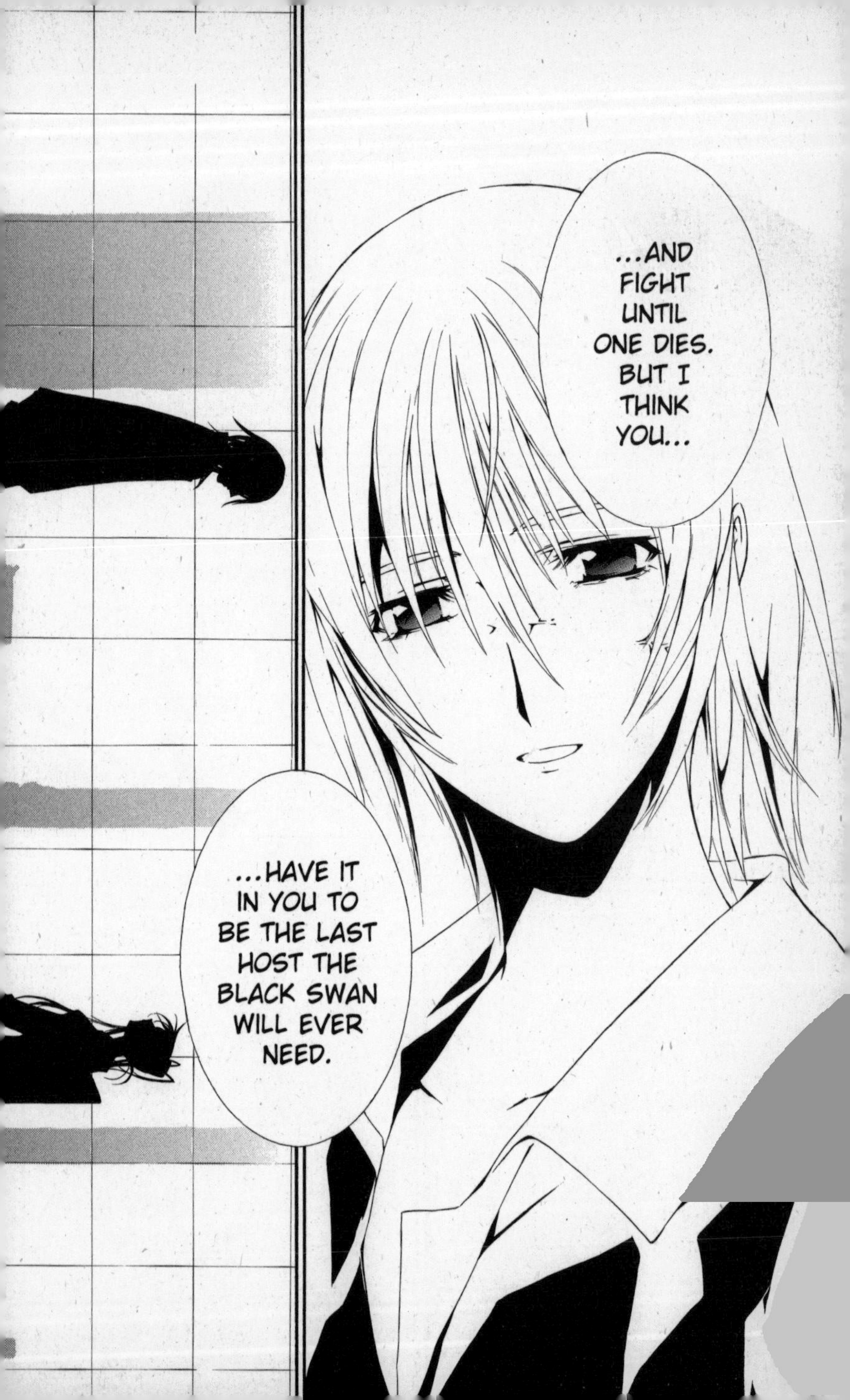
...AND FIGHT UNTIL ONE DIES. BUT I THINK YOU...
...HAVE IT IN YOU TO BE THE LAST HOST THE BLACK SWAN WILL EVER NEED.

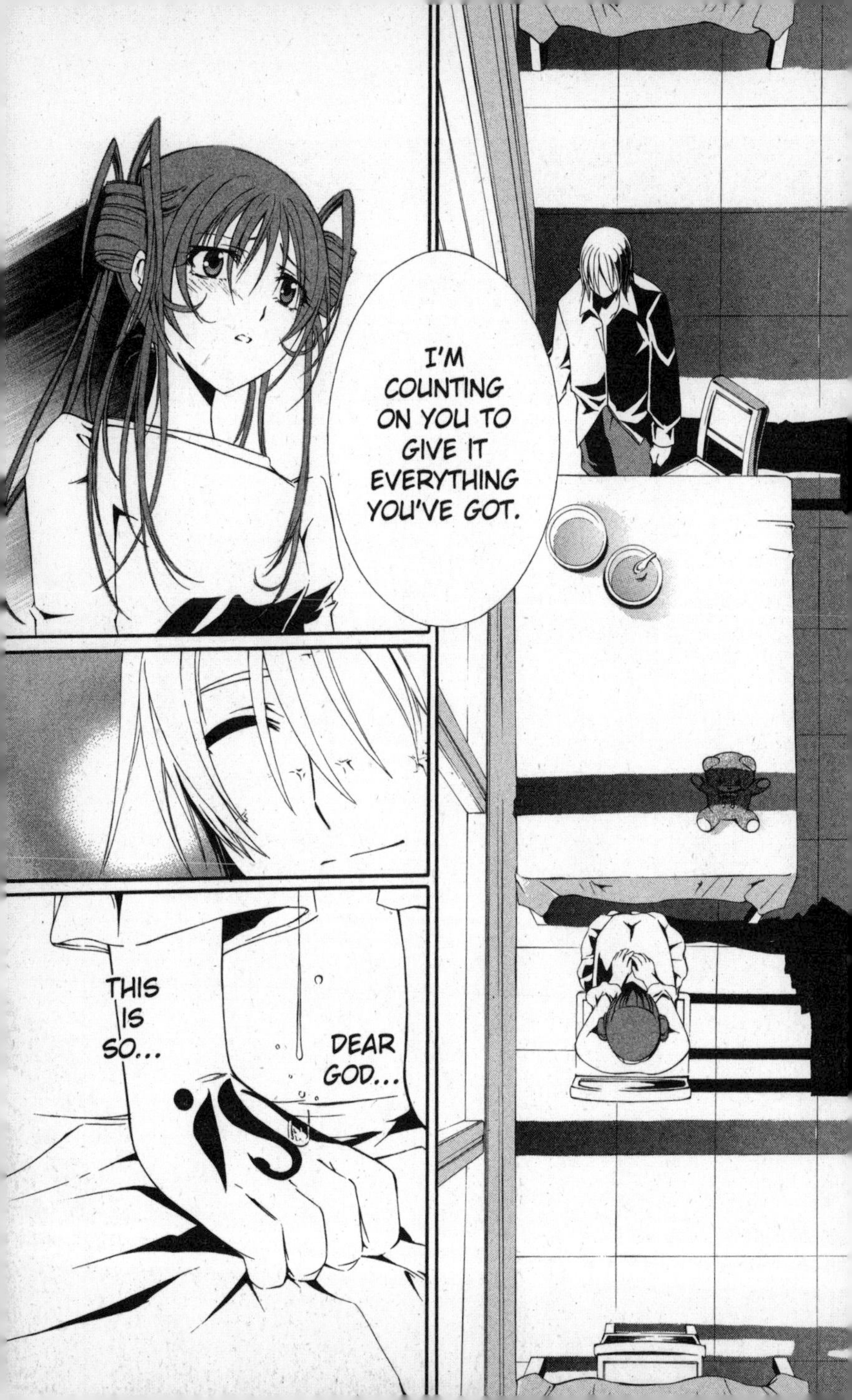
I'M COUNTING ON YOU TO GIVE IT EVERYTHING YOU'VE GOT.
DEAR GOD...
THIS IS SO...

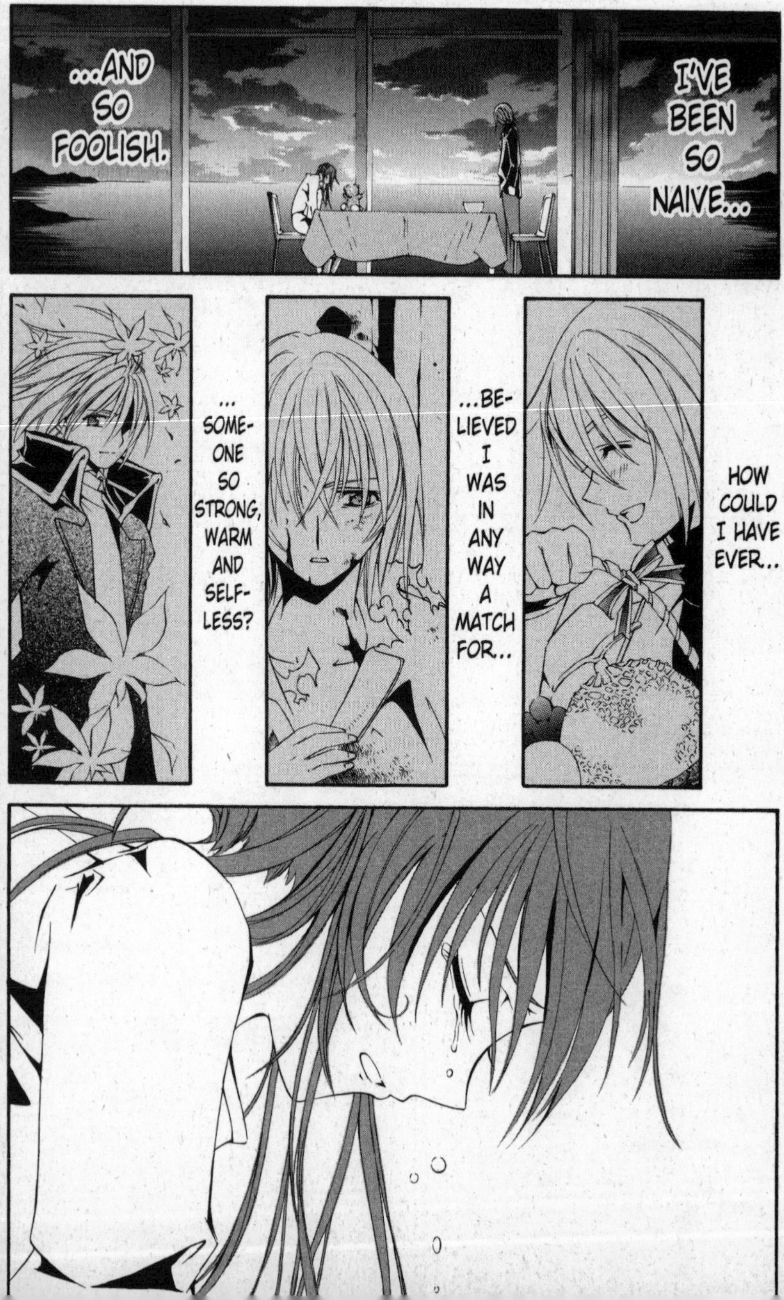
I'VE BEEN SO NAIVE...
...AND SO FOOLISH.
HOW COULD I HAVE EVER...
...BE-LIEVED I WAS IN ANY WAY A MATCH FOR...
...SOME-ONE SO STRONG, WARM AND SELF-LESS?

THE RECORD OF A
FALLEN VAMPIRE

THE RECORD OF A

FALLEN VAMPIRE

Chapter 40: A Tale of an Ordinary Girl

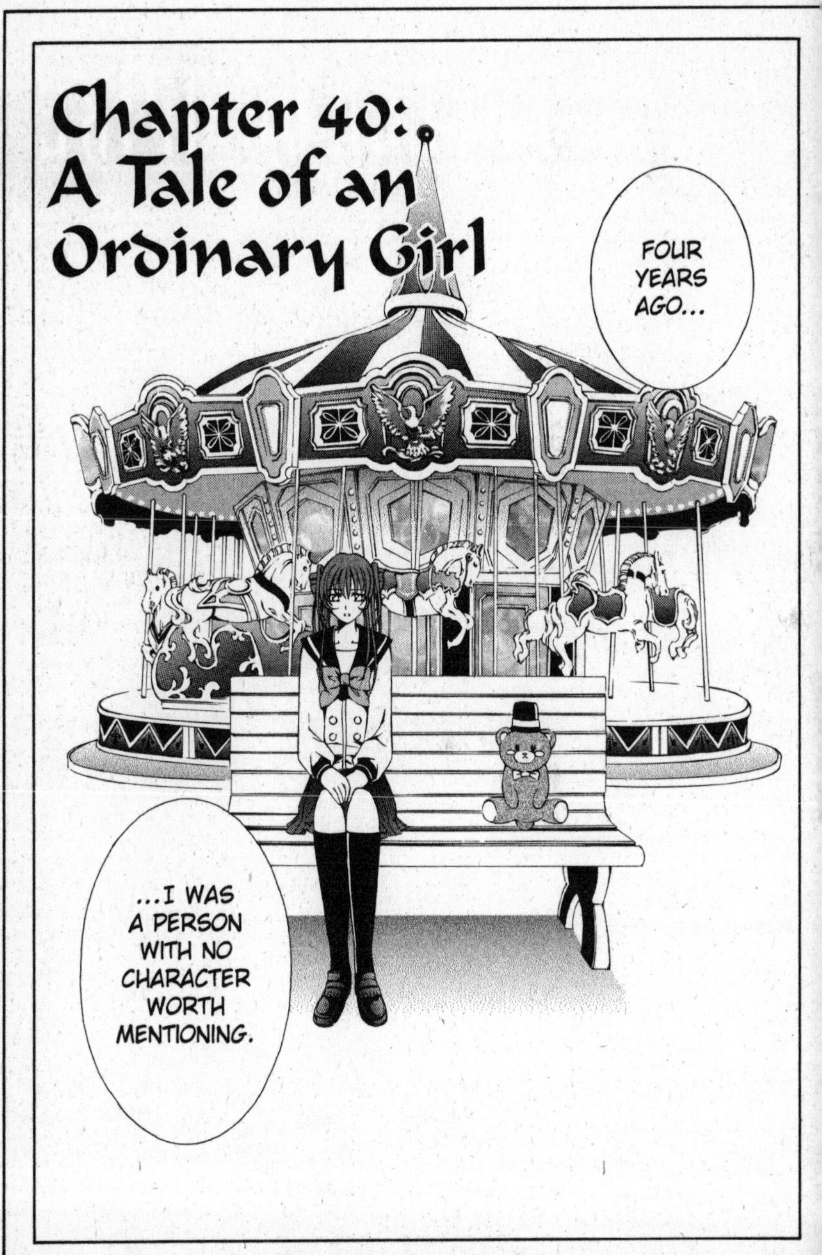
FOUR YEARS AGO...
...I WAS A PERSON WITH NO CHARACTER WORTH MENTIONING.

Confessions of the 50th Black Swan, Kayuki Hirasaka: Part One

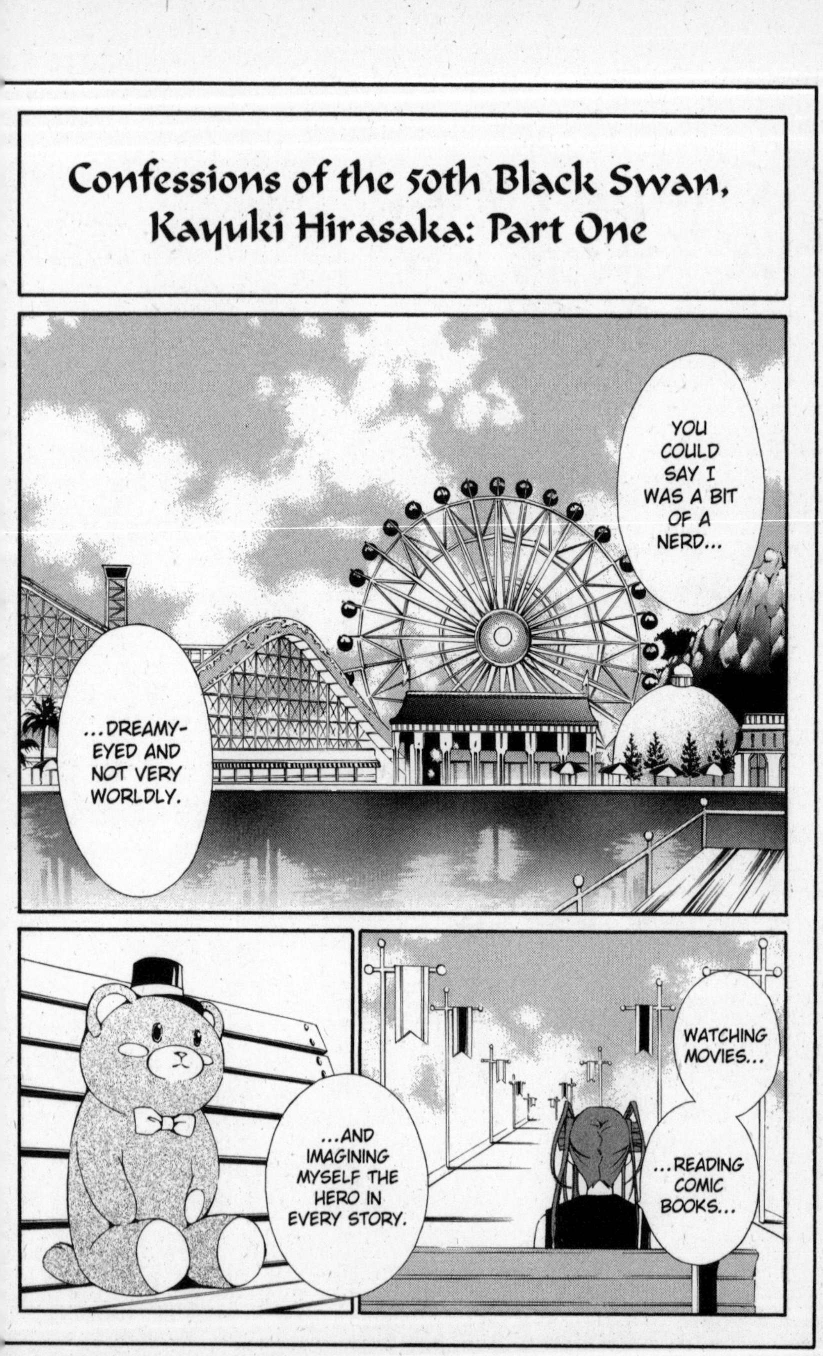
YOU COULD SAY I WAS A BIT OF A NERD...
...DREAMY-EYED AND NOT VERY WORLDLY.
WATCHING MOVIES...
...READING COMIC BOOKS...
...AND IMAGINING MYSELF THE HERO IN EVERY STORY.

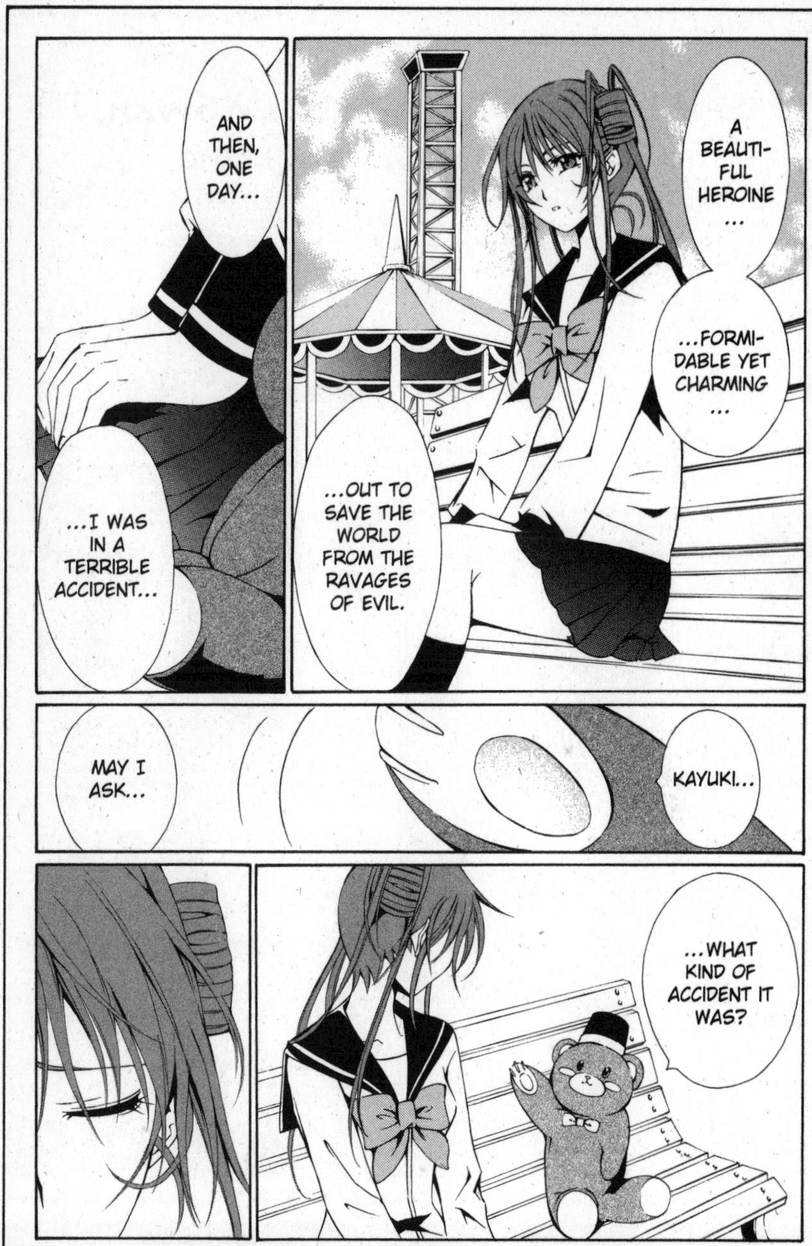
A BEAUTIFUL HEROINE...
...FORMIDABLE YET CHARMING...
...OUT TO SAVE THE WORLD FROM THE RAVAGES OF EVIL.
AND THEN, ONE DAY...
...I WAS IN A TERRIBLE ACCIDENT...
KAYUKI...
MAY I ASK...
...WHAT KIND OF ACCIDENT IT WAS?

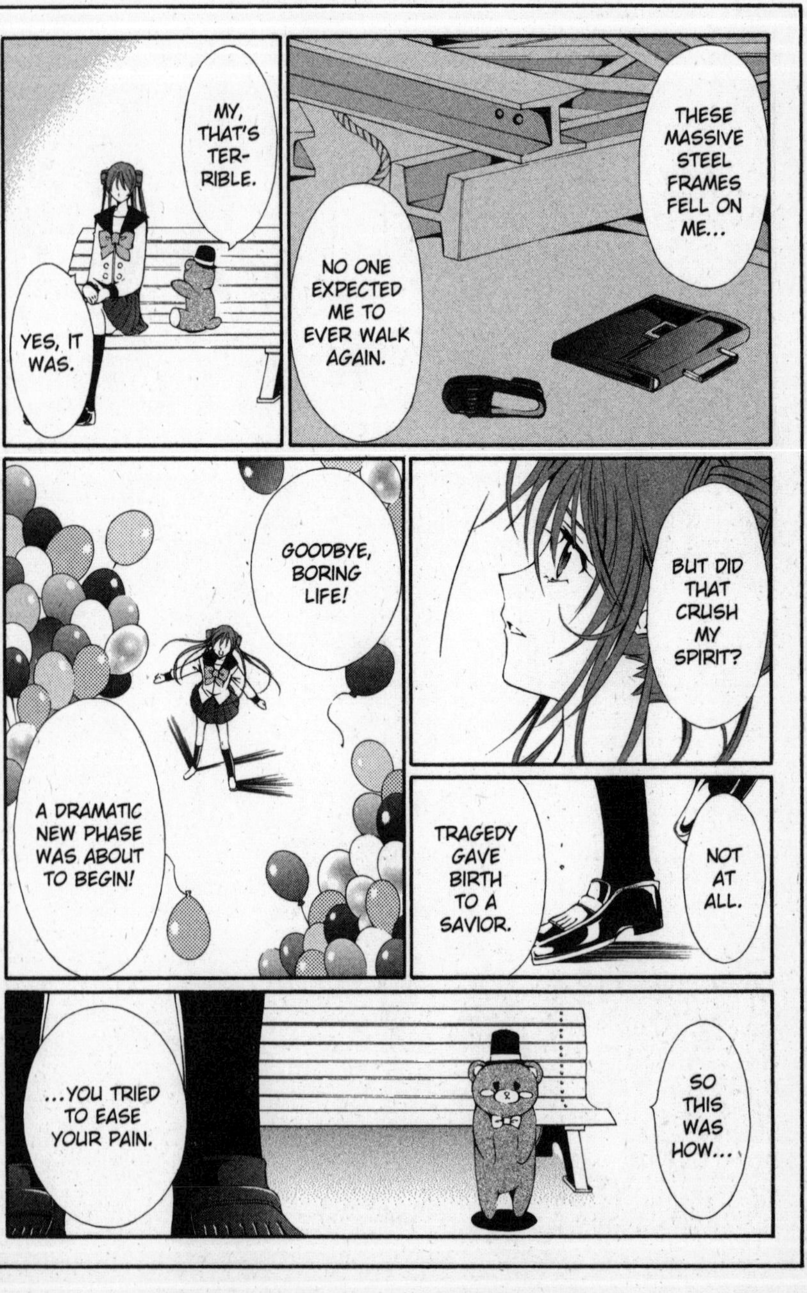
THESE MASSIVE STEEL FRAMES FELL ON ME...
NO ONE EXPECTED ME TO EVER WALK AGAIN.
MY, THAT'S TER-RIBLE.
YES, IT WAS.
BUT DID THAT CRUSH MY SPIRIT?
NOT AT ALL.
TRAGEDY GAVE BIRTH TO A SAVIOR.
GOODBYE, BORING LIFE!
A DRAMATIC NEW PHASE WAS ABOUT TO BEGIN!
SO THIS WAS HOW...
...YOU TRIED TO EASE YOUR PAIN.

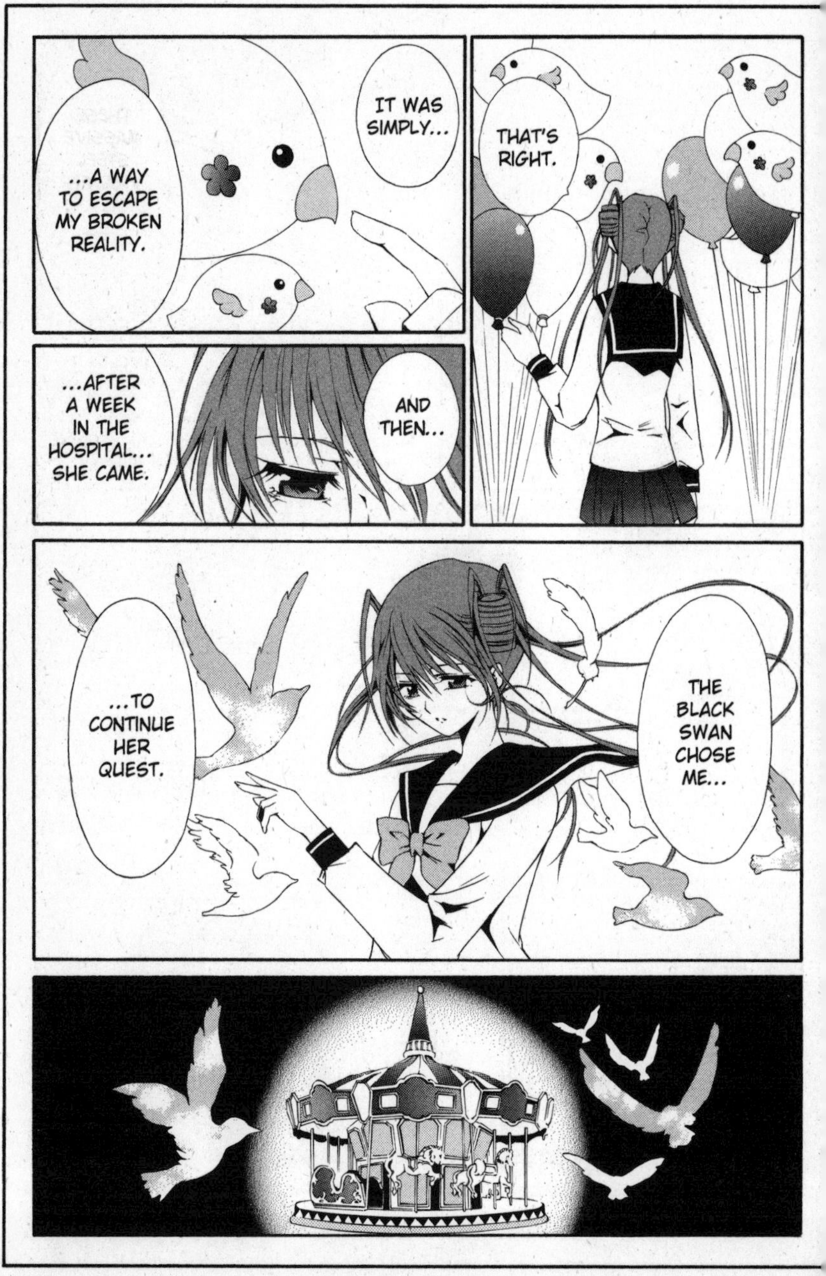
THAT'S RIGHT.
IT WAS SIMPLY...
...A WAY TO ESCAPE MY BROKEN REALITY.
AND THEN...
...AFTER A WEEK IN THE HOSPITAL... SHE CAME.
THE BLACK SWAN CHOSE ME...
...TO CONTINUE HER QUEST.

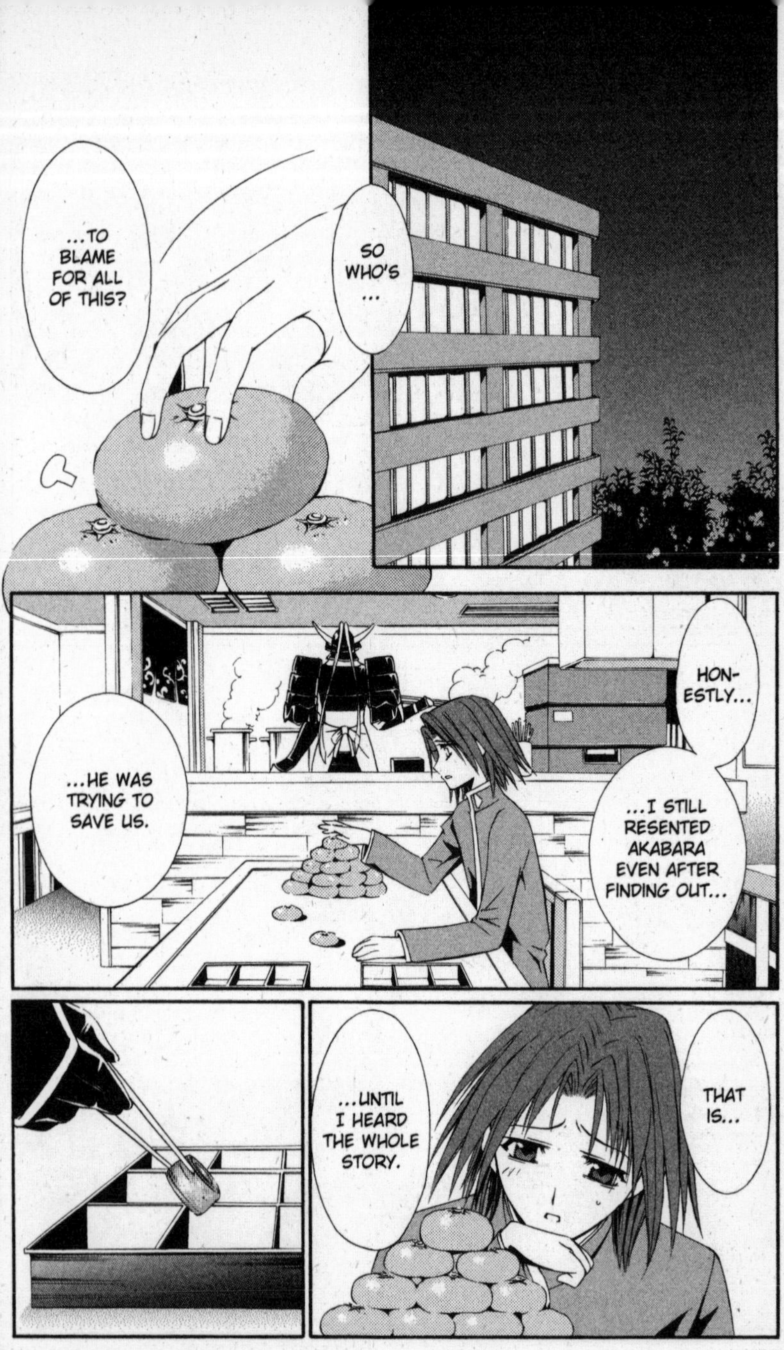
SO WHO'S ...
...TO BLAME FOR ALL OF THIS?
HON-ESTLY...
...I STILL RESENTED AKABARA EVEN AFTER FINDING OUT...
...HE WAS TRYING TO SAVE US.
THAT IS...
...UNTIL I HEARD THE WHOLE STORY.

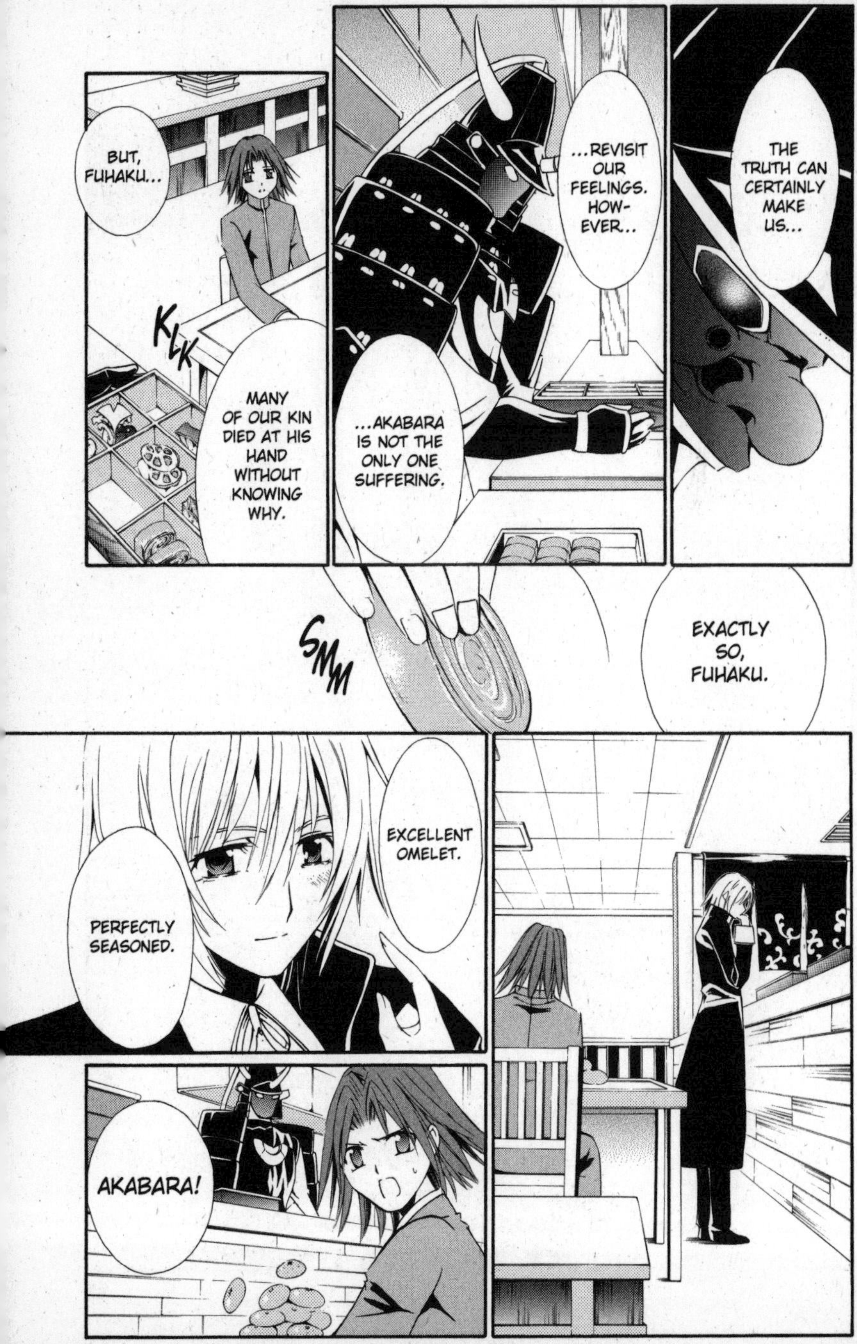
THE TRUTH CAN CERTAINLY MAKE US...
...REVISIT OUR FEELINGS. HOW-EVER...
...AKABARA IS NOT THE ONLY ONE SUFFERING.
BUT, FUHAKU...
KLK
MANY OF OUR KIN DIED AT HIS HAND WITHOUT KNOWING WHY.
EXACTLY SO, FUHAKU.
SMM
EXCELLENT OMELET.
PERFECTLY SEASONED.
AKABARA!

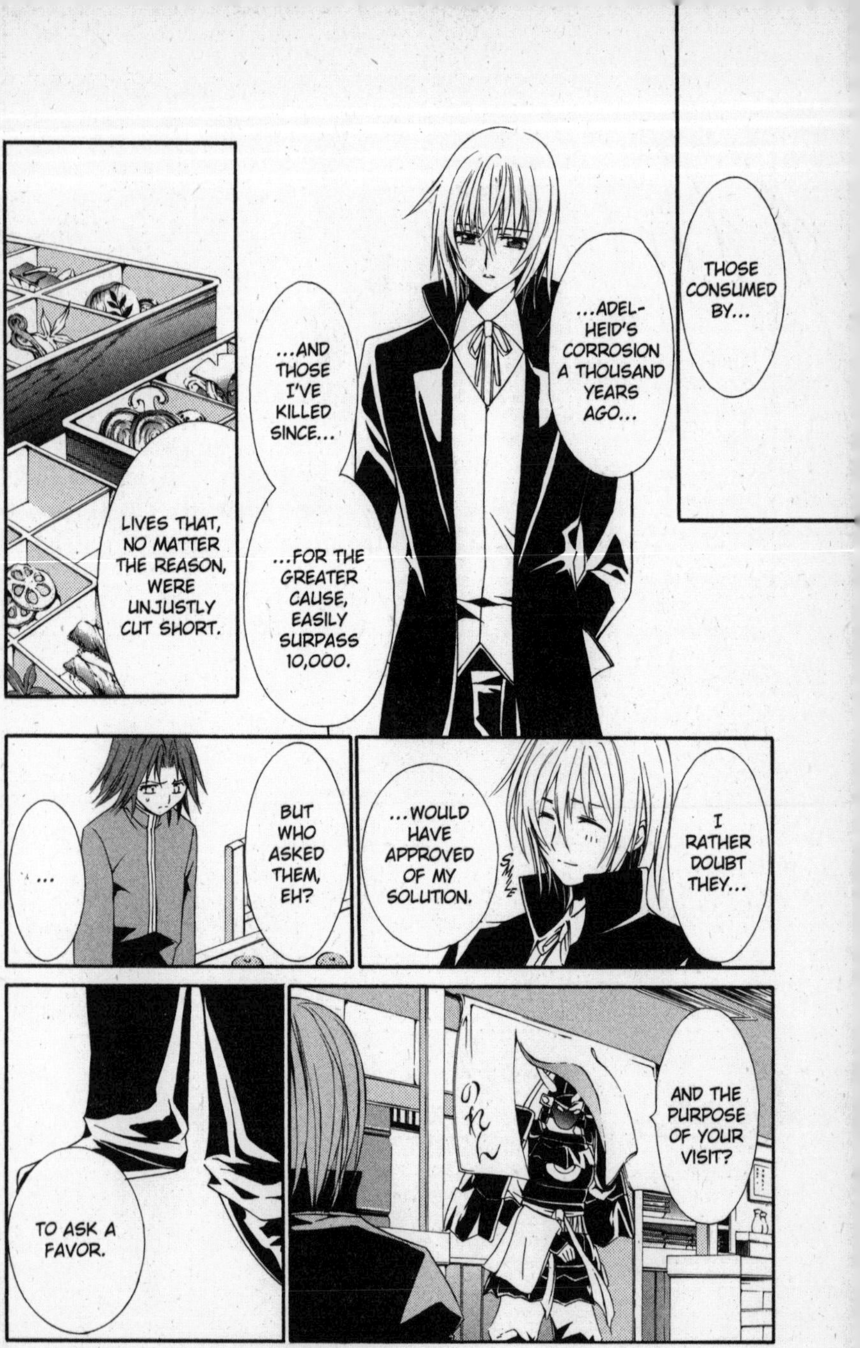
THOSE CONSUMED BY...
...ADEL-HEID'S CORROSION A THOUSAND YEARS AGO...
...AND THOSE I'VE KILLED SINCE...
...FOR THE GREATER CAUSE, EASILY SURPASS 10,000.
LIVES THAT, NO MATTER THE REASON, WERE UNJUSTLY CUT SHORT.
I RATHER DOUBT THEY...
SMILE
...WOULD HAVE APPROVED OF MY SOLUTION.
BUT WHO ASKED THEM, EH?
...
AND THE PURPOSE OF YOUR VISIT?
のれん
TO ASK A FAVOR.

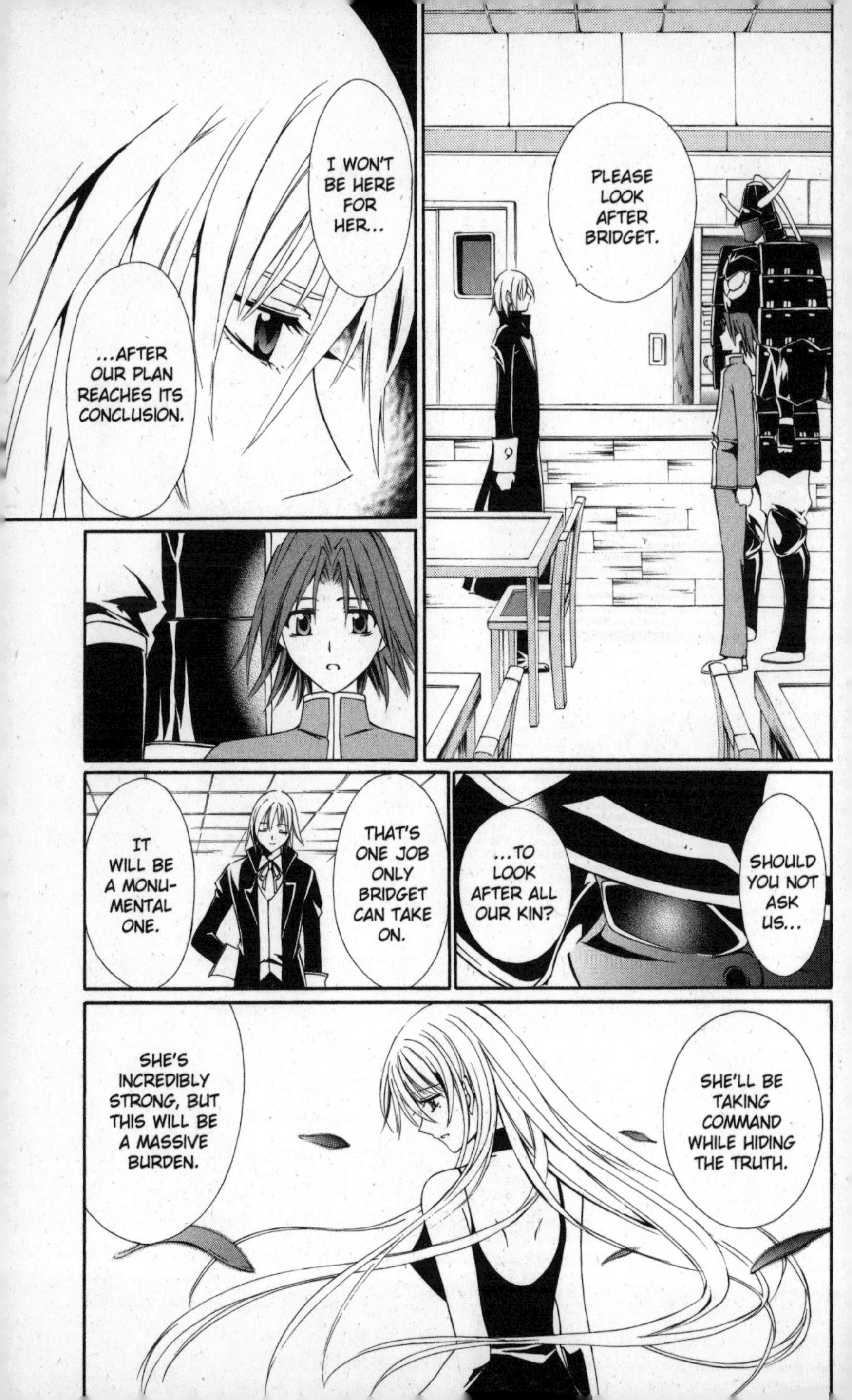
PLEASE LOOK AFTER BRIDGET.
I WON'T BE HERE FOR HER...
...AFTER OUR PLAN REACHES ITS CONCLUSION.
SHOULD YOU NOT ASK US...
...TO LOOK AFTER ALL OUR KIN?
THAT'S ONE JOB ONLY BRIDGET CAN TAKE ON.
IT WILL BE A MONU-MENTAL ONE.
SHE'LL BE TAKING COMMAND WHILE HIDING THE TRUTH.
SHE'S INCREDIBLY STRONG, BUT THIS WILL BE A MASSIVE BURDEN.

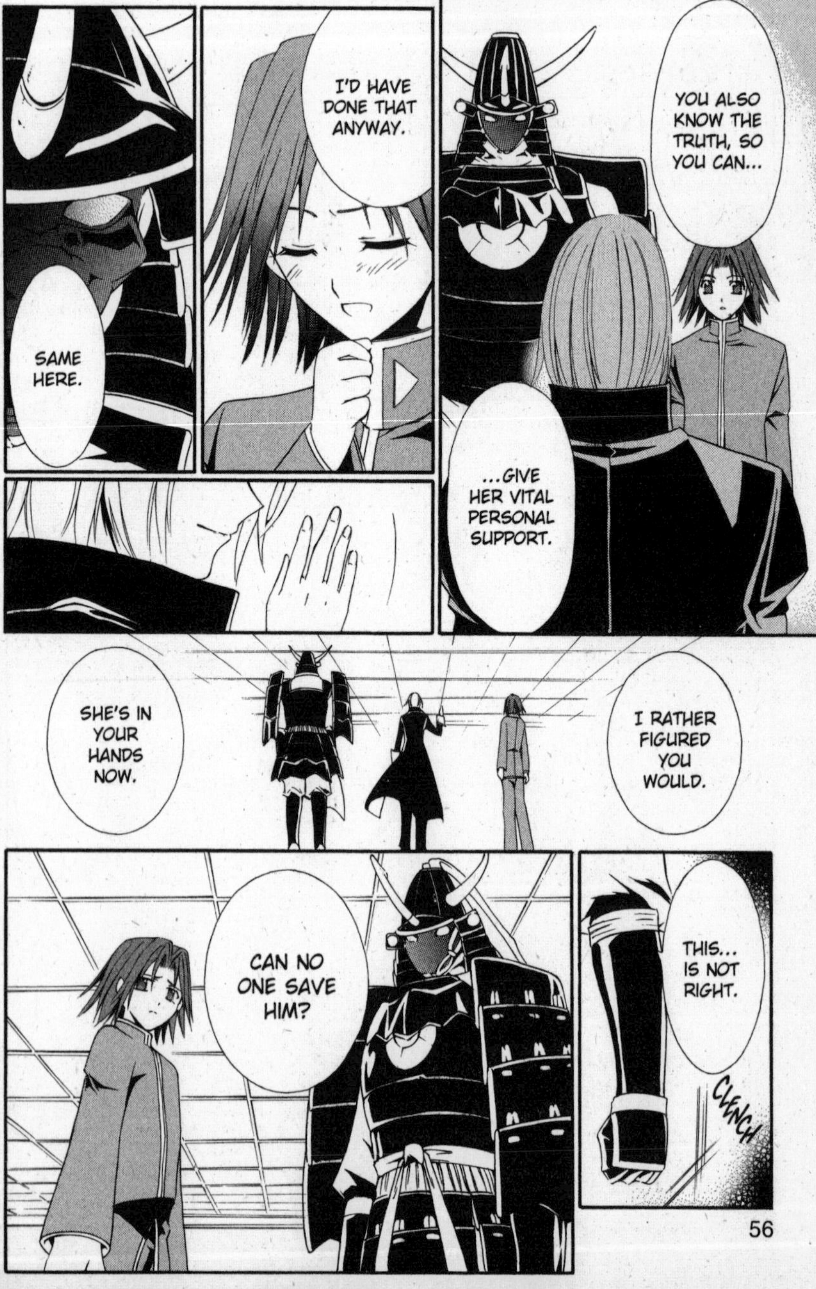
YOU ALSO KNOW THE TRUTH, SO YOU CAN...
...GIVE HER VITAL PERSONAL SUPPORT.
I'D HAVE DONE THAT ANYWAY.
SAME HERE.
I RATHER FIGURED YOU WOULD.
SHE'S IN YOUR HANDS NOW.
THIS... IS NOT RIGHT.
CLENCH
CAN NO ONE SAVE HIM?

Confessions of the 50th Black Swan, Kayuki Hirasaka: Part Two

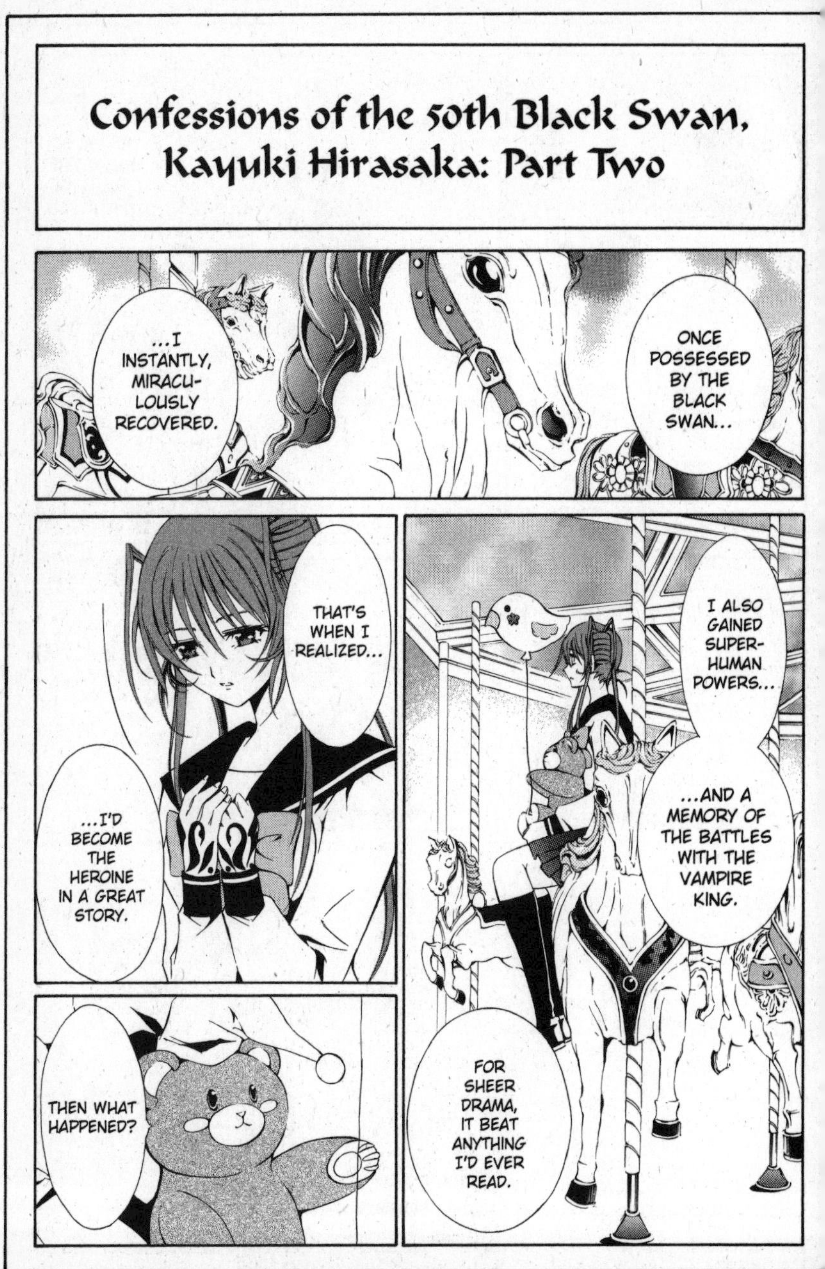
ONCE POSSESSED BY THE BLACK SWAN...
...I INSTANTLY, MIRACULOUSLY RECOVERED.
I ALSO GAINED SUPER-HUMAN POWERS...
...AND A MEMORY OF THE BATTLES WITH THE VAMPIRE KING.
FOR SHEER DRAMA, IT BEAT ANYTHING I'D EVER READ.
THAT'S WHEN I REALIZED...
...I'D BECOME THE HEROINE IN A GREAT STORY.
THEN WHAT HAPPENED?

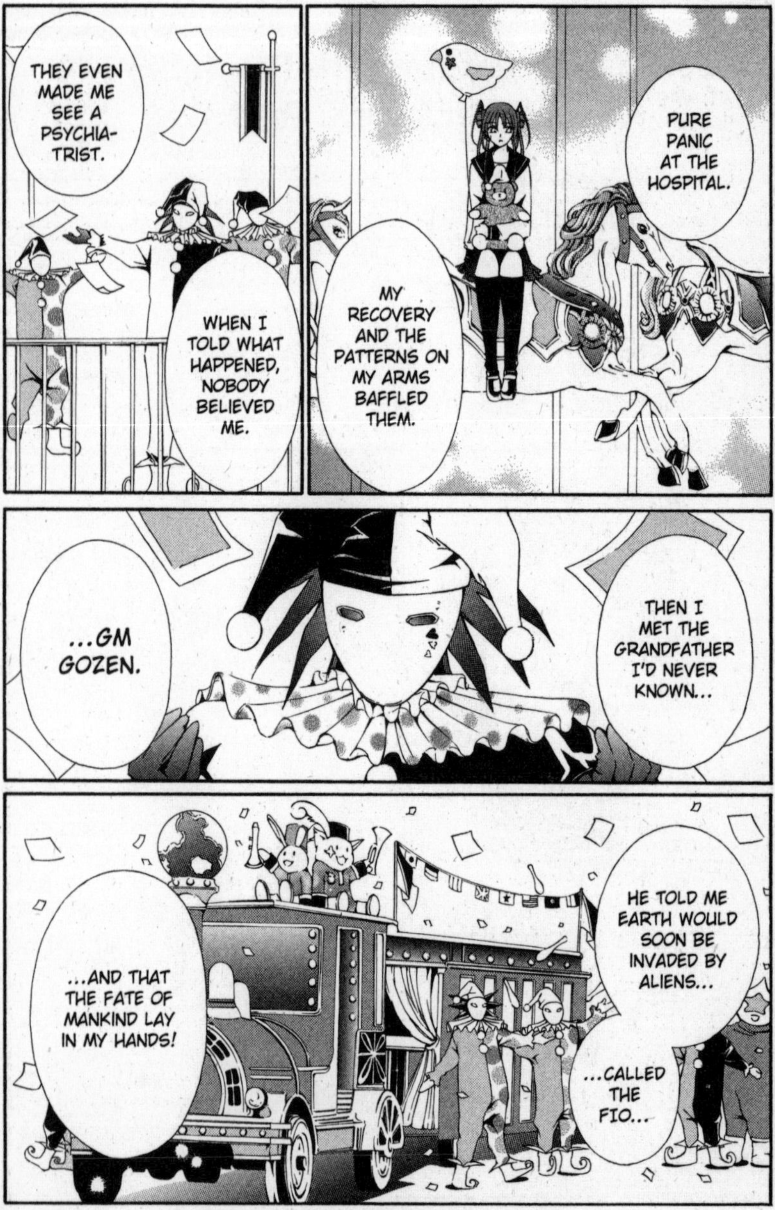
PURE PANIC AT THE HOSPITAL.
MY RECOVERY AND THE PATTERNS ON MY ARMS BAFFLED THEM.
WHEN I TOLD WHAT HAPPENED, NOBODY BELIEVED ME.
THEY EVEN MADE ME SEE A PSYCHIA-TRIST.
THEN I MET THE GRANDFATHER I'D NEVER KNOWN...
...GM GOZEN.
HE TOLD ME EARTH WOULD SOON BE INVADED BY ALIENS...
...CALLED THE FIO...
...AND THAT THE FATE OF MANKIND LAY IN MY HANDS!

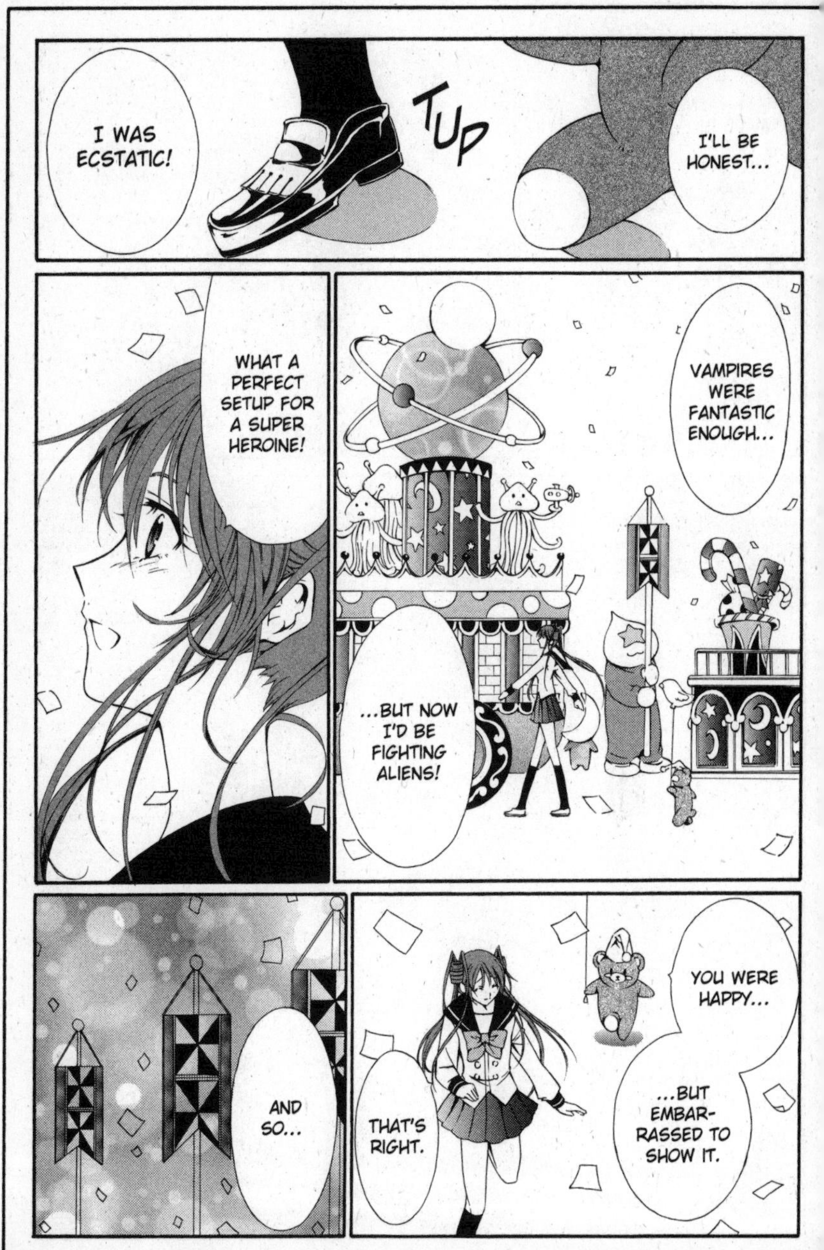
I'LL BE HONEST...
TUP
I WAS ECSTATIC!
VAMPIRES WERE FANTASTIC ENOUGH...
...BUT NOW I'D BE FIGHTING ALIENS!
WHAT A PERFECT SETUP FOR A SUPER HEROINE!
YOU WERE HAPPY...
...BUT EMBAR-RASSED TO SHOW IT.
THAT'S RIGHT.
AND SO...

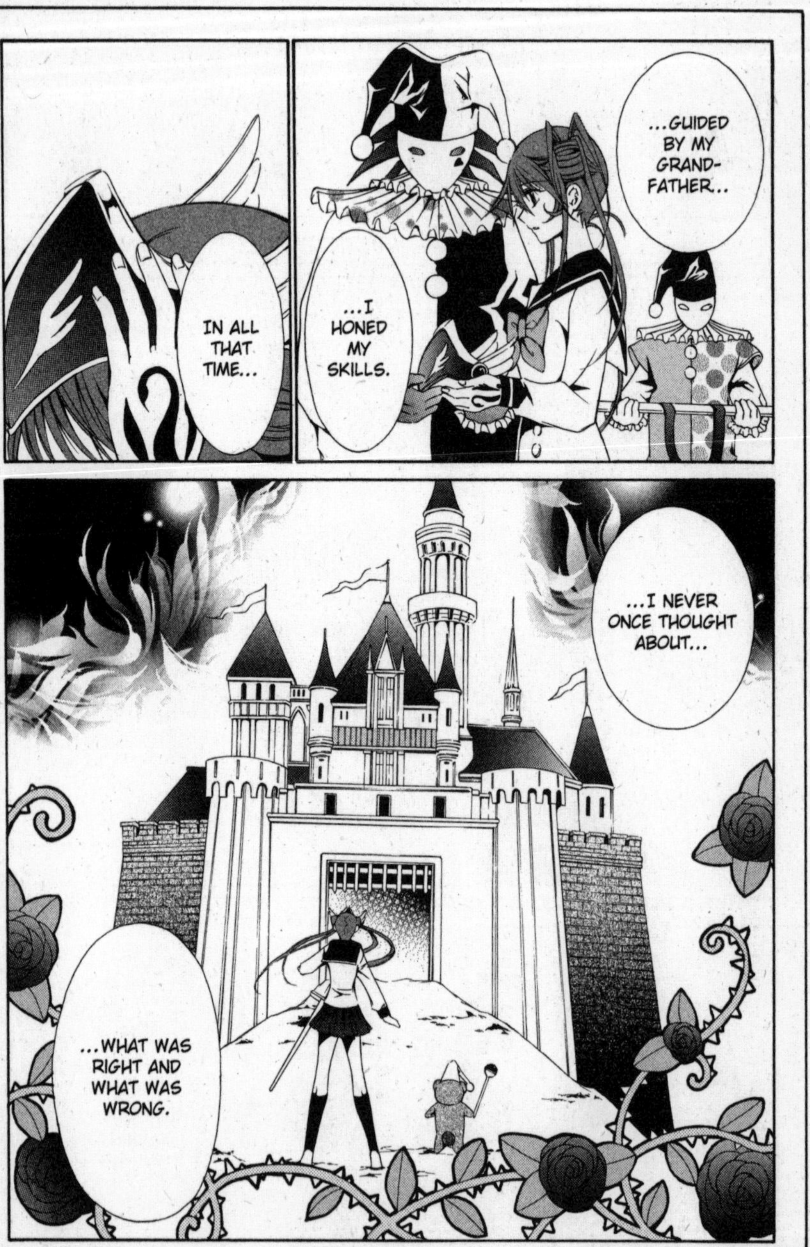
...GUIDED BY MY GRAND-FATHER...
...I HONED MY SKILLS.
IN ALL THAT TIME...
...I NEVER ONCE THOUGHT ABOUT...
...WHAT WAS RIGHT AND WHAT WAS WRONG.

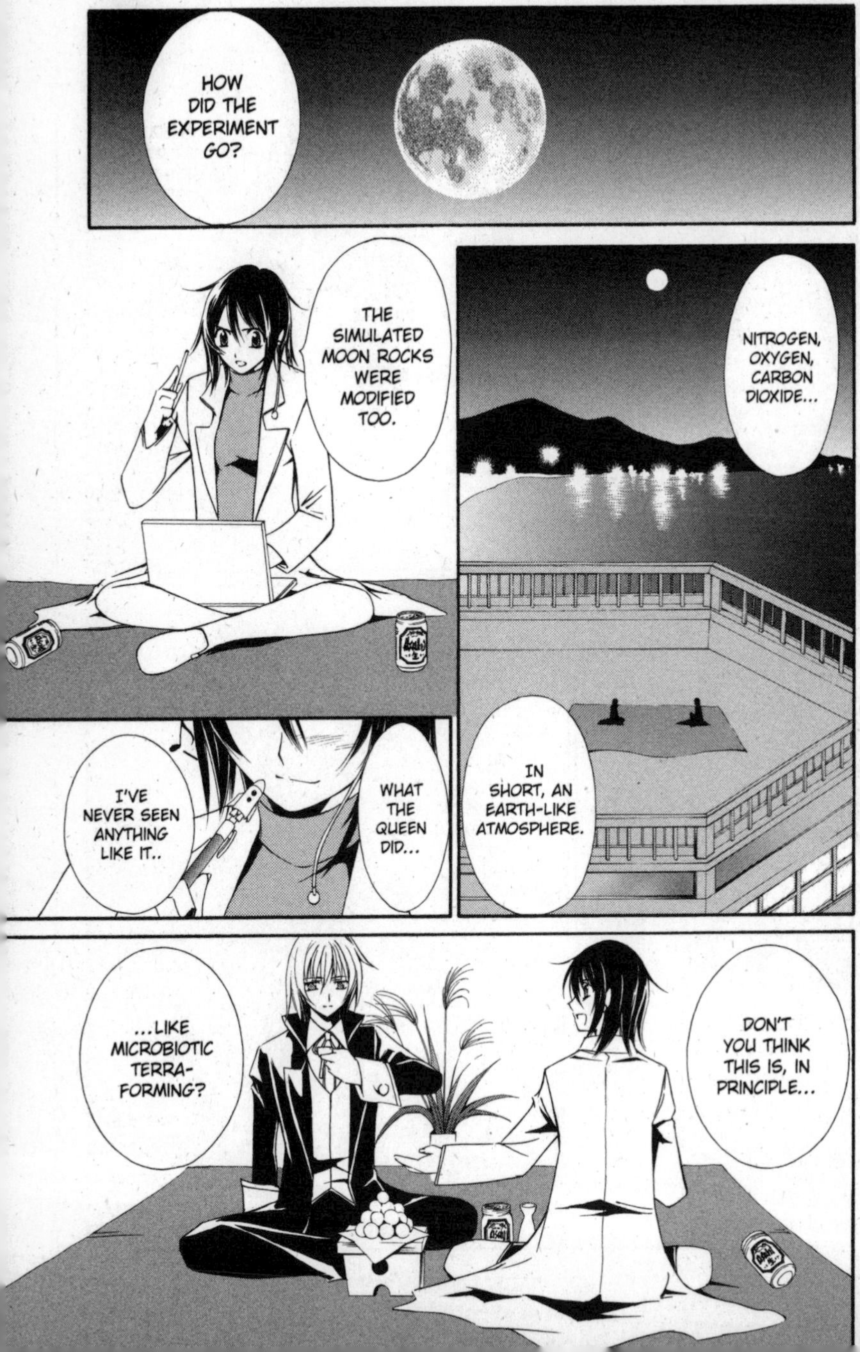
HOW DID THE EXPERIMENT GO?
NITROGEN, OXYGEN, CARBON DIOXIDE...
IN SHORT, AN EARTH-LIKE ATMOSPHERE.
THE SIMULATED MOON ROCKS WERE MODIFIED TOO.
WHAT THE QUEEN DID...
I'VE NEVER SEEN ANYTHING LIKE IT..
DON'T YOU THINK THIS IS, IN PRINCIPLE...
...LIKE MICROBIOTIC TERRA-FORMING?

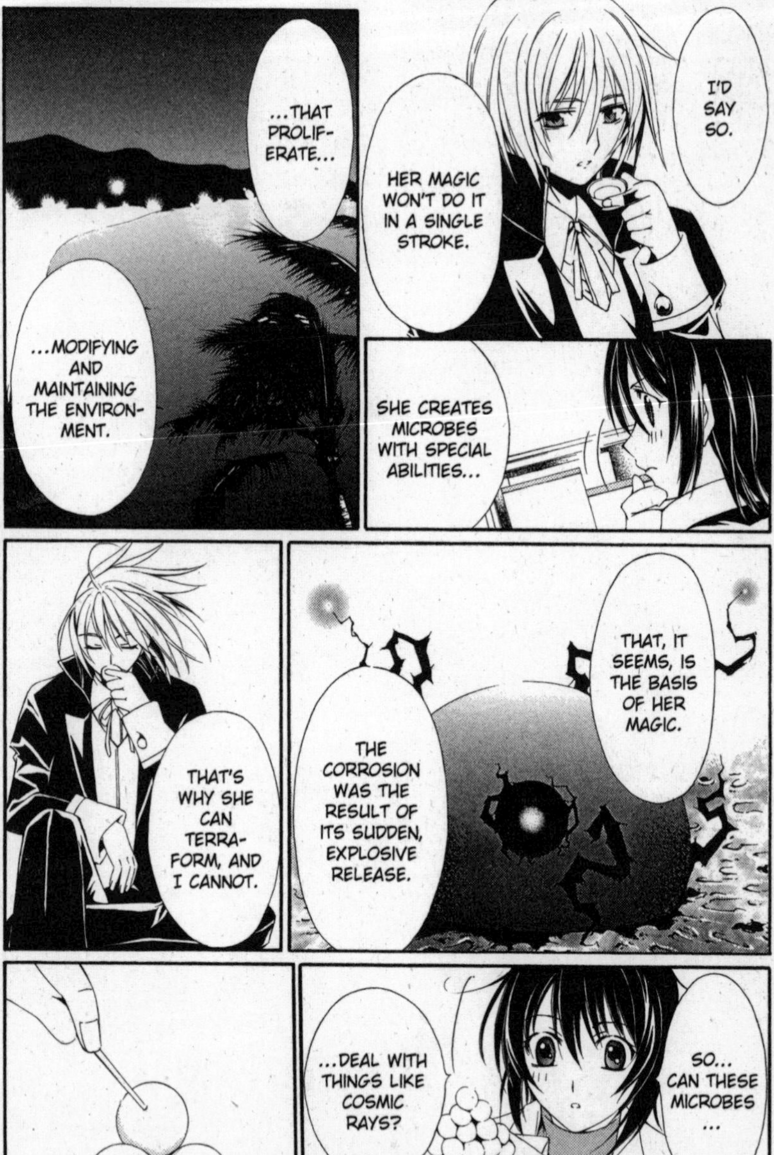
I'D SAY SO.
HER MAGIC WON'T DO IT IN A SINGLE STROKE.
SHE CREATES MICROBES WITH SPECIAL ABILITIES...
...THAT PROLIF-ERATE...
...MODIFYING AND MAINTAINING THE ENVIRON-MENT.
THAT, IT SEEMS, IS THE BASIS OF HER MAGIC.
THE CORROSION WAS THE RESULT OF ITS SUDDEN, EXPLOSIVE RELEASE.
THAT'S WHY SHE CAN TERRA-FORM, AND I CANNOT.
SO... CAN THESE MICROBES ...
...DEAL WITH THINGS LIKE COSMIC RAYS?

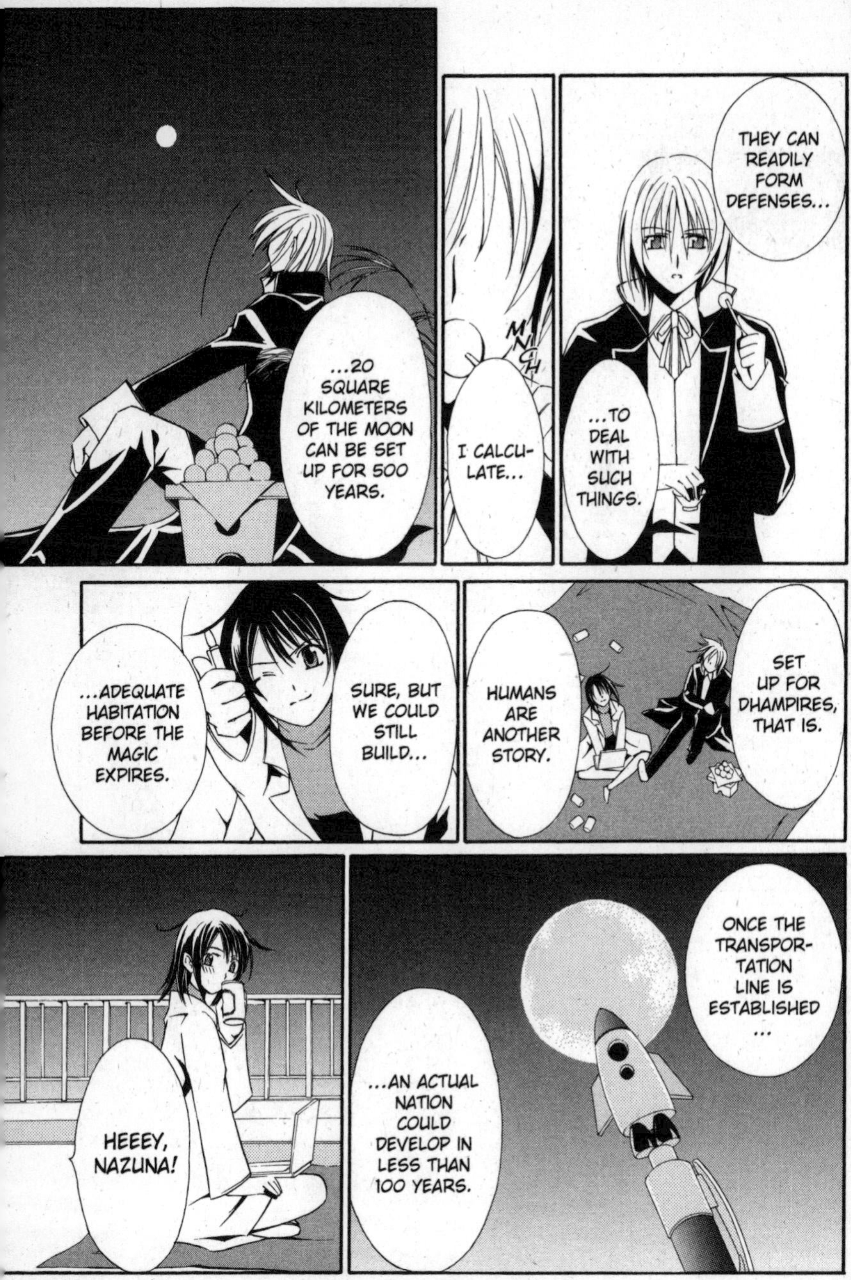
THEY CAN READILY FORM DEFENSES...
...TO DEAL WITH SUCH THINGS.
MNCH
I CALCULATE...
...20 SQUARE KILOMETERS OF THE MOON CAN BE SET UP FOR 500 YEARS.
SET UP FOR DHAMPIRES, THAT IS.
HUMANS ARE ANOTHER STORY.
SURE, BUT WE COULD STILL BUILD...
...ADEQUATE HABITATION BEFORE THE MAGIC EXPIRES.
ONCE THE TRANSPORTATION LINE IS ESTABLISHED...
...AN ACTUAL NATION COULD DEVELOP IN LESS THAN 100 YEARS.
HEEEY, NAZUNA!

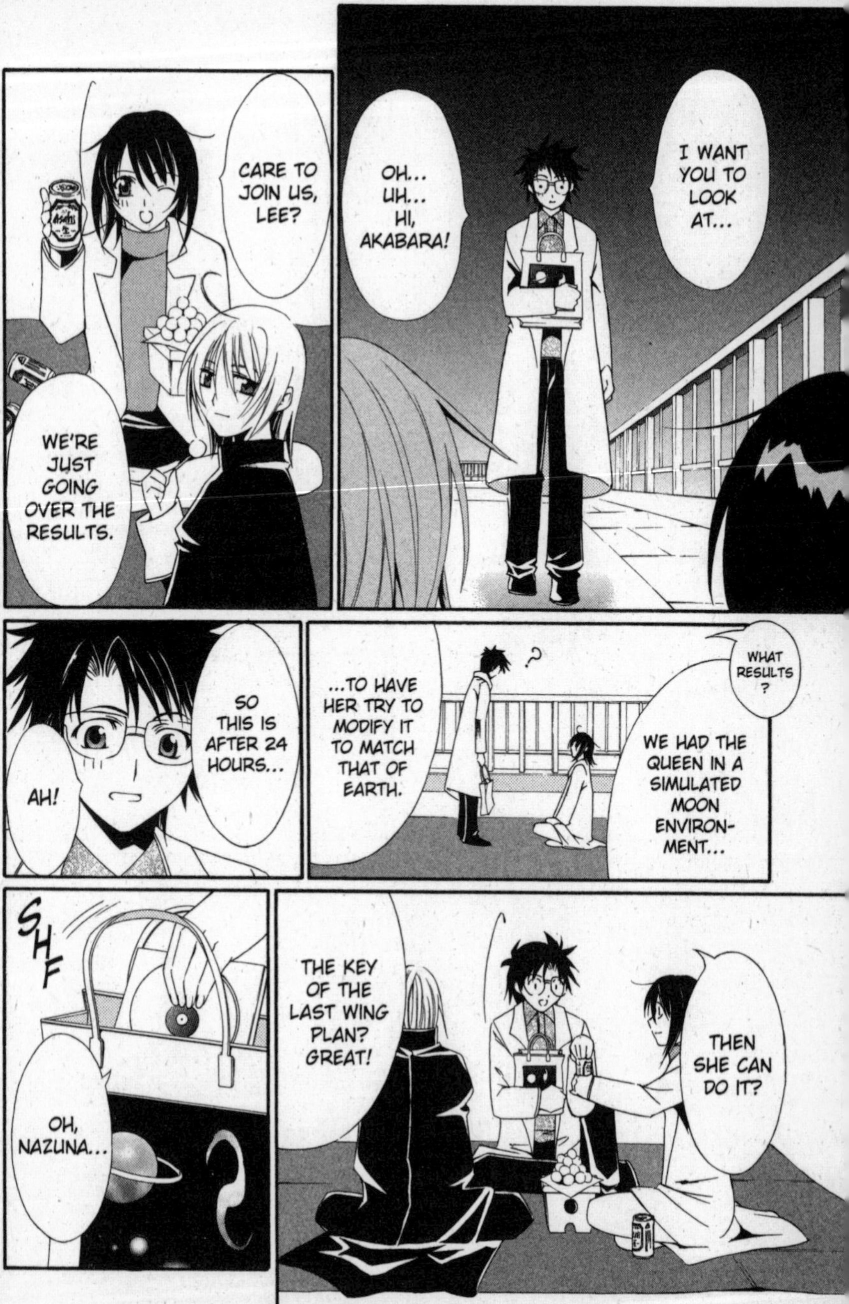
I WANT YOU TO LOOK AT...
OH... UH... HI, AKABARA!
CARE TO JOIN US, LEE?
WE'RE JUST GOING OVER THE RESULTS.
WHAT RESULTS?
WE HAD THE QUEEN IN A SIMULATED MOON ENVIRON-MENT...
...TO HAVE HER TRY TO MODIFY IT TO MATCH THAT OF EARTH.
SO THIS IS AFTER 24 HOURS...
AH!
THEN SHE CAN DO IT?
THE KEY OF THE LAST WING PLAN? GREAT!
SHF
OH, NAZUNA...

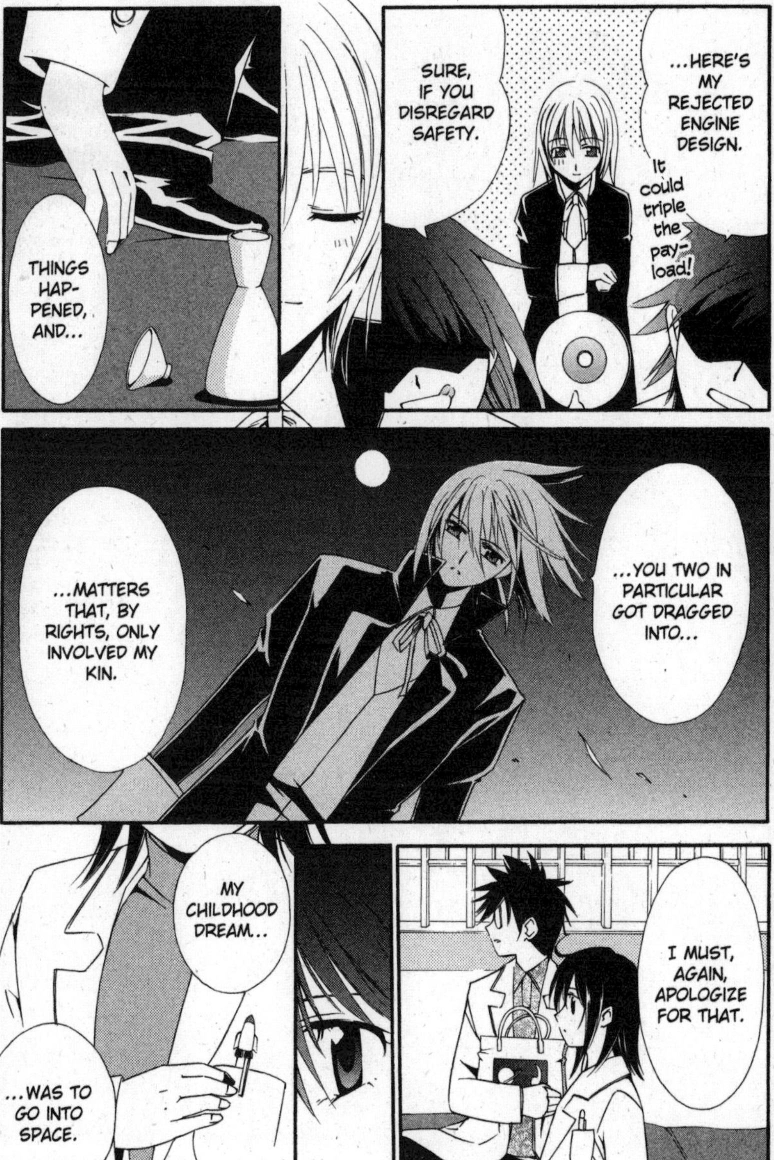
...HERE'S MY REJECTED ENGINE DESIGN.
It could triple the pay-load!
SURE, IF YOU DISREGARD SAFETY.
THINGS HAP-PENED, AND...
...YOU TWO IN PARTICULAR GOT DRAGGED INTO...
...MATTERS THAT, BY RIGHTS, ONLY INVOLVED MY KIN.
I MUST, AGAIN, APOLOGIZE FOR THAT.
MY CHILDHOOD DREAM...
...WAS TO GO INTO SPACE.

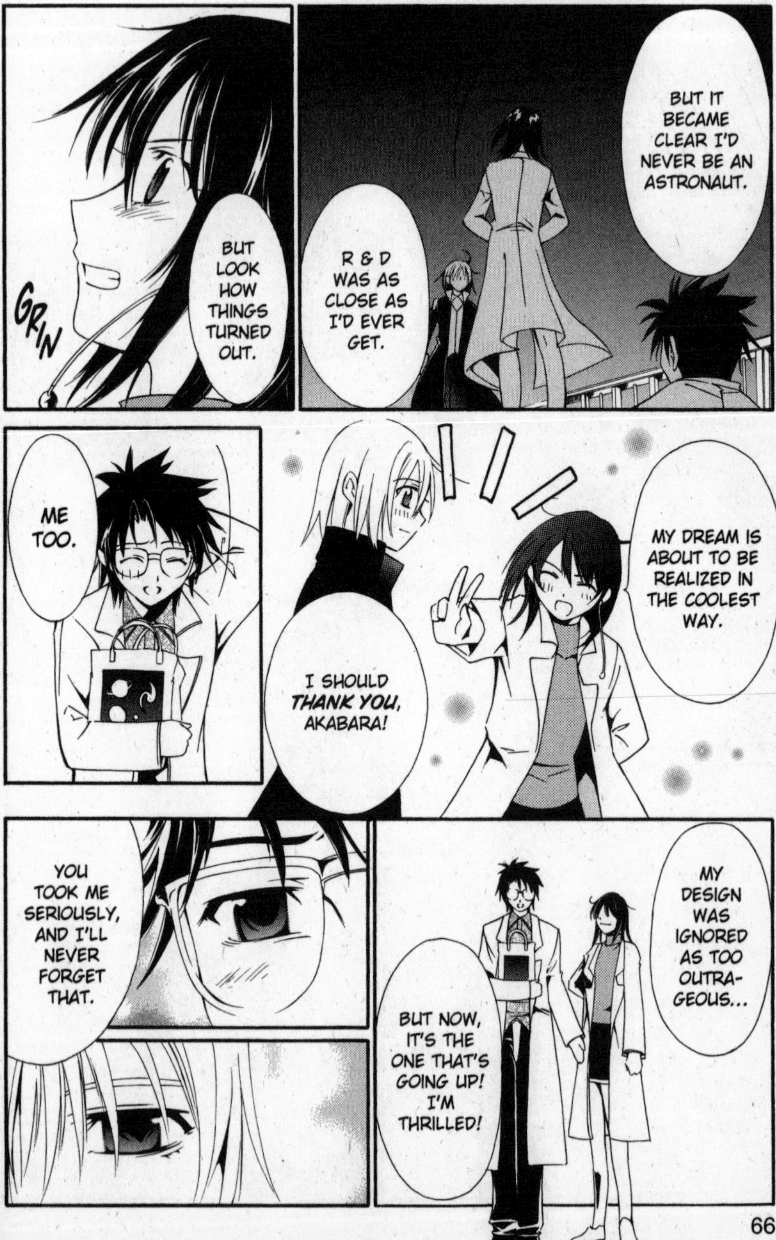
BUT IT BECAME CLEAR I'D NEVER BE AN ASTRONAUT.
R & D WAS AS CLOSE AS I'D EVER GET.
BUT LOOK HOW THINGS TURNED OUT.
GRIN
MY DREAM IS ABOUT TO BE REALIZED IN THE COOLEST WAY.
I SHOULD *THANK YOU*, AKABARA!
ME TOO.
MY DESIGN WAS IGNORED AS TOO OUTRA-GEOUS...
BUT NOW, IT'S THE ONE THAT'S GOING UP! I'M THRILLED!
YOU TOOK ME SERIOUSLY, AND I'LL NEVER FORGET THAT.

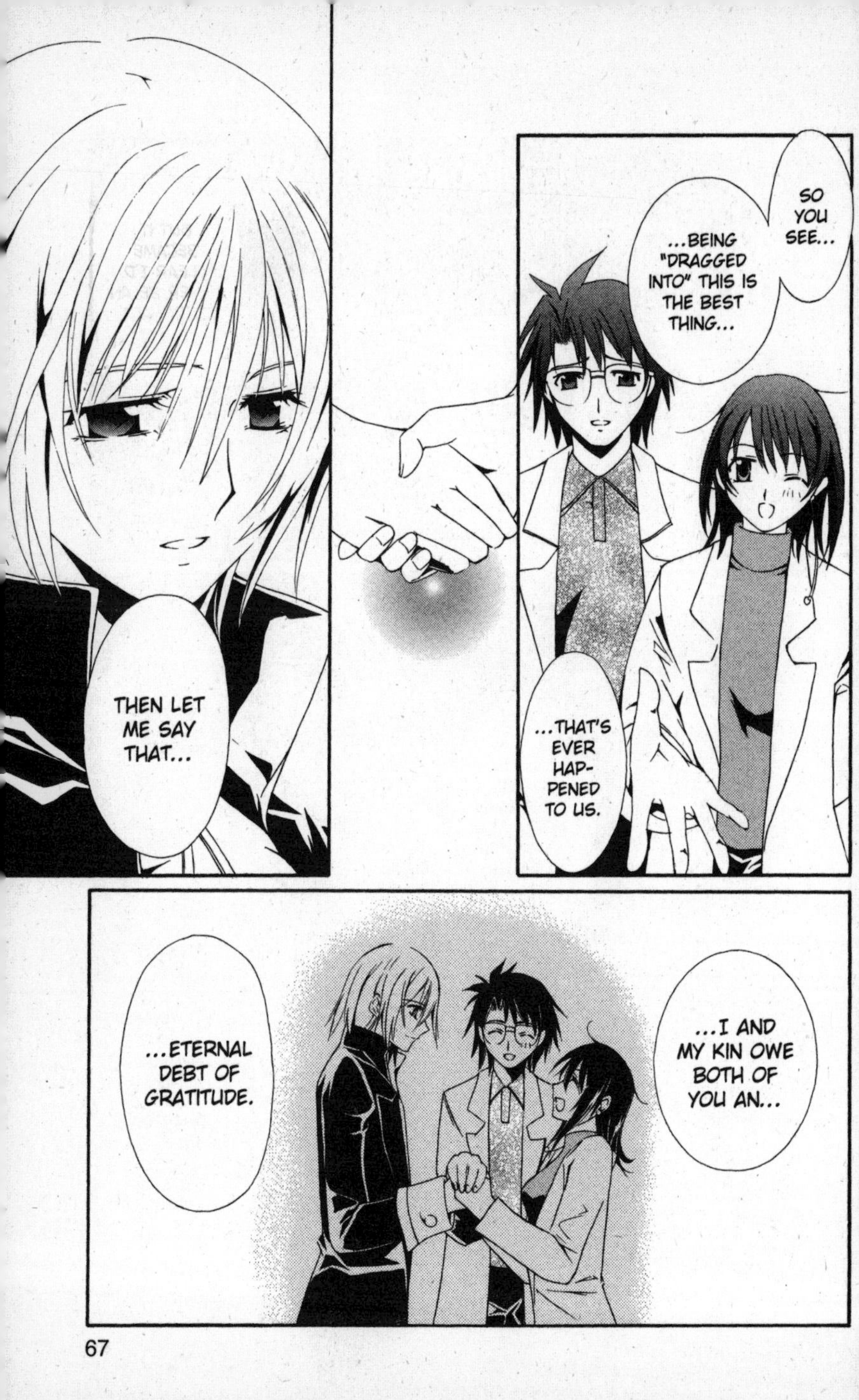
SO YOU SEE...
...BEING "DRAGGED INTO" THIS IS THE BEST THING...
...THAT'S EVER HAP-PENED TO US.
THEN LET ME SAY THAT...
...I AND MY KIN OWE BOTH OF YOU AN...
...ETERNAL DEBT OF GRATITUDE.

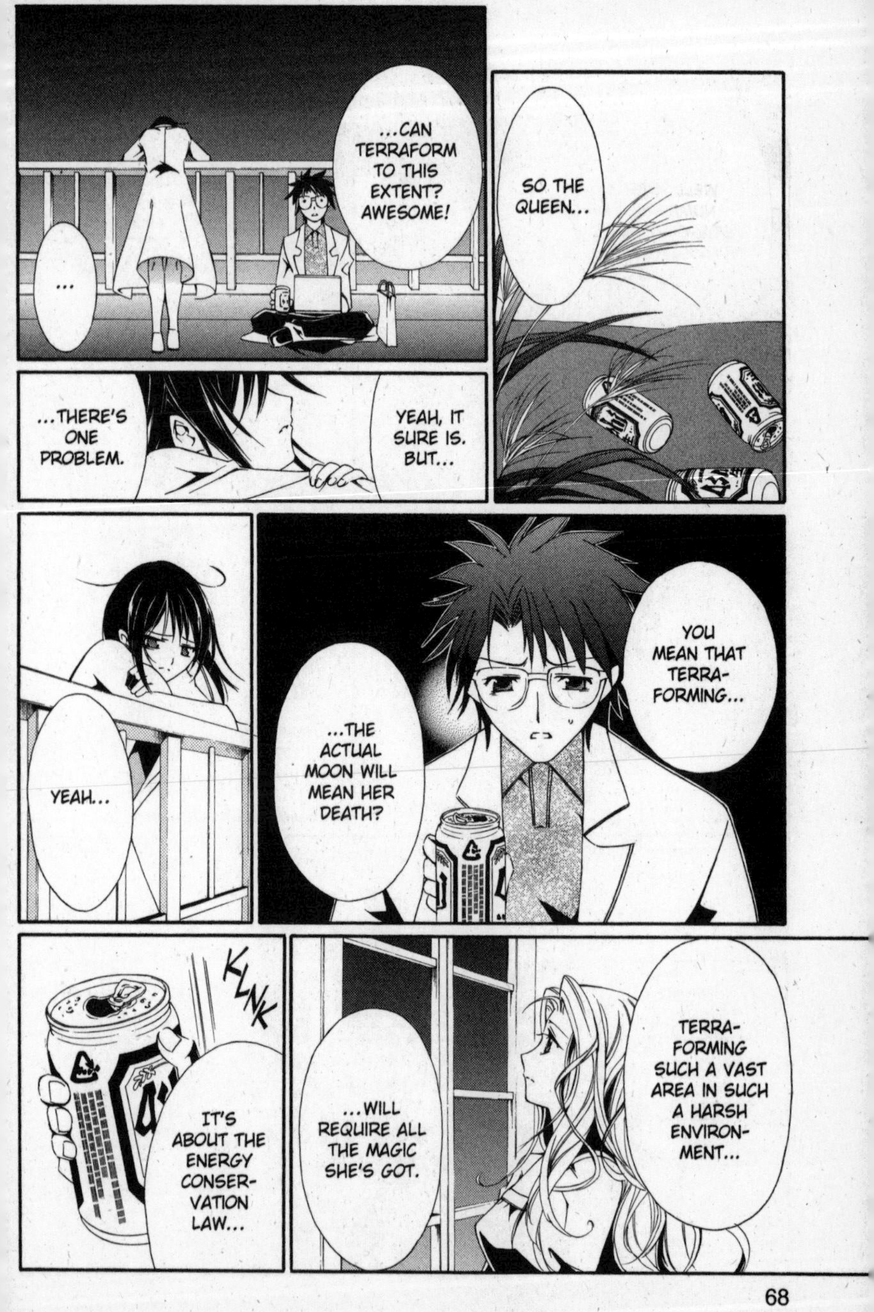
SO THE QUEEN...
...CAN TERRAFORM TO THIS EXTENT? AWESOME!
...
YEAH, IT SURE IS. BUT...
...THERE'S ONE PROBLEM.
YOU MEAN THAT TERRA-FORMING...
...THE ACTUAL MOON WILL MEAN HER DEATH?
YEAH...
TERRA-FORMING SUCH A VAST AREA IN SUCH A HARSH ENVIRON-MENT...
...WILL REQUIRE ALL THE MAGIC SHE'S GOT.
KLNK
IT'S ABOUT THE ENERGY CONSER-VATION LAW...

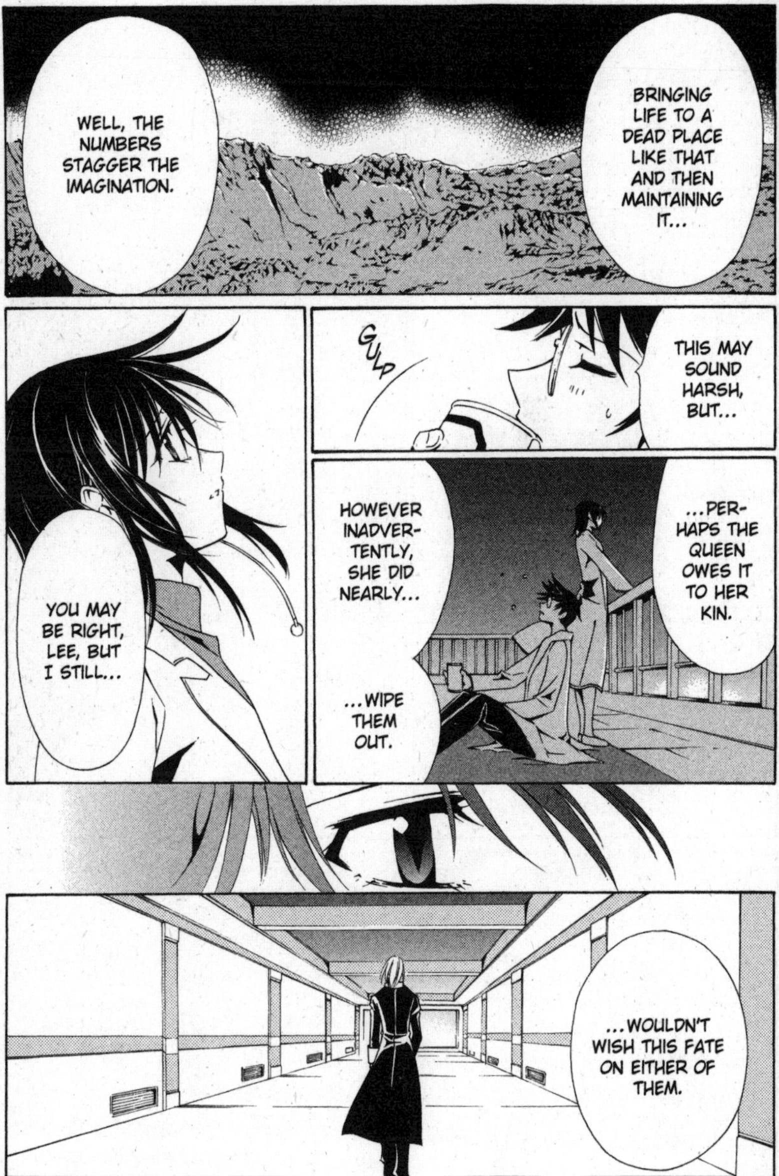
BRINGING LIFE TO A DEAD PLACE LIKE THAT AND THEN MAINTAINING IT...
WELL, THE NUMBERS STAGGER THE IMAGINATION.
THIS MAY SOUND HARSH, BUT...
GULP
...PER-HAPS THE QUEEN OWES IT TO HER KIN.
HOWEVER INADVER-TENTLY, SHE DID NEARLY...
...WIPE THEM OUT.
YOU MAY BE RIGHT, LEE, BUT I STILL...
...WOULDN'T WISH THIS FATE ON EITHER OF THEM.

Confessions of the 50th Black Swan, Kayuki Hirasaka: Part Three

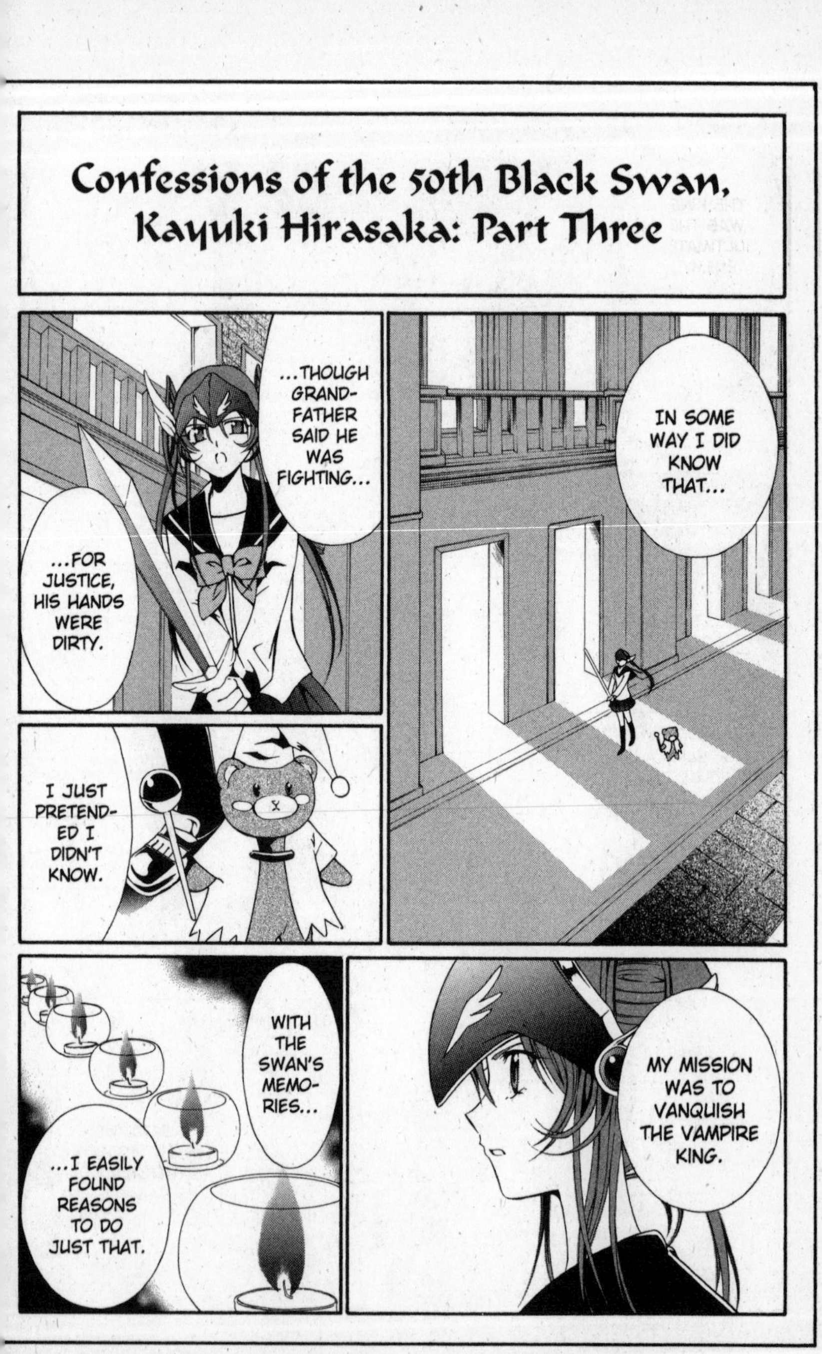
IN SOME WAY I DID KNOW THAT...
...THOUGH GRANDFATHER SAID HE WAS FIGHTING...
...FOR JUSTICE, HIS HANDS WERE DIRTY.
I JUST PRETENDED I DIDN'T KNOW.
MY MISSION WAS TO VANQUISH THE VAMPIRE KING.
WITH THE SWAN'S MEMORIES...
...I EASILY FOUND REASONS TO DO JUST THAT.

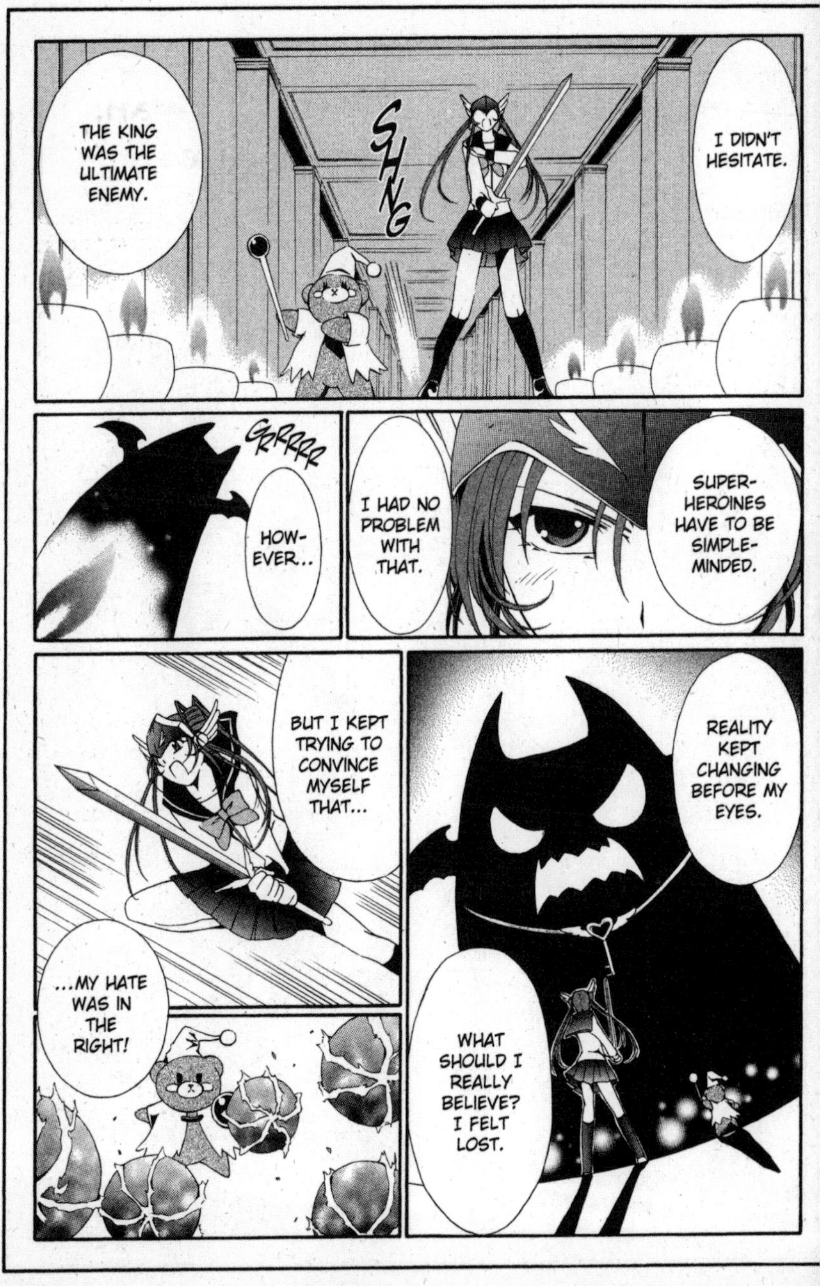
I DIDN'T HESITATE.
THE KING WAS THE ULTIMATE ENEMY.
SHNG
SUPER-HEROINES HAVE TO BE SIMPLE-MINDED.
I HAD NO PROBLEM WITH THAT.
GRRRRR
HOW-EVER...
REALITY KEPT CHANGING BEFORE MY EYES.
WHAT SHOULD I REALLY BELIEVE? I FELT LOST.
BUT I KEPT TRYING TO CONVINCE MYSELF THAT...
...MY HATE WAS IN THE RIGHT!

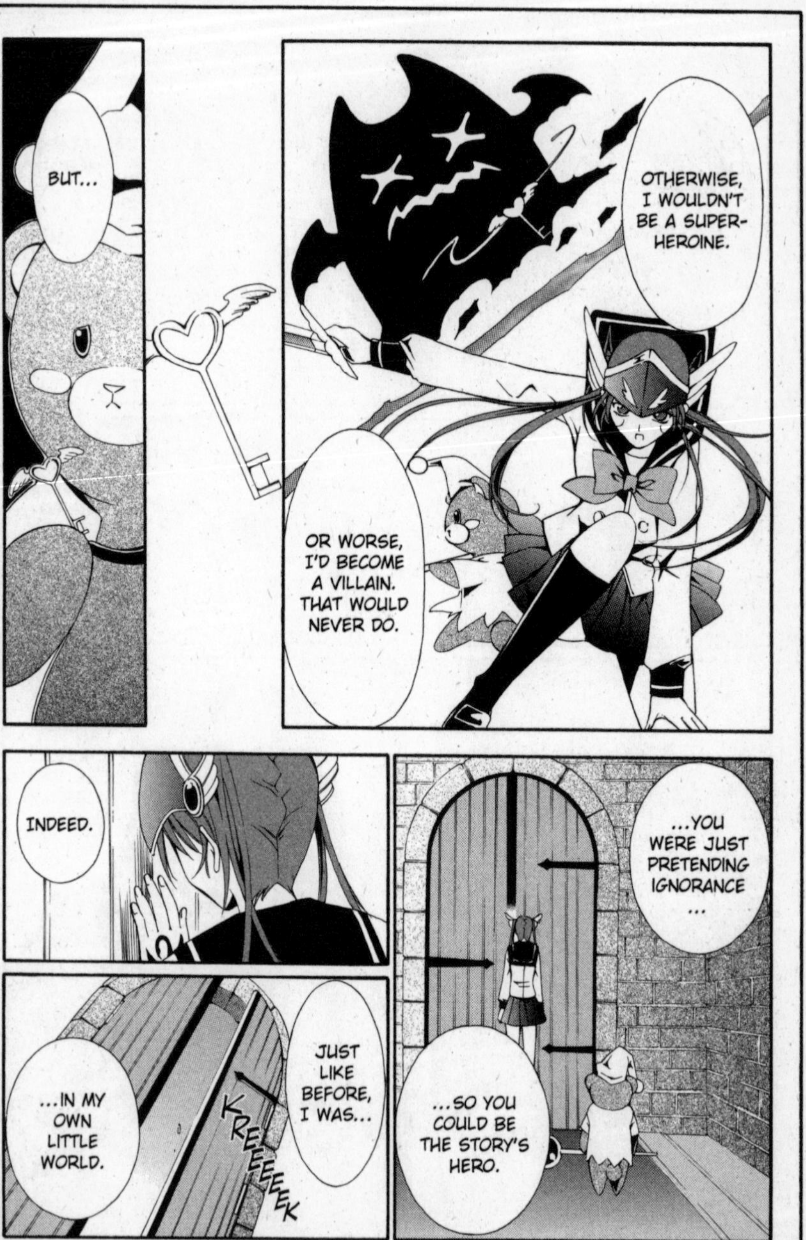
OTHERWISE, I WOULDN'T BE A SUPER-HEROINE.
OR WORSE, I'D BECOME A VILLAIN. THAT WOULD NEVER DO.
BUT...
...YOU WERE JUST PRETENDING IGNORANCE ...
...SO YOU COULD BE THE STORY'S HERO.
INDEED.
JUST LIKE BEFORE, I WAS...
KREEEEEK
...IN MY OWN LITTLE WORLD.

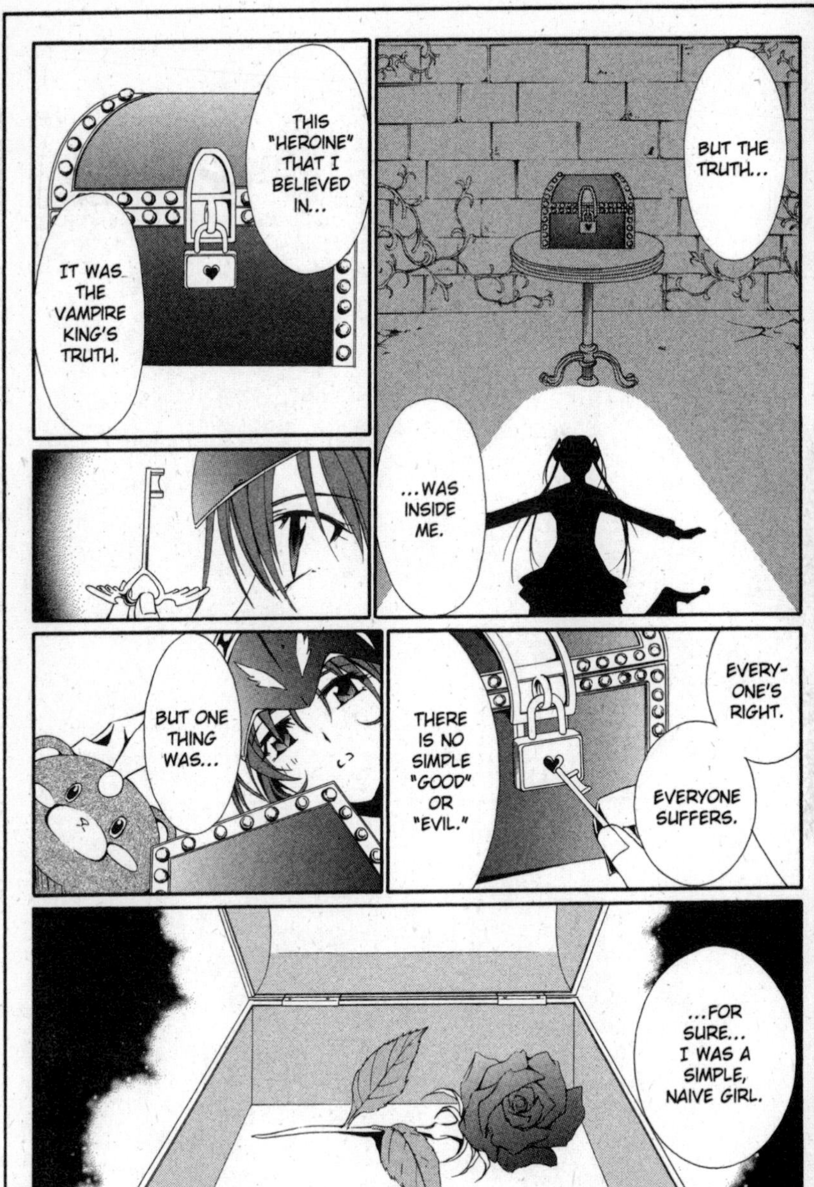
BUT THE TRUTH...
...WAS INSIDE ME.
THIS "HEROINE" THAT I BELIEVED IN...
IT WAS THE VAMPIRE KING'S TRUTH.
EVERYONE'S RIGHT.
EVERYONE SUFFERS.
THERE IS NO SIMPLE "GOOD" OR "EVIL."
BUT ONE THING WAS...
...FOR SURE... I WAS A SIMPLE, NAIVE GIRL.

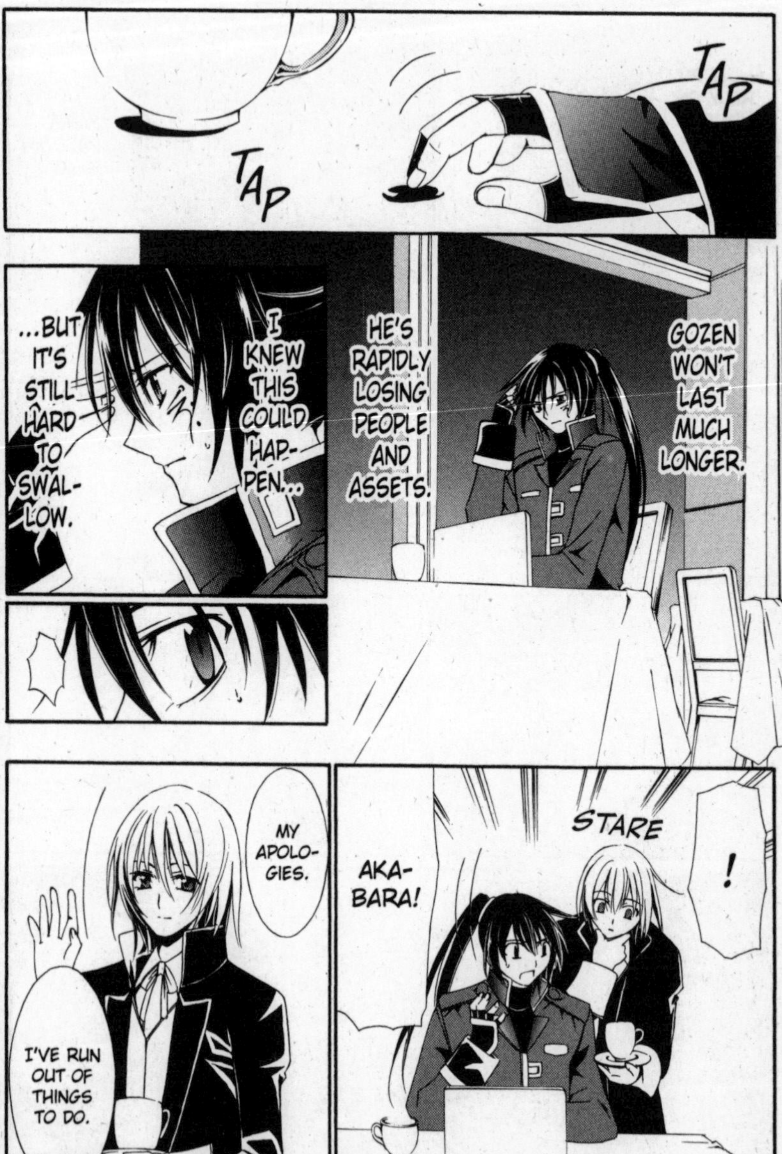
TAP
TAP
GOZEN WON'T LAST MUCH LONGER.
HE'S RAPIDLY LOSING PEOPLE AND ASSETS.
I KNEW THIS COULD HAP-PEN...
...BUT IT'S STILL HARD TO SWAL-LOW.
!
STARE
AKA-BARA!
MY APOLO-GIES.
I'VE RUN OUT OF THINGS TO DO.

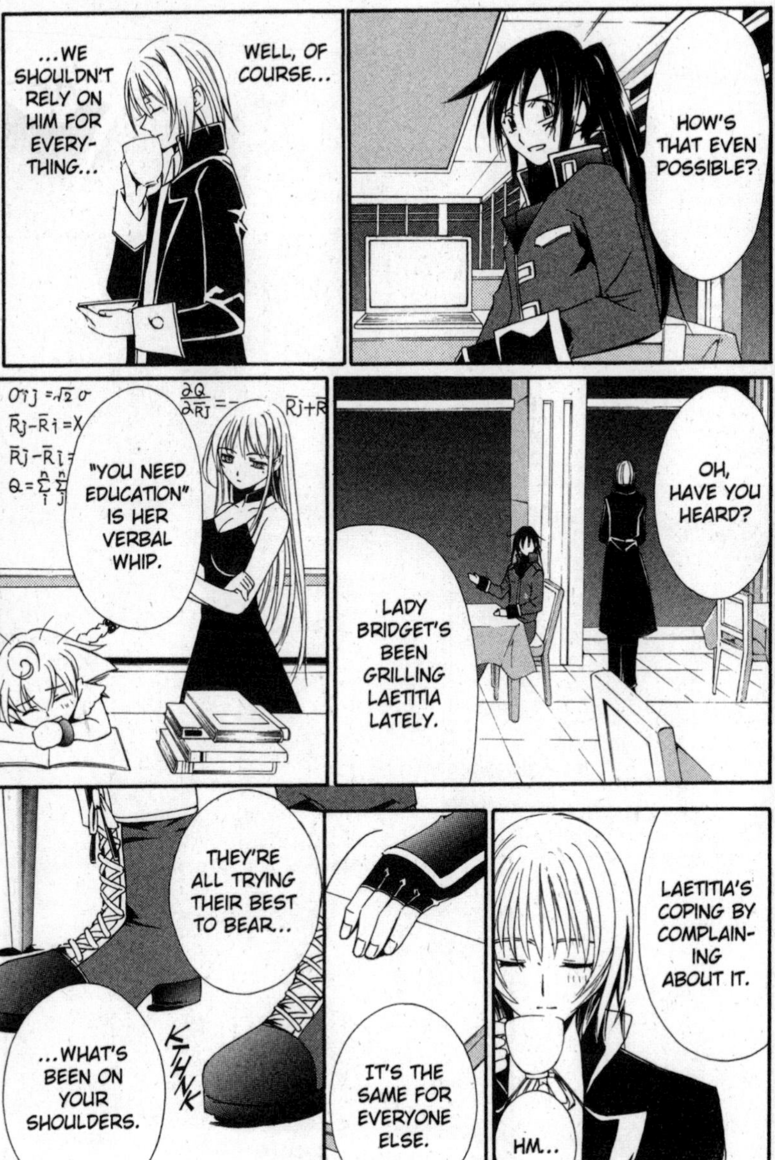
HOW'S THAT EVEN POSSIBLE?
WELL, OF COURSE...
...WE SHOULDN'T RELY ON HIM FOR EVERY-THING...
OH, HAVE YOU HEARD?
LADY BRIDGET'S BEEN GRILLING LAETITIA LATELY.
"YOU NEED EDUCATION" IS HER VERBAL WHIP.
LAETITIA'S COPING BY COMPLAIN-ING ABOUT IT.
HM...
IT'S THE SAME FOR EVERYONE ELSE.
THEY'RE ALL TRYING THEIR BEST TO BEAR...
KTHNK
...WHAT'S BEEN ON YOUR SHOULDERS.

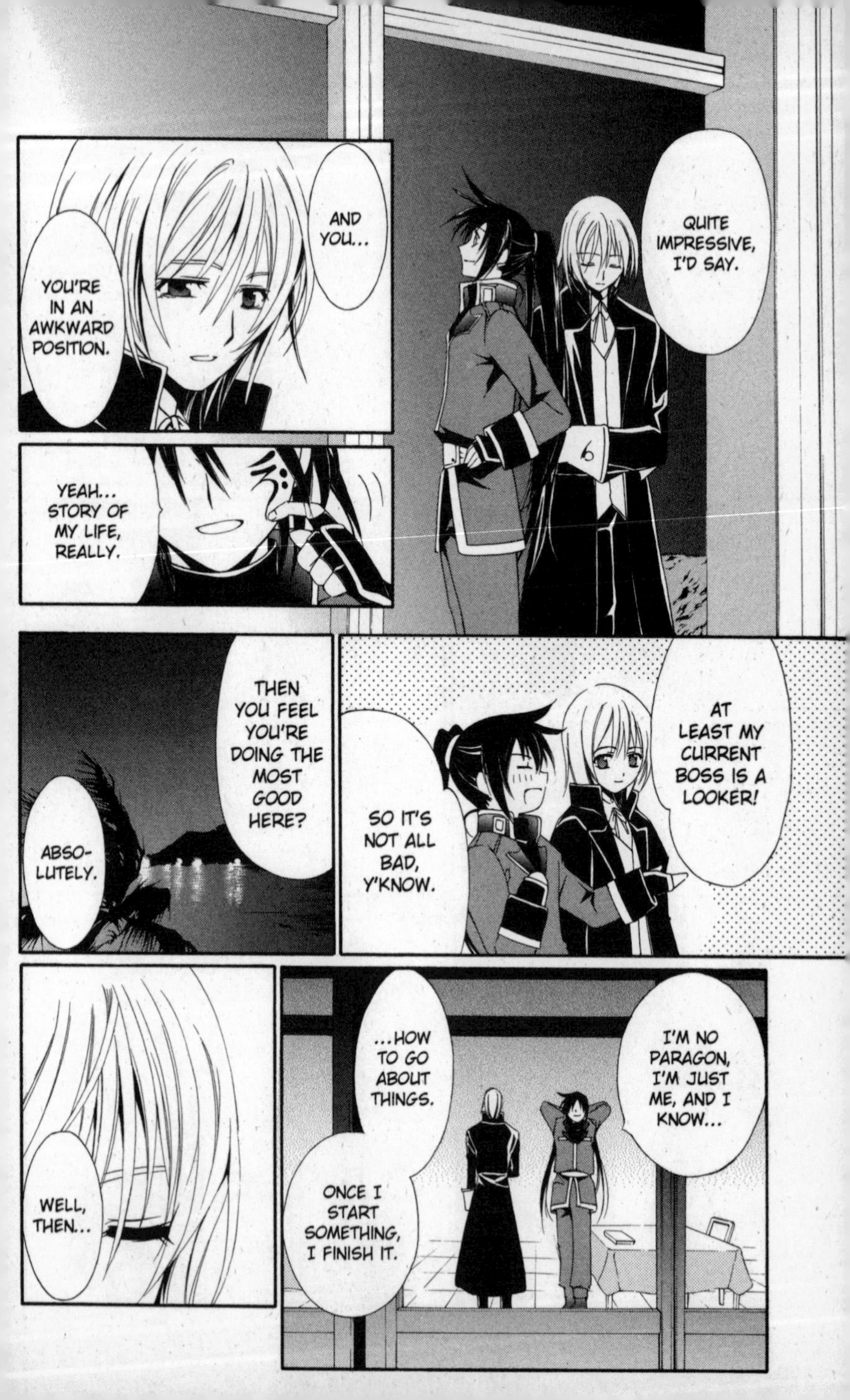
QUITE IMPRESSIVE, I'D SAY.
AND YOU...
YOU'RE IN AN AWKWARD POSITION.
YEAH... STORY OF MY LIFE, REALLY.
AT LEAST MY CURRENT BOSS IS A LOOKER!
SO IT'S NOT ALL BAD, Y'KNOW.
THEN YOU FEEL YOU'RE DOING THE MOST GOOD HERE?
ABSO-LUTELY.
I'M NO PARAGON, I'M JUST ME, AND I KNOW...
...HOW TO GO ABOUT THINGS.
ONCE I START SOMETHING, I FINISH IT.
WELL, THEN...

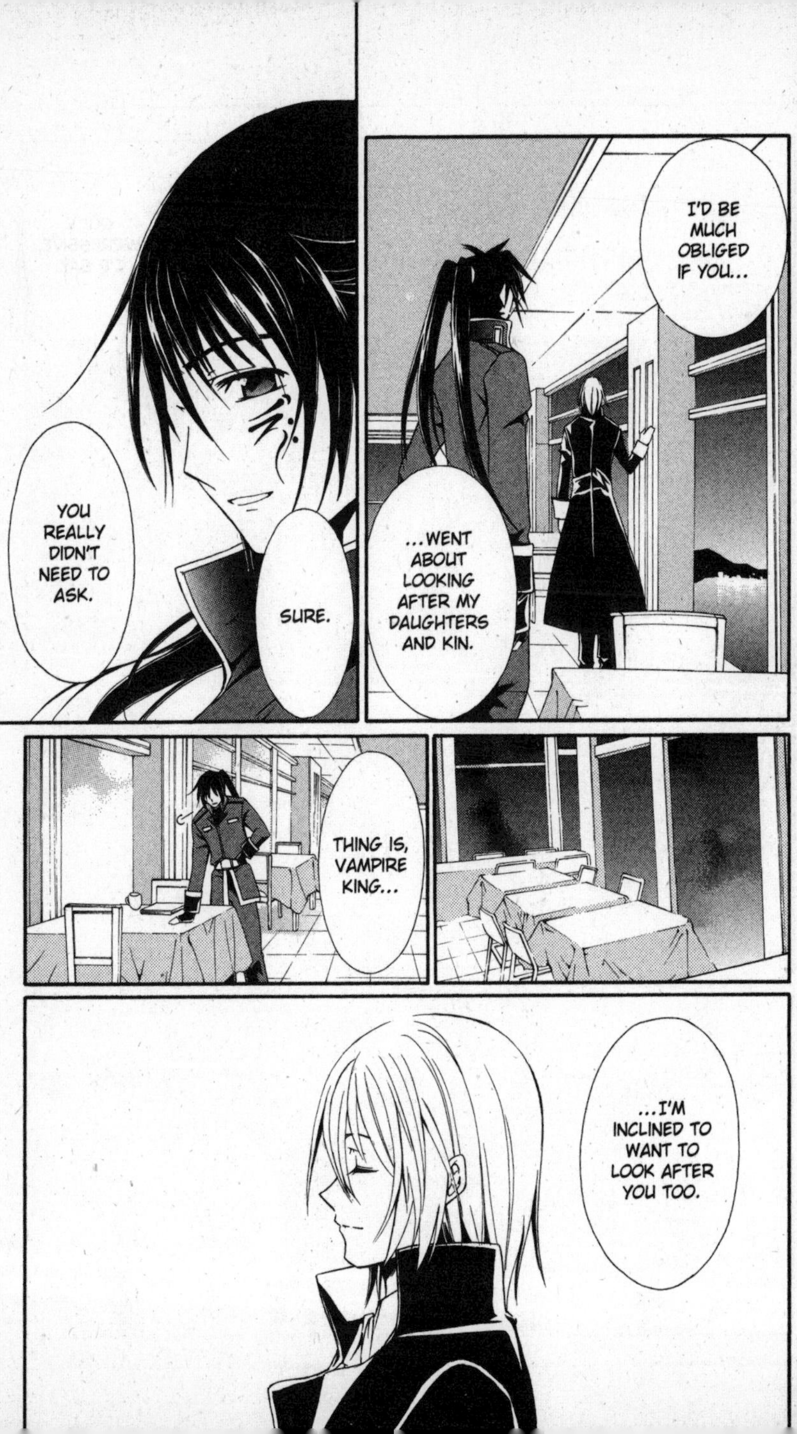
I'D BE MUCH OBLIGED IF YOU...
...WENT ABOUT LOOKING AFTER MY DAUGHTERS AND KIN.
SURE.
YOU REALLY DIDN'T NEED TO ASK.
THING IS, VAMPIRE KING...
...I'M INCLINED TO WANT TO LOOK AFTER YOU TOO.

Confessions of the 50th Black Swan, Kayuki Hirasaka: Part Four

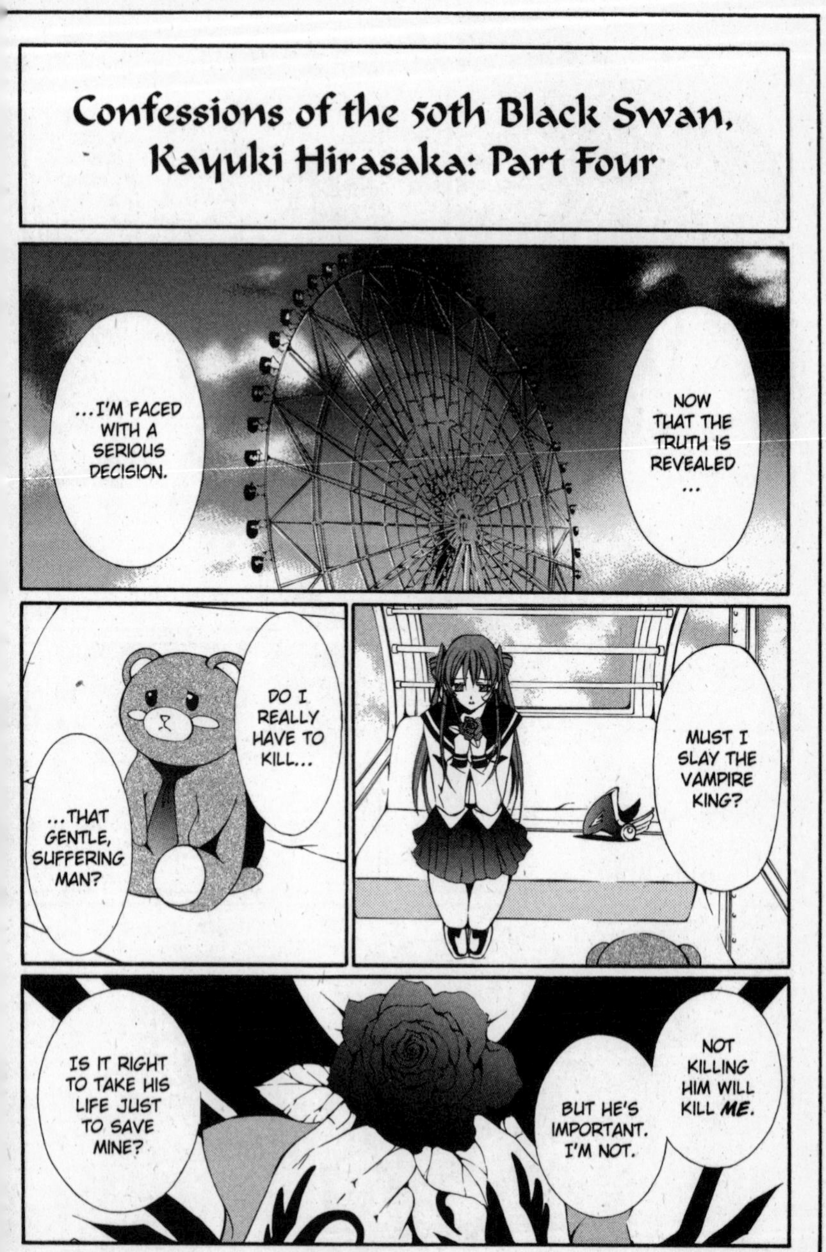
NOW THAT THE TRUTH IS REVEALED...
...I'M FACED WITH A SERIOUS DECISION.
MUST I SLAY THE VAMPIRE KING?
DO I REALLY HAVE TO KILL...
...THAT GENTLE, SUFFERING MAN?
NOT KILLING HIM WILL KILL ME.
BUT HE'S IMPORTANT. I'M NOT.
IS IT RIGHT TO TAKE HIS LIFE JUST TO SAVE MINE?

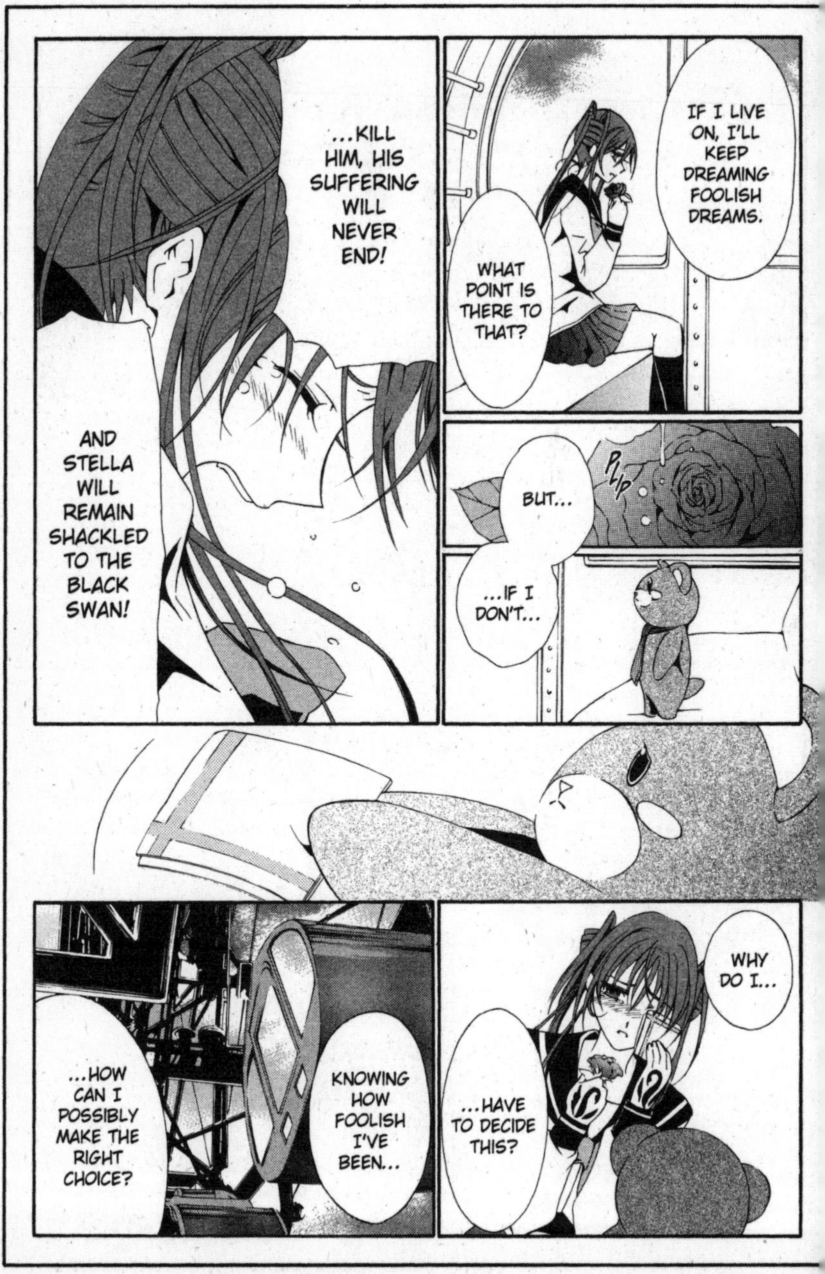
IF I LIVE ON, I'LL KEEP DREAMING FOOLISH DREAMS.
WHAT POINT IS THERE TO THAT?
PLIP
BUT...
...IF I DON'T...
...KILL HIM, HIS SUFFERING WILL NEVER END!
AND STELLA WILL REMAIN SHACKLED TO THE BLACK SWAN!
WHY DO I...
...HAVE TO DECIDE THIS?
KNOWING HOW FOOLISH I'VE BEEN...
...HOW CAN I POSSIBLY MAKE THE RIGHT CHOICE?

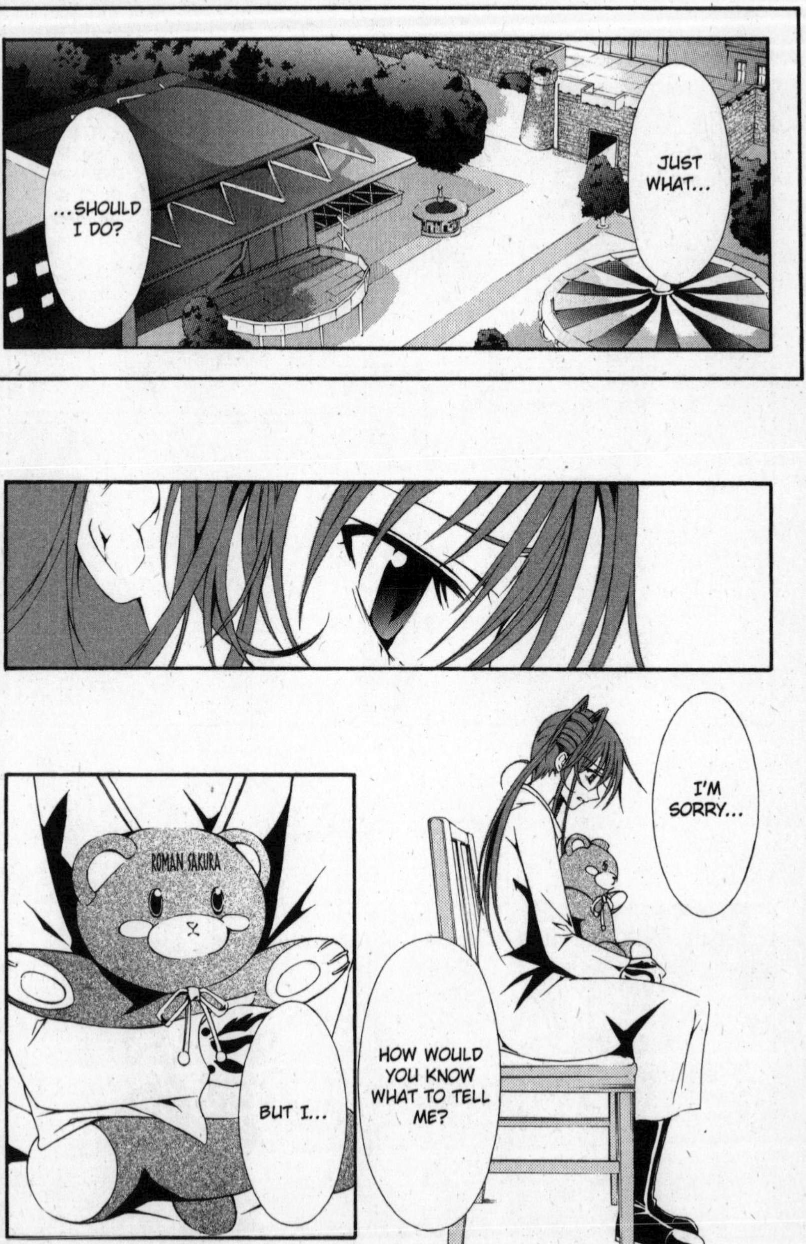
JUST WHAT...
...SHOULD I DO?
I'M SORRY...
HOW WOULD YOU KNOW WHAT TO TELL ME?
ROMAN SAKURA
BUT I...

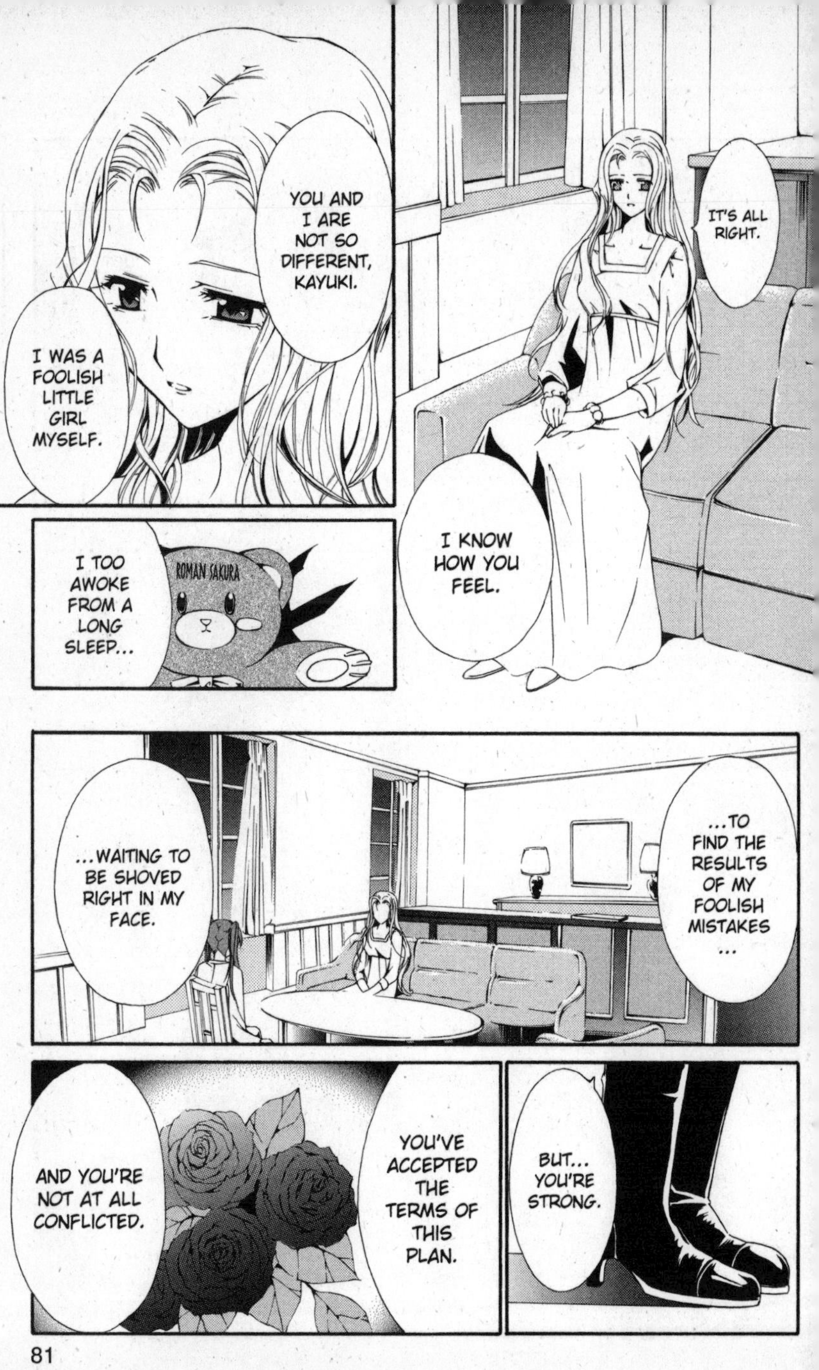
IT'S ALL RIGHT.
I KNOW HOW YOU FEEL.
YOU AND I ARE NOT SO DIFFERENT, KAYUKI.
I WAS A FOOLISH LITTLE GIRL MYSELF.
I TOO AWOKE FROM A LONG SLEEP...
ROMAN SAKURA
...TO FIND THE RESULTS OF MY FOOLISH MISTAKES...
...WAITING TO BE SHOVED RIGHT IN MY FACE.
BUT... YOU'RE STRONG.
YOU'VE ACCEPTED THE TERMS OF THIS PLAN.
AND YOU'RE NOT AT ALL CONFLICTED.

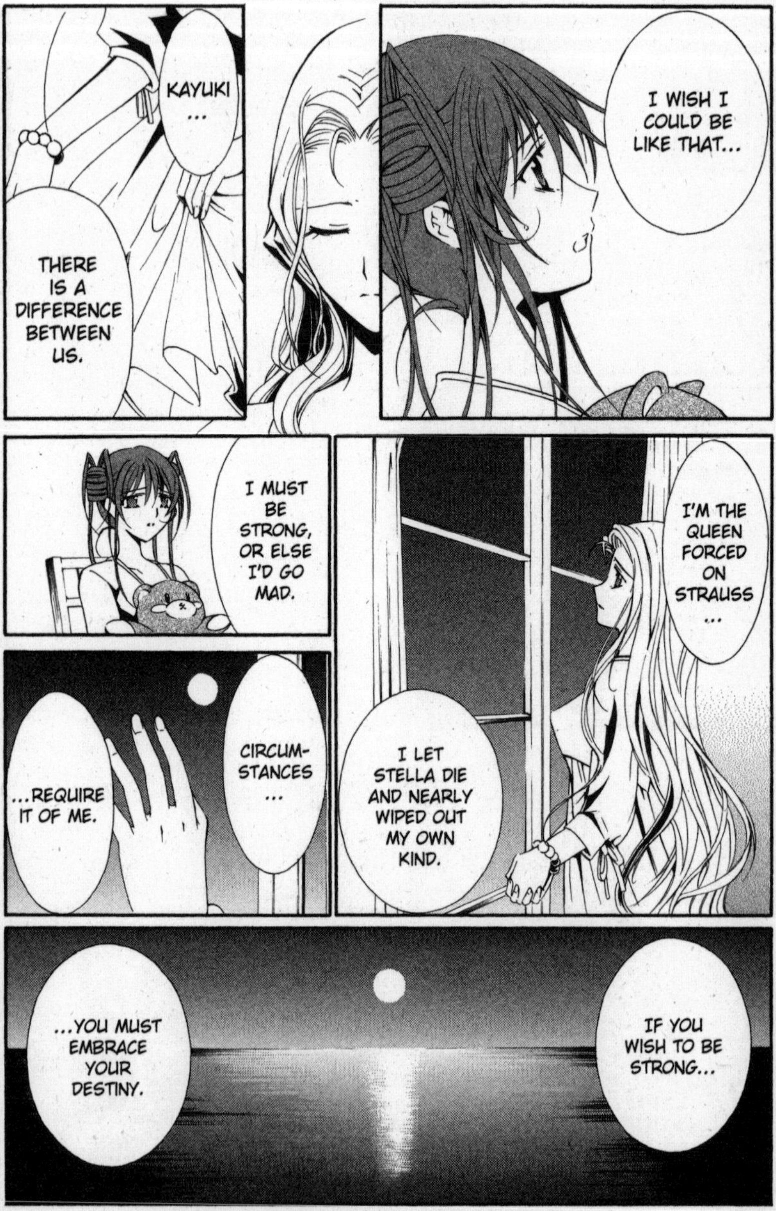
I WISH I COULD BE LIKE THAT...
KAYUKI ...
THERE IS A DIFFERENCE BETWEEN US.
I'M THE QUEEN FORCED ON STRAUSS ...
I LET STELLA DIE AND NEARLY WIPED OUT MY OWN KIND.
I MUST BE STRONG, OR ELSE I'D GO MAD.
CIRCUM-STANCES ...
...REQUIRE IT OF ME.
IF YOU WISH TO BE STRONG...
...YOU MUST EMBRACE YOUR DESTINY.

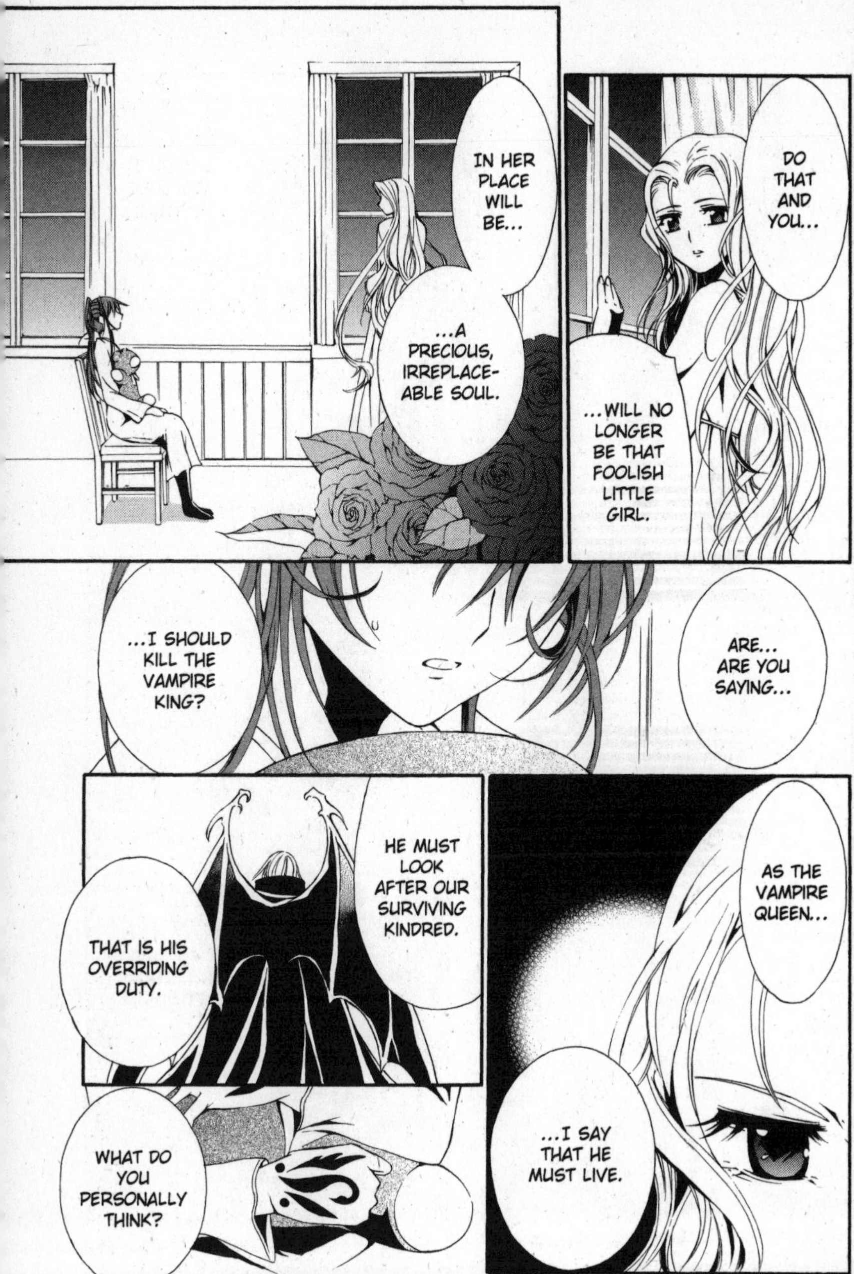
DO THAT AND YOU...
...WILL NO LONGER BE THAT FOOLISH LITTLE GIRL.
IN HER PLACE WILL BE...
...A PRECIOUS, IRREPLACE-ABLE SOUL.
ARE... ARE YOU SAYING...
...I SHOULD KILL THE VAMPIRE KING?
AS THE VAMPIRE QUEEN...
...I SAY THAT HE MUST LIVE.
HE MUST LOOK AFTER OUR SURVIVING KINDRED.
THAT IS HIS OVERRIDING DUTY.
WHAT DO YOU PERSONALLY THINK?

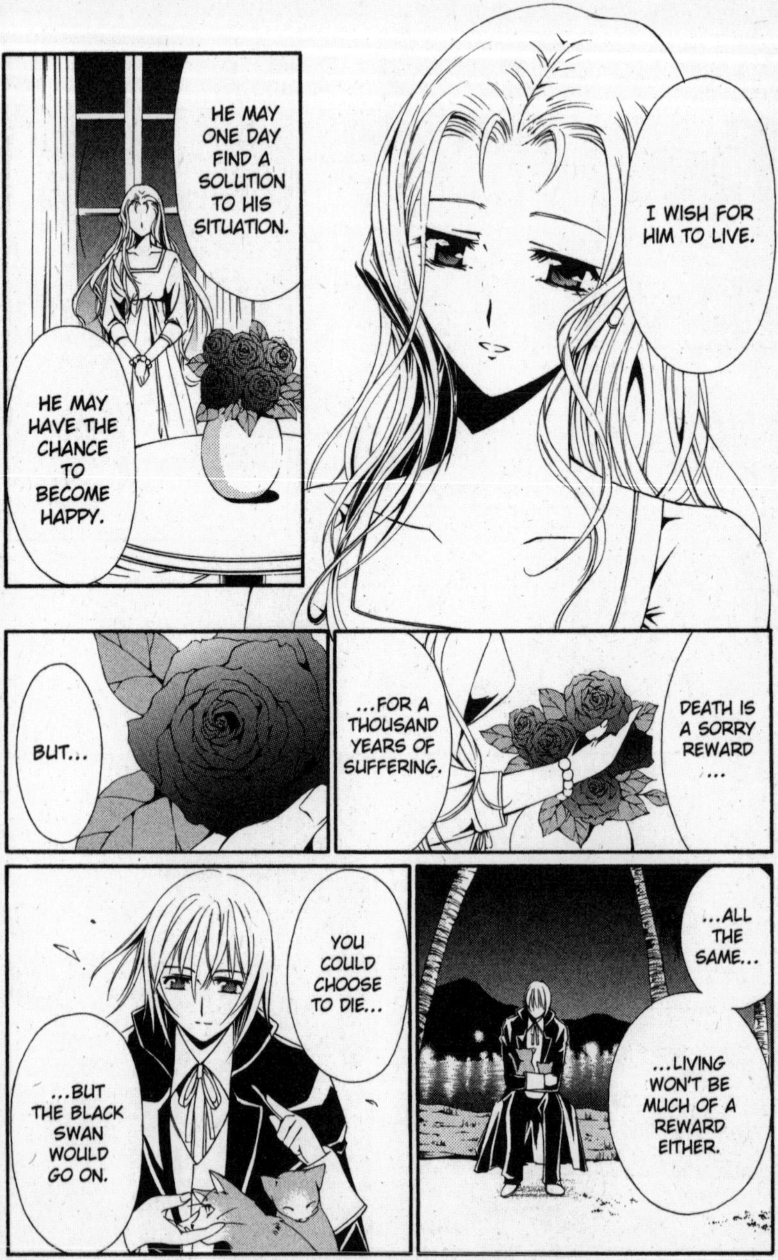
I WISH FOR HIM TO LIVE.
HE MAY ONE DAY FIND A SOLUTION TO HIS SITUATION.
HE MAY HAVE THE CHANCE TO BECOME HAPPY.
DEATH IS A SORRY REWARD...
...FOR A THOUSAND YEARS OF SUFFERING.
BUT...
...ALL THE SAME...
...LIVING WON'T BE MUCH OF A REWARD EITHER.
YOU COULD CHOOSE TO DIE...
...BUT THE BLACK SWAN WOULD GO ON.

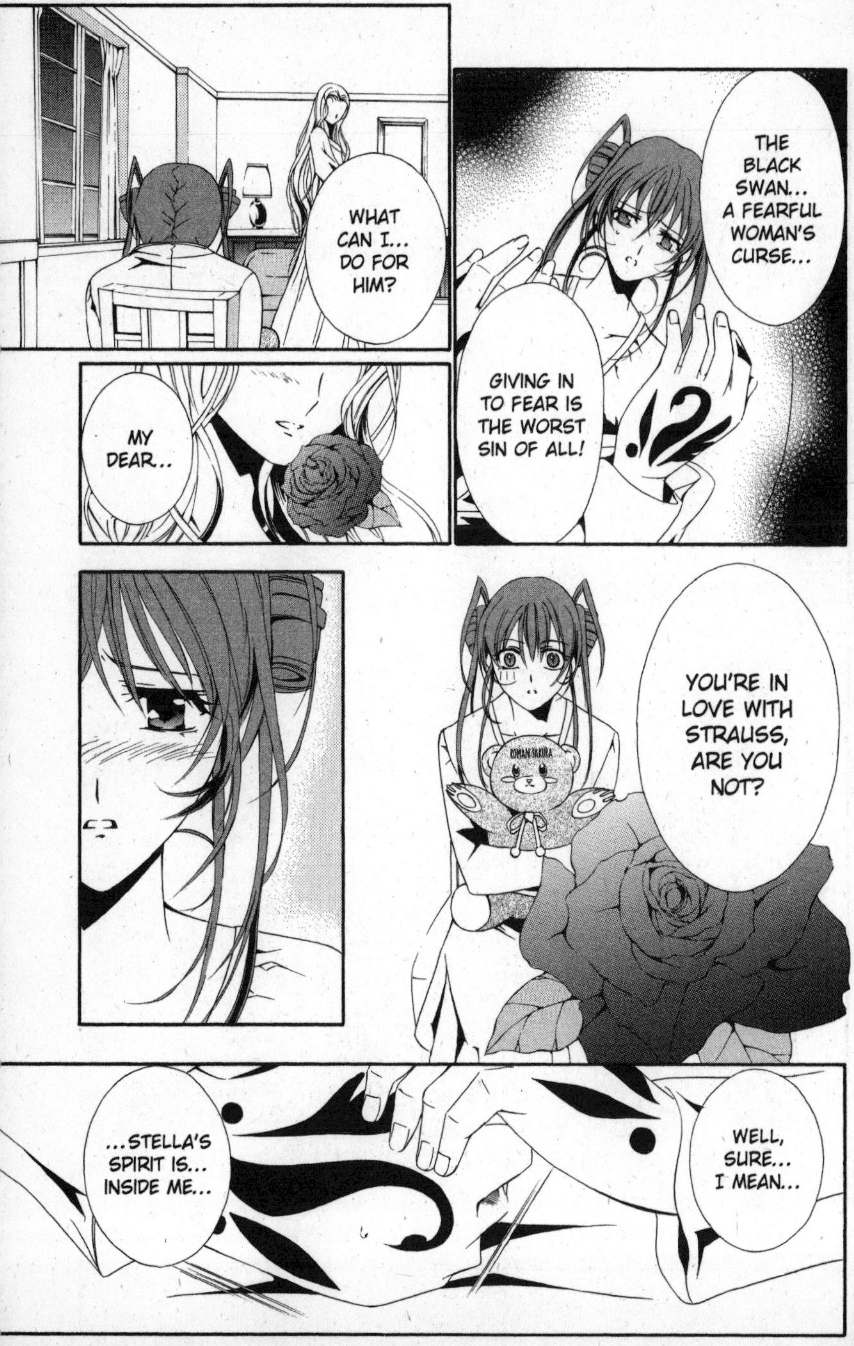
THE BLACK SWAN... A FEARFUL WOMAN'S CURSE...
GIVING IN TO FEAR IS THE WORST SIN OF ALL!
WHAT CAN I... DO FOR HIM?
MY DEAR...
YOU'RE IN LOVE WITH STRAUSS, ARE YOU NOT?
ROMAN SAKURA
WELL, SURE... I MEAN...
...STELLA'S SPIRIT IS... INSIDE ME...

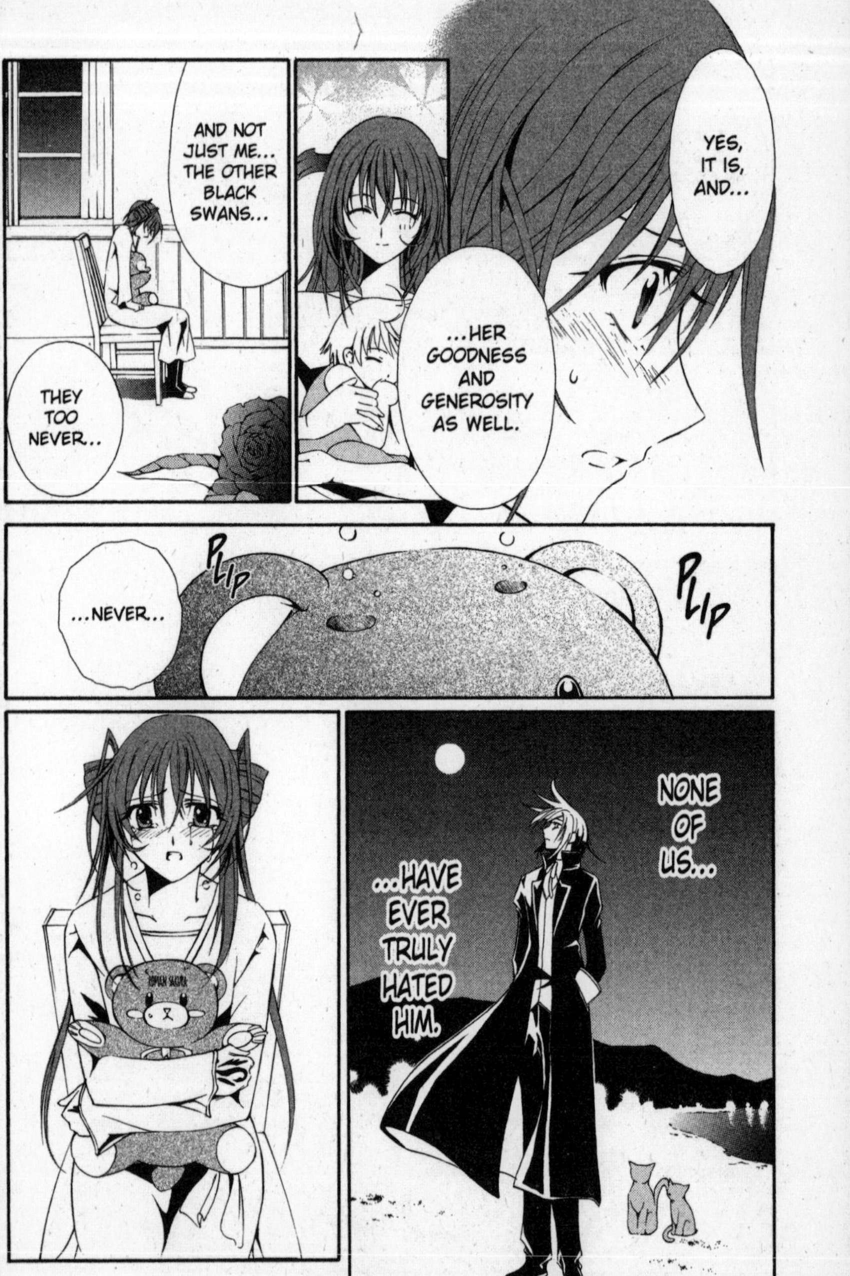
YES, IT IS, AND...
...HER GOODNESS AND GENEROSITY AS WELL.
AND NOT JUST ME... THE OTHER BLACK SWANS...
THEY TOO NEVER...
PLIP
PLIP
...NEVER...
NONE OF US...
...HAVE EVER TRULY HATED HIM.

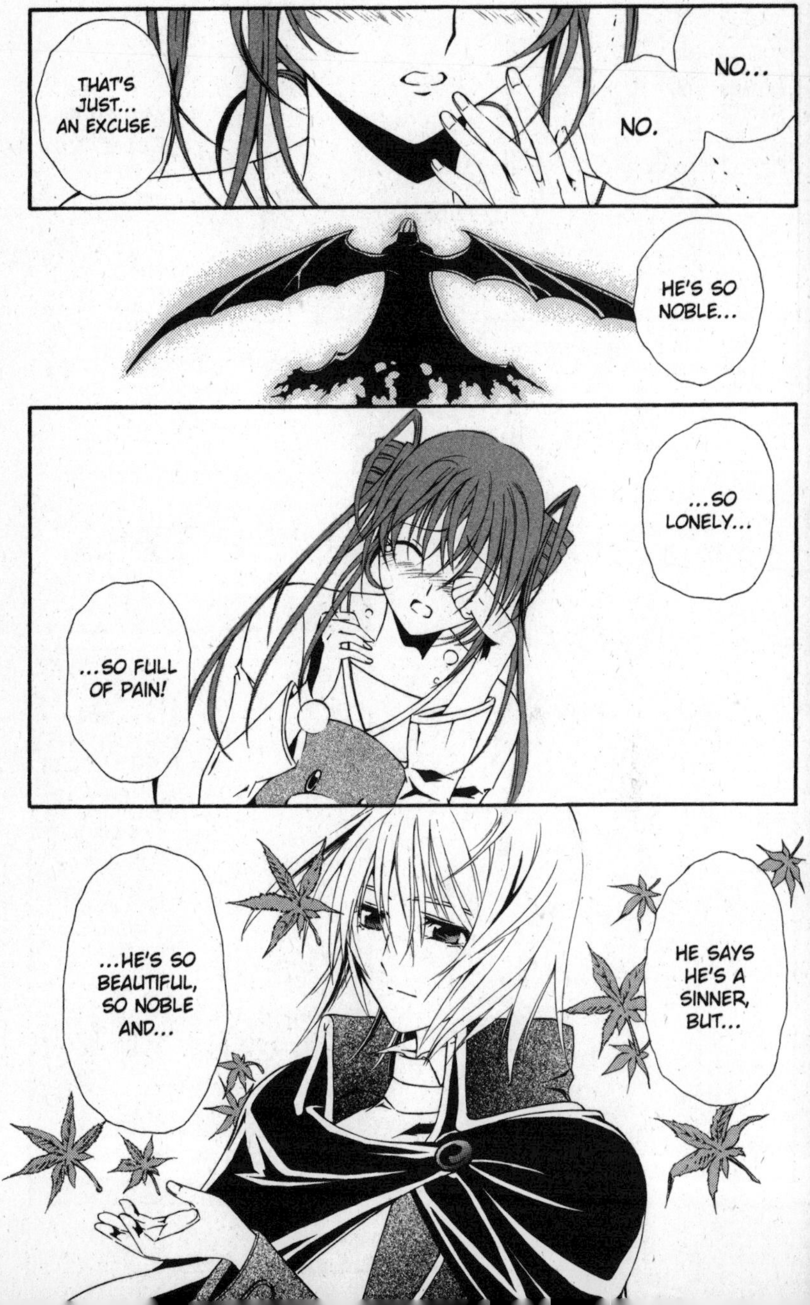
NO...
NO.
THAT'S JUST... AN EXCUSE.
HE'S SO NOBLE...
...SO LONELY...
...SO FULL OF PAIN!
HE SAYS HE'S A SINNER, BUT...
...HE'S SO BEAUTIFUL, SO NOBLE AND...

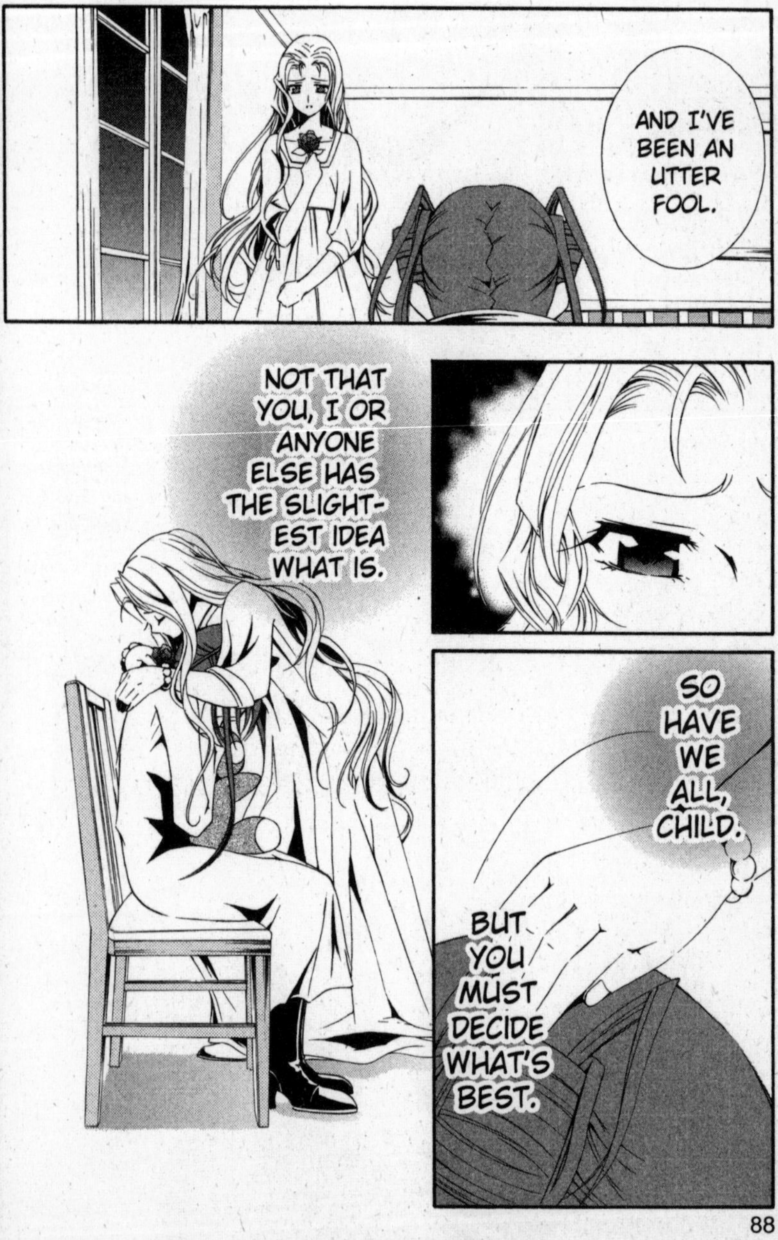
AND I'VE BEEN AN UTTER FOOL.
SO HAVE WE ALL, CHILD.
BUT YOU MUST DECIDE WHAT'S BEST.
NOT THAT YOU, I OR ANYONE ELSE HAS THE SLIGHT-EST IDEA WHAT IS.

THE RECORD OF A
FALLEN VAMPIRE

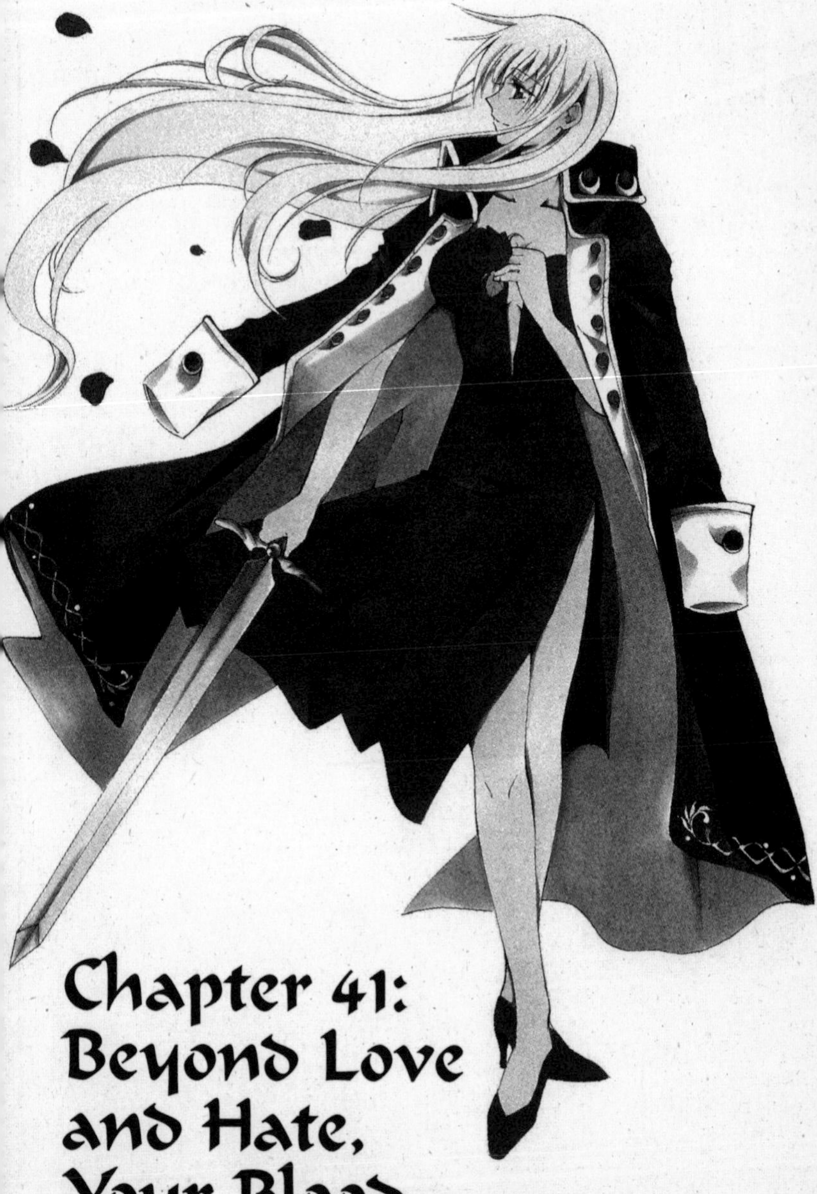

Chapter 41: Beyond Love and Hate, Your Blood

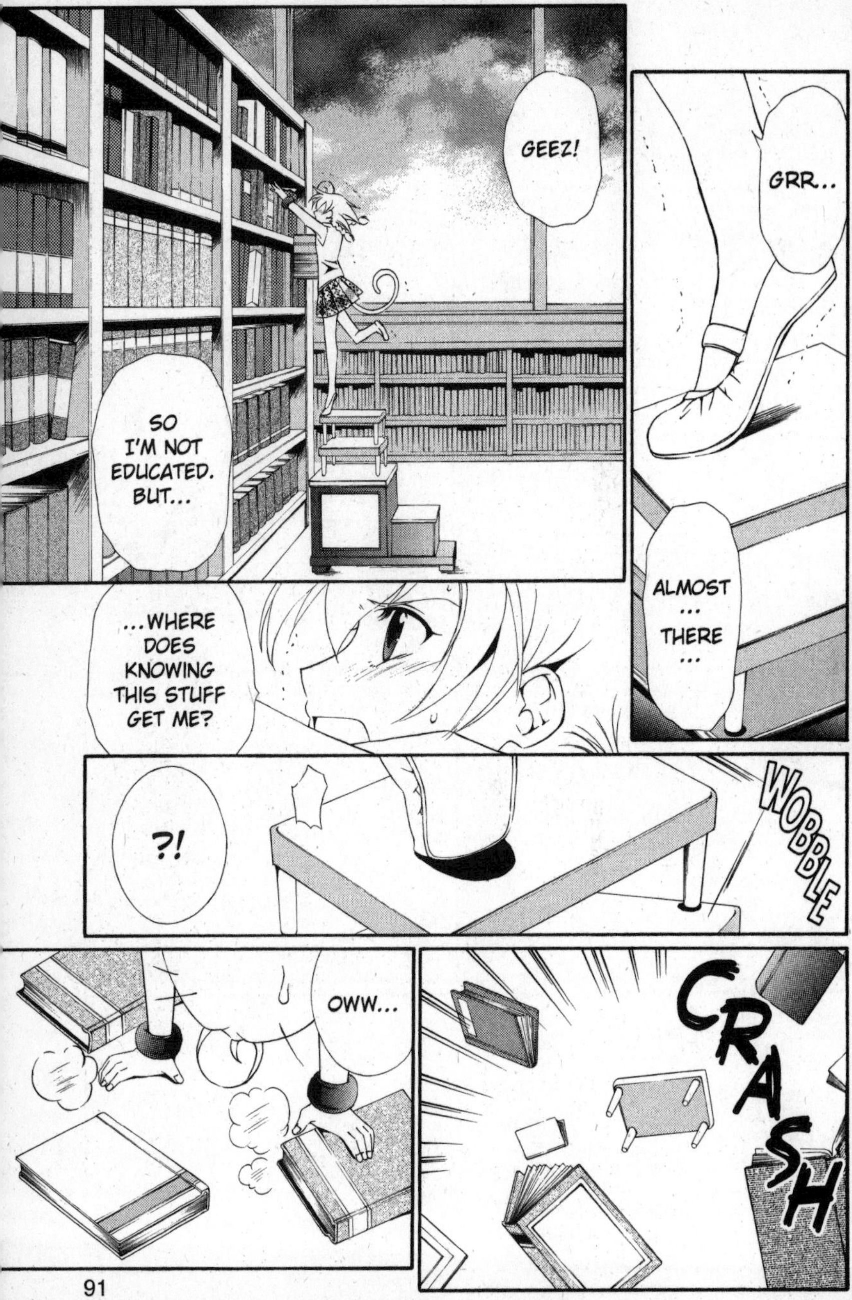
GRR...
ALMOST ... THERE ...
GEEZ!
SO I'M NOT EDUCATED. BUT...
...WHERE DOES KNOWING THIS STUFF GET ME?
WOBBLE
?!
CRASH
OWW...

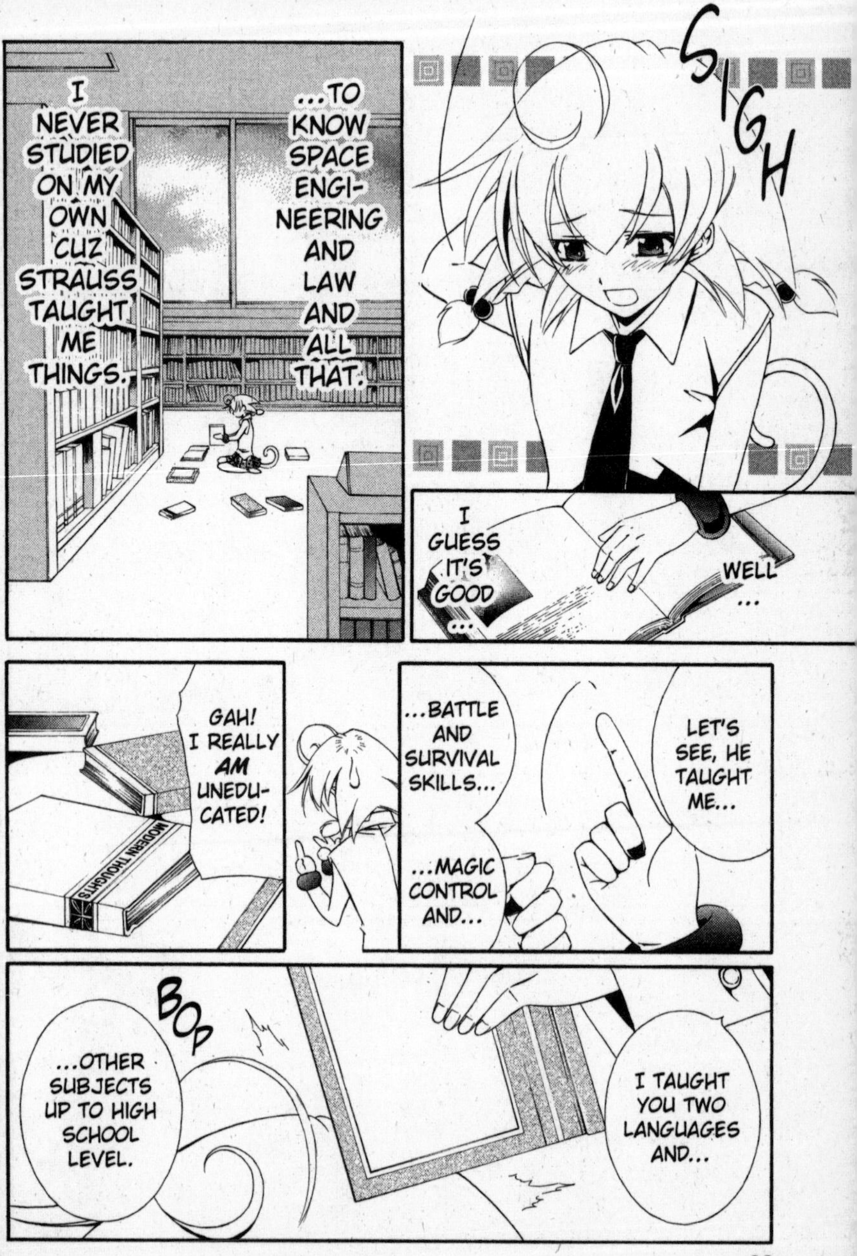
SIGH
WELL...
I GUESS IT'S GOOD...
I NEVER STUDIED ON MY OWN CUZ STRAUSS TAUGHT ME THINGS.
...TO KNOW SPACE ENGINEERING AND LAW AND ALL THAT.
LET'S SEE, HE TAUGHT ME...
...BATTLE AND SURVIVAL SKILLS...
...MAGIC CONTROL AND...
GAH! I REALLY AM UNEDUCATED!
MODERN THOUGHTS
I TAUGHT YOU TWO LANGUAGES AND...
BOP
...OTHER SUBJECTS UP TO HIGH SCHOOL LEVEL.

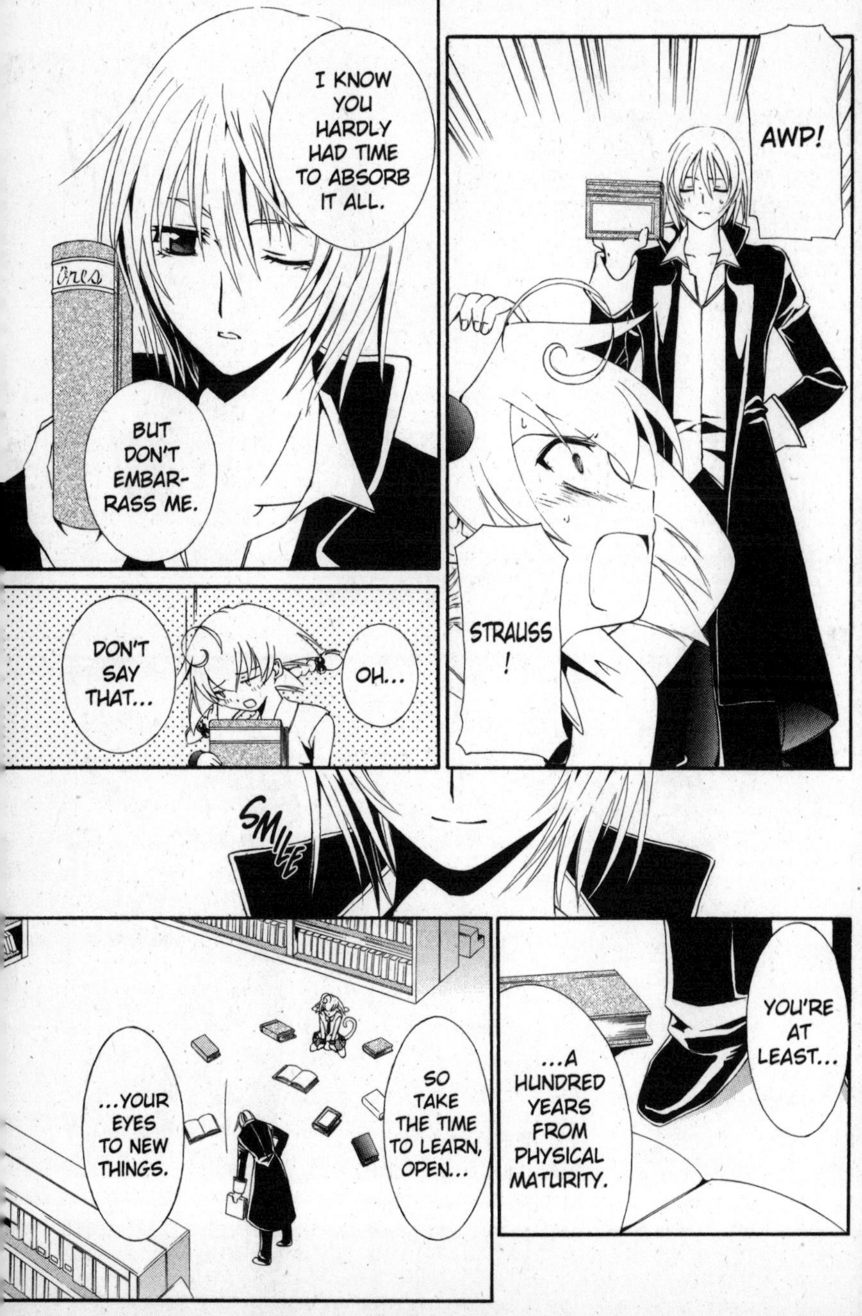
AWP!
STRAUSS!
I KNOW YOU HARDLY HAD TIME TO ABSORB IT ALL.
BUT DON'T EMBARRASS ME.
OH...
DON'T SAY THAT...
SMILE
YOU'RE AT LEAST...
...A HUNDRED YEARS FROM PHYSICAL MATURITY.
SO TAKE THE TIME TO LEARN, OPEN...
...YOUR EYES TO NEW THINGS.

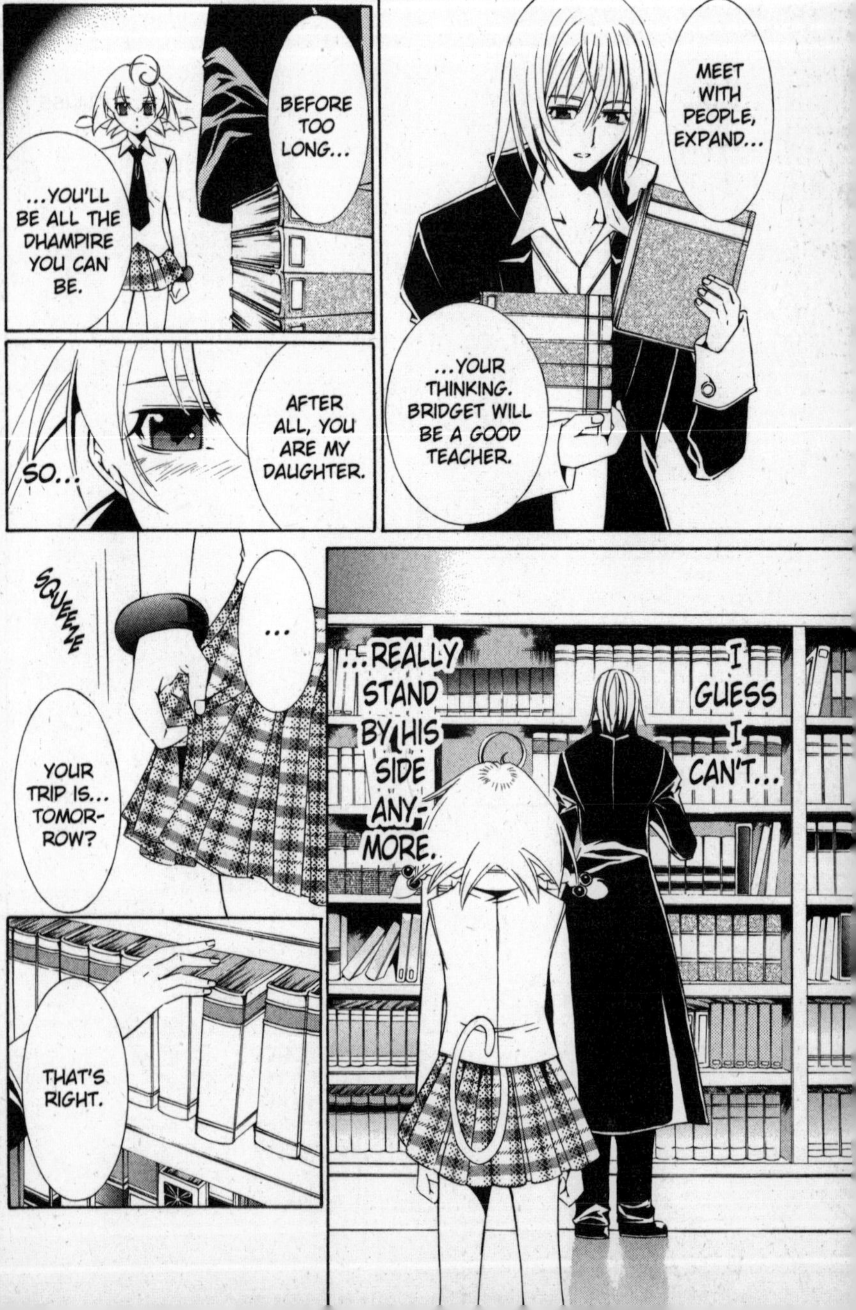
MEET WITH PEOPLE, EXPAND...
...YOUR THINKING. BRIDGET WILL BE A GOOD TEACHER.
BEFORE TOO LONG...
...YOU'LL BE ALL THE DHAMPIRE YOU CAN BE.
AFTER ALL, YOU ARE MY DAUGHTER.
SO...
I GUESS I CAN'T...
...REALLY STAND BY HIS SIDE ANYMORE.
SQUEEZE
...
YOUR TRIP IS... TOMORROW?
THAT'S RIGHT.

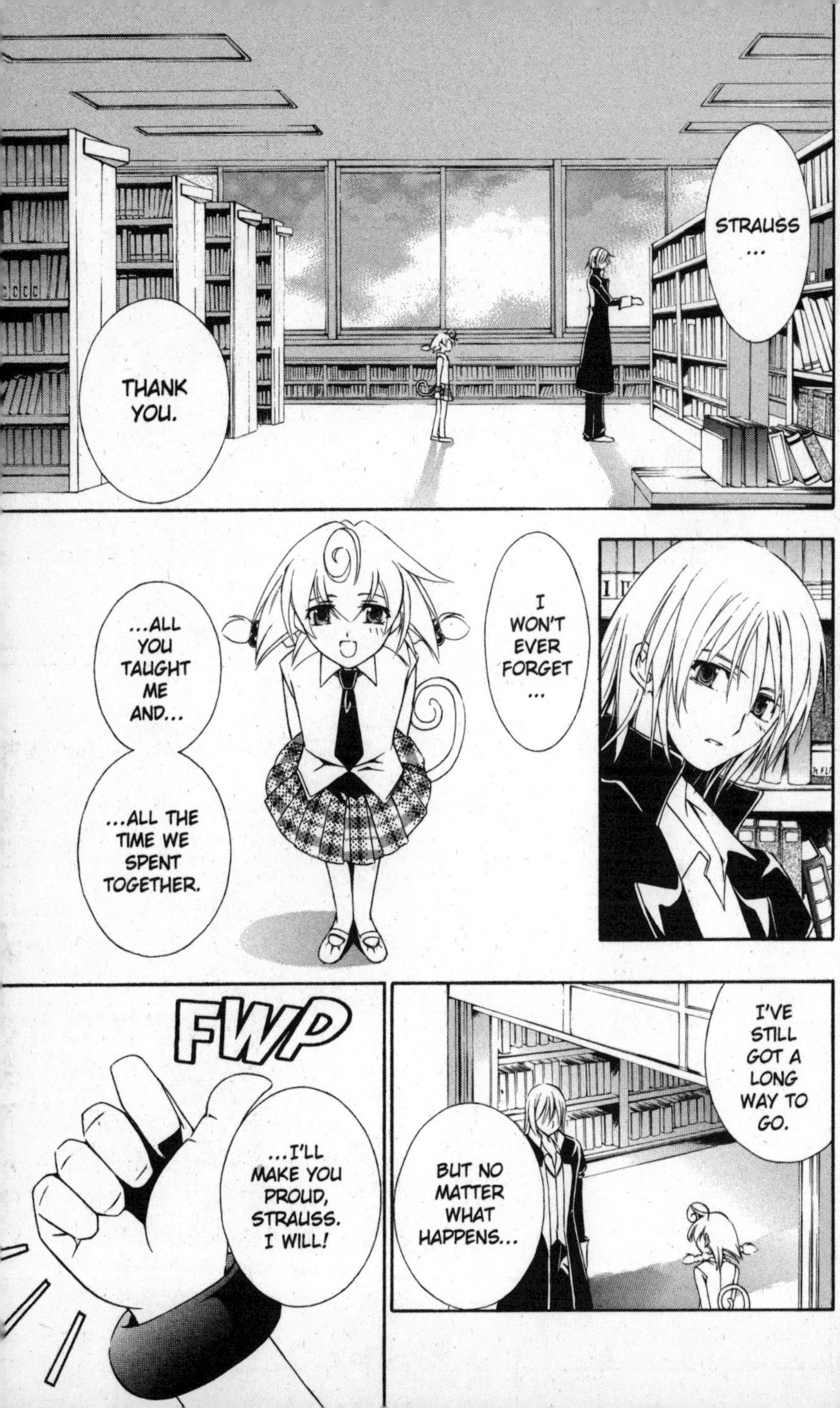
STRAUSS...
THANK YOU.
I WON'T EVER FORGET...
...ALL YOU TAUGHT ME AND...
...ALL THE TIME WE SPENT TOGETHER.
I'VE STILL GOT A LONG WAY TO GO.
BUT NO MATTER WHAT HAPPENS...
FWP
...I'LL MAKE YOU PROUD, STRAUSS. I WILL!

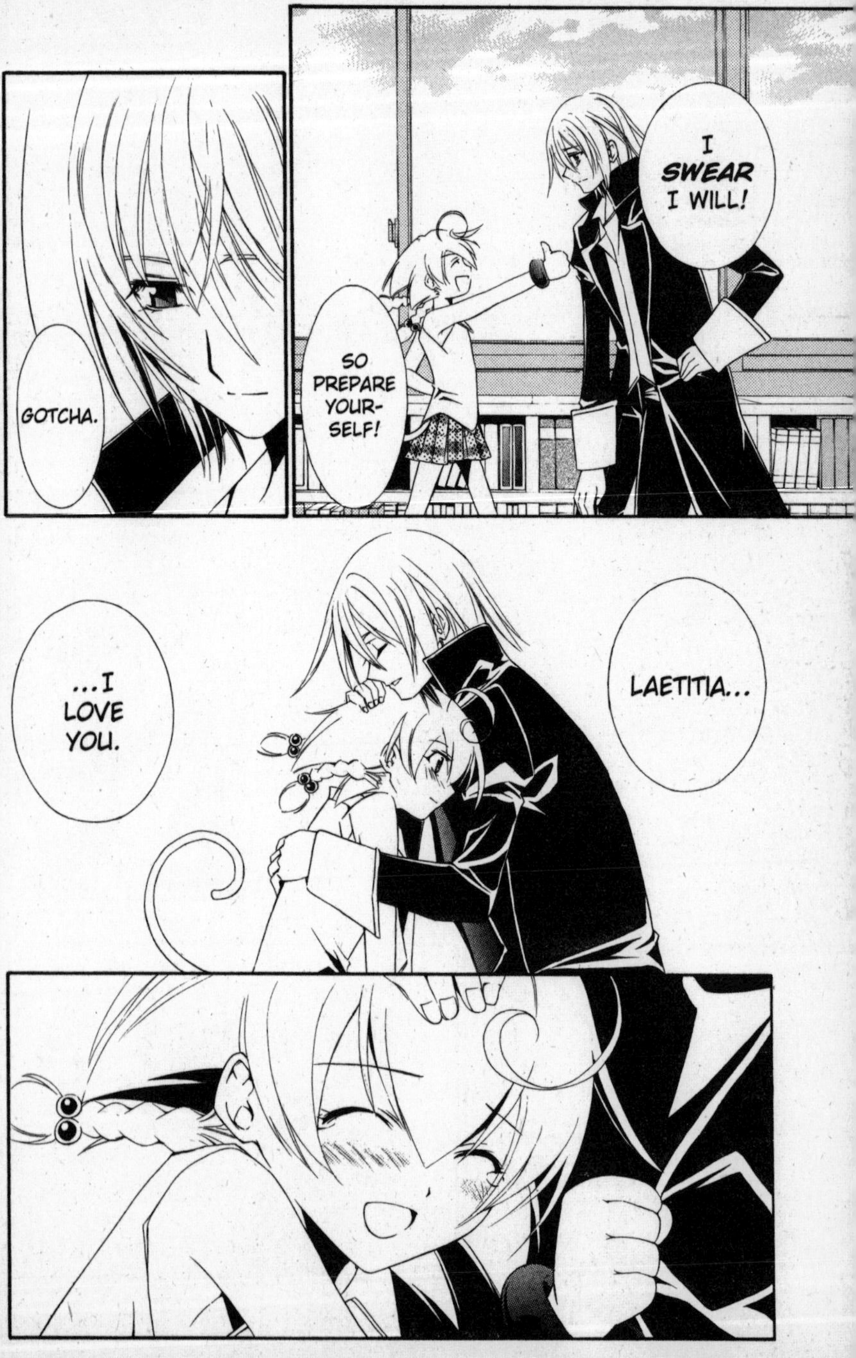
I SWEAR I WILL!
SO PREPARE YOUR-SELF!
GOTCHA.
LAETITIA...
...I LOVE YOU.

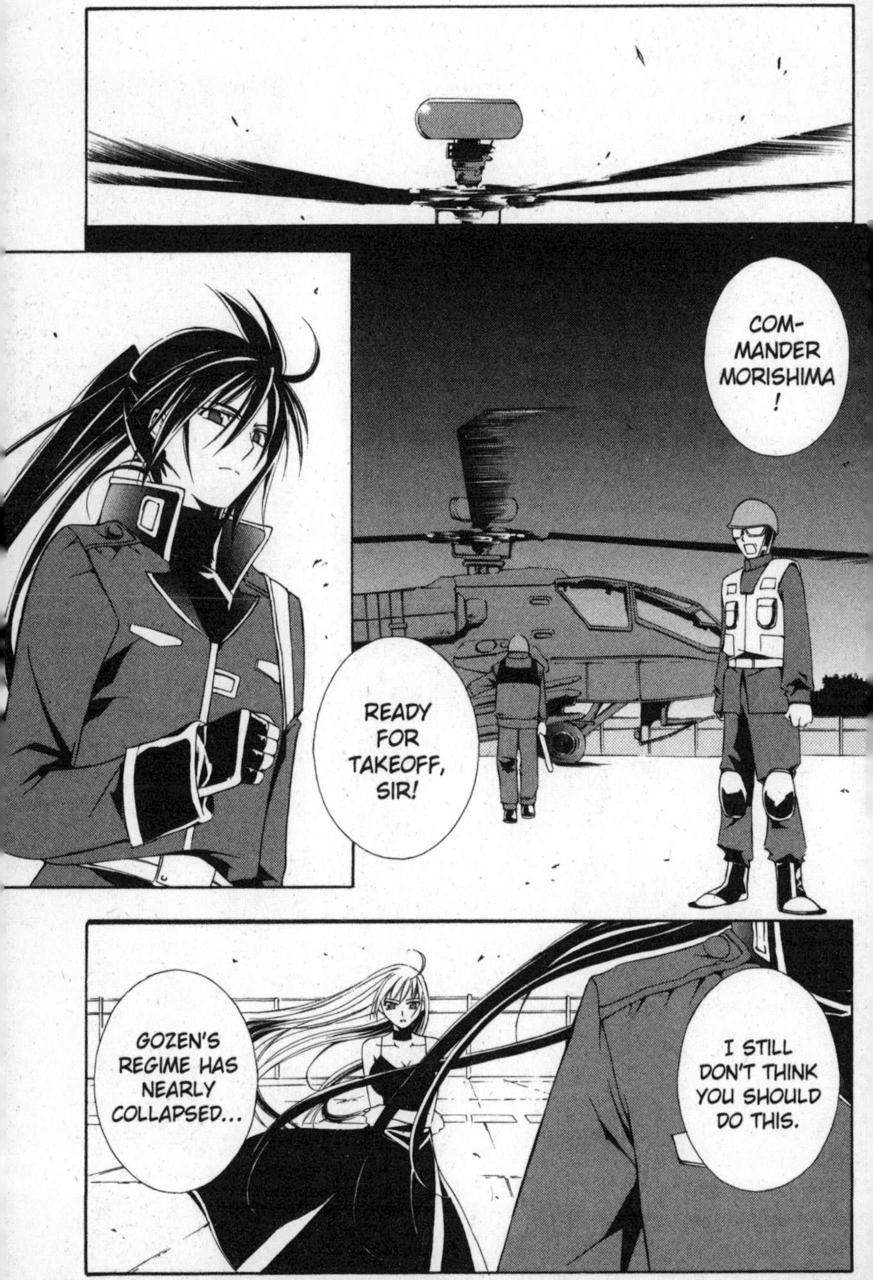
COM-MANDER MORISHIMA!
READY FOR TAKEOFF, SIR!
I STILL DON'T THINK YOU SHOULD DO THIS.
GOZEN'S REGIME HAS NEARLY COLLAPSED...

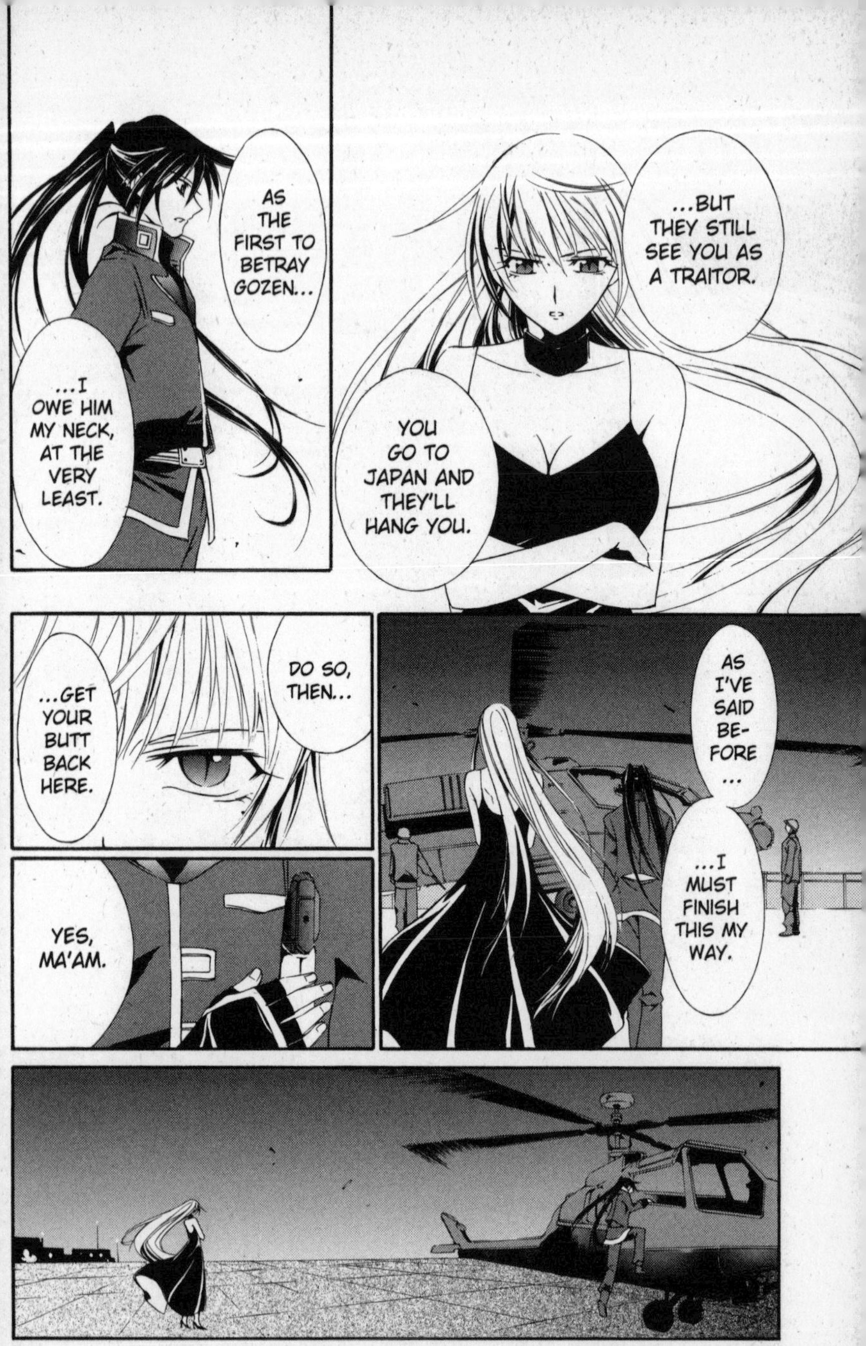
...BUT THEY STILL SEE YOU AS A TRAITOR.
YOU GO TO JAPAN AND THEY'LL HANG YOU.
AS THE FIRST TO BETRAY GOZEN...
...I OWE HIM MY NECK, AT THE VERY LEAST.
AS I'VE SAID BE- FORE ...
...I MUST FINISH THIS MY WAY.
DO SO, THEN...
...GET YOUR BUTT BACK HERE.
YES, MA'AM.

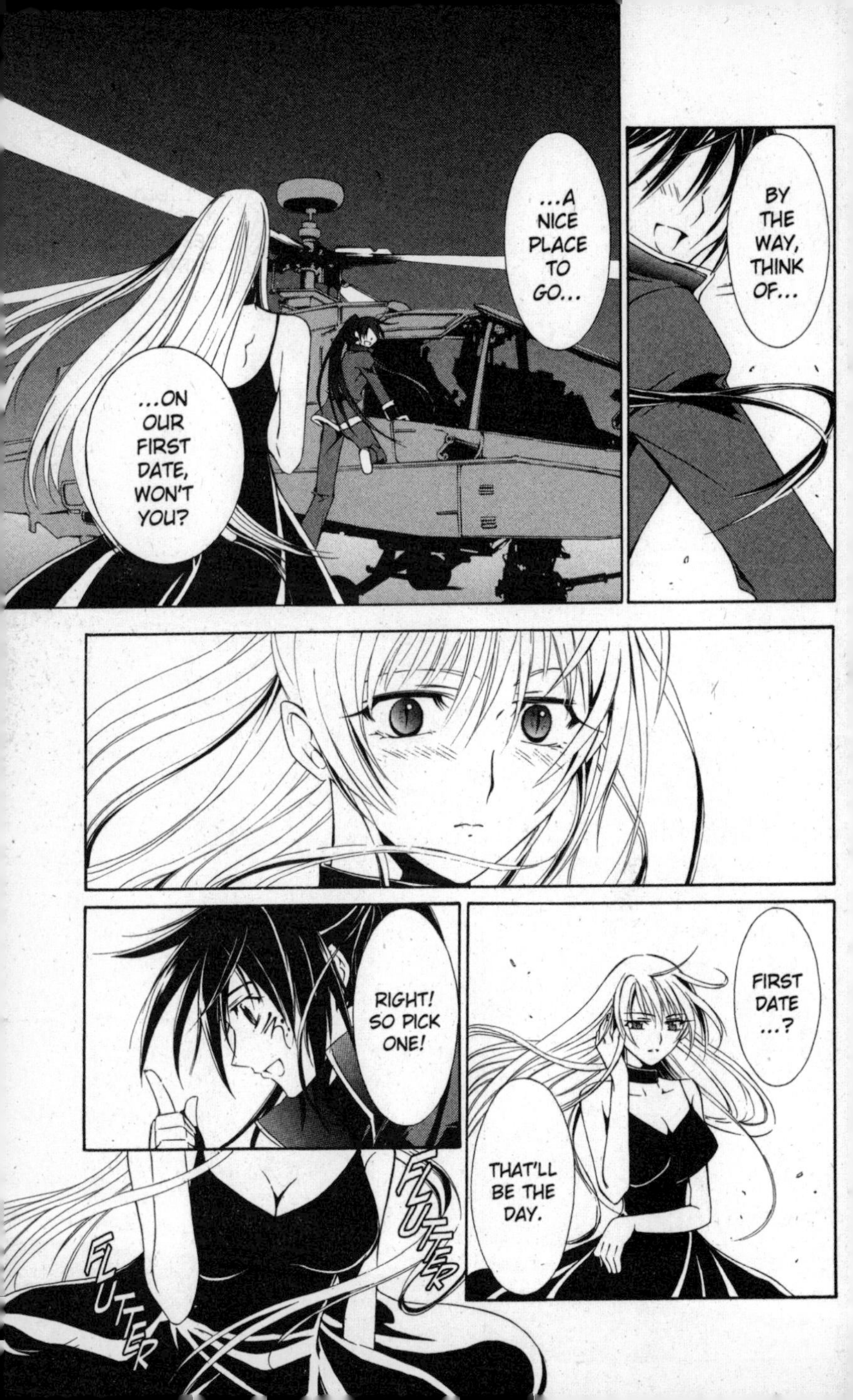
BY THE WAY, THINK OF...
...A NICE PLACE TO GO...
...ON OUR FIRST DATE, WON'T YOU?
FIRST DATE ...?
RIGHT! SO PICK ONE!
THAT'LL BE THE DAY.
FLUTTER
FLUTTER

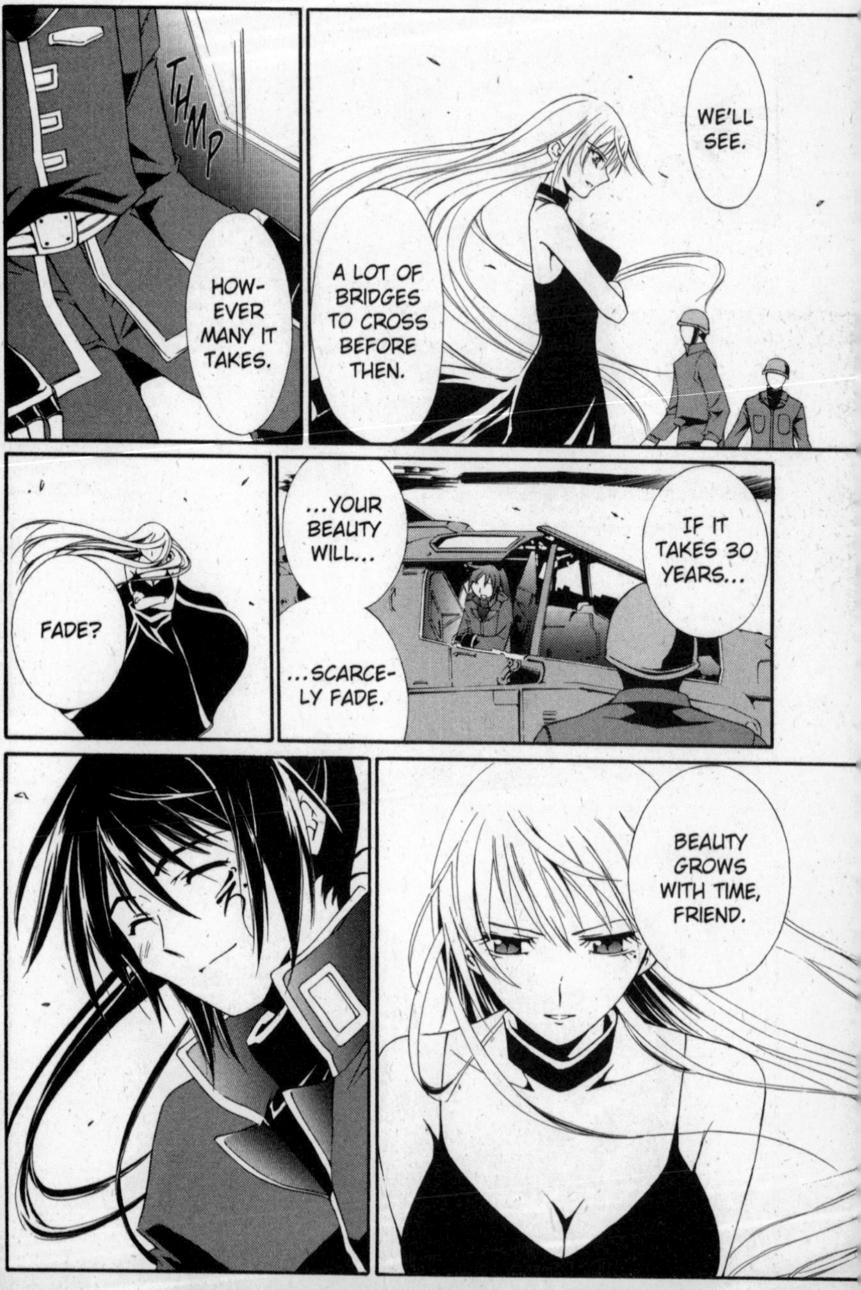
WE'LL SEE.
A LOT OF BRIDGES TO CROSS BEFORE THEN.
THMP
HOW-EVER MANY IT TAKES.
IF IT TAKES 30 YEARS...
...YOUR BEAUTY WILL...
...SCARCE-LY FADE.
FADE?
BEAUTY GROWS WITH TIME, FRIEND.

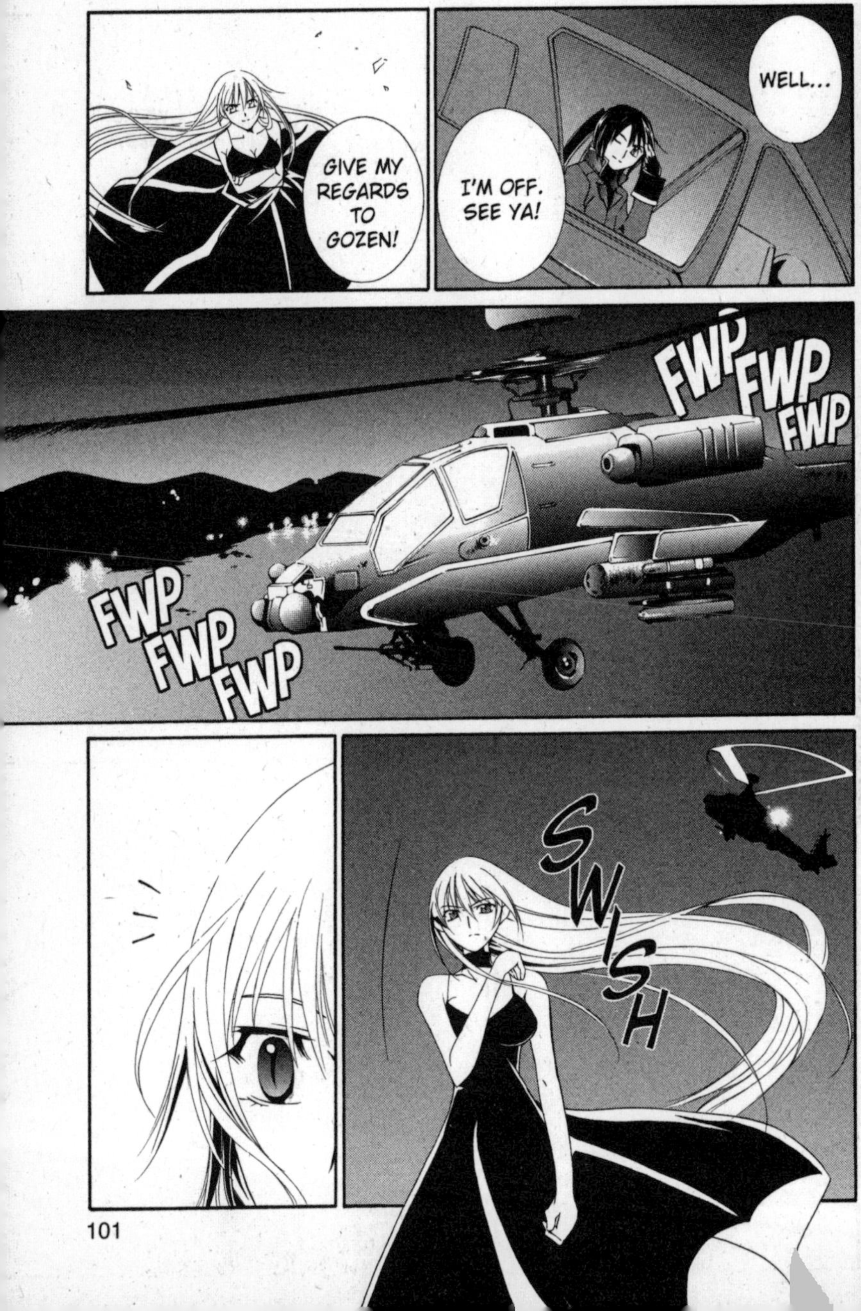
WELL...
I'M OFF. SEE YA!
GIVE MY REGARDS TO GOZEN!
FWP FWP FWP
FWP FWP FWP
SWISH

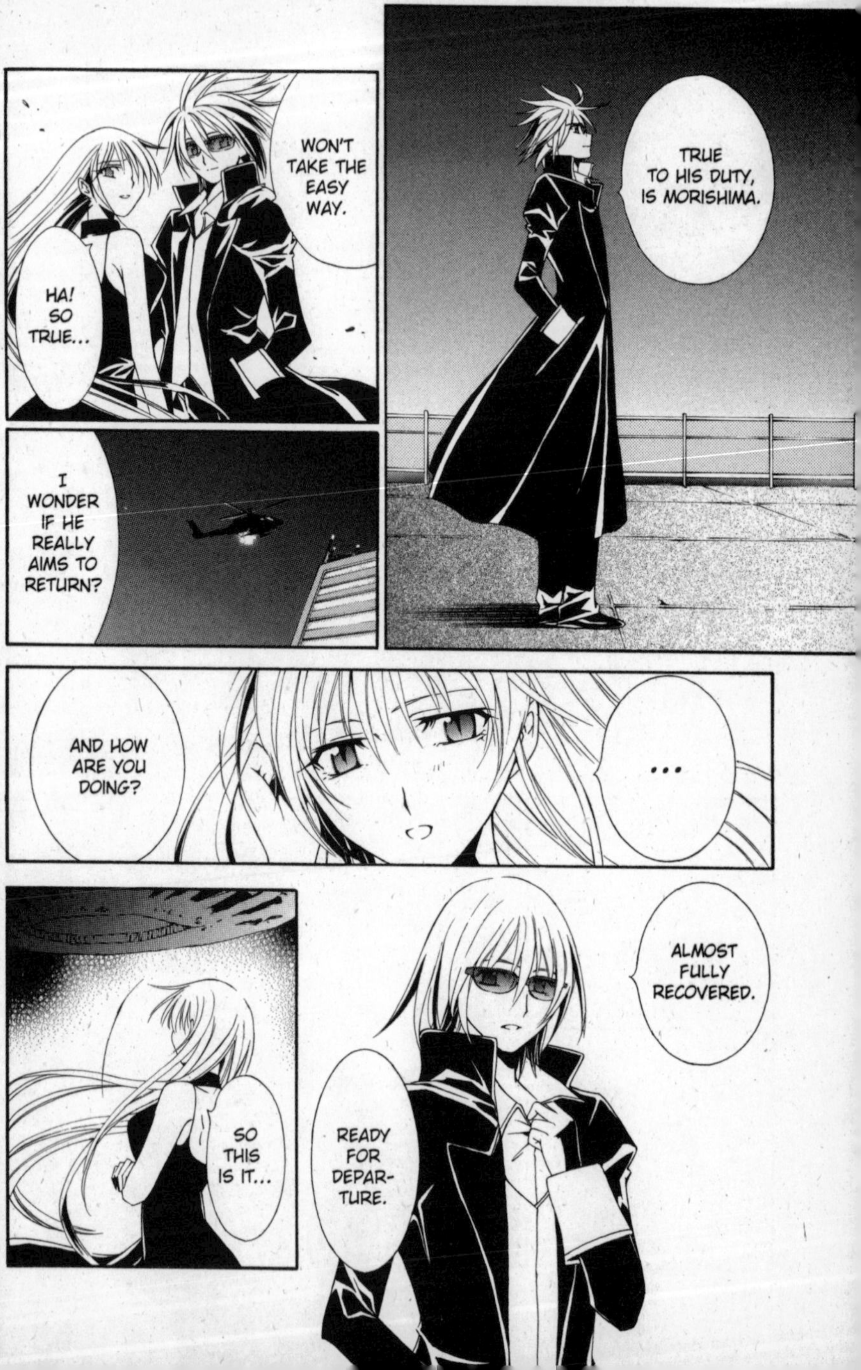
TRUE TO HIS DUTY, IS MORISHIMA.
WON'T TAKE THE EASY WAY.
HA! SO TRUE...
I WONDER IF HE REALLY AIMS TO RETURN?
...
AND HOW ARE YOU DOING?
ALMOST FULLY RECOVERED.
READY FOR DEPAR-TURE.
SO THIS IS IT...

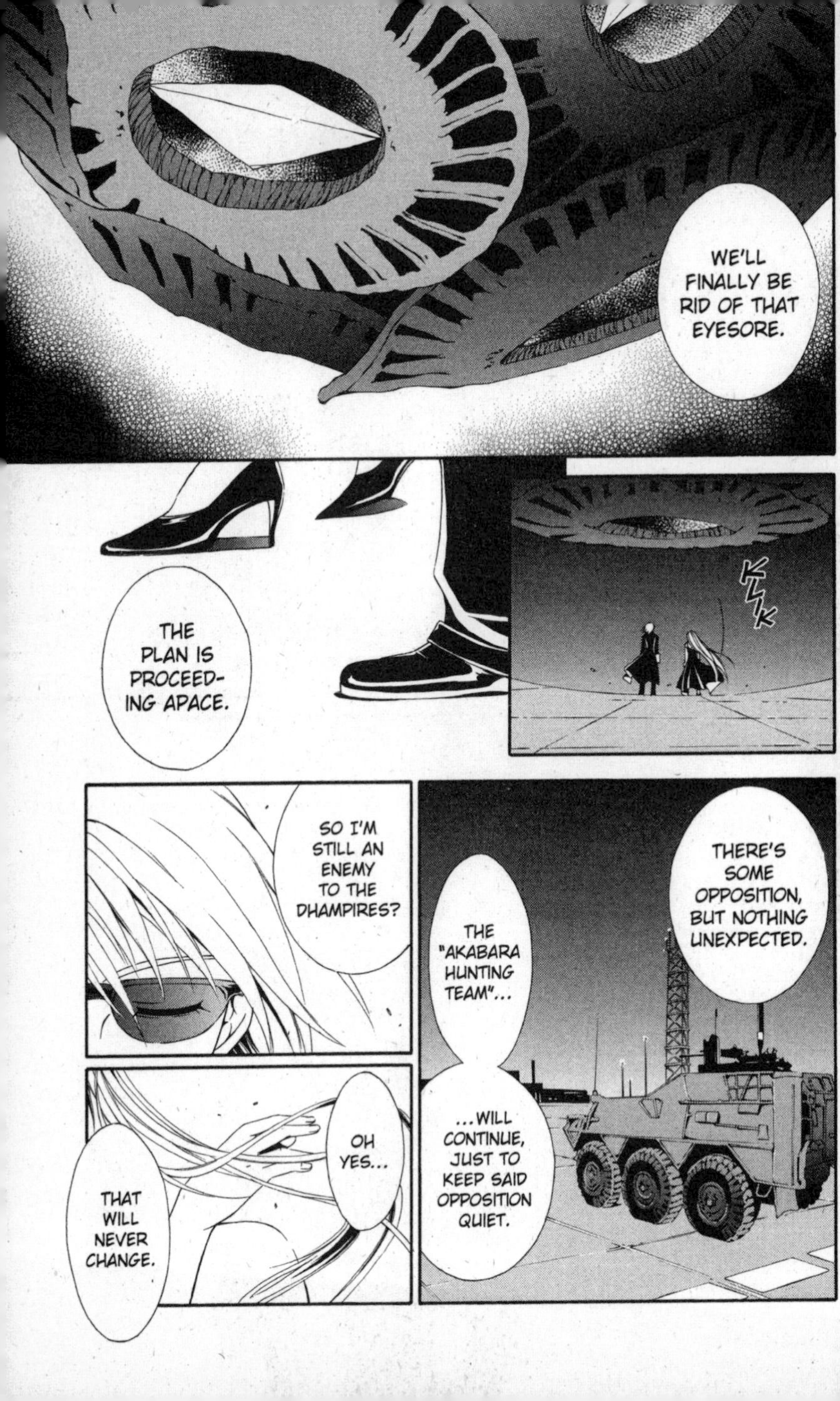
WE'LL FINALLY BE RID OF THAT EYESORE.
KLIK
THE PLAN IS PROCEED-ING APACE.
THERE'S SOME OPPOSITION, BUT NOTHING UNEXPECTED.
THE "AKABARA HUNTING TEAM"...
...WILL CONTINUE, JUST TO KEEP SAID OPPOSITION QUIET.
SO I'M STILL AN ENEMY TO THE DHAMPIRES?
OH YES...
THAT WILL NEVER CHANGE.

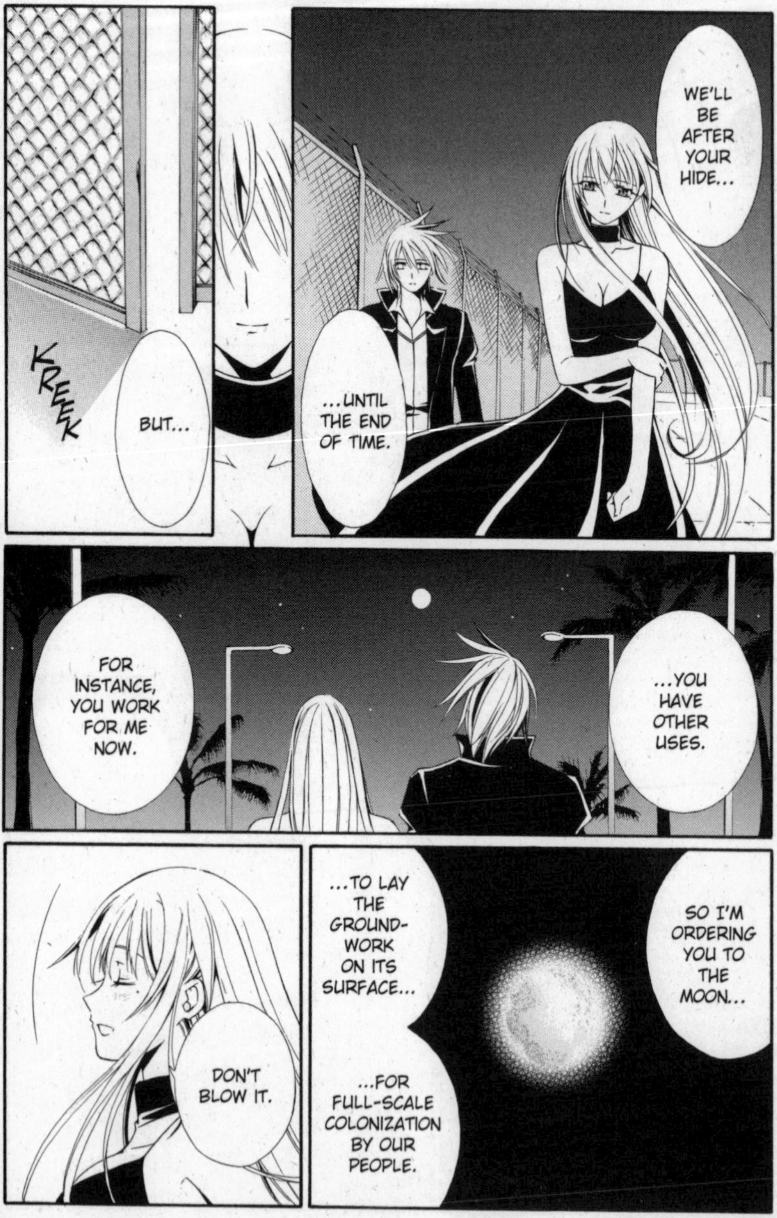
WE'LL BE AFTER YOUR HIDE...
...UNTIL THE END OF TIME.
KREEK
BUT...
...YOU HAVE OTHER USES.
FOR INSTANCE, YOU WORK FOR ME NOW.
SO I'M ORDERING YOU TO THE MOON...
...TO LAY THE GROUND-WORK ON ITS SURFACE...
...FOR FULL-SCALE COLONIZATION BY OUR PEOPLE.
DON'T BLOW IT.

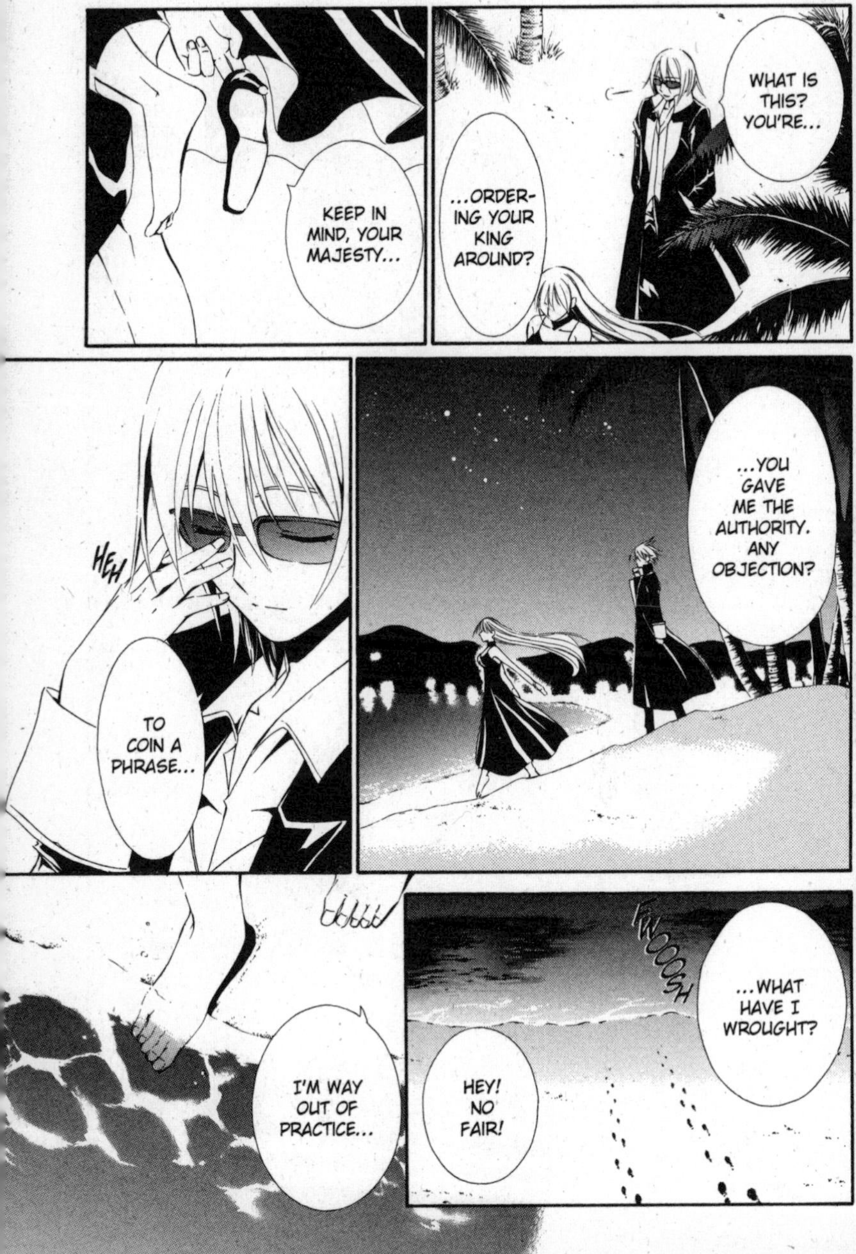
WHAT IS THIS? YOU'RE...
...ORDERING YOUR KING AROUND?
KEEP IN MIND, YOUR MAJESTY...
...YOU GAVE ME THE AUTHORITY. ANY OBJECTION?
HEH
TO COIN A PHRASE...
FWOOOSH
...WHAT HAVE I WROUGHT?
HEY! NO FAIR!
I'M WAY OUT OF PRACTICE...

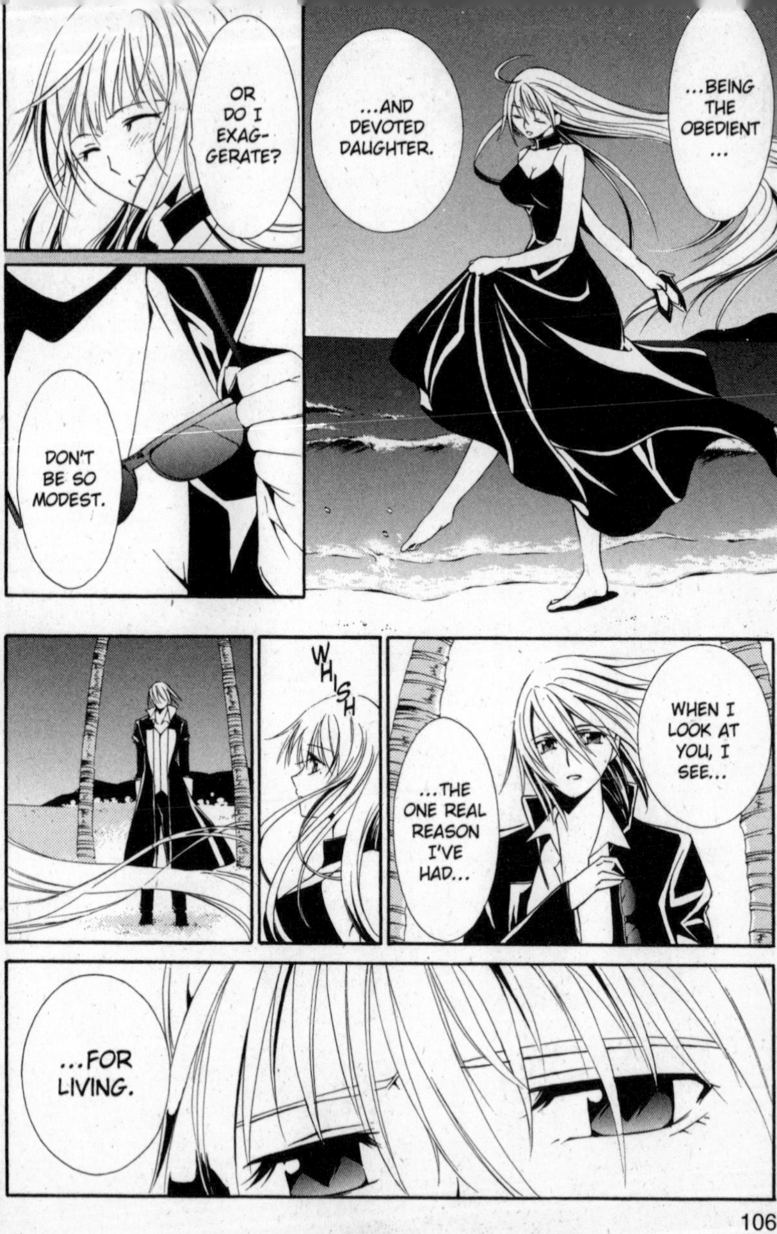
...BEING THE OBEDIENT ...
...AND DEVOTED DAUGHTER.
OR DO I EXAG-GERATE?
DON'T BE SO MODEST.
WHEN I LOOK AT YOU, I SEE...
...THE ONE REAL REASON I'VE HAD...
WHISH
...FOR LIVING.

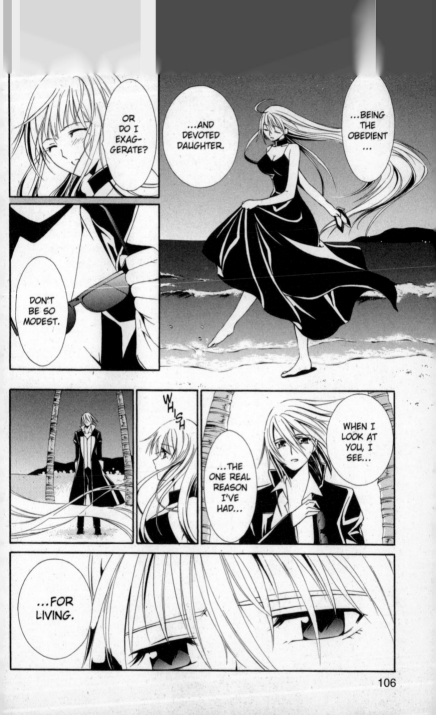

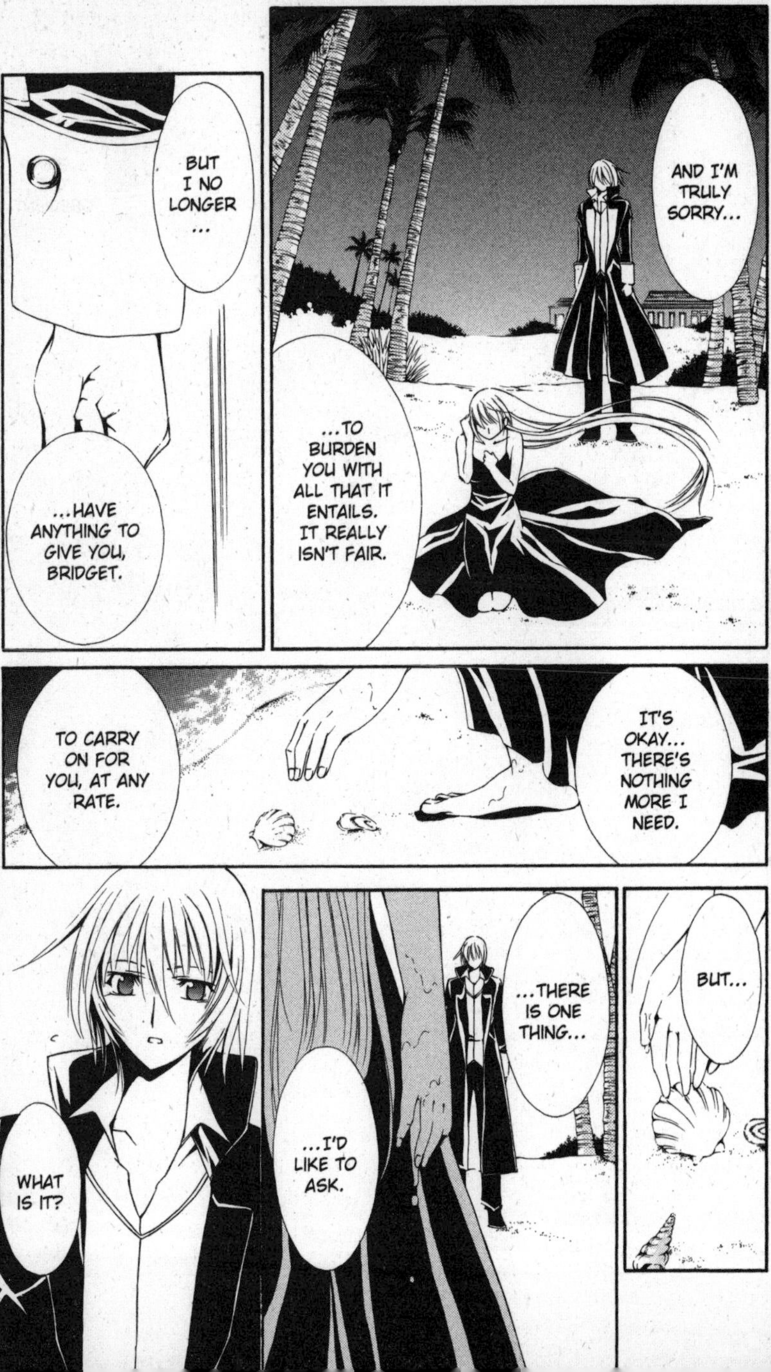
AND I'M TRULY SORRY...
...TO BURDEN YOU WITH ALL THAT IT ENTAILS. IT REALLY ISN'T FAIR.
BUT I NO LONGER ...
...HAVE ANYTHING TO GIVE YOU, BRIDGET.
IT'S OKAY... THERE'S NOTHING MORE I NEED.
TO CARRY ON FOR YOU, AT ANY RATE.
BUT...
...THERE IS ONE THING...
...I'D LIKE TO ASK.
WHAT IS IT?

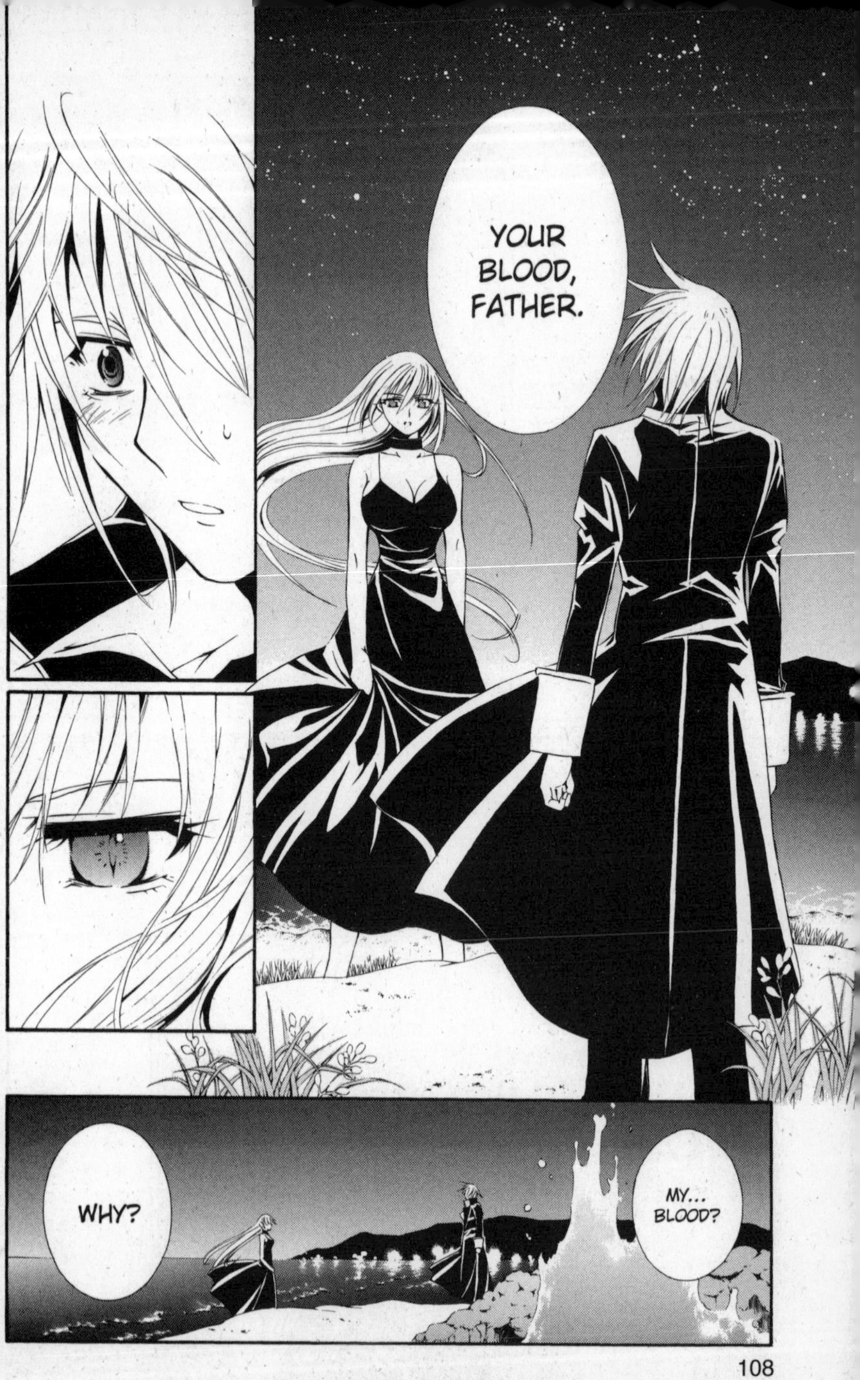
YOUR BLOOD, FATHER.
MY... BLOOD?
WHY?

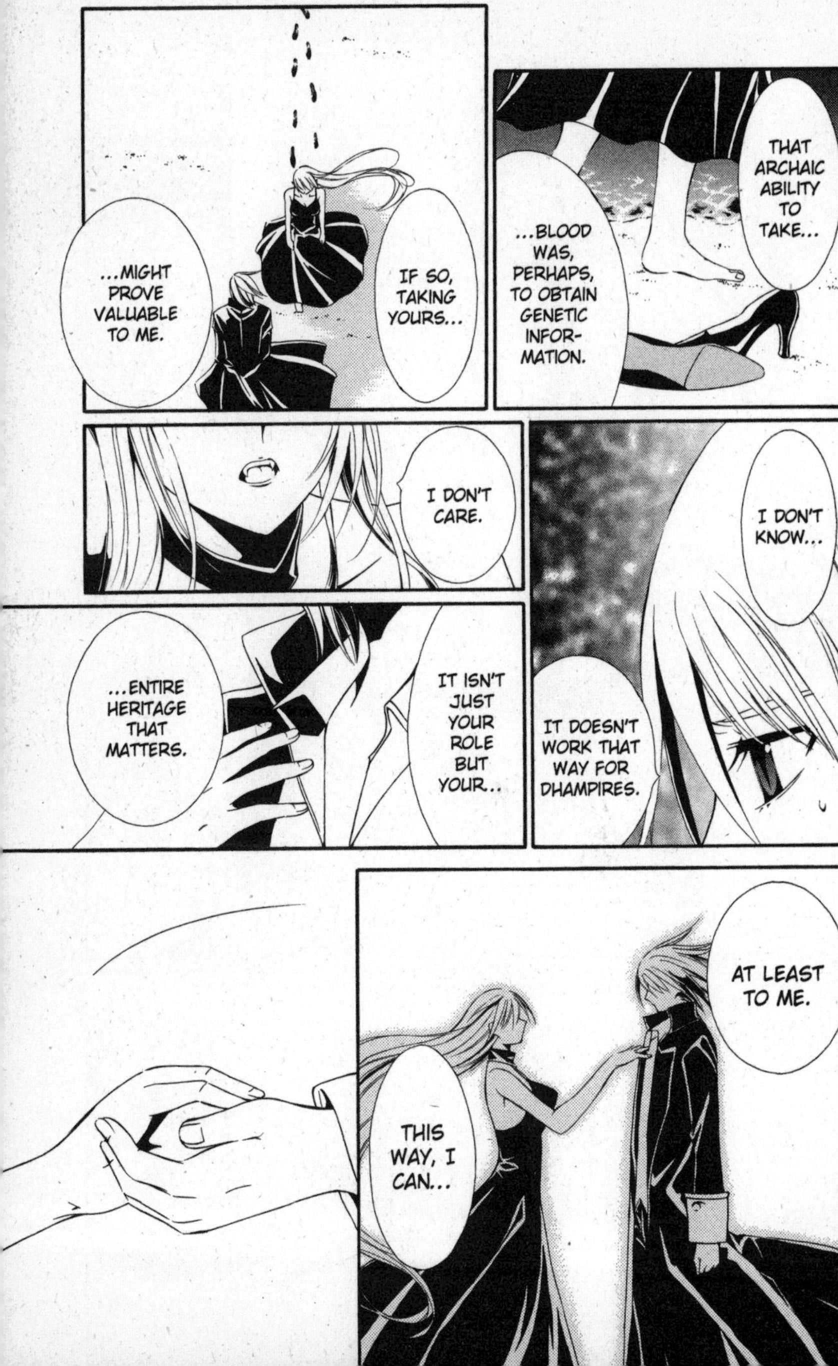
THAT ARCHAIC ABILITY TO TAKE...
...BLOOD WAS, PERHAPS, TO OBTAIN GENETIC INFOR-MATION.
IF SO, TAKING YOURS...
...MIGHT PROVE VALUABLE TO ME.
I DON'T KNOW...
IT DOESN'T WORK THAT WAY FOR DHAMPIRES.
I DON'T CARE.
IT ISN'T JUST YOUR ROLE BUT YOUR...
...ENTIRE HERITAGE THAT MATTERS.
AT LEAST TO ME.
THIS WAY, I CAN...

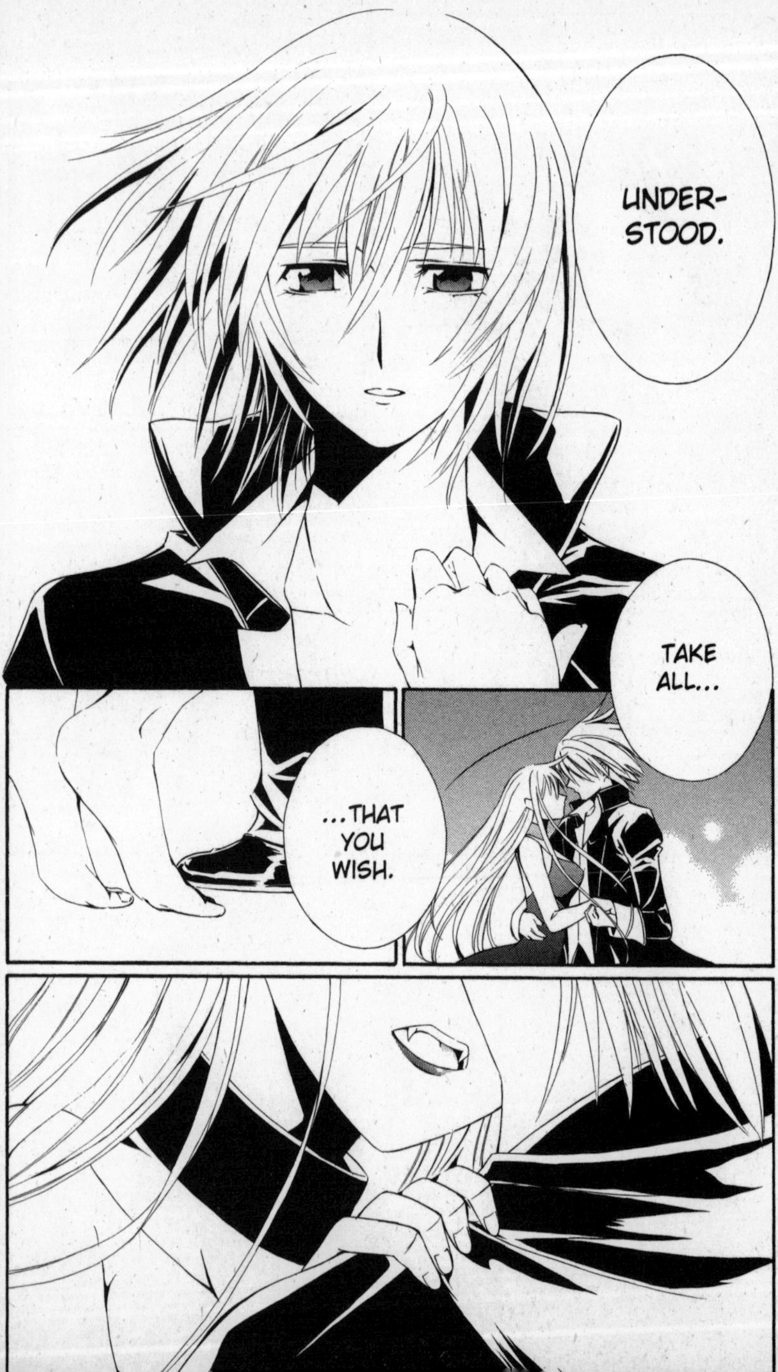
UNDER-
STOOD.
TAKE ALL...
...THAT YOU WISH.

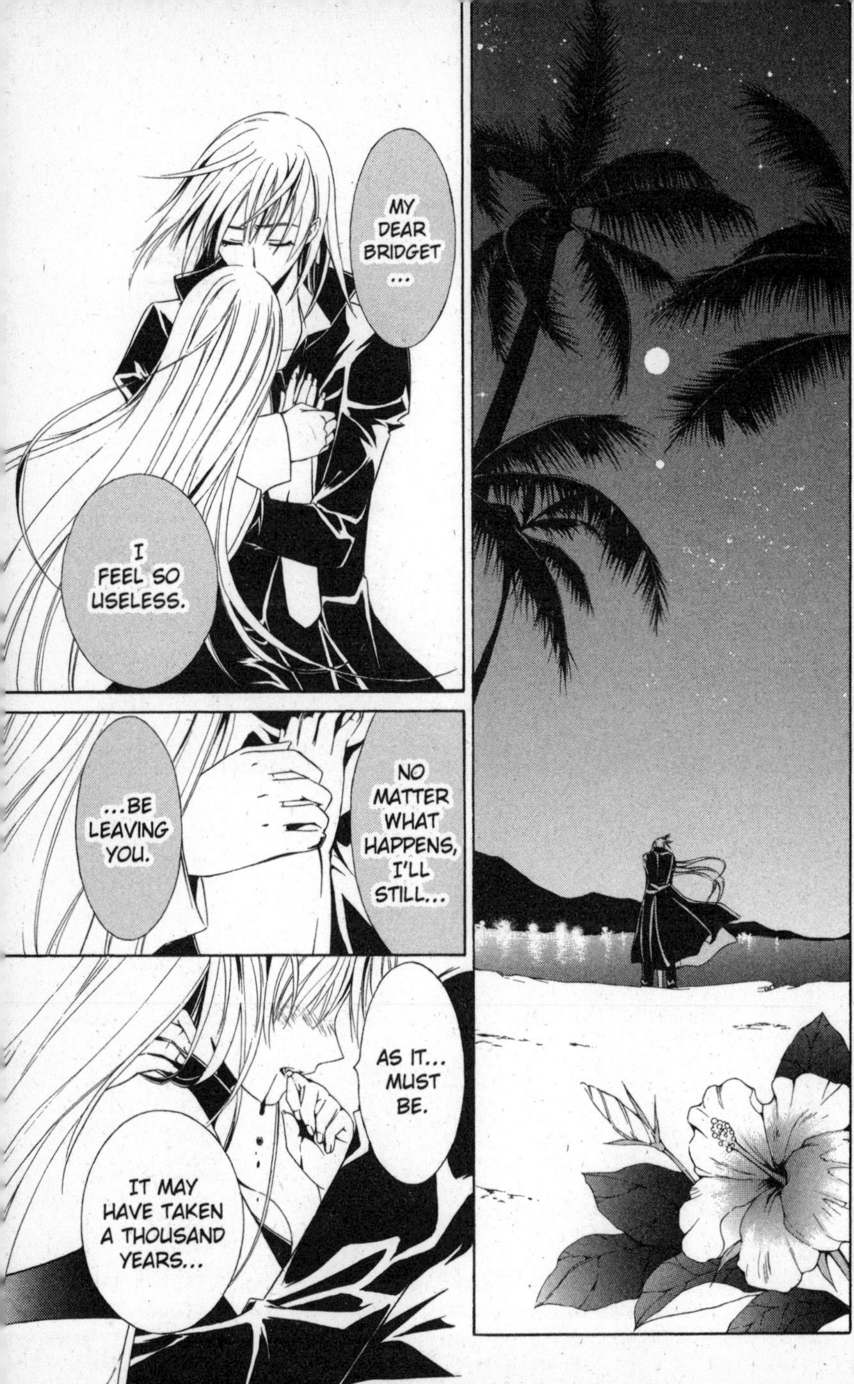
MY DEAR BRIDGET ...
I FEEL SO USELESS.
NO MATTER WHAT HAPPENS, I'LL STILL...
...BE LEAVING YOU.
AS IT... MUST BE.
IT MAY HAVE TAKEN A THOUSAND YEARS...

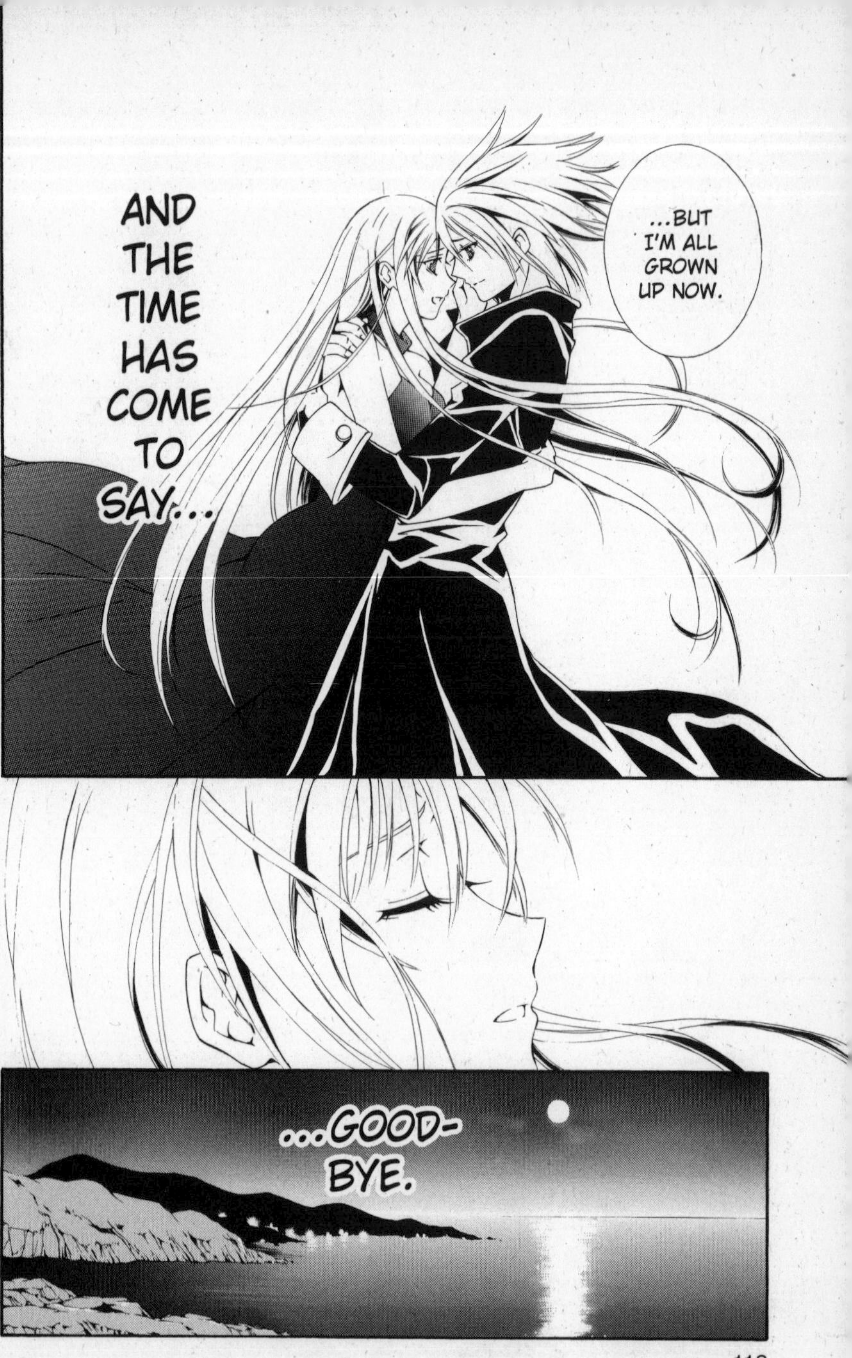
...BUT I'M ALL GROWN UP NOW.
AND THE TIME HAS COME TO SAY...
...GOOD-BYE.

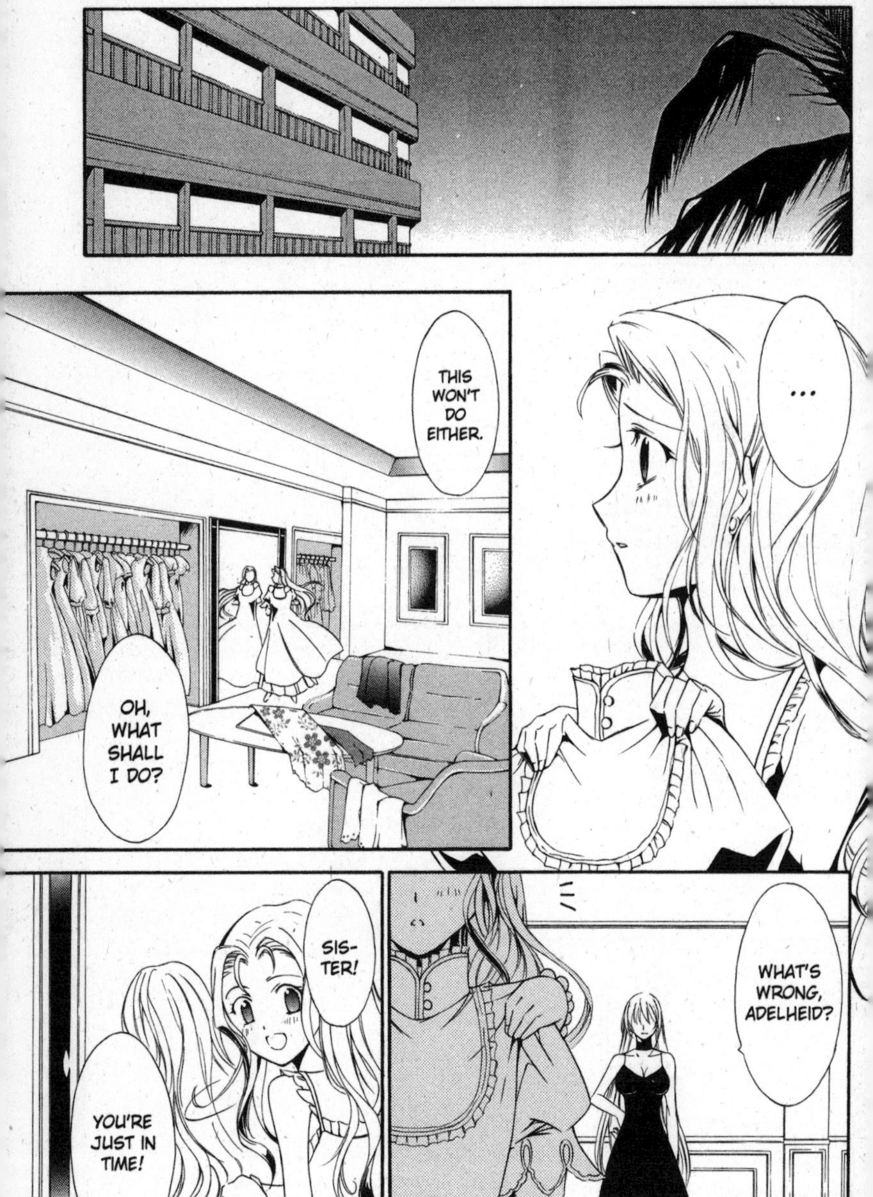
...
THIS WON'T DO EITHER.
OH, WHAT SHALL I DO?
WHAT'S WRONG, ADELHEID?
SIS-TER!
YOU'RE JUST IN TIME!

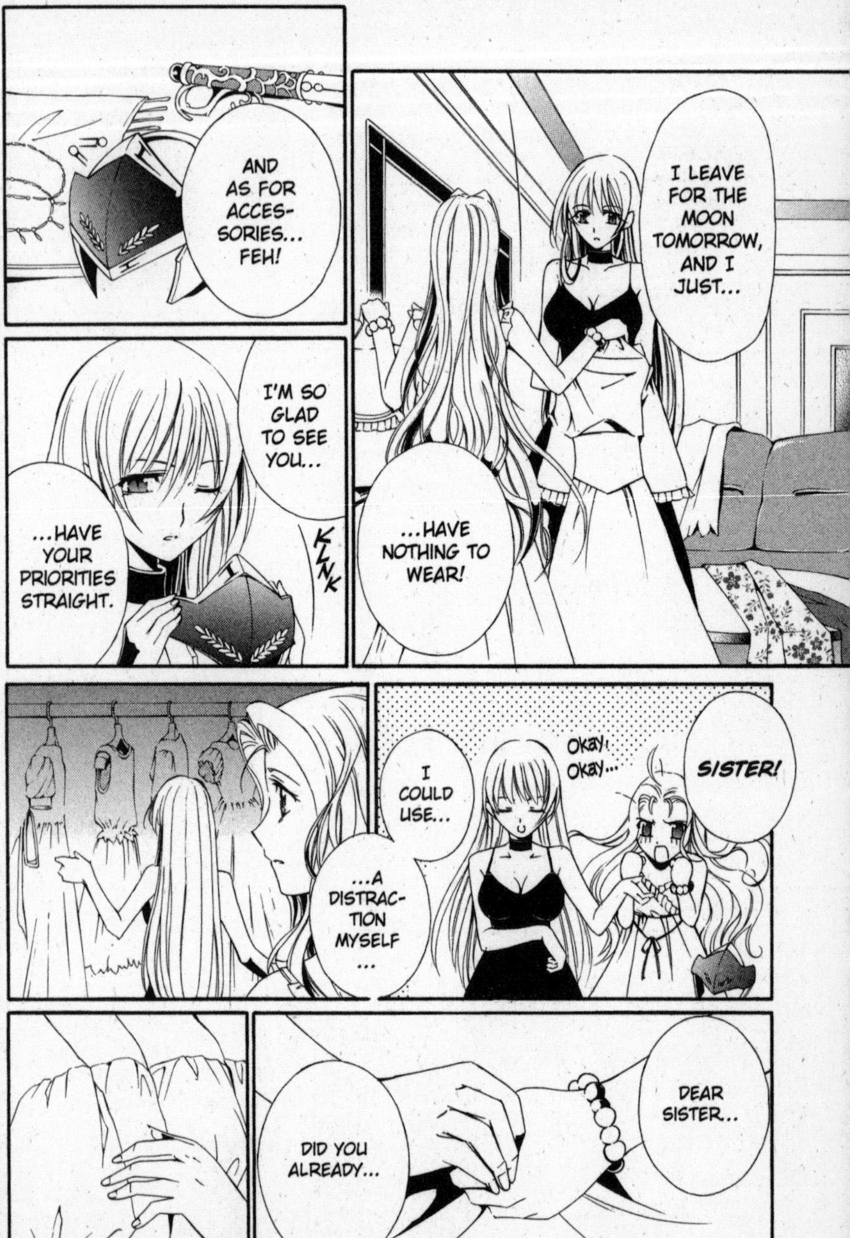

I LEAVE FOR THE MOON TOMORROW, AND I JUST...
...HAVE NOTHING TO WEAR!
AND AS FOR ACCES-SORIES... FEH!
I'M SO GLAD TO SEE YOU...
KLNK
...HAVE YOUR PRIORITIES STRAIGHT.
SISTER!
Okay! Okay...
I COULD USE...
...A DISTRAC-TION MYSELF...
DEAR SISTER...
DID YOU ALREADY...

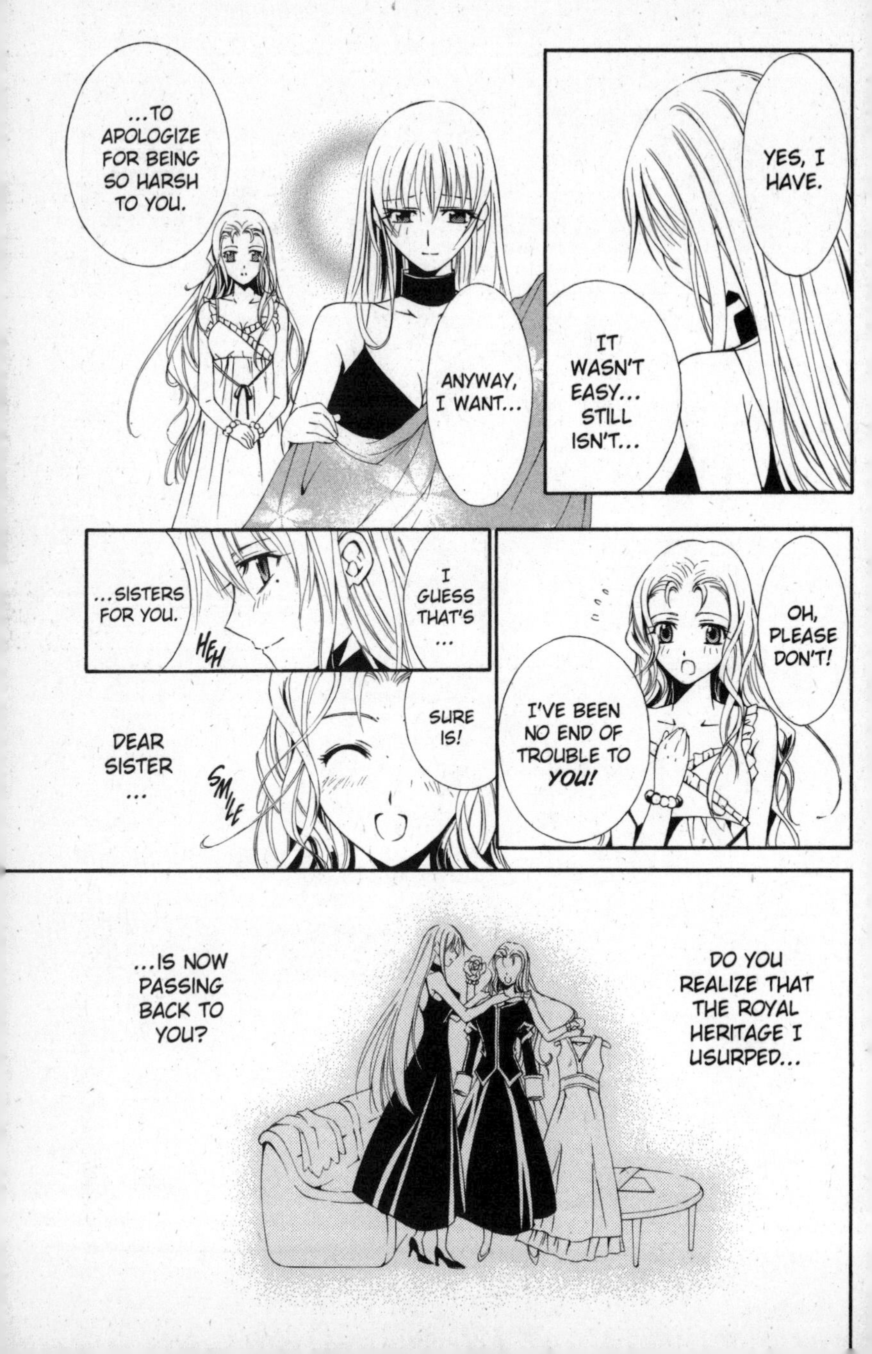
YES, I HAVE.
IT WASN'T EASY... STILL ISN'T...
ANYWAY, I WANT...
...TO APOLOGIZE FOR BEING SO HARSH TO YOU.
OH, PLEASE DON'T!
I'VE BEEN NO END OF TROUBLE TO YOU!
I GUESS THAT'S...
...SISTERS FOR YOU.
HEH
SURE IS!
SMILE
DEAR SISTER...
DO YOU REALIZE THAT THE ROYAL HERITAGE I USURPED...
...IS NOW PASSING BACK TO YOU?

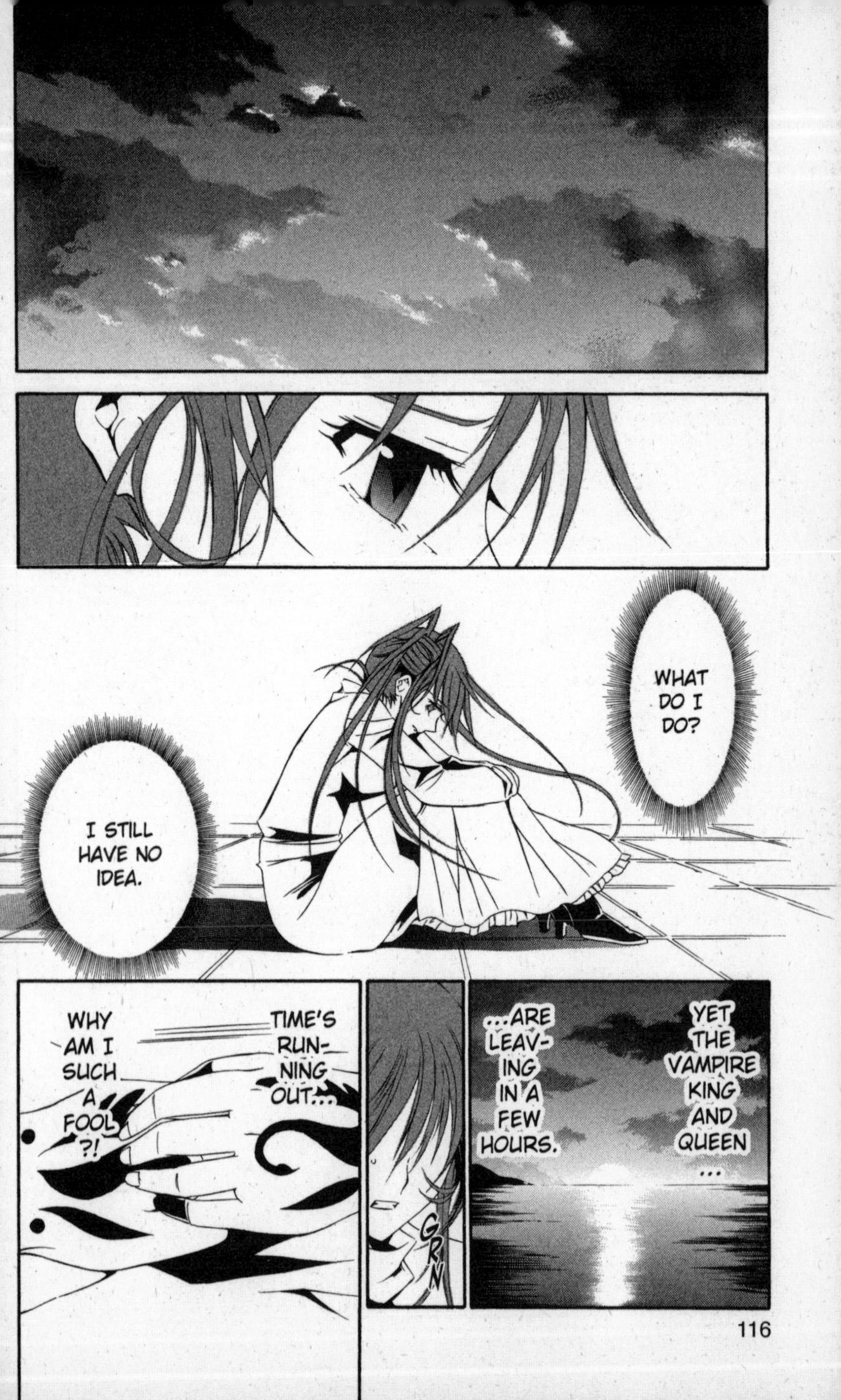
WHAT DO I DO?
I STILL HAVE NO IDEA.
YET THE VAMPIRE KING AND QUEEN...
...ARE LEAVING IN A FEW HOURS.
GRN
TIME'S RUNNING OUT...
WHY AM I SUCH A FOOL?!

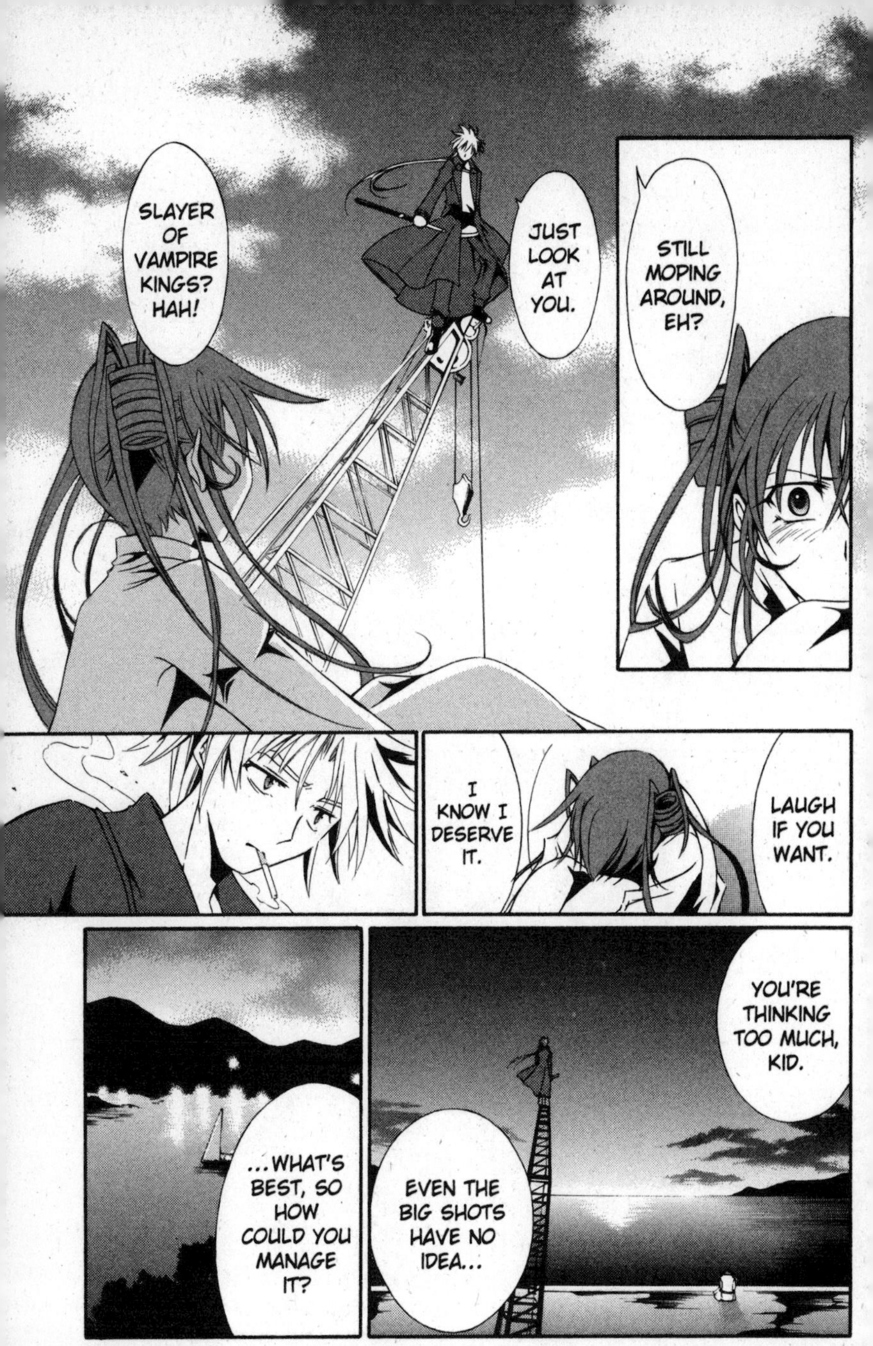
STILL MOPING AROUND, EH?
JUST LOOK AT YOU.
SLAYER OF VAMPIRE KINGS? HAH!
LAUGH IF YOU WANT.
I KNOW I DESERVE IT.
YOU'RE THINKING TOO MUCH, KID.
EVEN THE BIG SHOTS HAVE NO IDEA...
...WHAT'S BEST, SO HOW COULD YOU MANAGE IT?

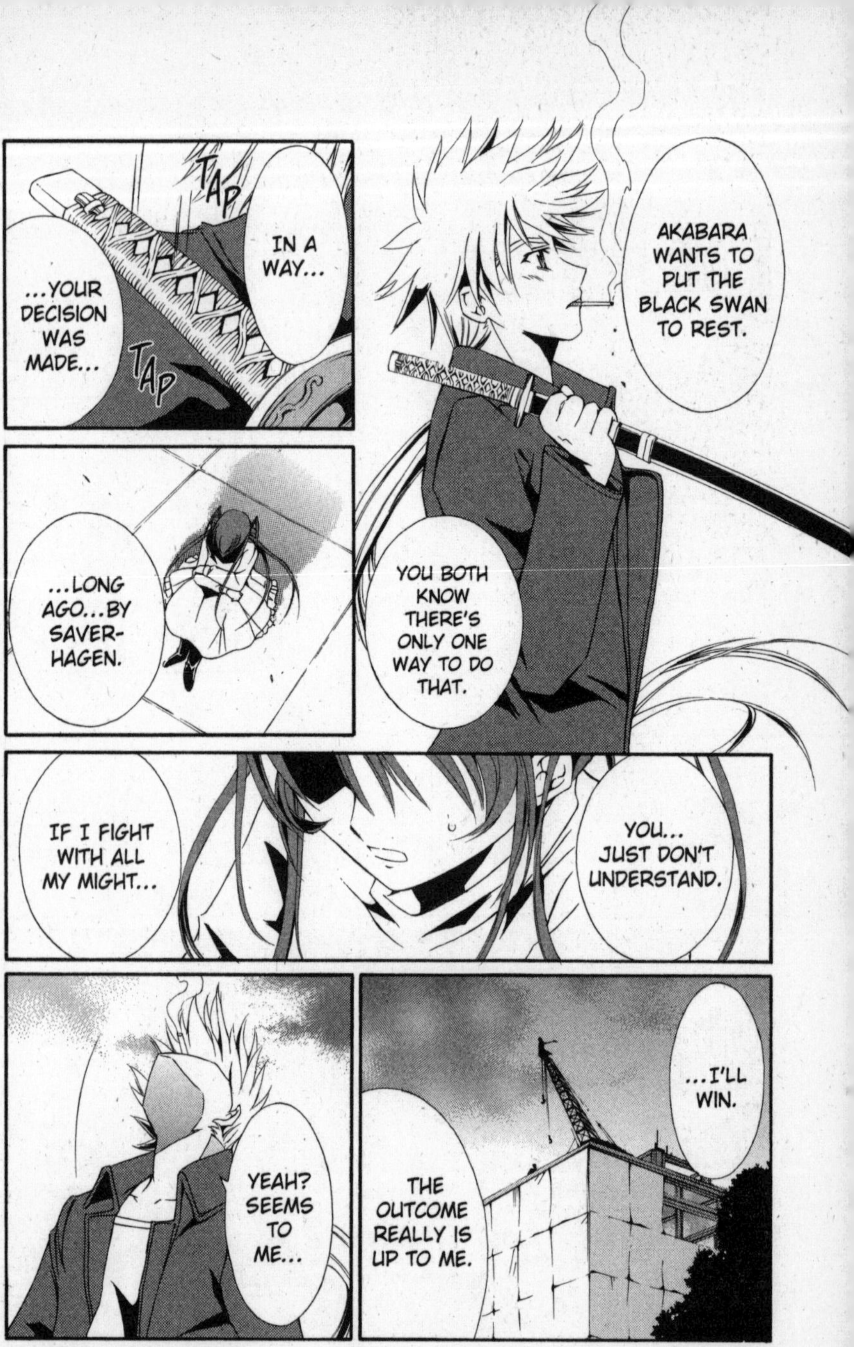
AKABARA WANTS TO PUT THE BLACK SWAN TO REST.
YOU BOTH KNOW THERE'S ONLY ONE WAY TO DO THAT.
TAP
IN A WAY...
TAP
...YOUR DECISION WAS MADE...
...LONG AGO...BY SAVER-HAGEN.
YOU... JUST DON'T UNDERSTAND.
IF I FIGHT WITH ALL MY MIGHT...
...I'LL WIN.
THE OUTCOME REALLY IS UP TO ME.
YEAH? SEEMS TO ME...

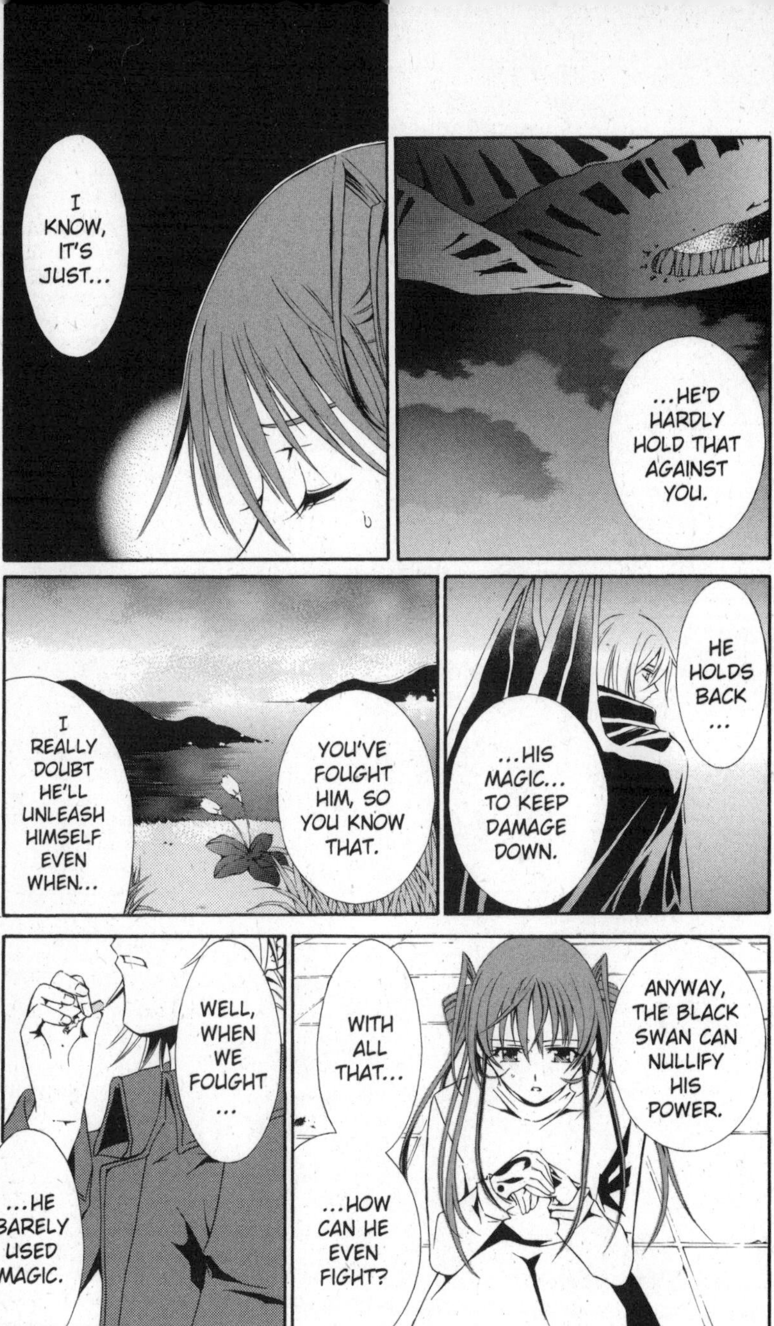
...HE'D HARDLY HOLD THAT AGAINST YOU.
I KNOW, IT'S JUST...
HE HOLDS BACK...
...HIS MAGIC... TO KEEP DAMAGE DOWN.
YOU'VE FOUGHT HIM, SO YOU KNOW THAT.
I REALLY DOUBT HE'LL UNLEASH HIMSELF EVEN WHEN...
ANYWAY, THE BLACK SWAN CAN NULLIFY HIS POWER.
WITH ALL THAT...
...HOW CAN HE EVEN FIGHT?
WELL, WHEN WE FOUGHT...
...HE BARELY USED MAGIC.

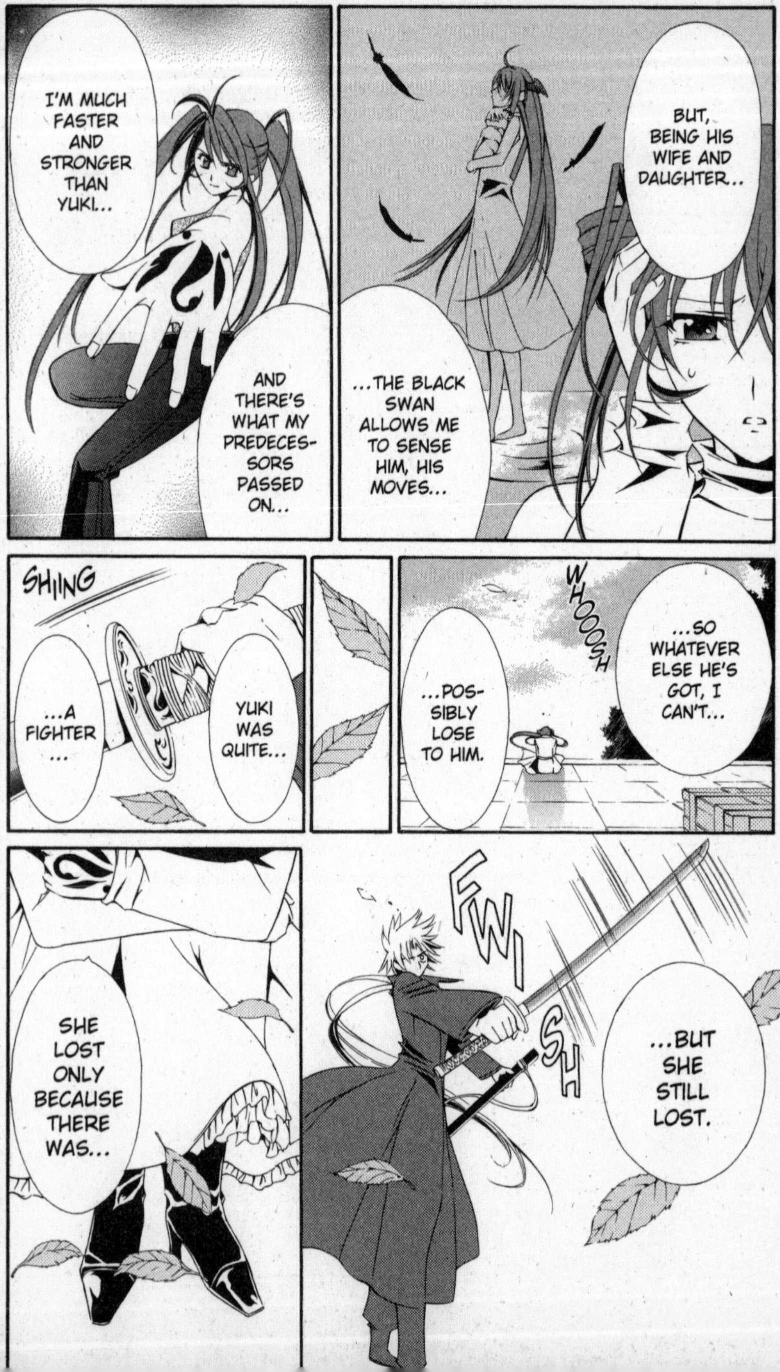
BUT, BEING HIS WIFE AND DAUGHTER...
...THE BLACK SWAN ALLOWS ME TO SENSE HIM, HIS MOVES...
I'M MUCH FASTER AND STRONGER THAN YUKI...
AND THERE'S WHAT MY PREDECES-SORS PASSED ON...
WHOOOSH
...SO WHATEVER ELSE HE'S GOT, I CAN'T...
...POS-SIBLY LOSE TO HIM.
SHIING
YUKI WAS QUITE...
...A FIGHTER...
FWISH
...BUT SHE STILL LOST.
SHE LOST ONLY BECAUSE THERE WAS...

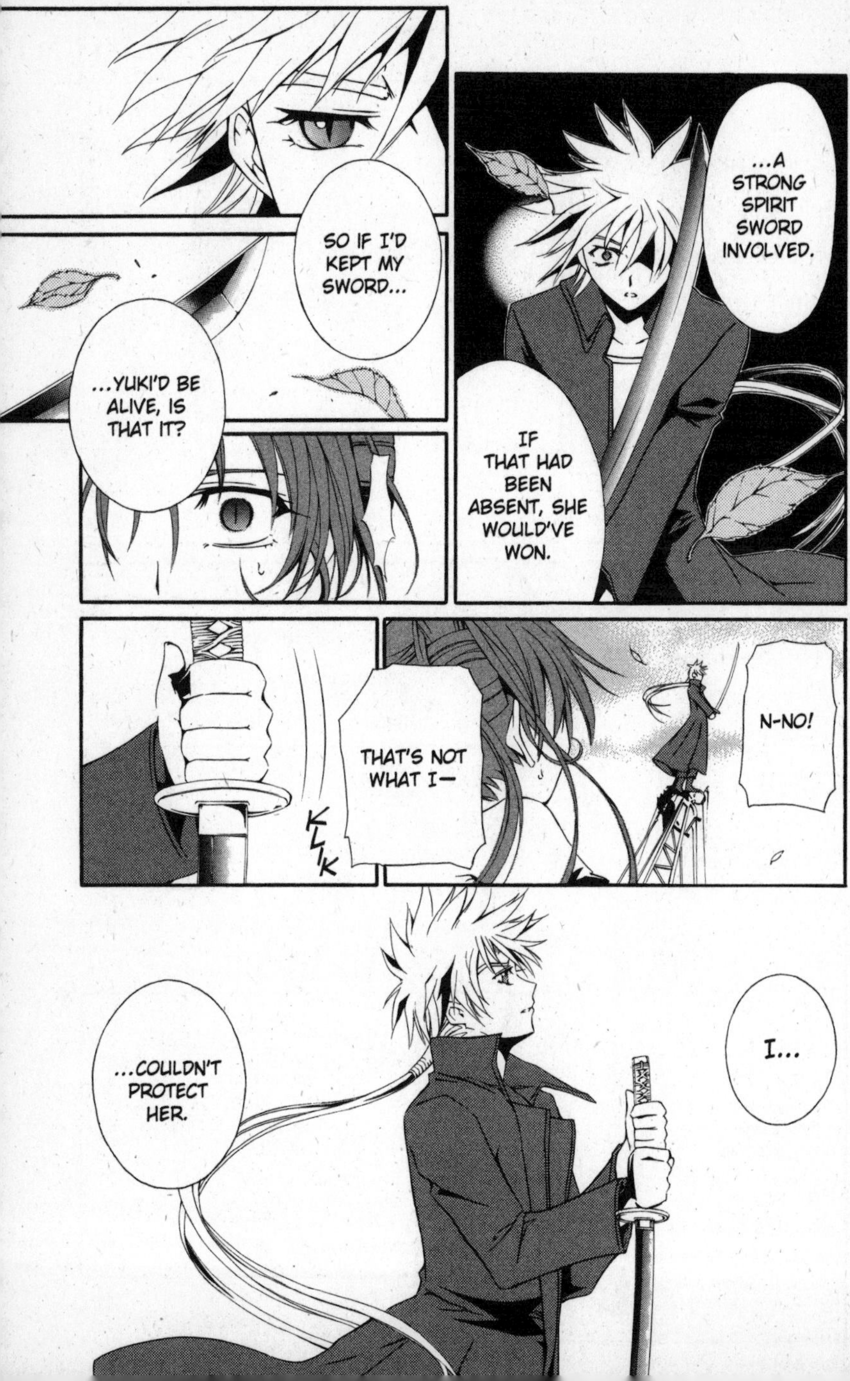
...A STRONG SPIRIT SWORD INVOLVED.
IF THAT HAD BEEN ABSENT, SHE WOULD'VE WON.
SO IF I'D KEPT MY SWORD...
...YUKI'D BE ALIVE, IS THAT IT?
N-NO!
THAT'S NOT WHAT I—
KLIK
I...
...COULDN'T PROTECT HER.

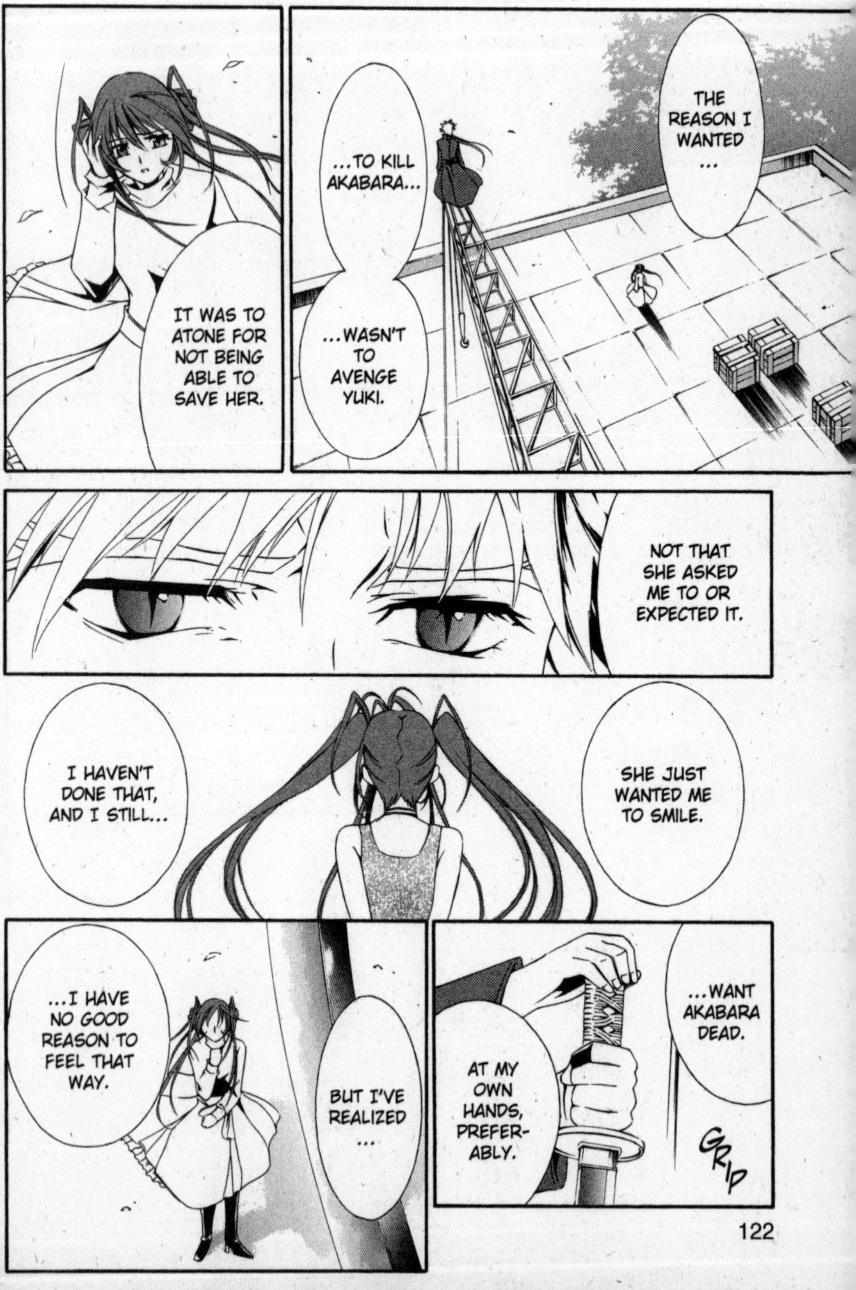
THE REASON I WANTED ...
...TO KILL AKABARA...
...WASN'T TO AVENGE YUKI.
IT WAS TO ATONE FOR NOT BEING ABLE TO SAVE HER.
NOT THAT SHE ASKED ME TO OR EXPECTED IT.
SHE JUST WANTED ME TO SMILE.
I HAVEN'T DONE THAT, AND I STILL...
...WANT AKABARA DEAD.
AT MY OWN HANDS, PREFER-ABLY.
GRIP
BUT I'VE REALIZED ...
...I HAVE NO GOOD REASON TO FEEL THAT WAY.

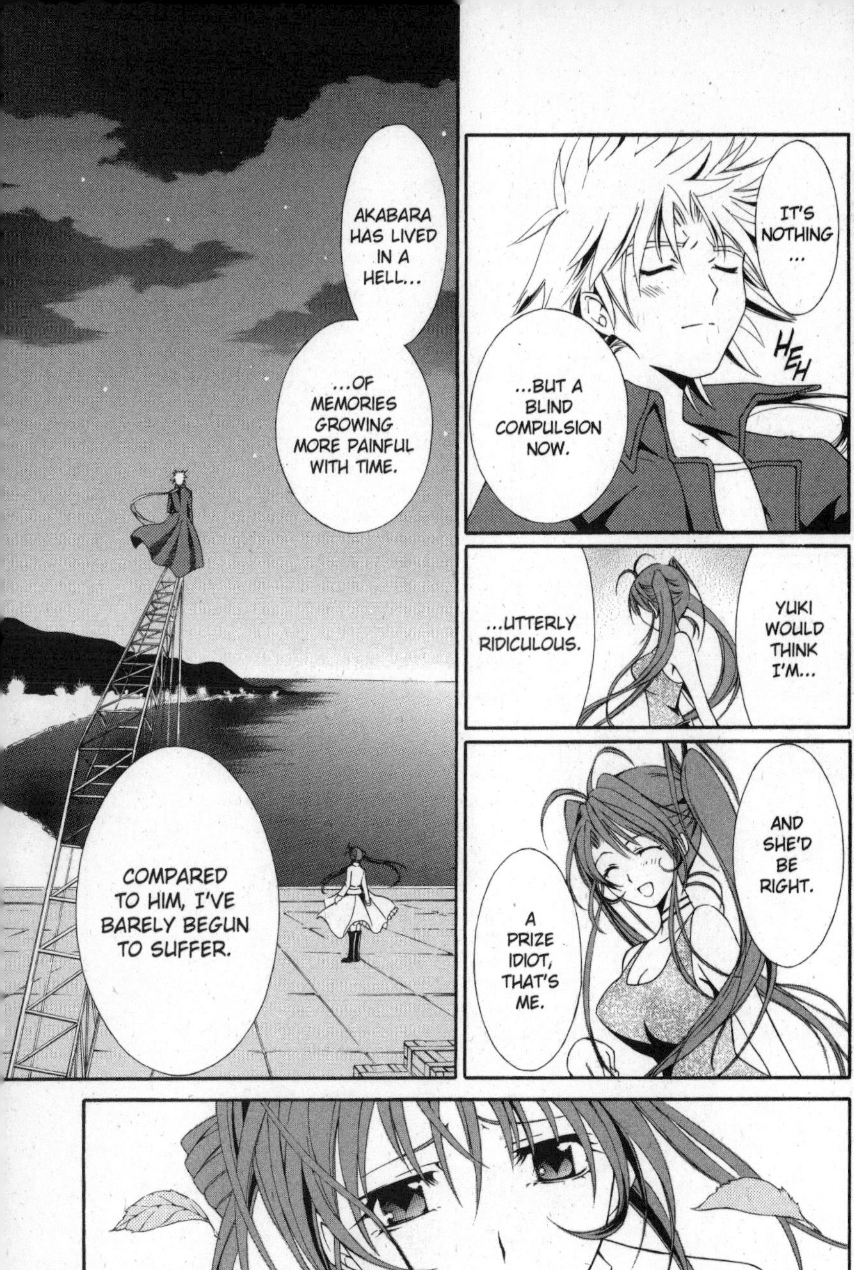
IT'S NOTHING...
...BUT A BLIND COMPULSION NOW.
HEH
YUKI WOULD THINK I'M...
...UTTERLY RIDICULOUS.
AND SHE'D BE RIGHT.
A PRIZE IDIOT, THAT'S ME.
AKABARA HAS LIVED IN A HELL...
...OF MEMORIES GROWING MORE PAINFUL WITH TIME.
COMPARED TO HIM, I'VE BARELY BEGUN TO SUFFER.

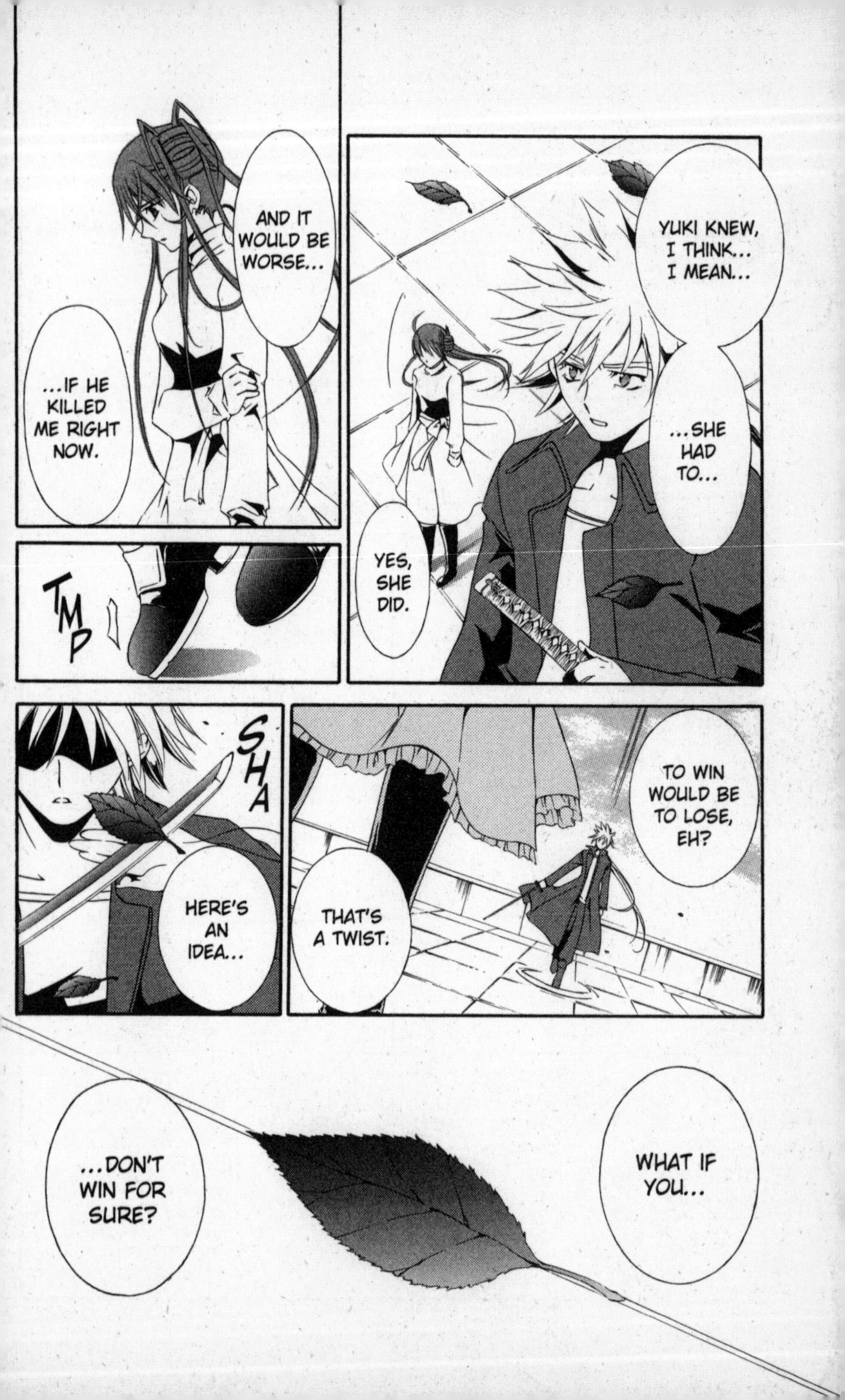
YUKI KNEW, I THINK... I MEAN...
...SHE HAD TO...
YES, SHE DID.
AND IT WOULD BE WORSE...
...IF HE KILLED ME RIGHT NOW.
TMP
TO WIN WOULD BE TO LOSE, EH?
THAT'S A TWIST.
SHA
HERE'S AN IDEA...
WHAT IF YOU...
...DON'T WIN FOR SURE?

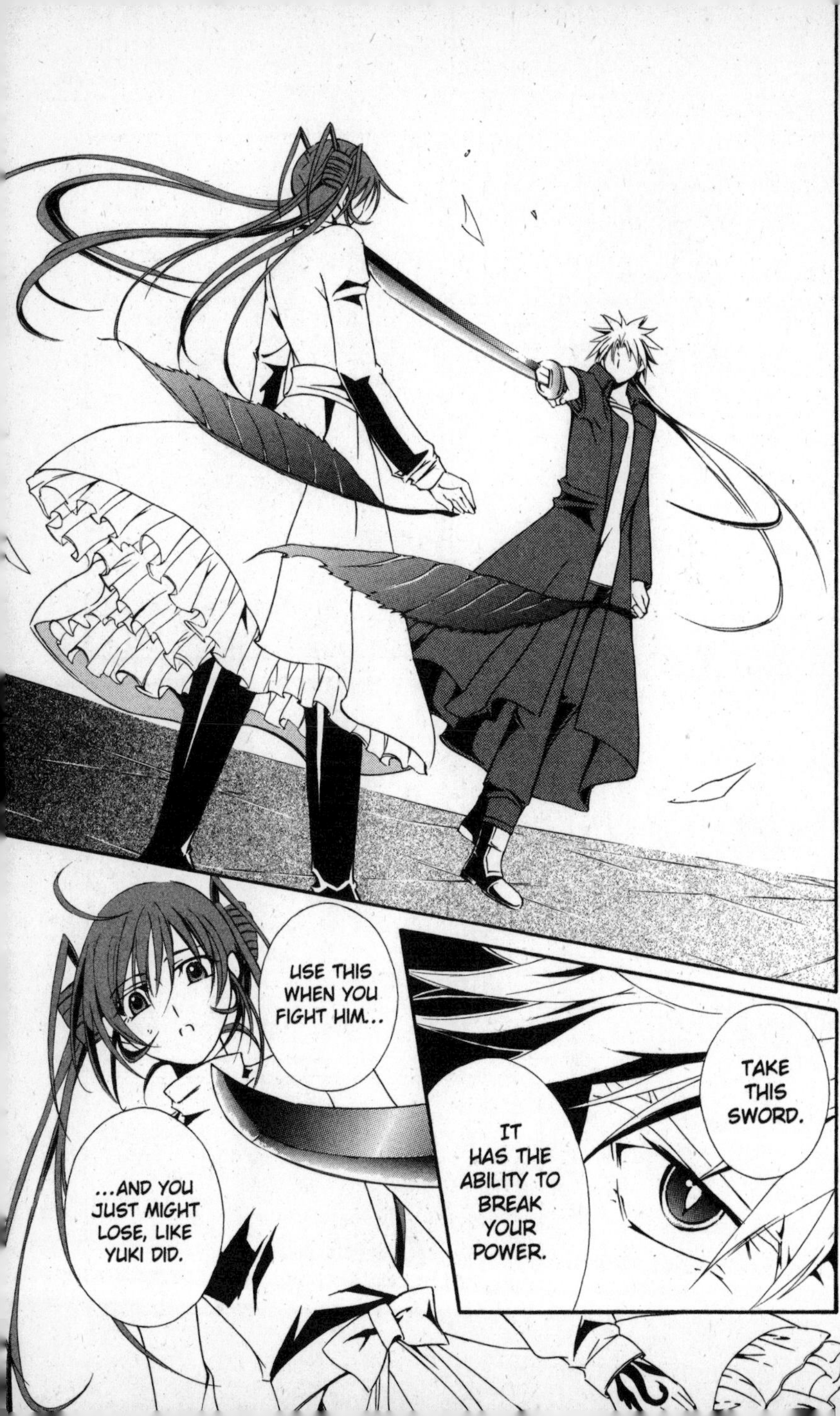
TAKE THIS SWORD.
IT HAS THE ABILITY TO BREAK YOUR POWER.
USE THIS WHEN YOU FIGHT HIM...
...AND YOU JUST MIGHT LOSE, LIKE YUKI DID.

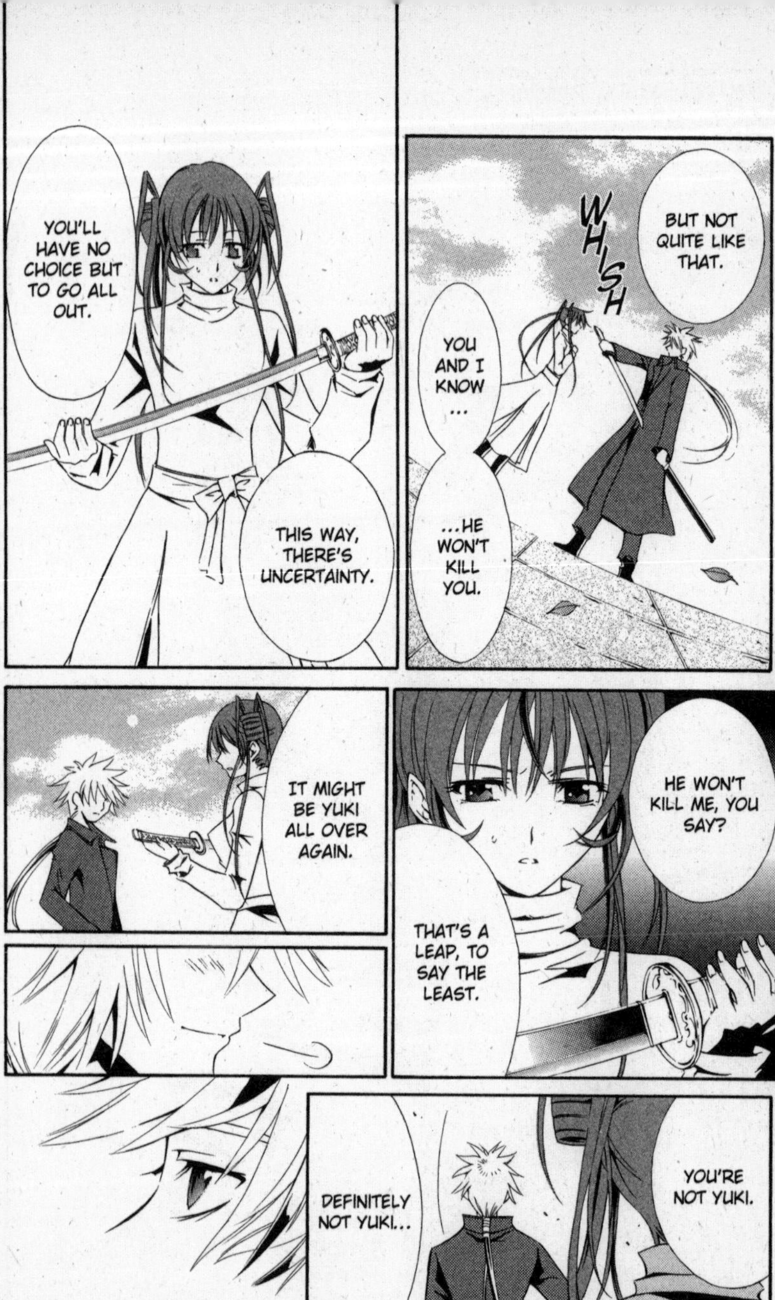
BUT NOT QUITE LIKE THAT.
WHISH
YOU AND I KNOW...
...HE WON'T KILL YOU.
YOU'LL HAVE NO CHOICE BUT TO GO ALL OUT.
THIS WAY, THERE'S UNCERTAINTY.
HE WON'T KILL ME, YOU SAY?
THAT'S A LEAP, TO SAY THE LEAST.
IT MIGHT BE YUKI ALL OVER AGAIN.
YOU'RE NOT YUKI.
DEFINITELY NOT YUKI...

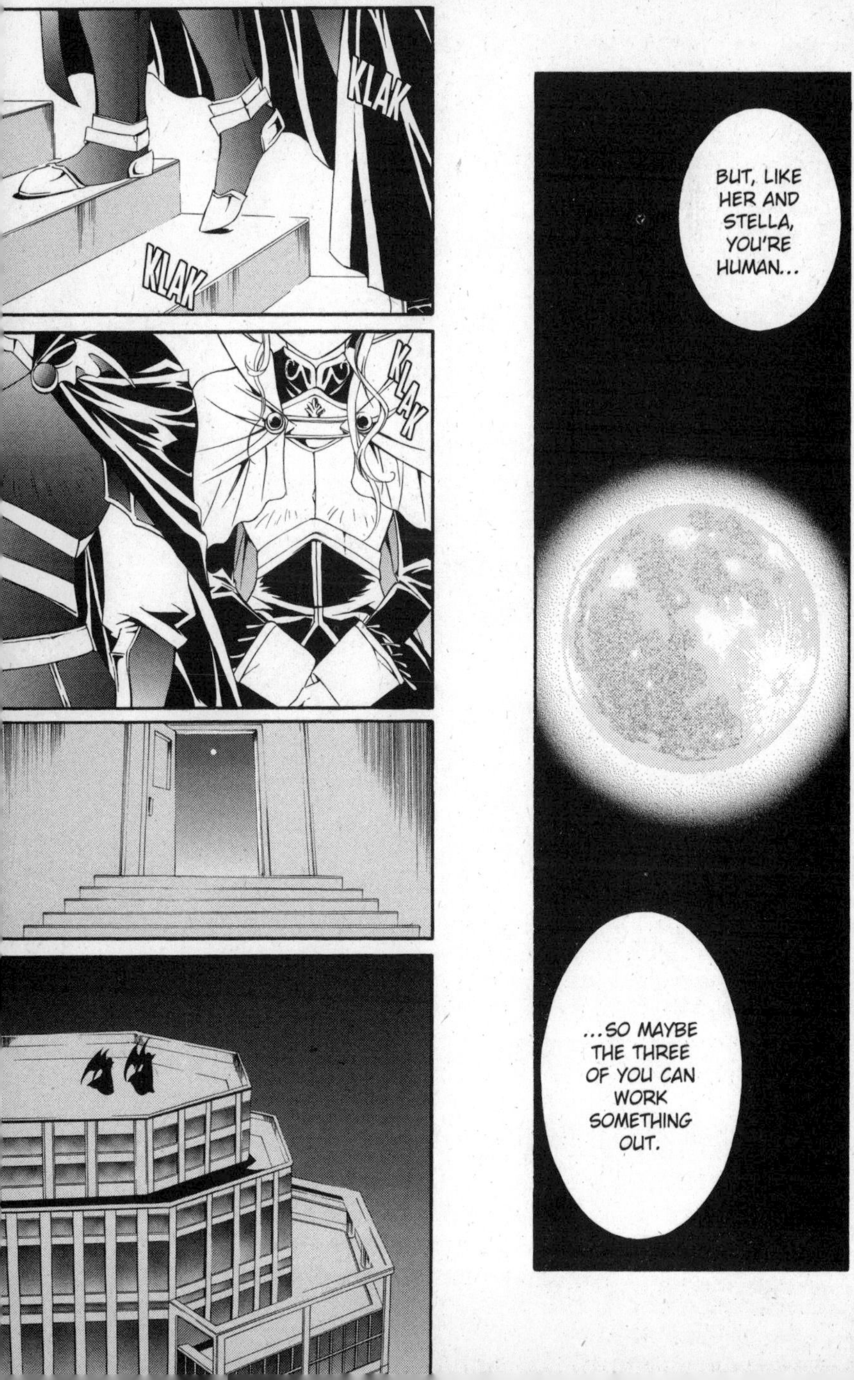
BUT, LIKE HER AND STELLA, YOU'RE HUMAN...
...SO MAYBE THE THREE OF YOU CAN WORK SOMETHING OUT.
KLAK
KLAK
KLAK

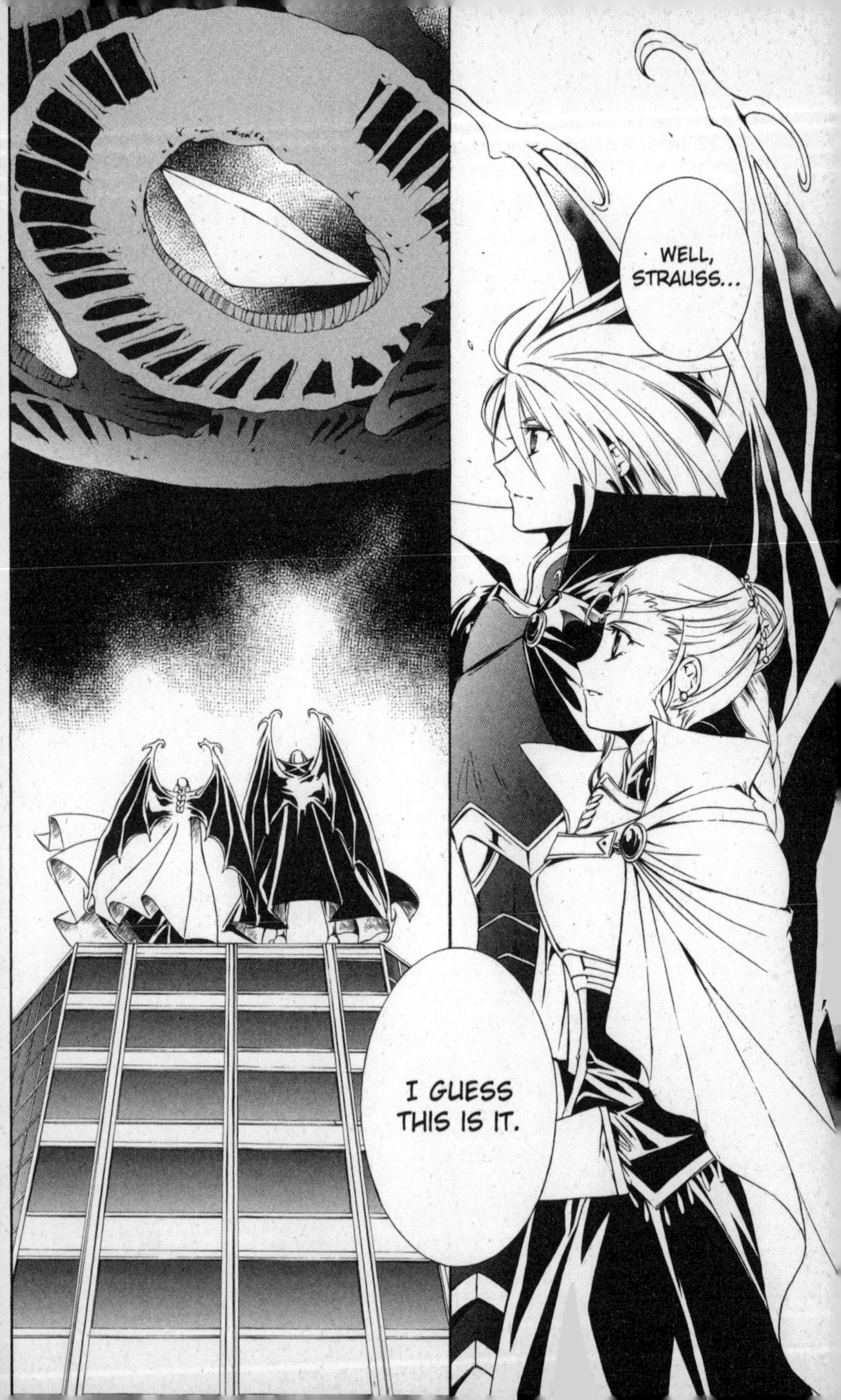
WELL, STRAUSS...
I GUESS THIS IS IT.

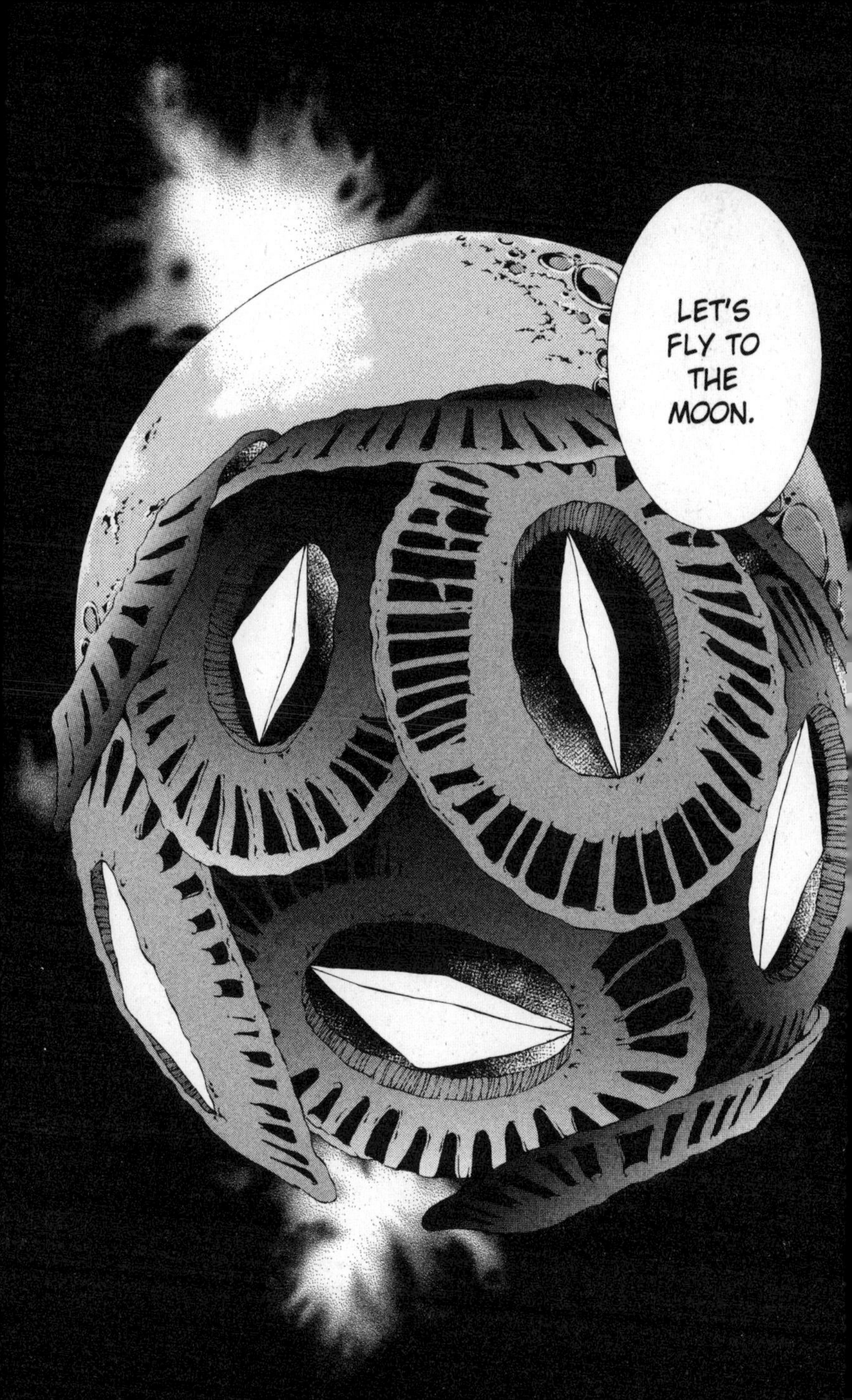
LET'S FLY TO THE MOON.

THE RECORD OF A

FALLEN VAMPIRE

Chapter 42: Pavane for an Endless Night

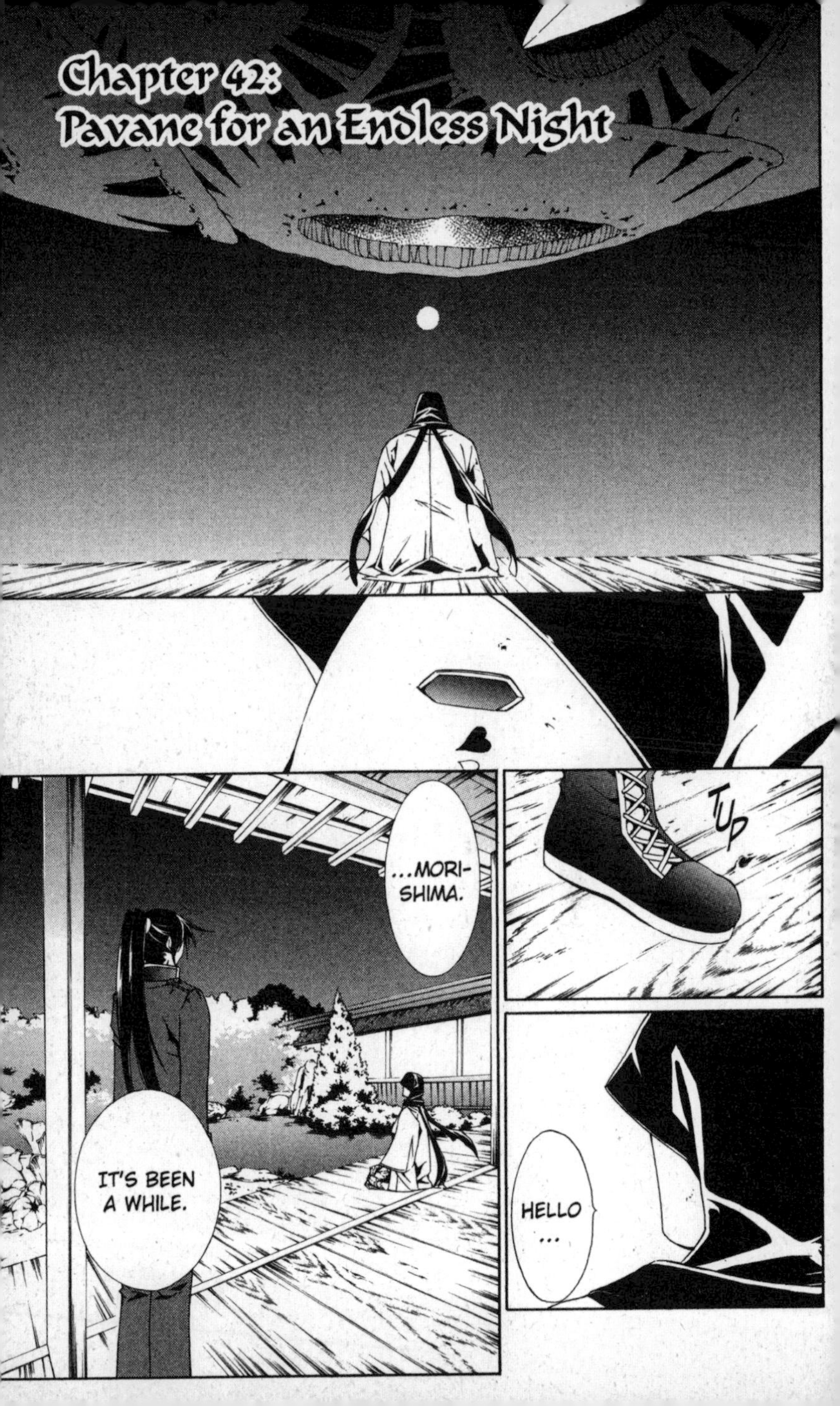
TUP
HELLO ...
...MORI-SHIMA.
IT'S BEEN A WHILE.

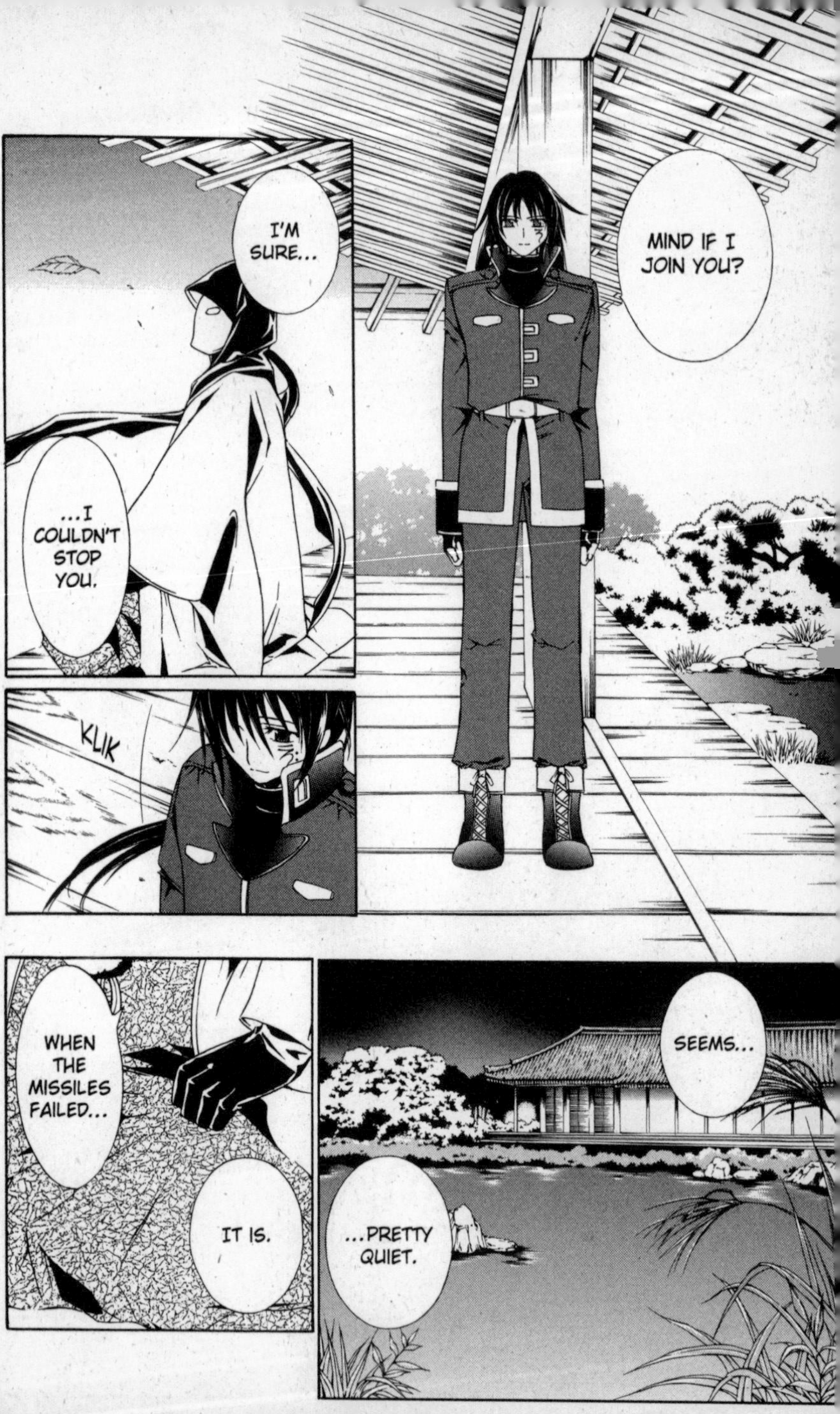
MIND IF I JOIN YOU?
I'M SURE...
...I COULDN'T STOP YOU.
KLIK
SEEMS...
...PRETTY QUIET.
WHEN THE MISSILES FAILED...
IT IS.

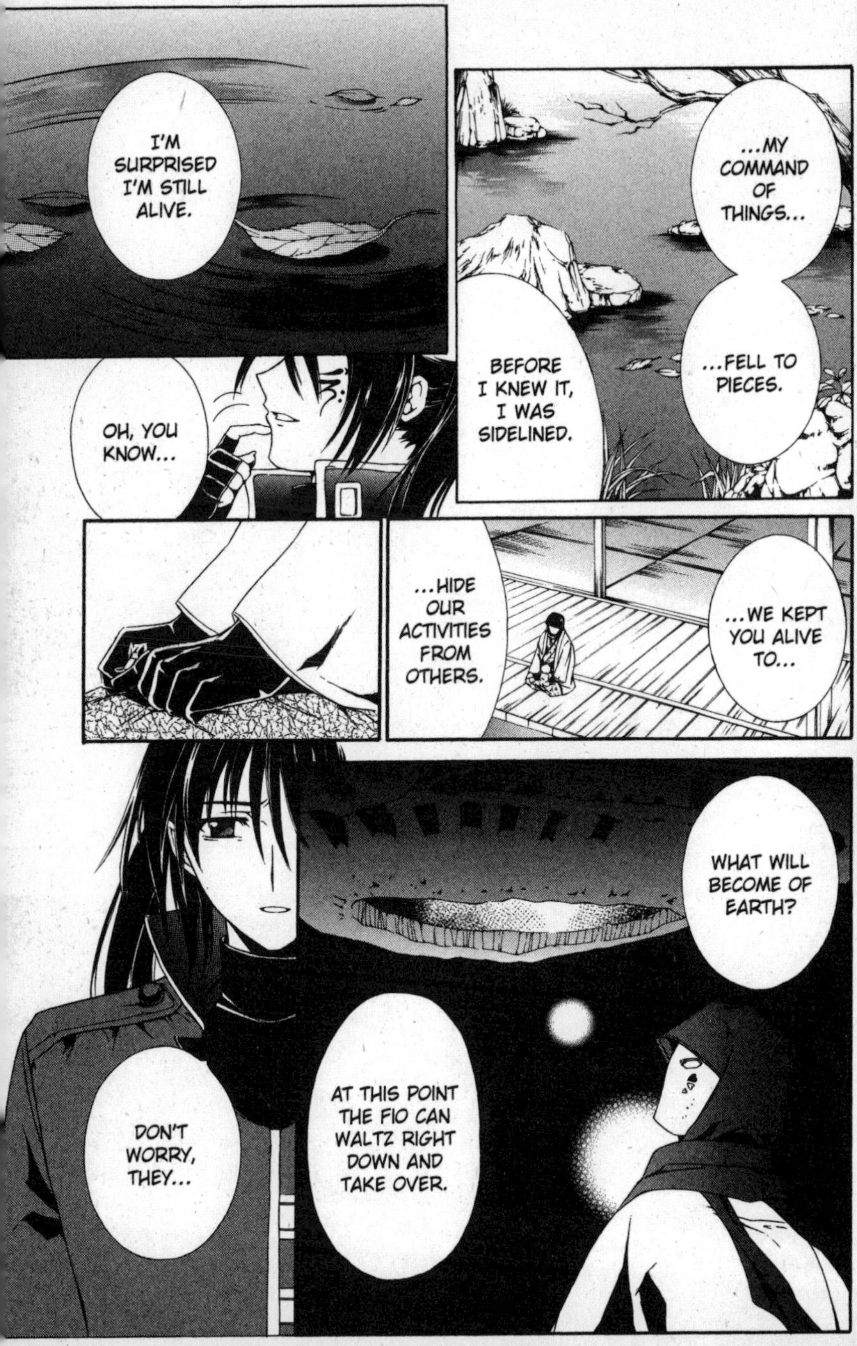
...MY COMMAND OF THINGS...
...FELL TO PIECES.
BEFORE I KNEW IT, I WAS SIDELINED.
I'M SURPRISED I'M STILL ALIVE.
OH, YOU KNOW...
...WE KEPT YOU ALIVE TO...
...HIDE OUR ACTIVITIES FROM OTHERS.
WHAT WILL BECOME OF EARTH?
AT THIS POINT THE FIO CAN WALTZ RIGHT DOWN AND TAKE OVER.
DON'T WORRY, THEY...

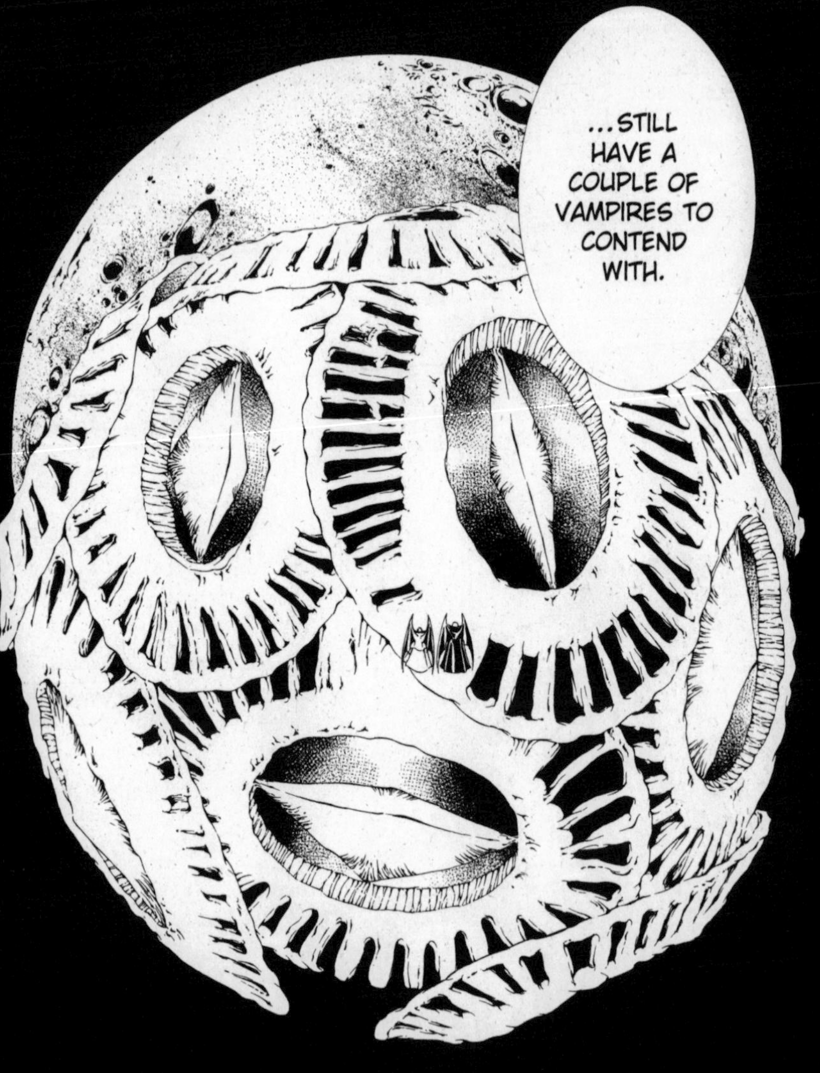
...STILL HAVE A COUPLE OF VAMPIRES TO CONTEND WITH.

Chapter 42:
Pavane for an Endless Night

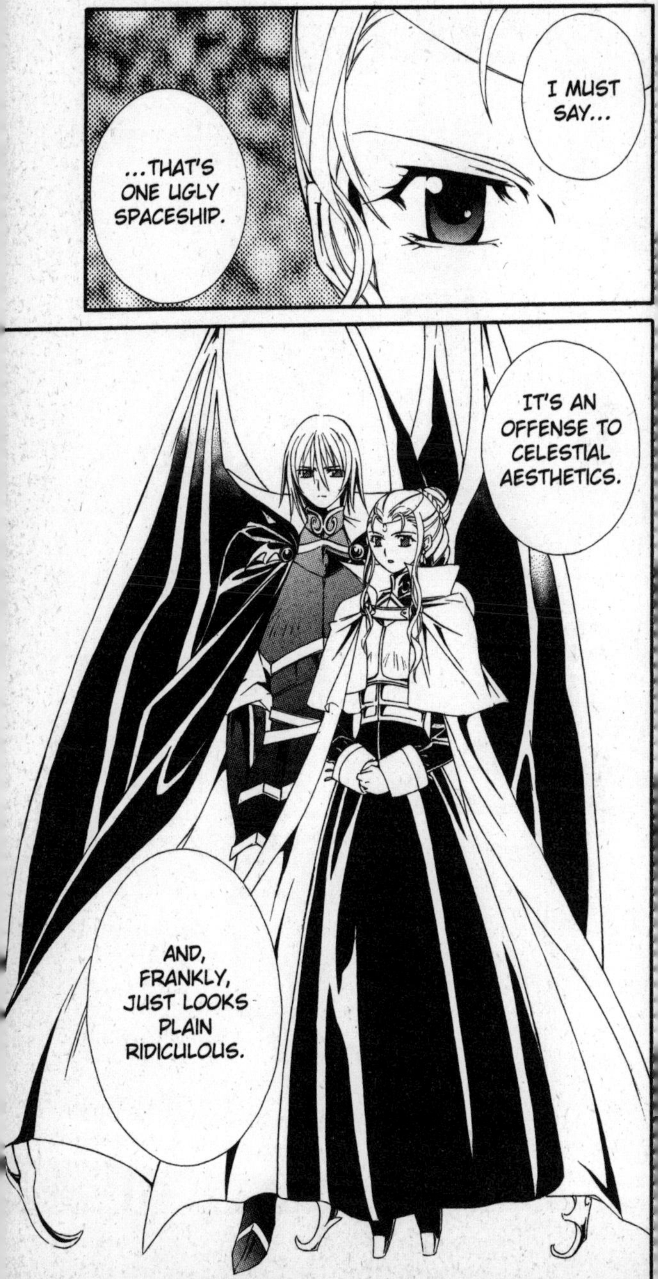
I MUST SAY...
...THAT'S ONE UGLY SPACESHIP.
IT'S AN OFFENSE TO CELESTIAL AESTHETICS.
AND, FRANKLY, JUST LOOKS PLAIN RIDICULOUS.

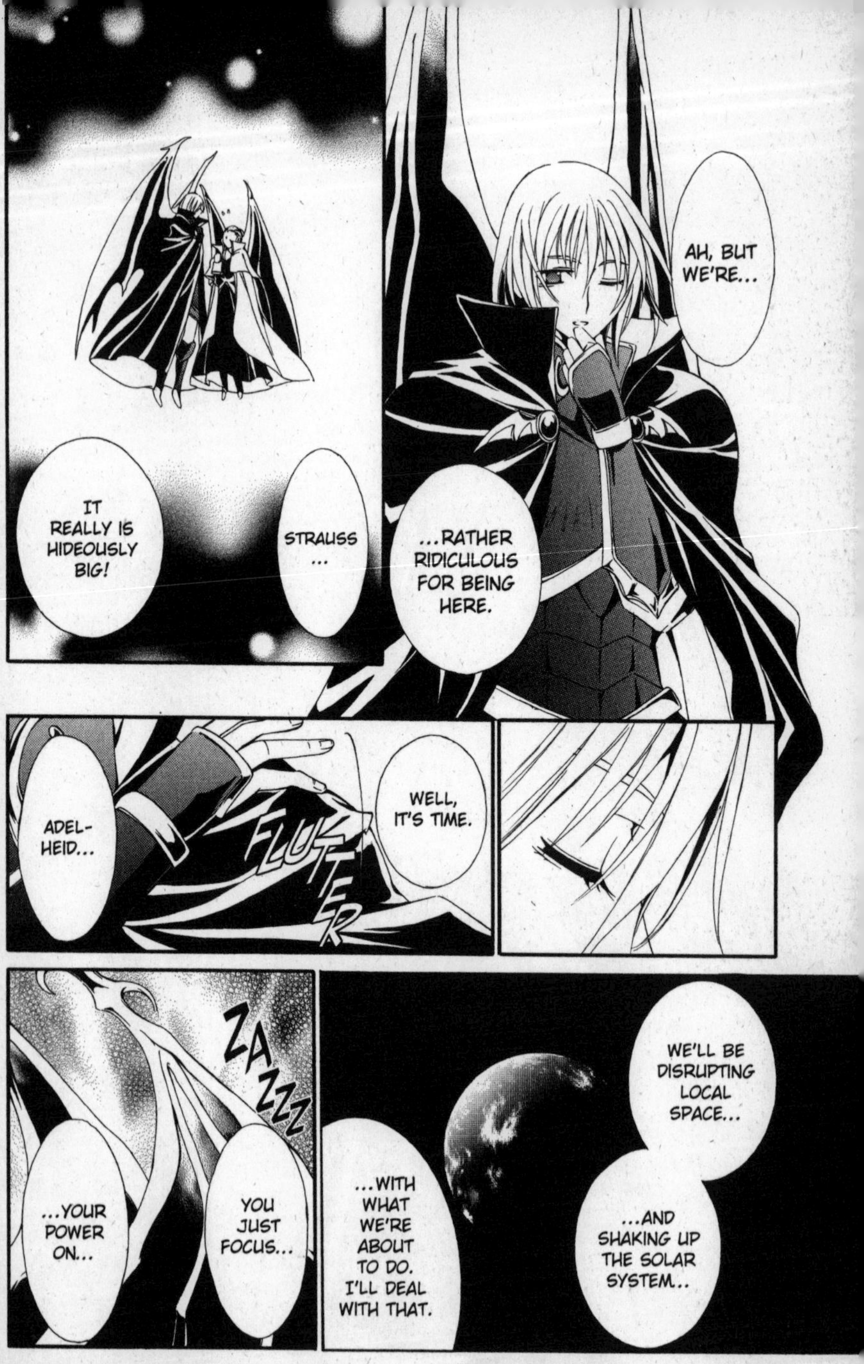
AH, BUT WE'RE...
...RATHER RIDICULOUS FOR BEING HERE.
STRAUSS ...
IT REALLY IS HIDEOUSLY BIG!
WELL, IT'S TIME.
FLUTTER
ADEL-HEID...
WE'LL BE DISRUPTING LOCAL SPACE...
...AND SHAKING UP THE SOLAR SYSTEM..
...WITH WHAT WE'RE ABOUT TO DO. I'LL DEAL WITH THAT.
ZAZZZ
YOU JUST FOCUS...
...YOUR POWER ON...

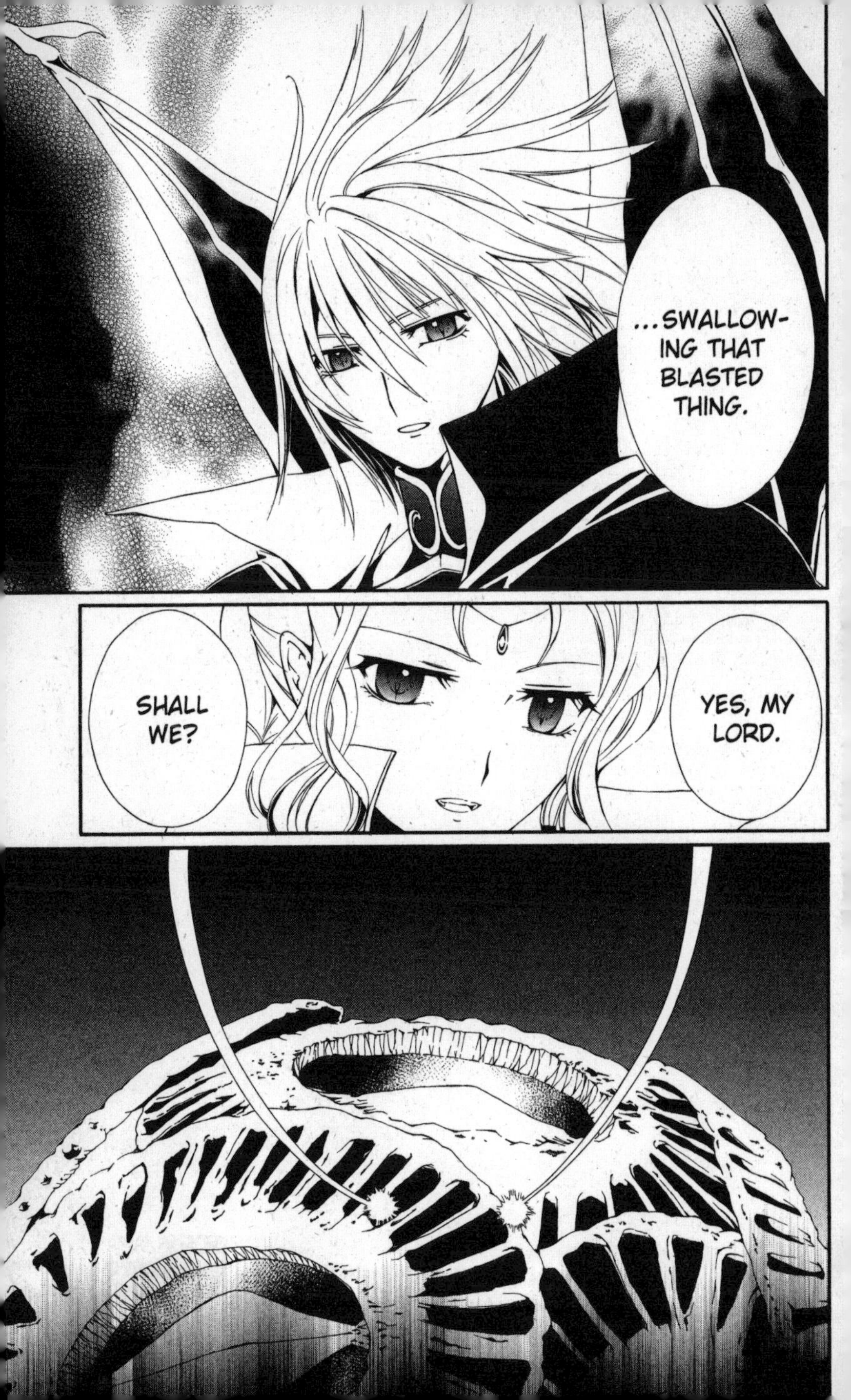
...SWALLOW-ING THAT BLASTED THING.
YES, MY LORD.
SHALL WE?

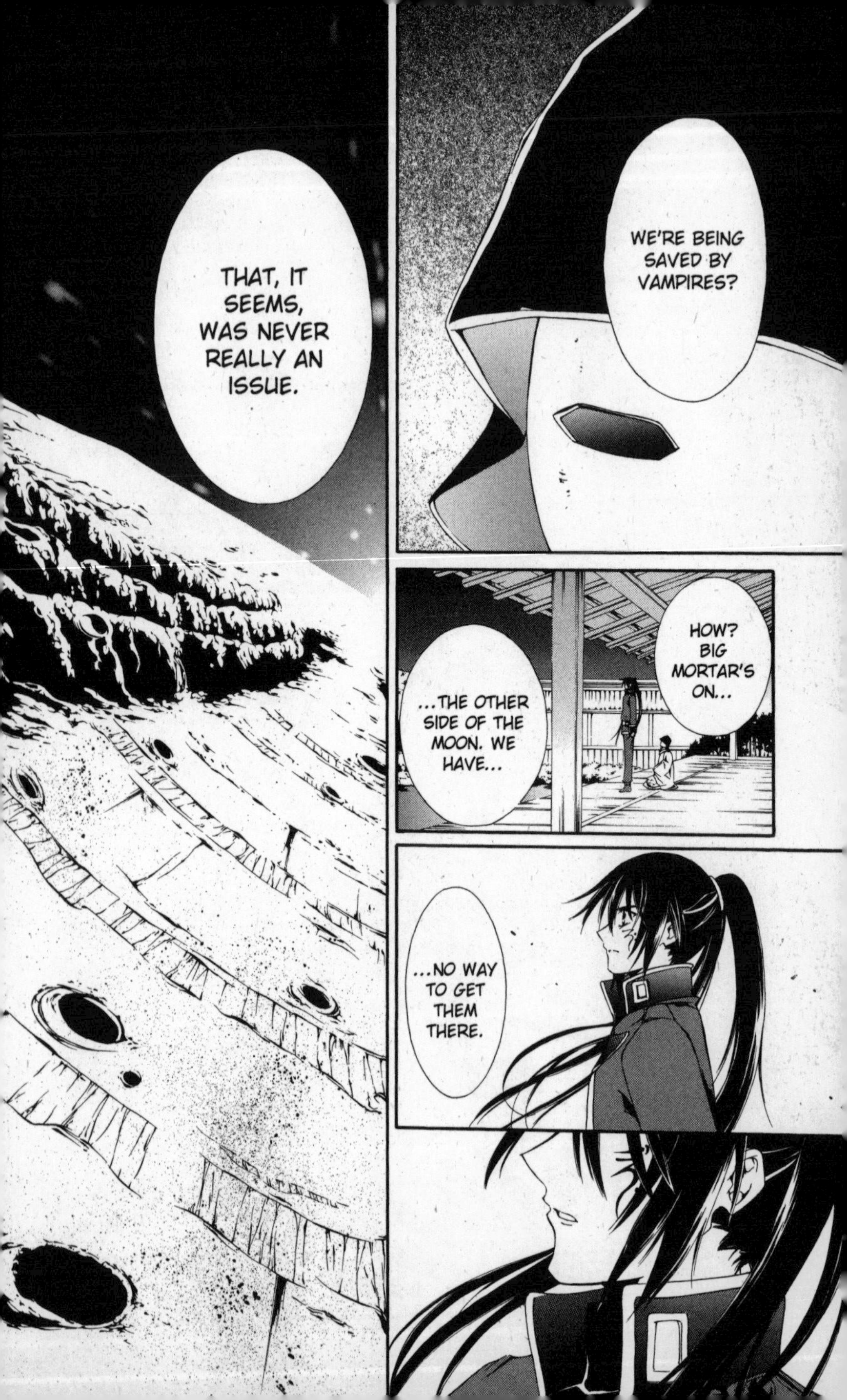
WE'RE BEING SAVED BY VAMPIRES?
HOW? BIG MORTAR'S ON...
...THE OTHER SIDE OF THE MOON. WE HAVE...
...NO WAY TO GET THEM THERE.
THAT, IT SEEMS, WAS NEVER REALLY AN ISSUE.

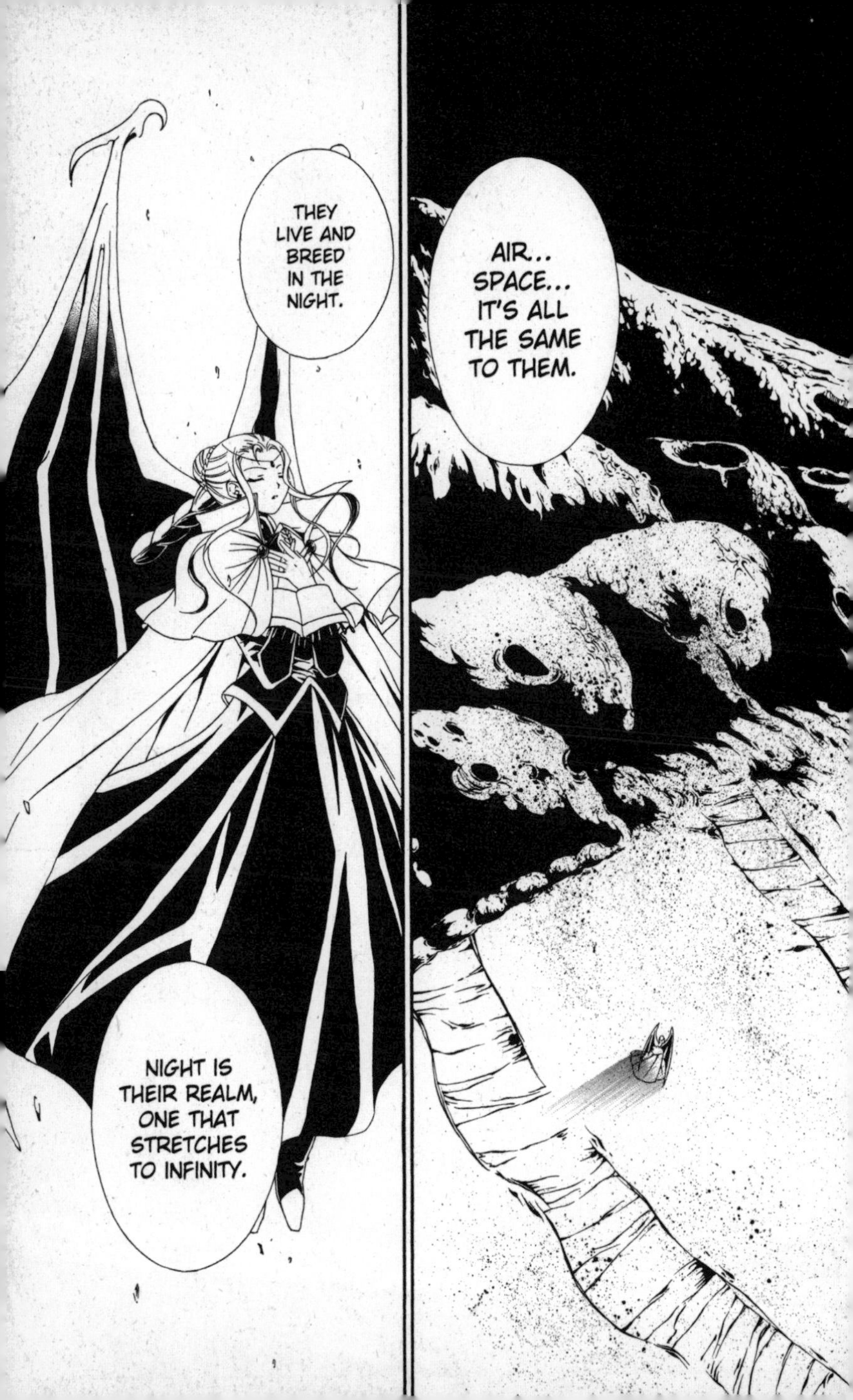
AIR... SPACE... IT'S ALL THE SAME TO THEM.
THEY LIVE AND BREED IN THE NIGHT.
NIGHT IS THEIR REALM, ONE THAT STRETCHES TO INFINITY.

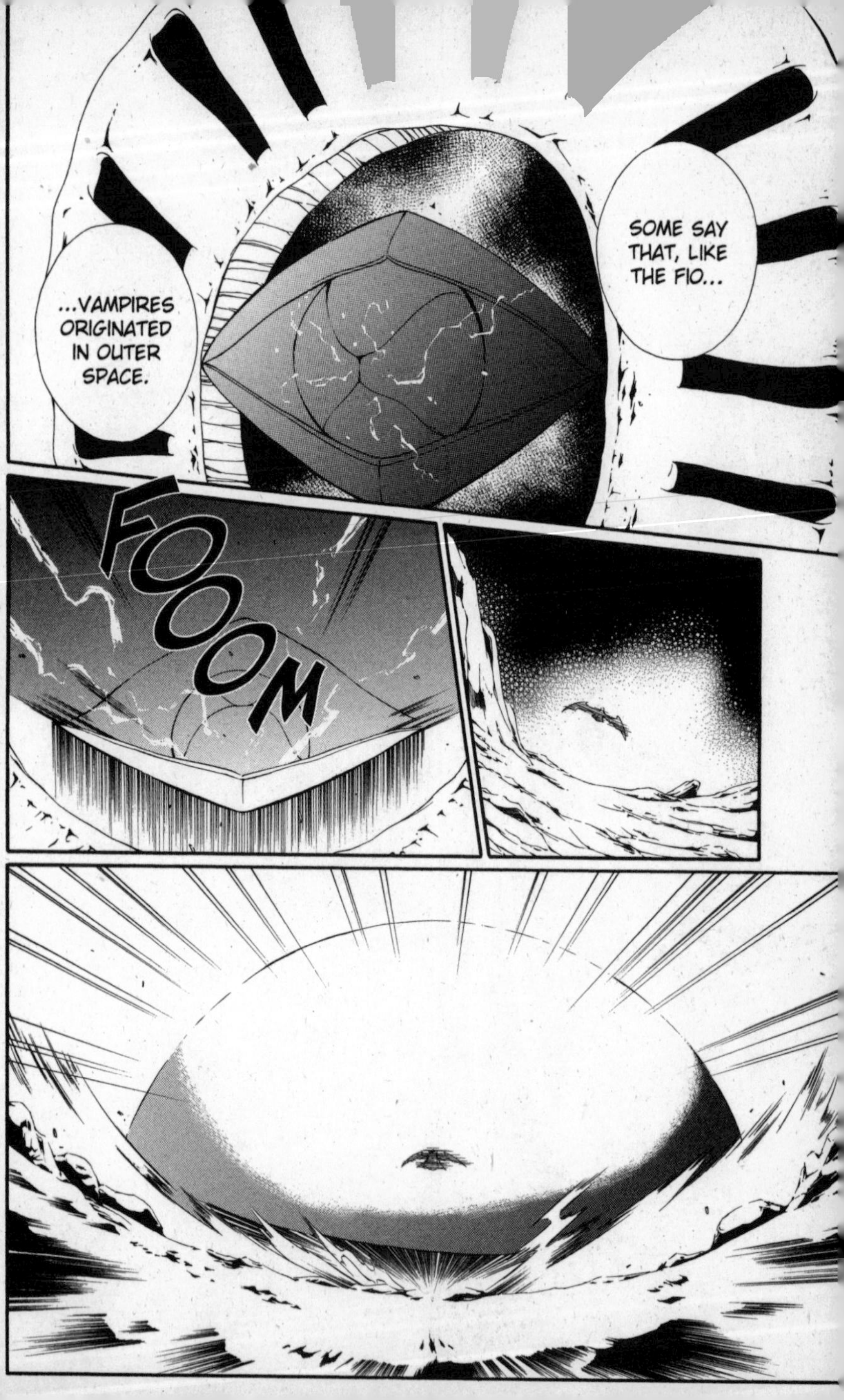
SOME SAY THAT, LIKE THE FIO...
...VAMPIRES ORIGINATED IN OUTER SPACE.
FOOOM

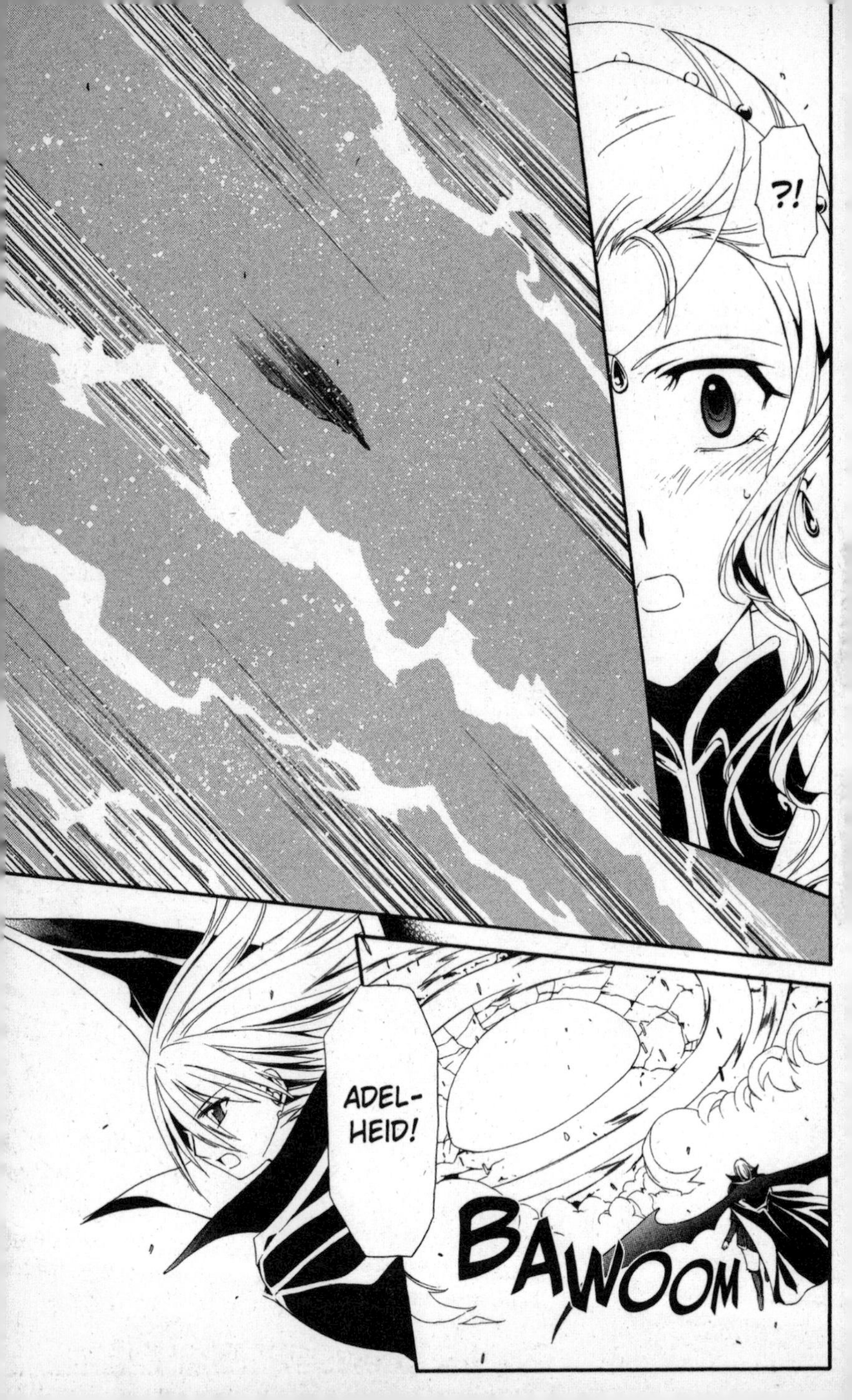
?!
ADEL-
HEID!
BAWOOM

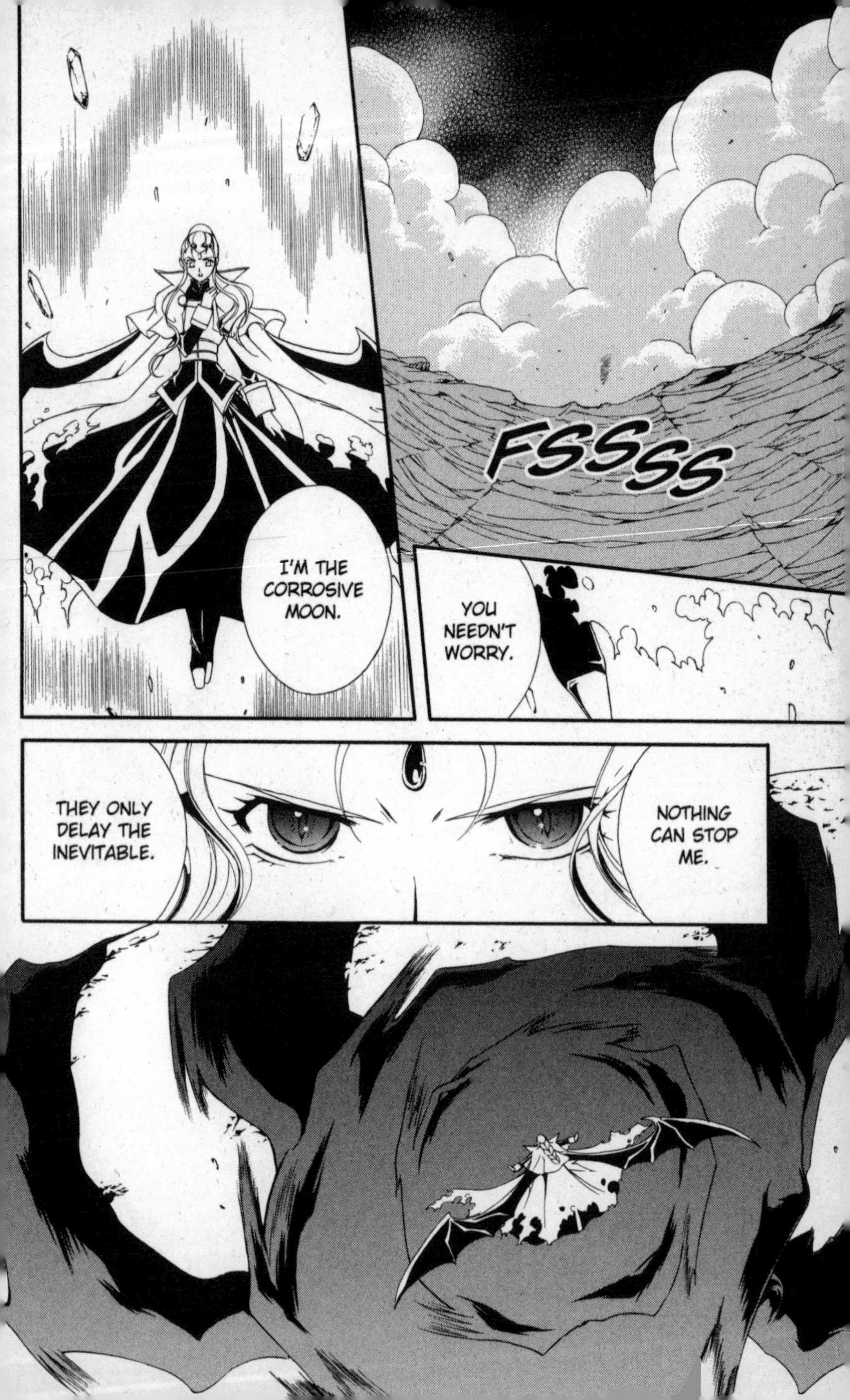
FSSSSS
YOU NEEDN'T WORRY.
I'M THE CORROSIVE MOON.
NOTHING CAN STOP ME.
THEY ONLY DELAY THE INEVITABLE.

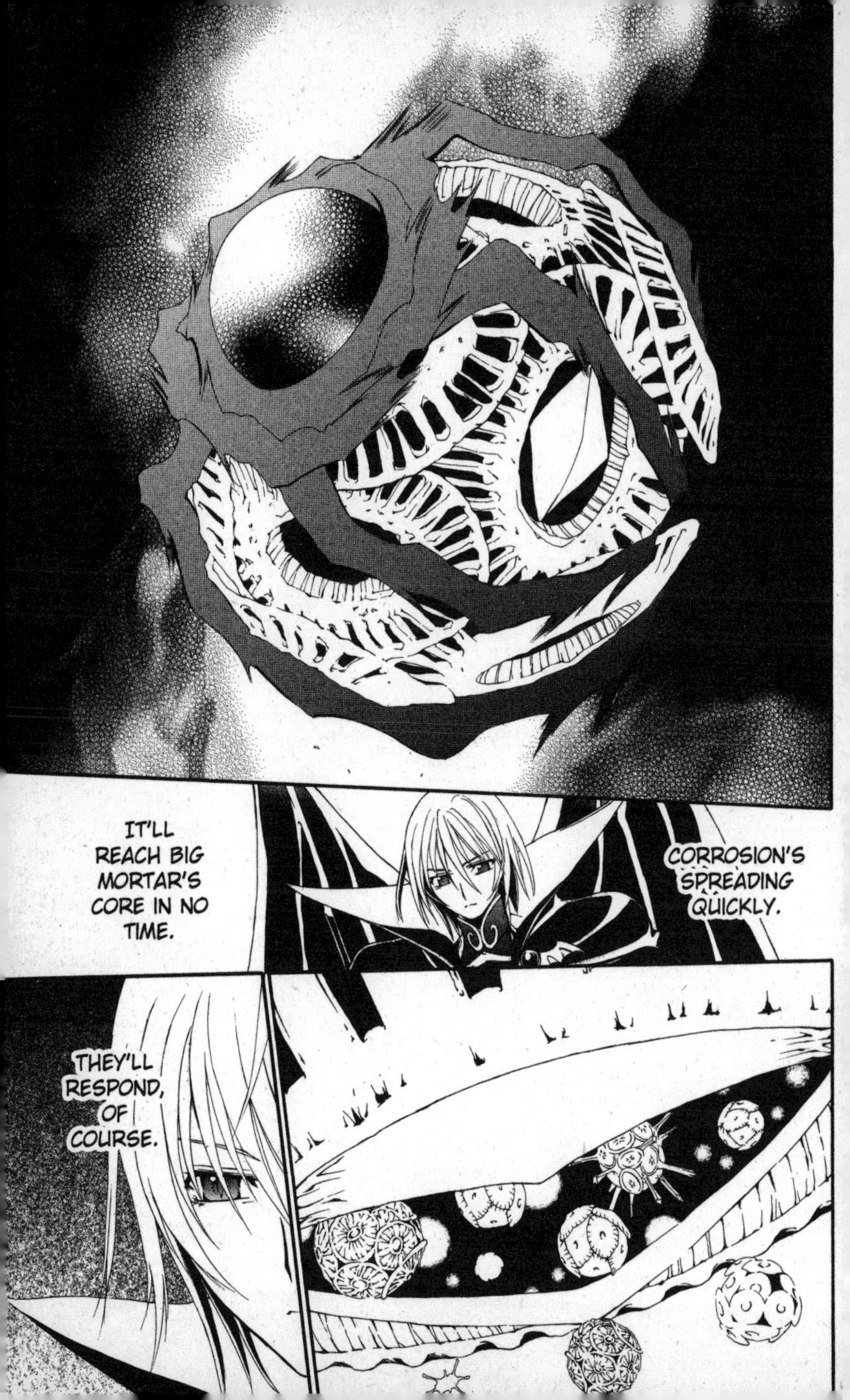
CORROSION'S SPREADING QUICKLY.
IT'LL REACH BIG MORTAR'S CORE IN NO TIME.
THEY'LL RESPOND, OF COURSE.

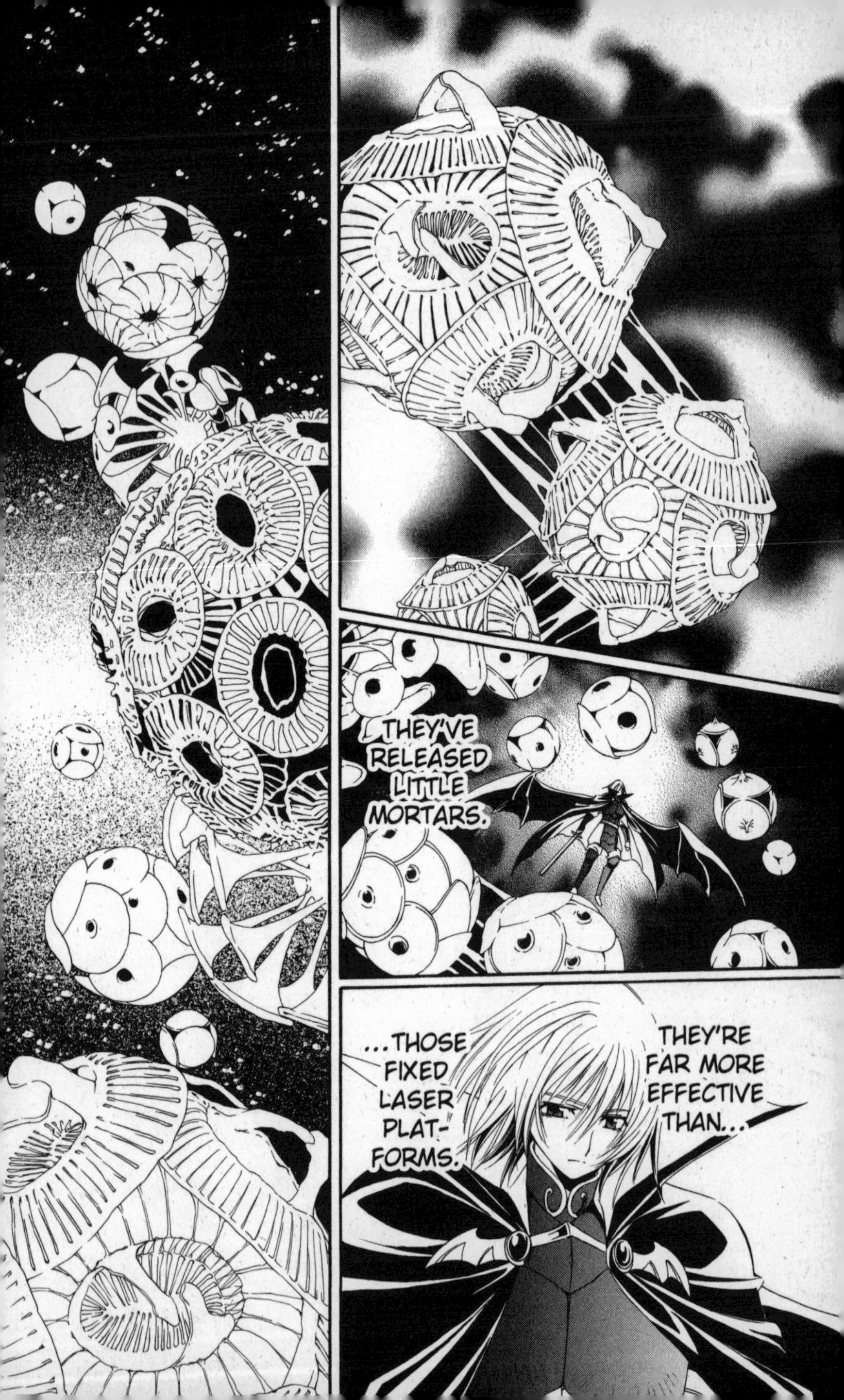
THEY'VE RELEASED LITTLE MORTARS.
THEY'RE FAR MORE EFFECTIVE THAN...
...THOSE FIXED LASER PLAT-FORMS.

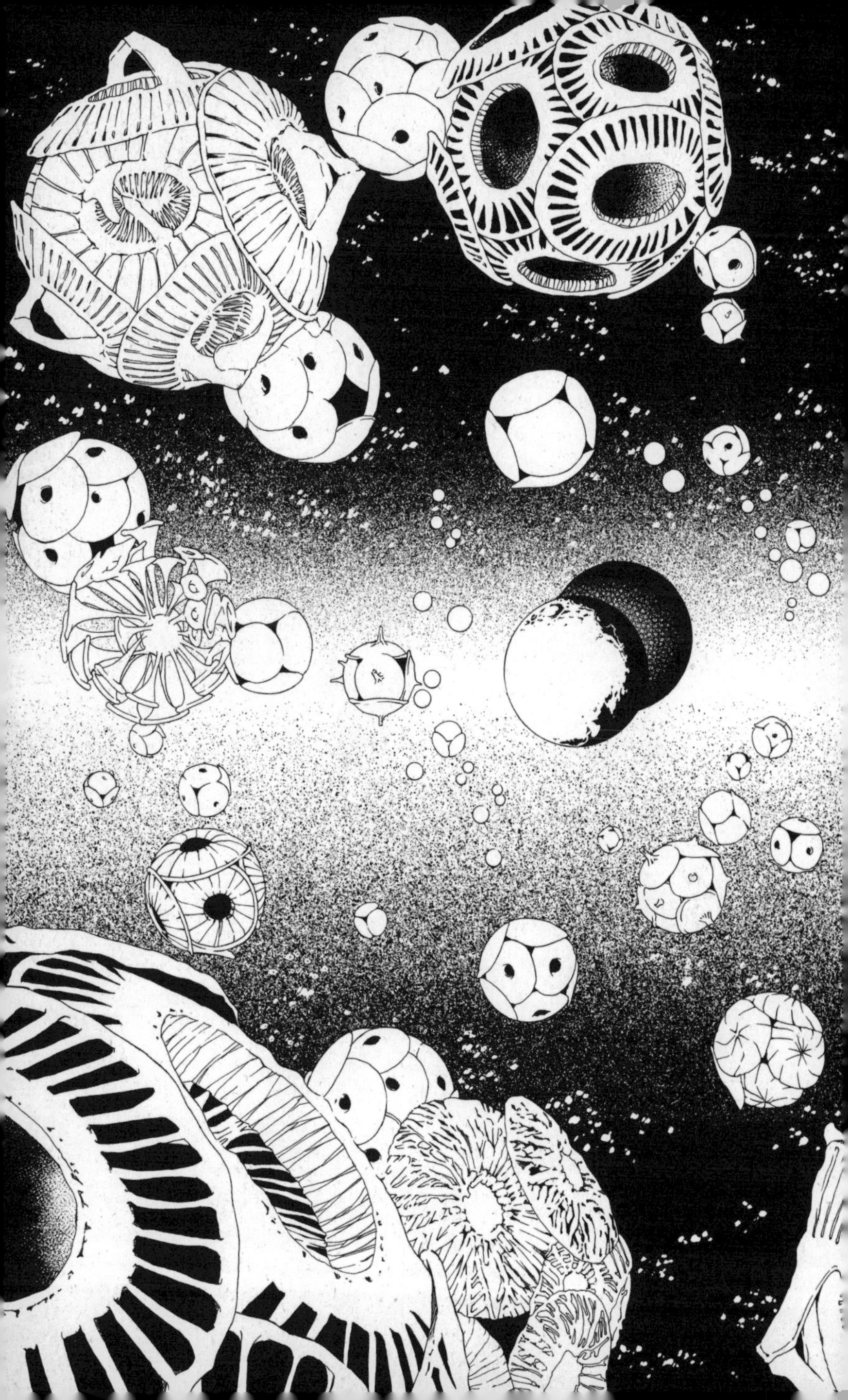

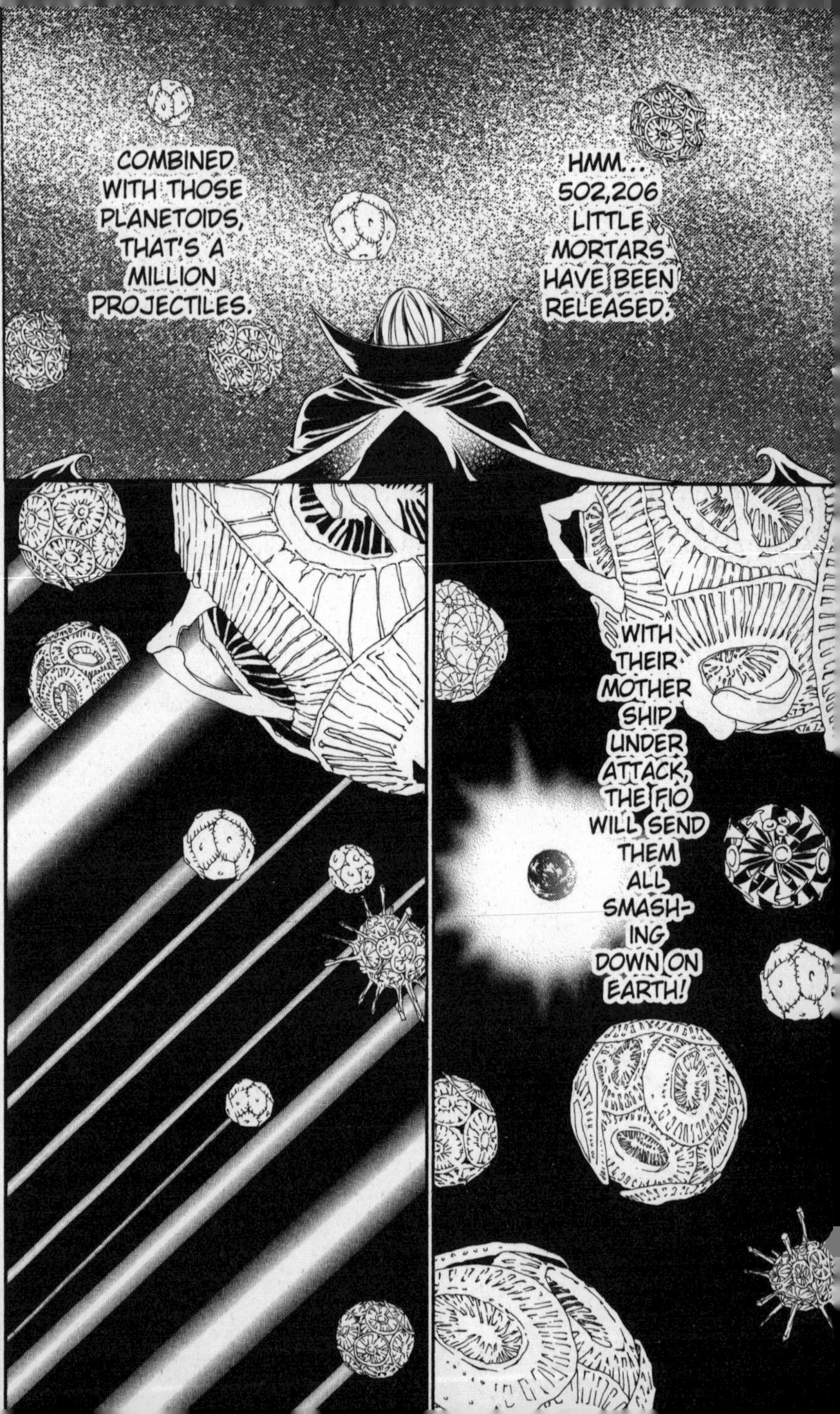
HMM... 502,206 LITTLE MORTARS HAVE BEEN RELEASED.
COMBINED WITH THOSE PLANETOIDS, THAT'S A MILLION PROJECTILES.
WITH THEIR MOTHER SHIP UNDER ATTACK, THE FIO WILL SEND THEM ALL SMASHING DOWN ON EARTH!

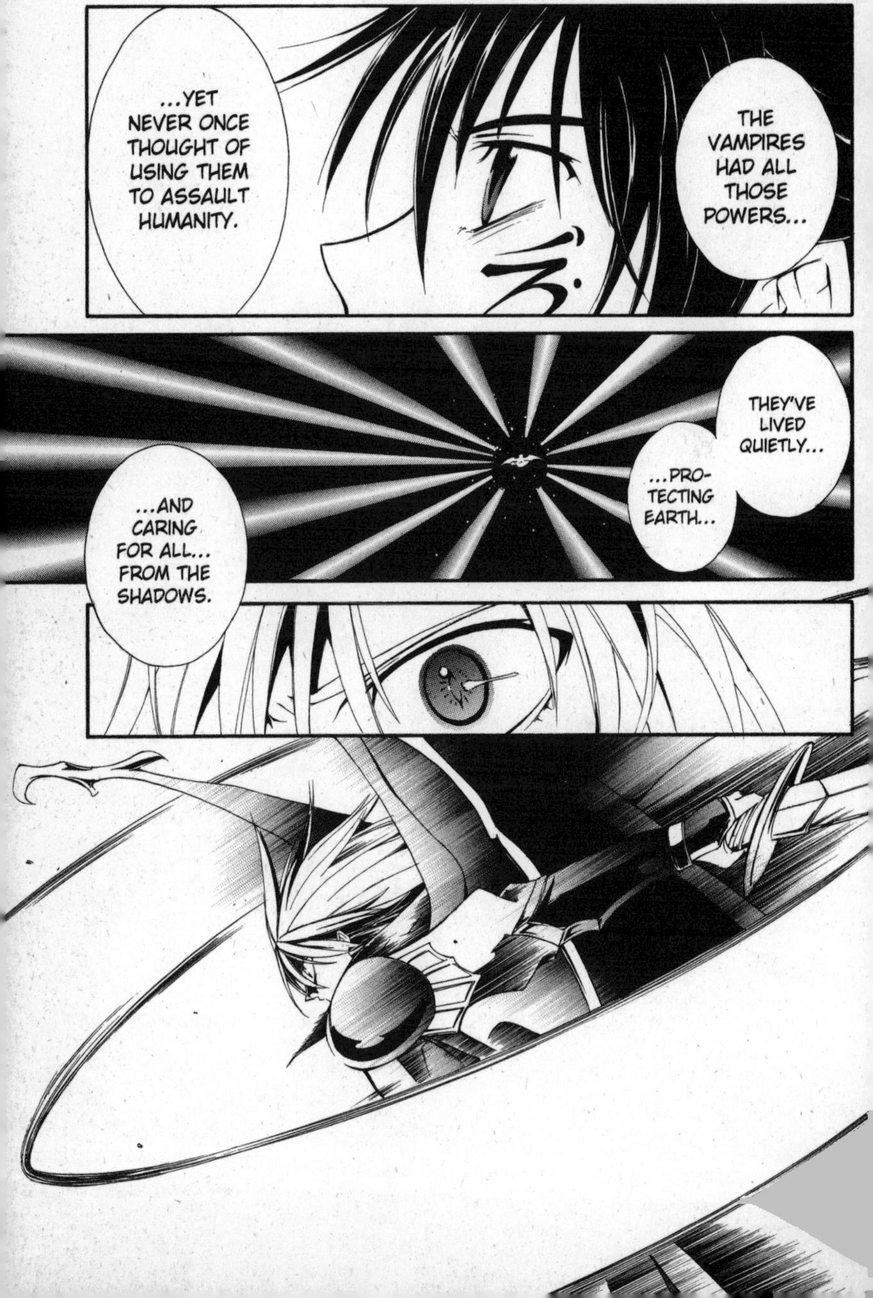
THE VAMPIRES HAD ALL THOSE POWERS...
...YET NEVER ONCE THOUGHT OF USING THEM TO ASSAULT HUMANITY.
THEY'VE LIVED QUIETLY...
...PRO-TECTING EARTH...
...AND CARING FOR ALL... FROM THE SHADOWS.

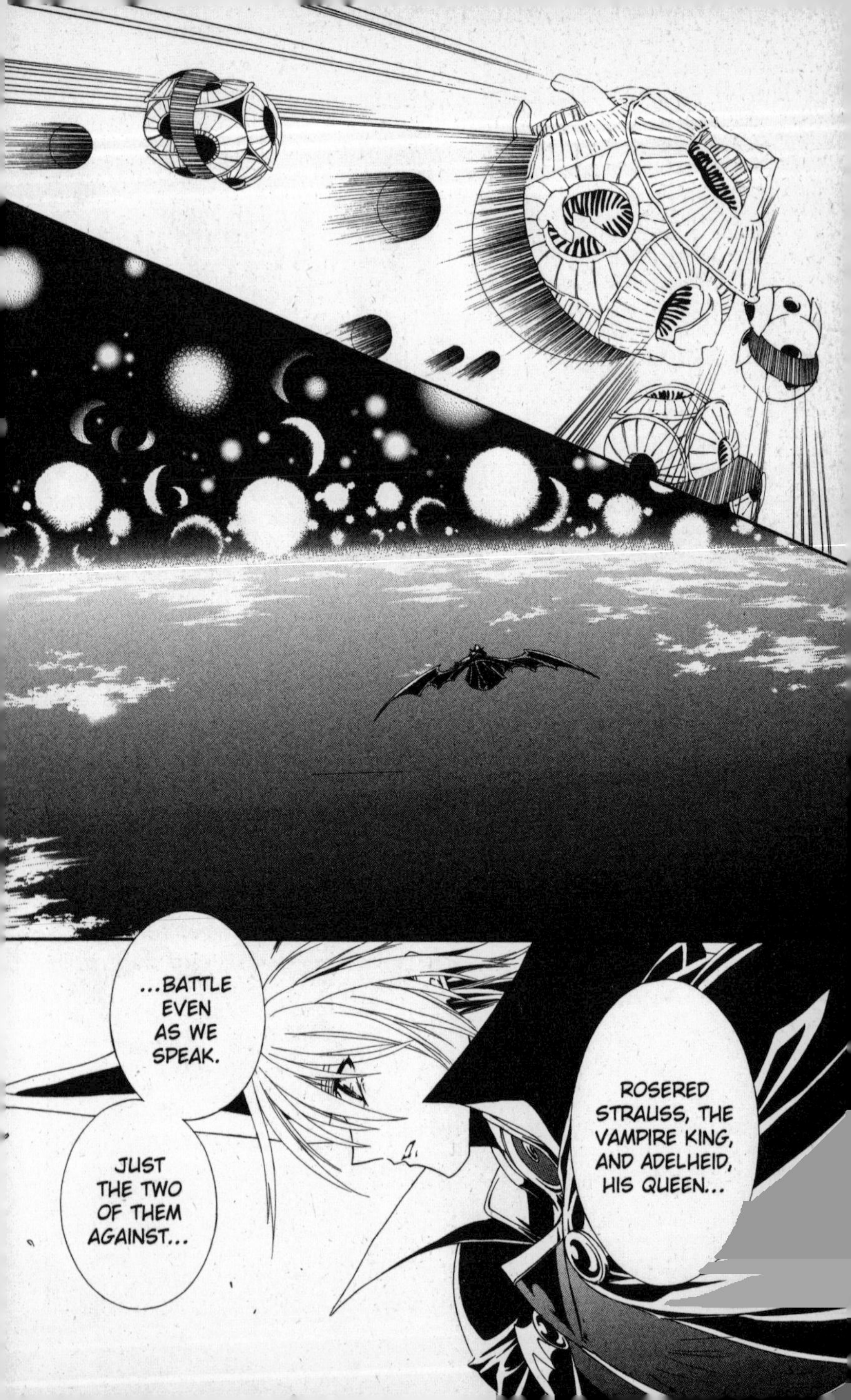
ROSERED STRAUSS, THE VAMPIRE KING, AND ADELHEID, HIS QUEEN...
...BATTLE EVEN AS WE SPEAK.
JUST THE TWO OF THEM AGAINST...

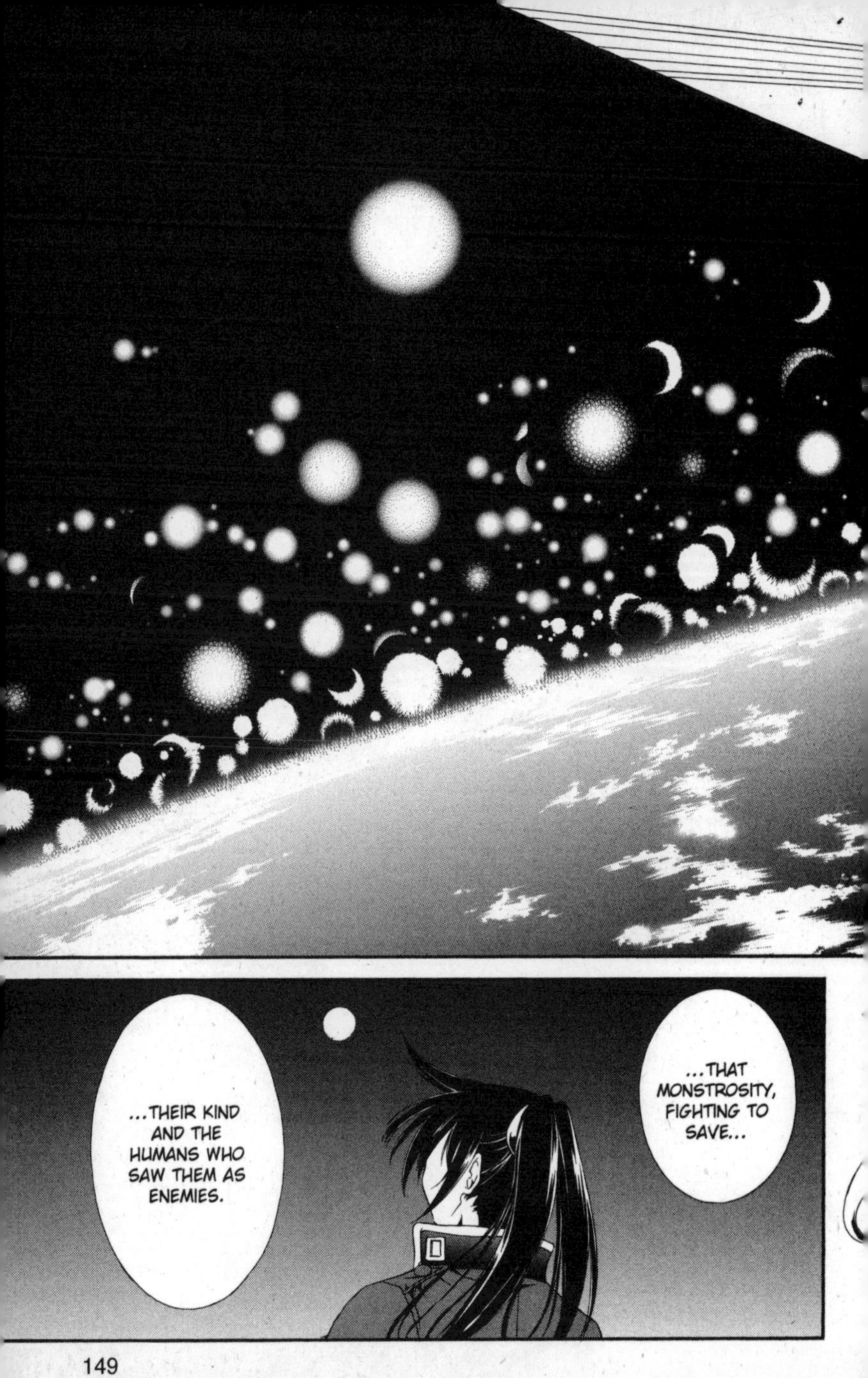
...THAT MONSTROSITY, FIGHTING TO SAVE...
...THEIR KIND AND THE HUMANS WHO SAW THEM AS ENEMIES.

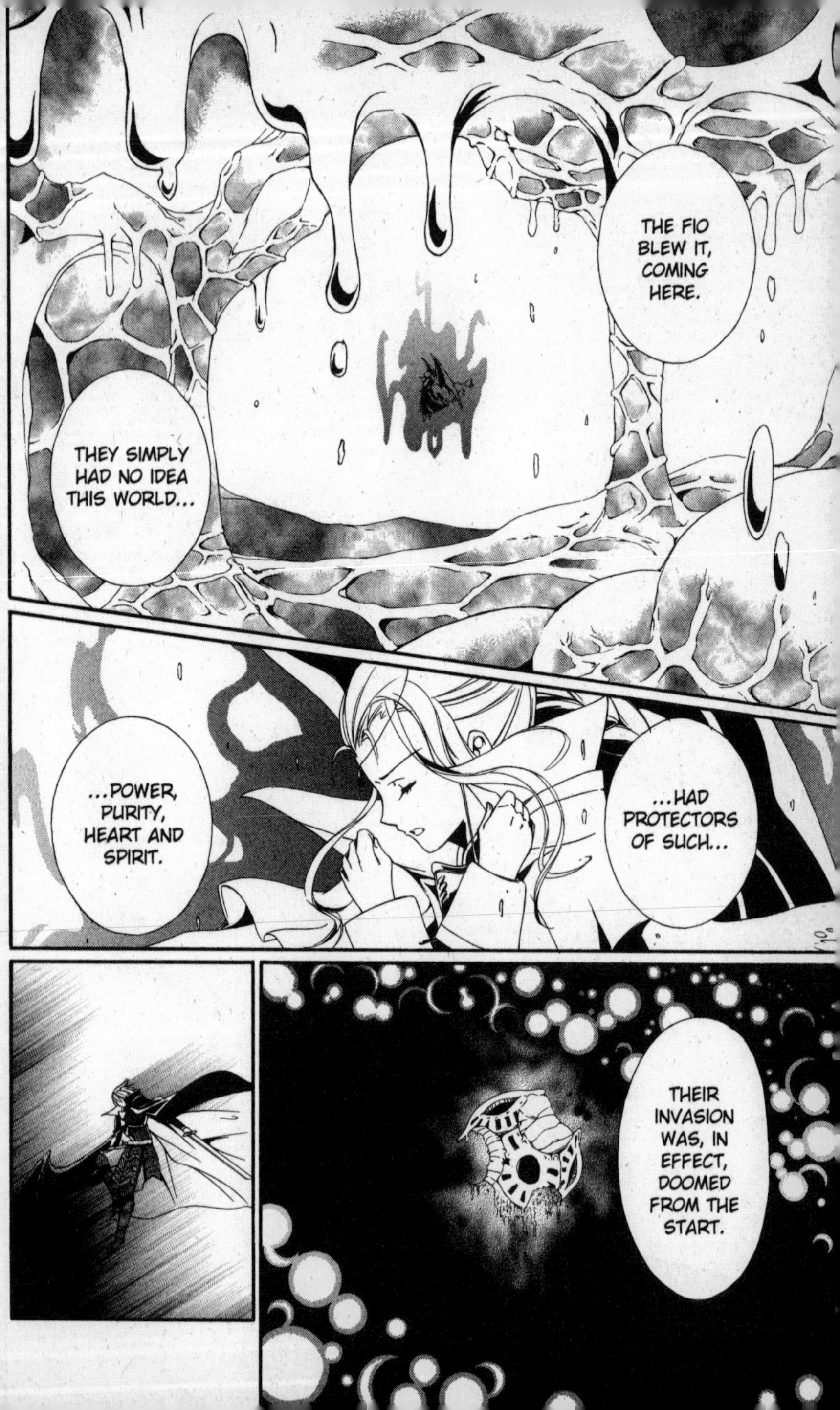
THE FIO BLEW IT, COMING HERE.
THEY SIMPLY HAD NO IDEA THIS WORLD...
...HAD PROTECTORS OF SUCH...
...POWER, PURITY, HEART AND SPIRIT.
THEIR INVASION WAS, IN EFFECT, DOOMED FROM THE START.

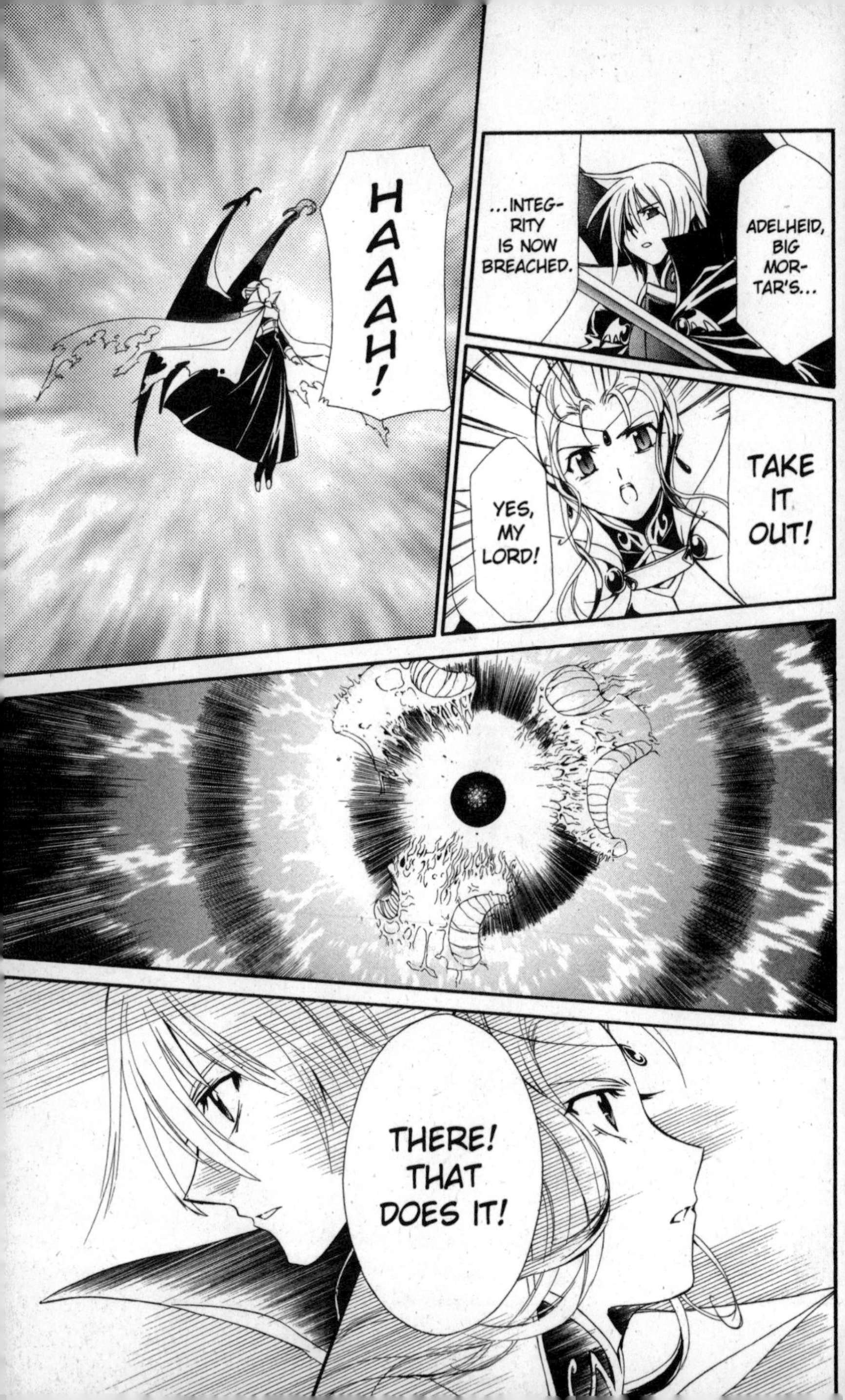
ADELHEID, BIG MOR-TAR'S...
...INTEG-RITY IS NOW BREACHED.
TAKE IT OUT!
YES, MY LORD!
HAAAH!
THERE! THAT DOES IT!

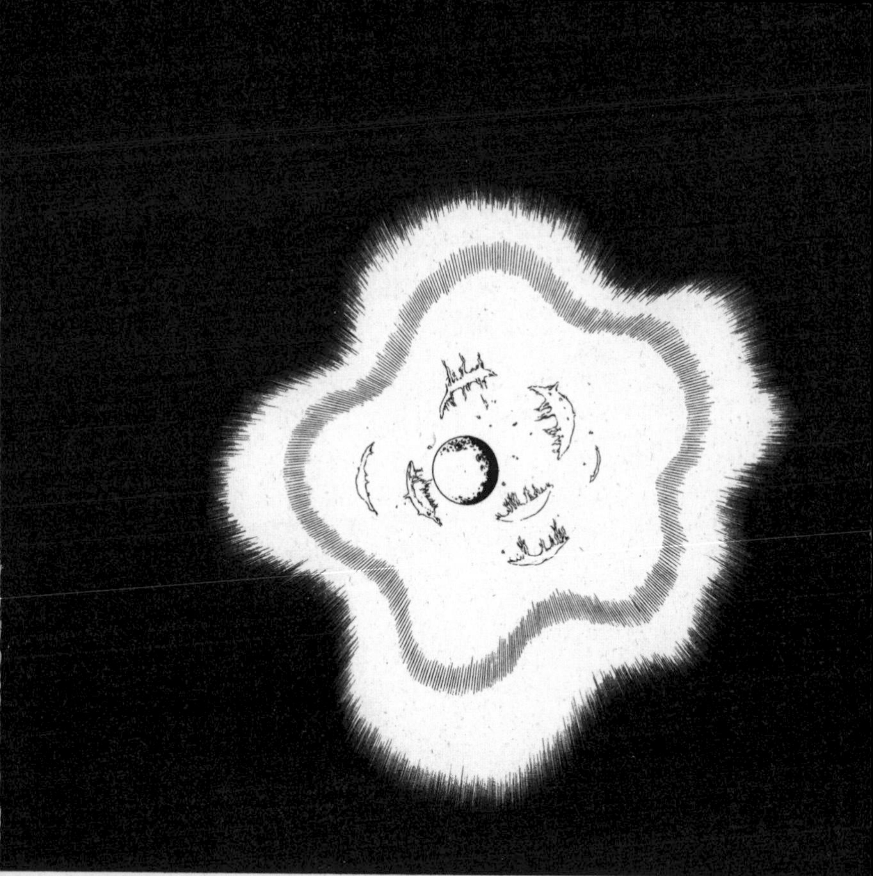
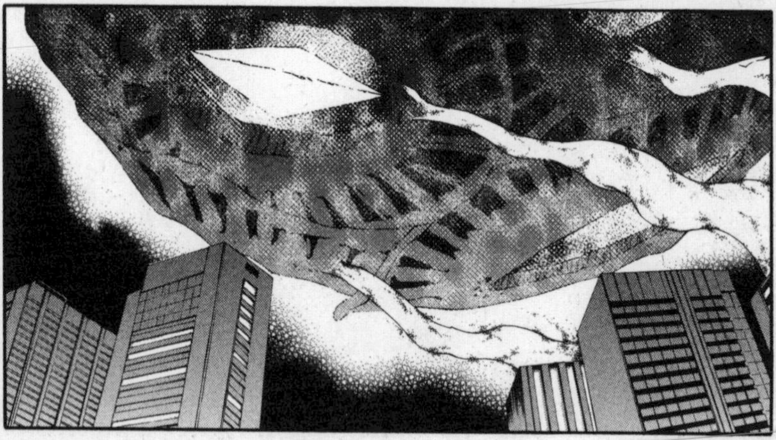

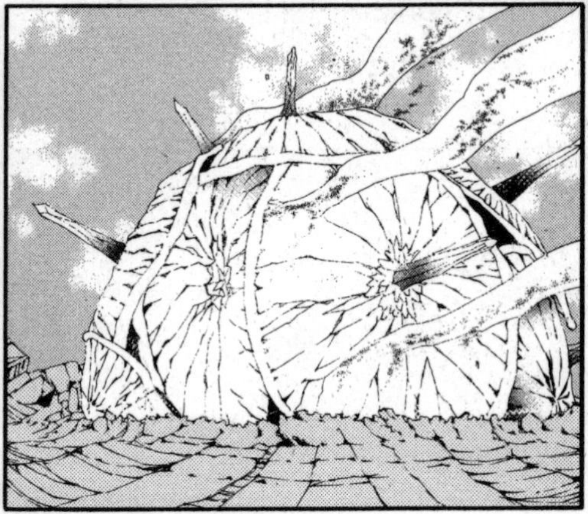
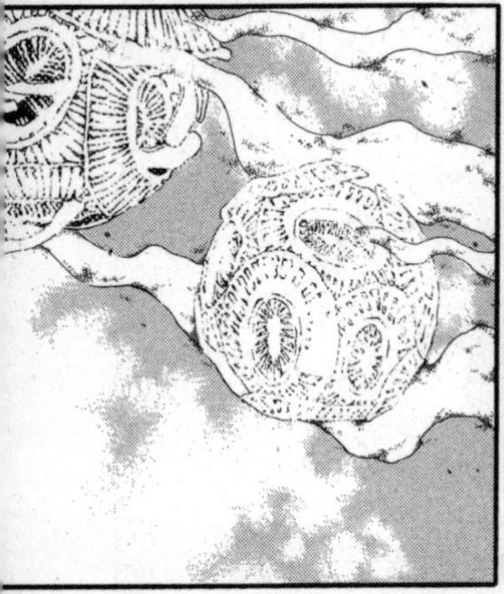

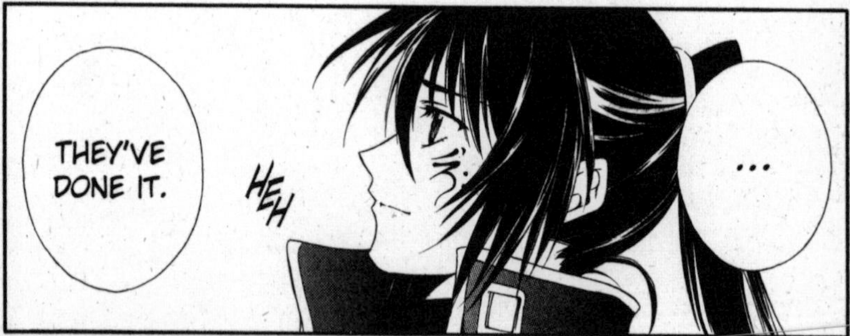
...
HEH
THEY'VE DONE IT.

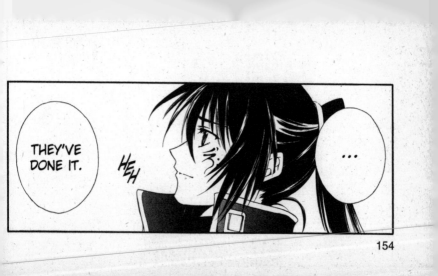

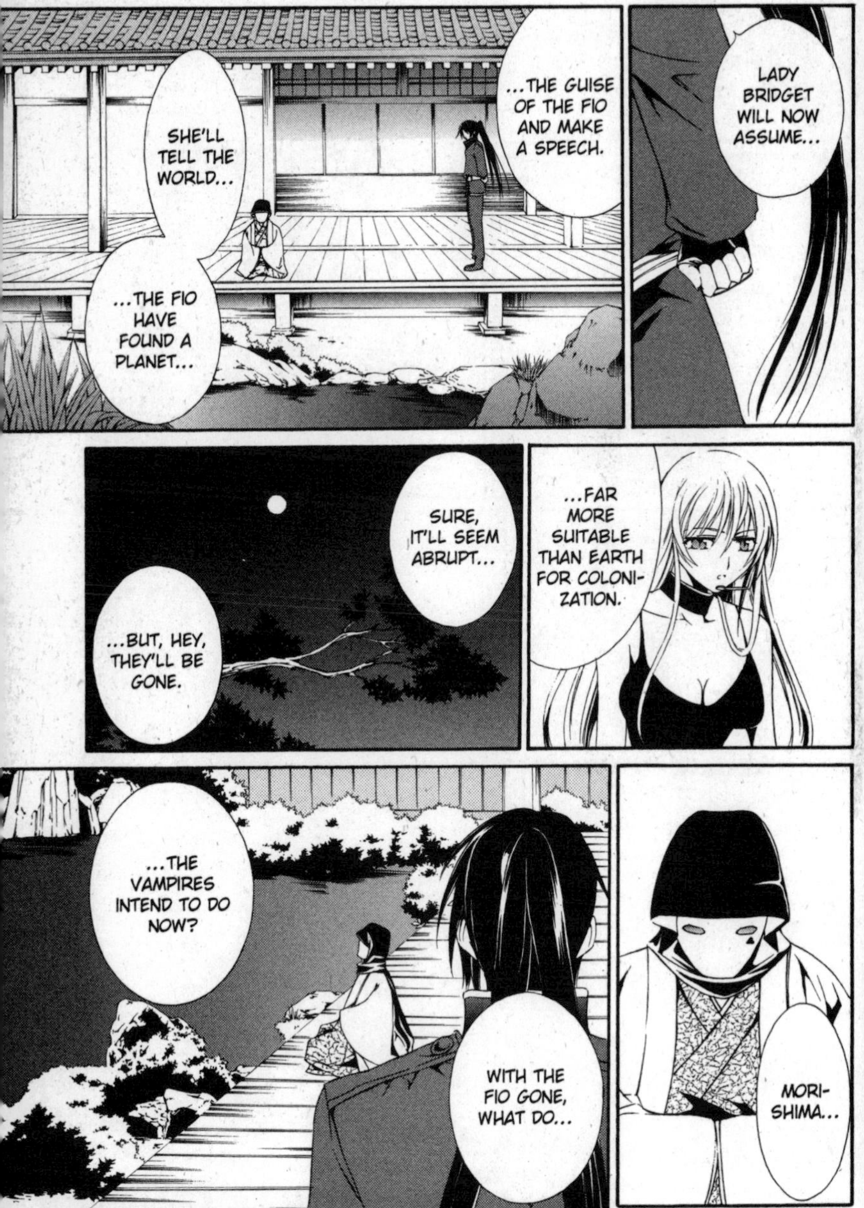
LADY BRIDGET WILL NOW ASSUME...
...THE GUISE OF THE FIO AND MAKE A SPEECH.
SHE'LL TELL THE WORLD...
...THE FIO HAVE FOUND A PLANET...
...FAR MORE SUITABLE THAN EARTH FOR COLONIZATION.
SURE, IT'LL SEEM ABRUPT...
...BUT, HEY, THEY'LL BE GONE.
MORISHIMA...
WITH THE FIO GONE, WHAT DO...
...THE VAMPIRES INTEND TO DO NOW?

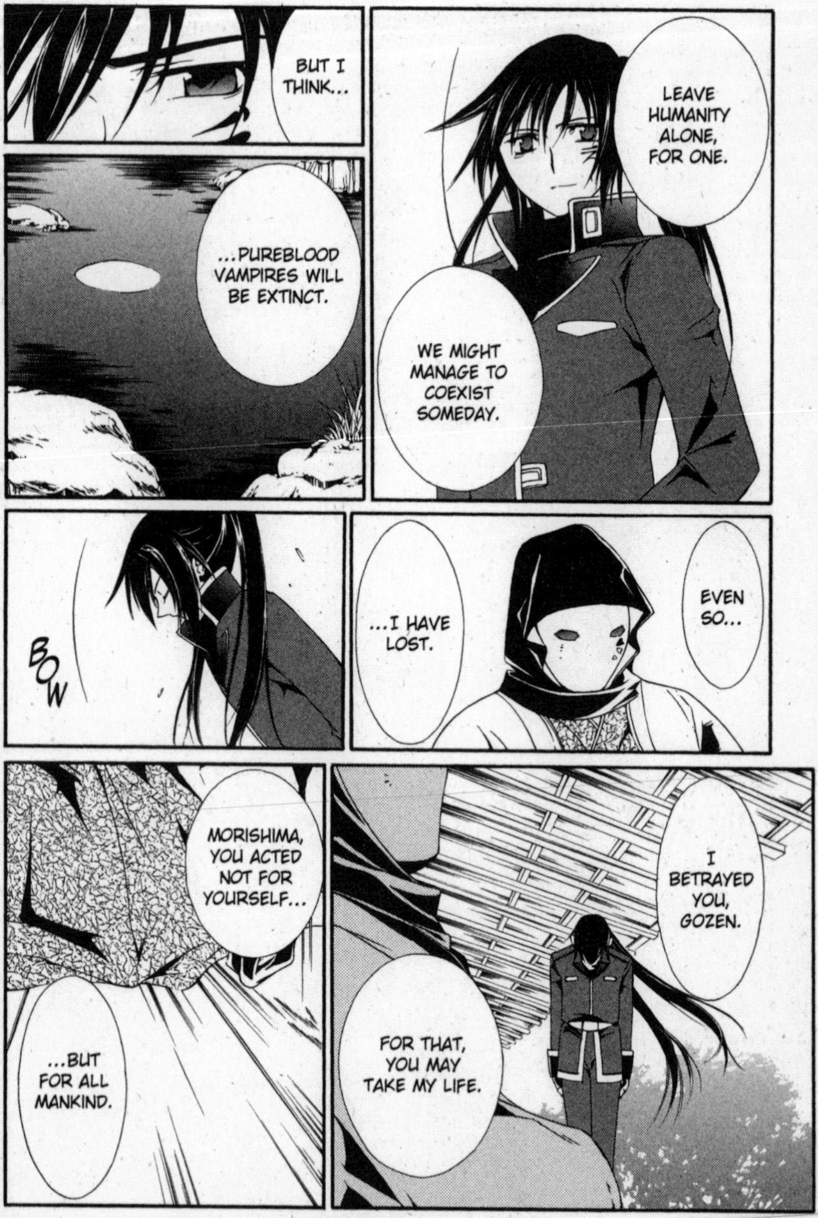
LEAVE HUMANITY ALONE, FOR ONE.
WE MIGHT MANAGE TO COEXIST SOMEDAY.
BUT I THINK...
...PUREBLOOD VAMPIRES WILL BE EXTINCT.
EVEN SO...
...I HAVE LOST.
BOW
I BETRAYED YOU, GOZEN.
FOR THAT, YOU MAY TAKE MY LIFE.
MORISHIMA, YOU ACTED NOT FOR YOURSELF...
...BUT FOR ALL MANKIND.

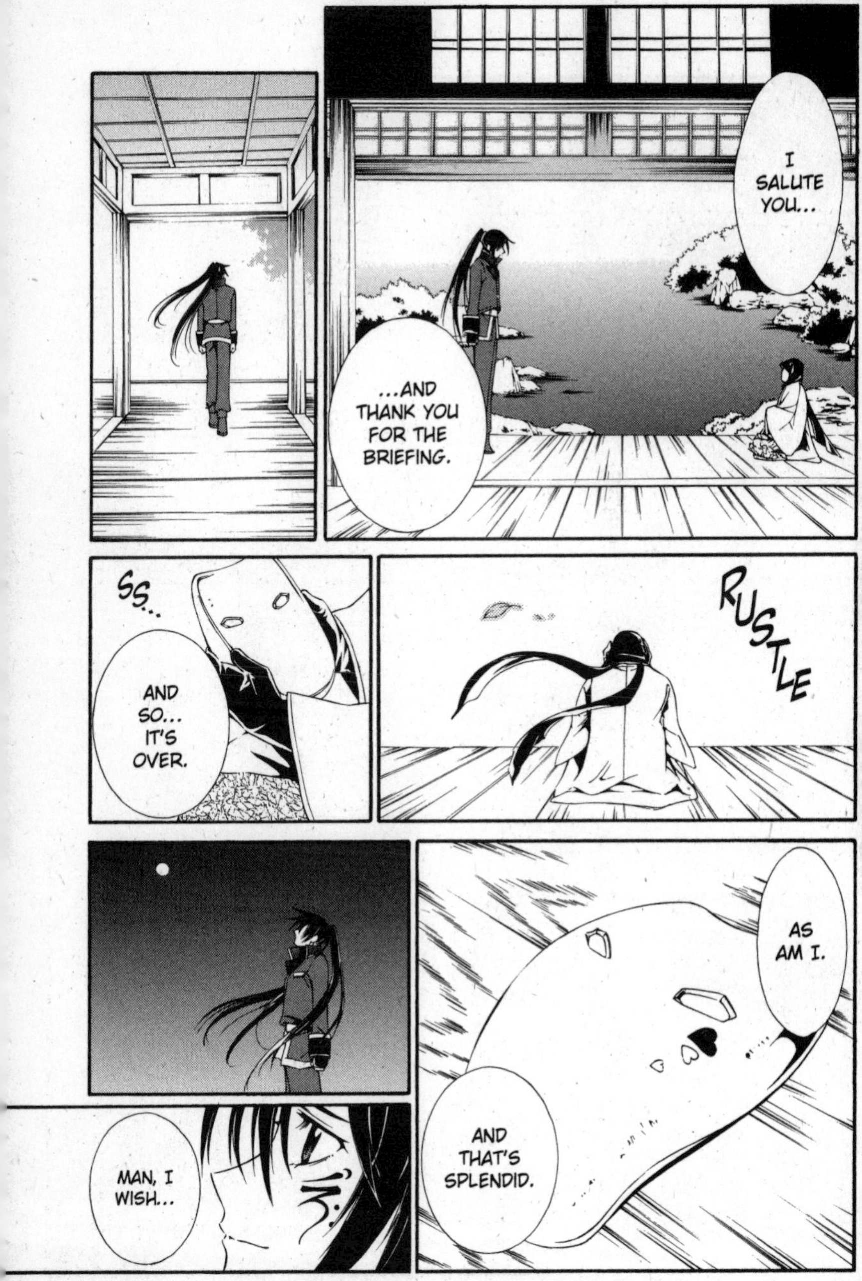
I SALUTE YOU...
...AND THANK YOU FOR THE BRIEFING.
RUSTLE
SS...
AND SO... IT'S OVER.
AS AM I.
AND THAT'S SPLENDID.
MAN, I WISH...

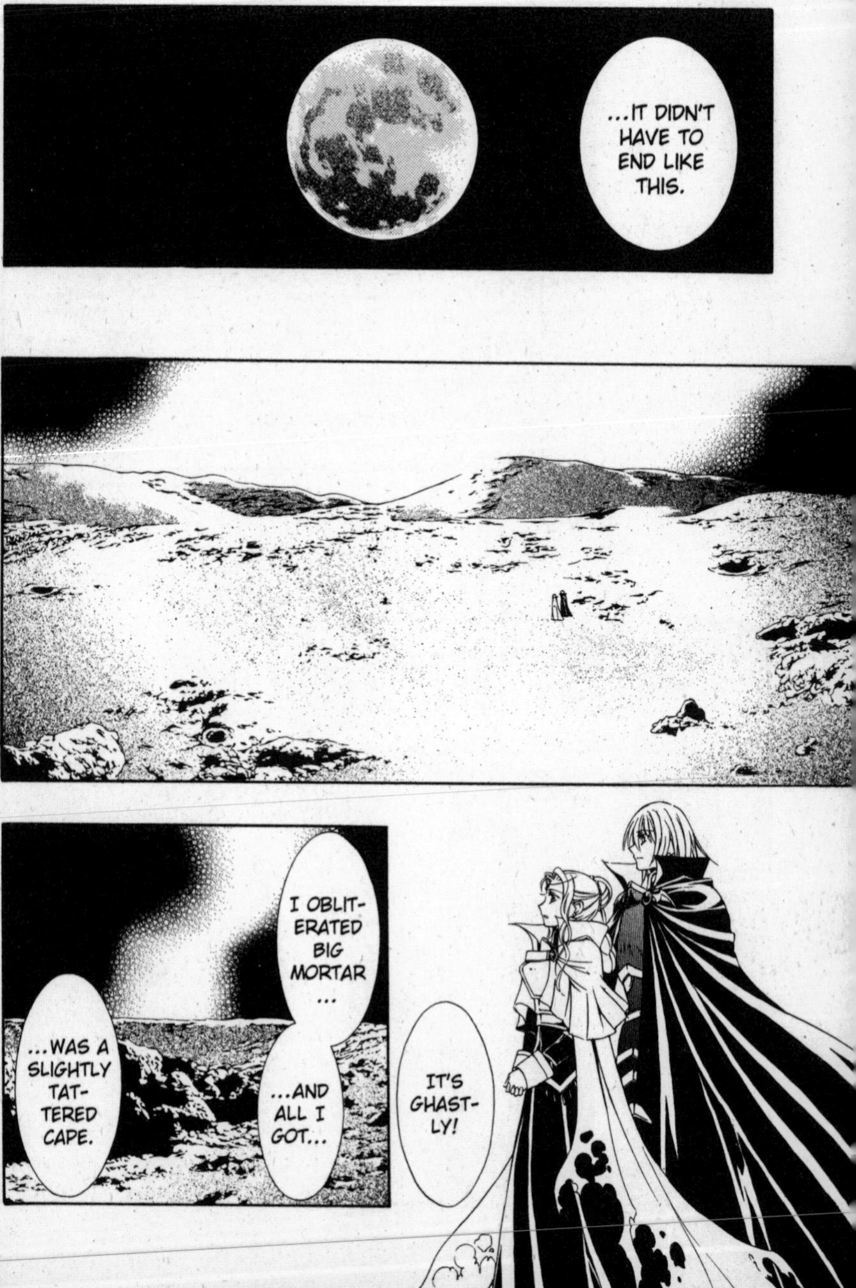
...IT DIDN'T HAVE TO END LIKE THIS.
IT'S GHASTLY!
I OBLITERATED BIG MORTAR...
...AND ALL I GOT...
...WAS A SLIGHTLY TATTERED CAPE.

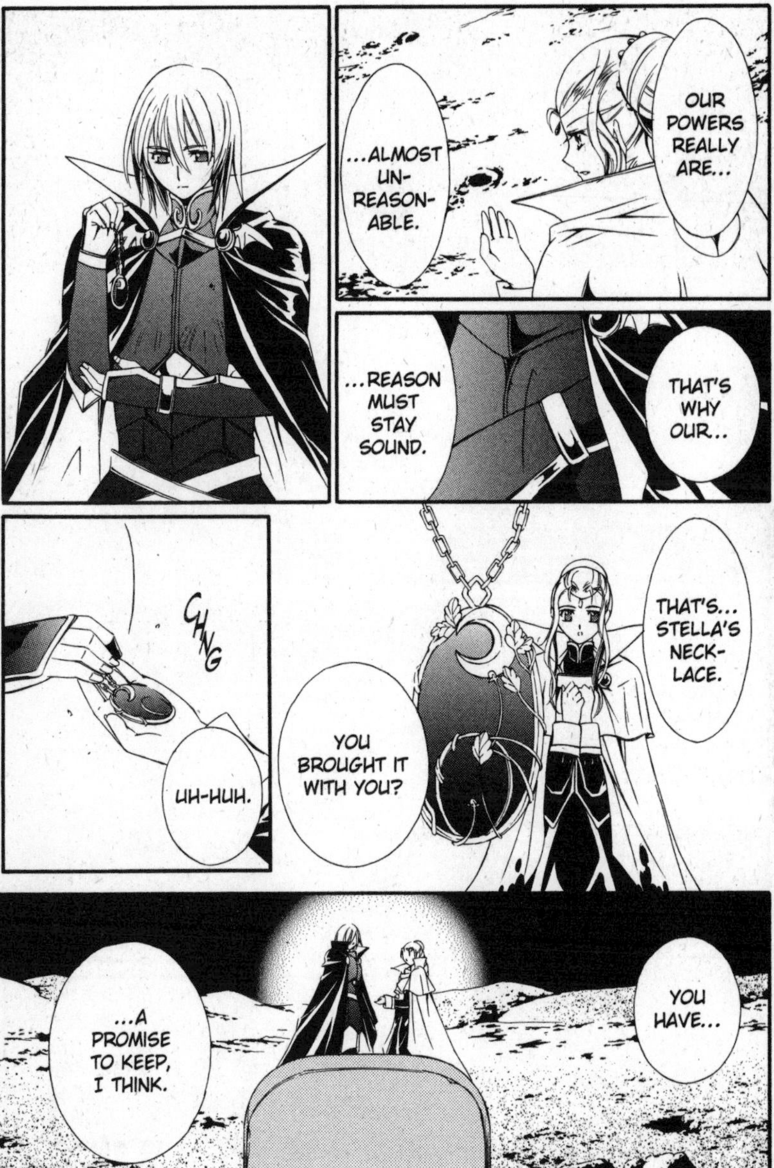
OUR POWERS REALLY ARE...
...ALMOST UN-REASONABLE.
THAT'S WHY OUR...
...REASON MUST STAY SOUND.
THAT'S... STELLA'S NECK-LACE.
YOU BROUGHT IT WITH YOU?
CHNG
UH-HUH.
YOU HAVE...
...A PROMISE TO KEEP, I THINK.

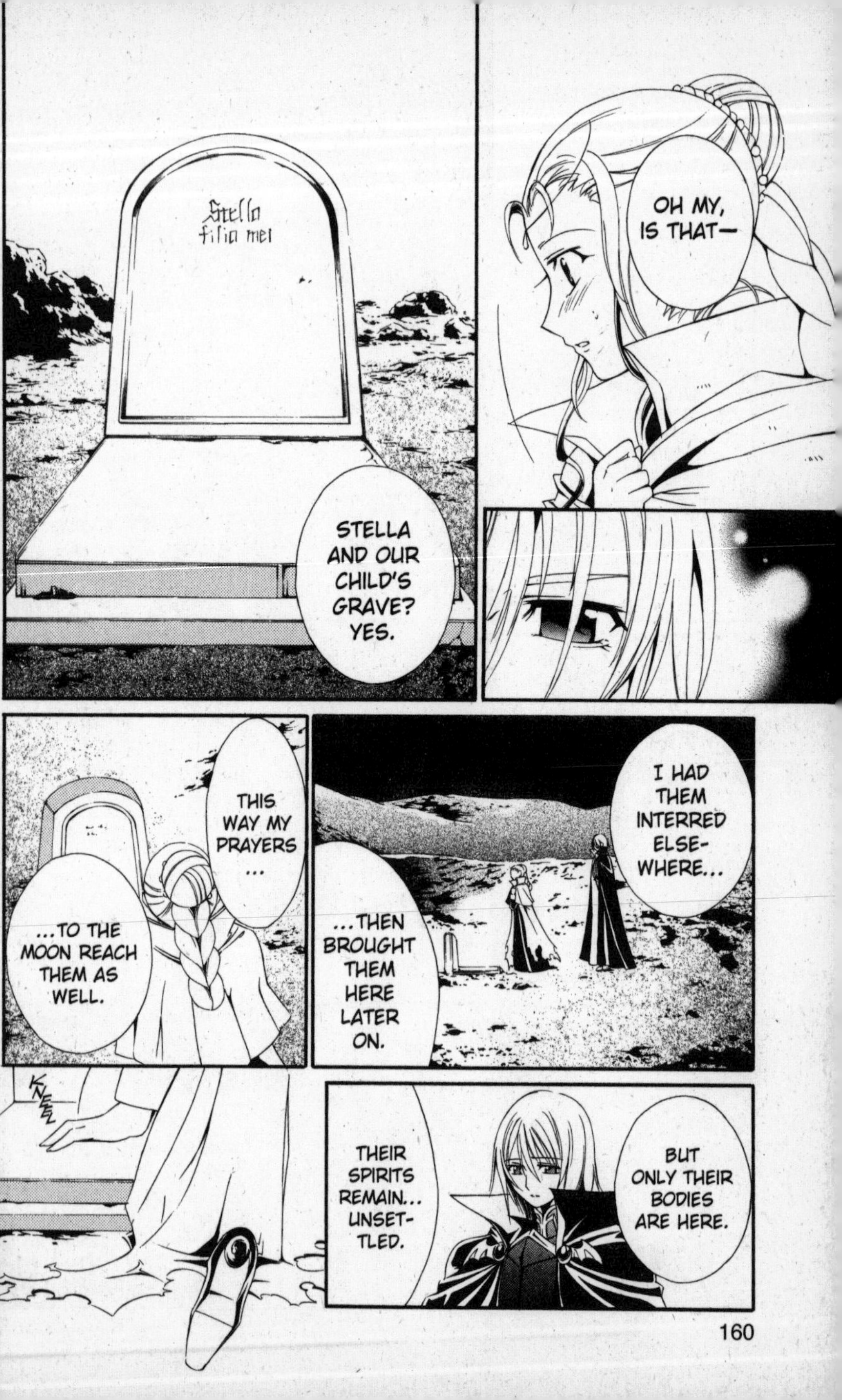
OH MY, IS THAT—
Stella filia mei
STELLA AND OUR CHILD'S GRAVE? YES.
I HAD THEM INTERRED ELSE-WHERE...
...THEN BROUGHT THEM HERE LATER ON.
THIS WAY MY PRAYERS ...
...TO THE MOON REACH THEM AS WELL.
BUT ONLY THEIR BODIES ARE HERE.
THEIR SPIRITS REMAIN... UNSET-TLED.
KNEEL

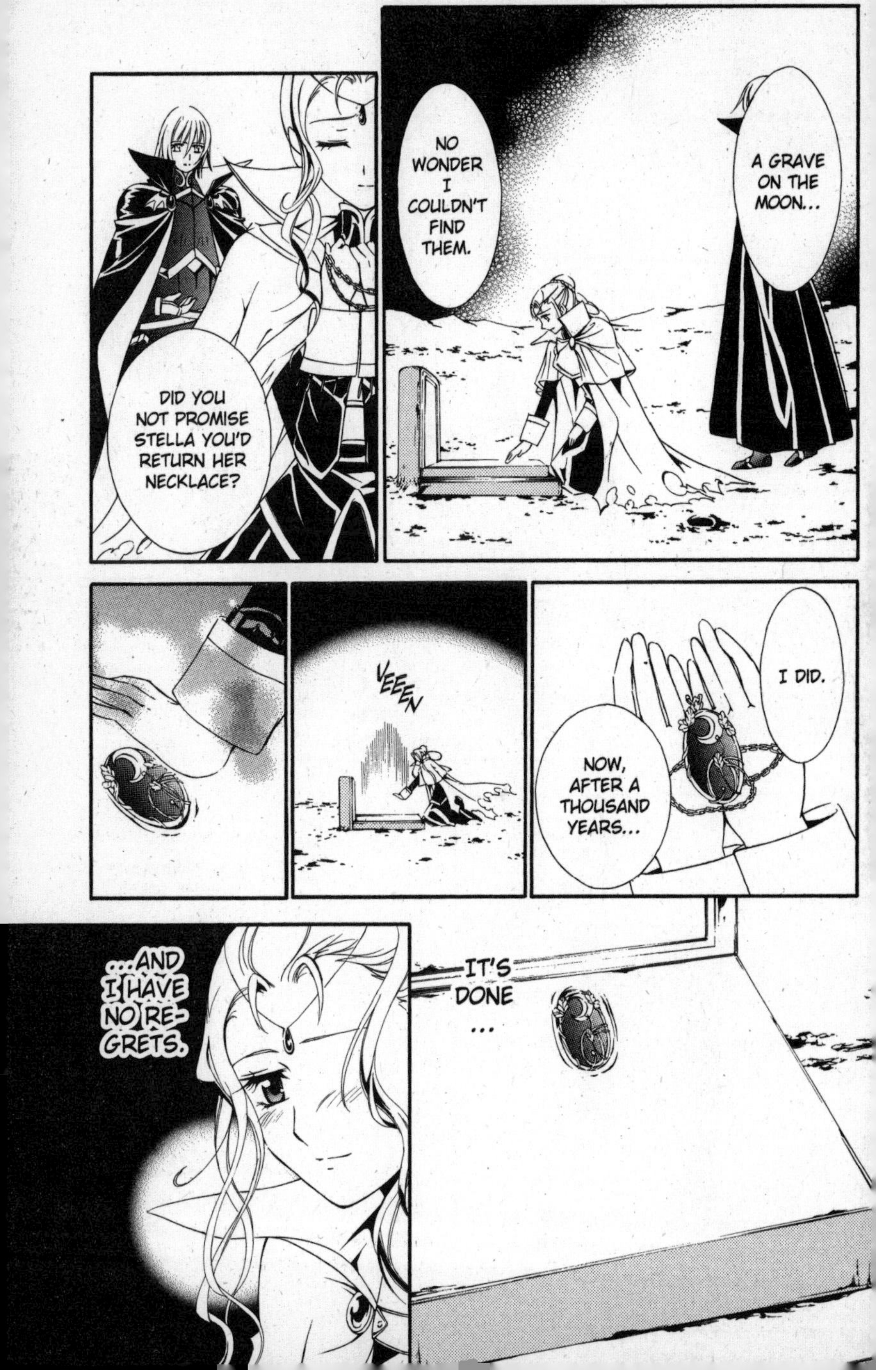
A GRAVE ON THE MOON...
NO WONDER I COULDN'T FIND THEM.
DID YOU NOT PROMISE STELLA YOU'D RETURN HER NECKLACE?
I DID.
NOW, AFTER A THOUSAND YEARS...
VEEEN
IT'S DONE ...
...AND I HAVE NO RE-GRETS.

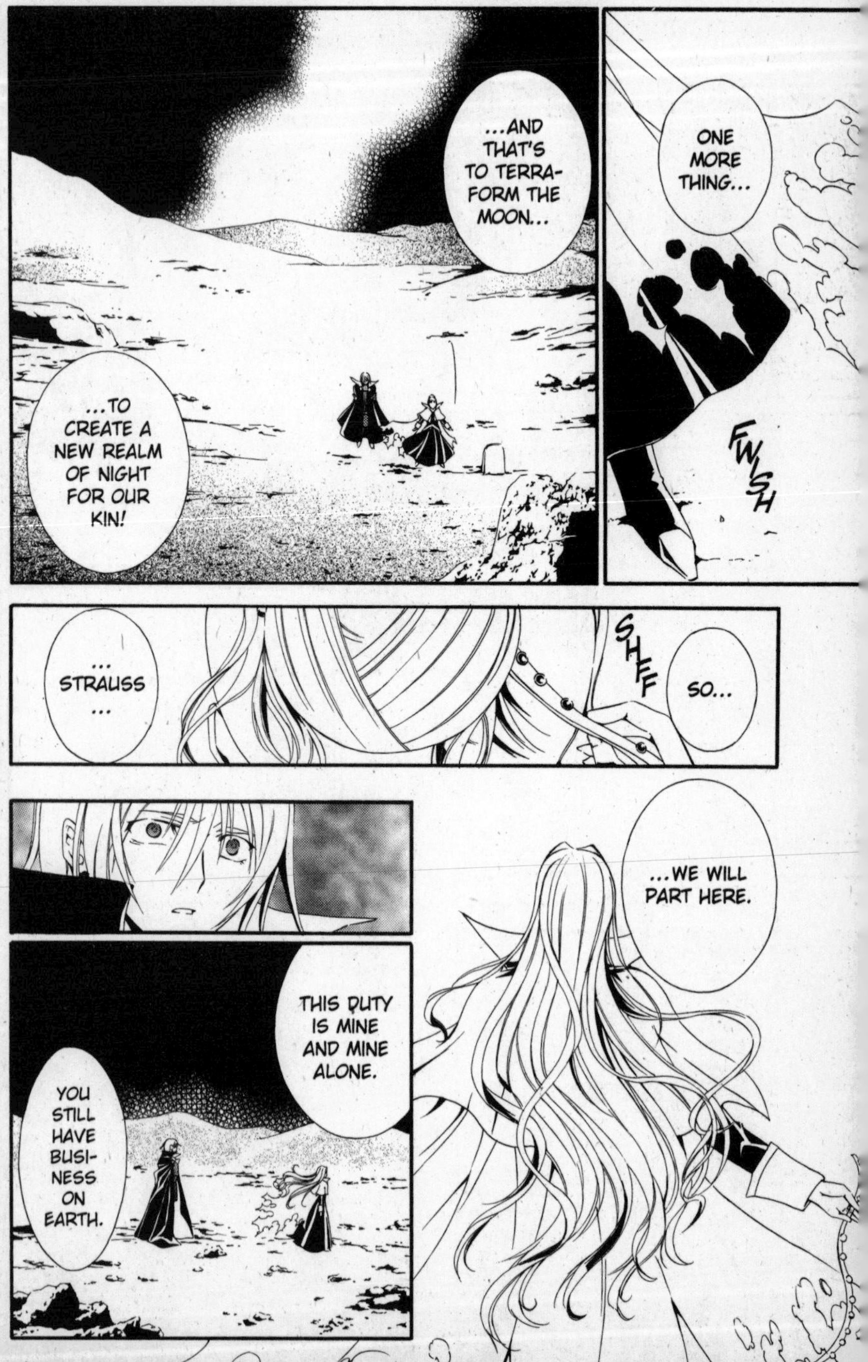
ONE MORE THING...
FWISH
...AND THAT'S TO TERRA-FORM THE MOON...
...TO CREATE A NEW REALM OF NIGHT FOR OUR KIN!
SHEF
SO...
...STRAUSS...
...WE WILL PART HERE.
THIS DUTY IS MINE AND MINE ALONE.
YOU STILL HAVE BUSINESS ON EARTH.

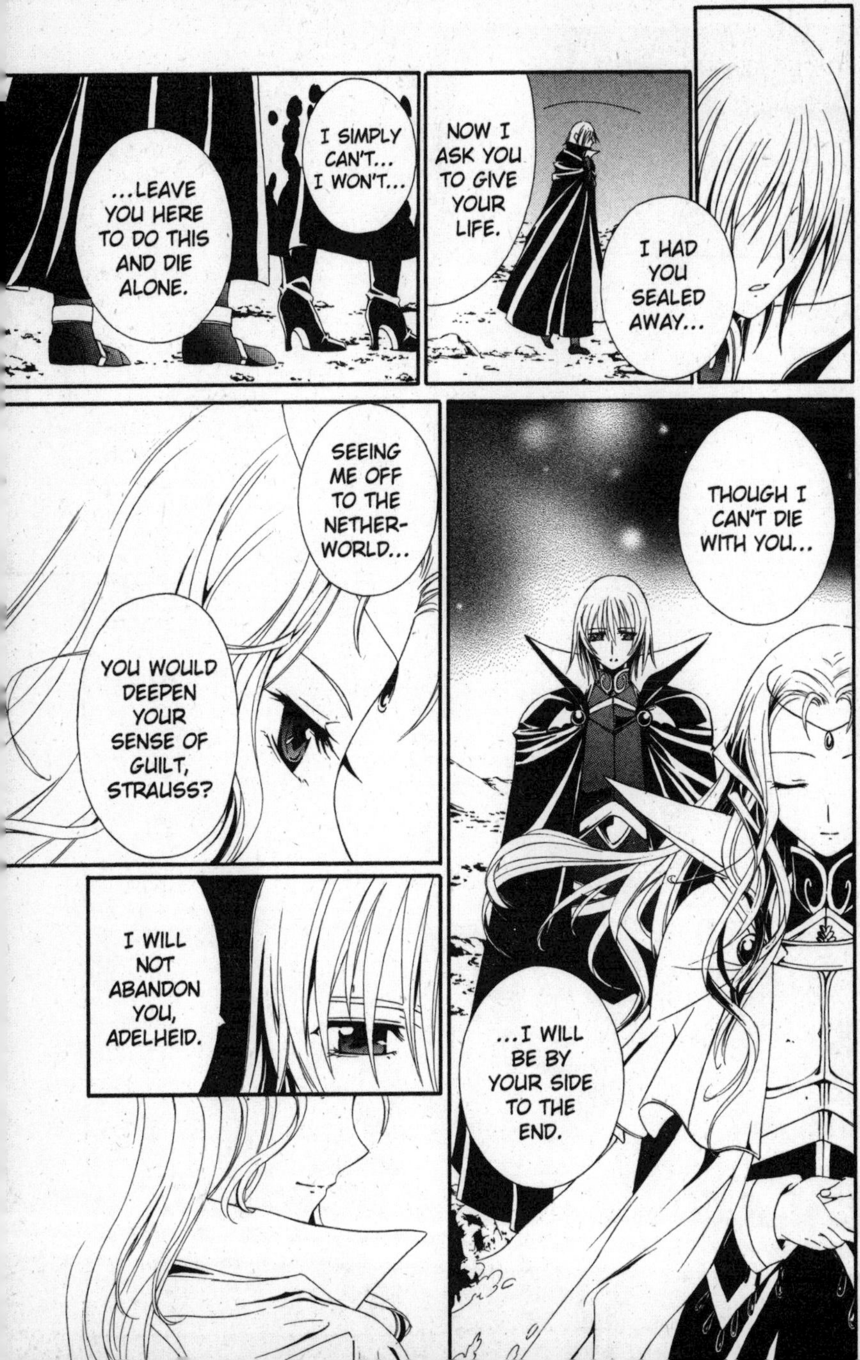
I HAD YOU SEALED AWAY...
NOW I ASK YOU TO GIVE YOUR LIFE.
I SIMPLY CAN'T... I WON'T...
...LEAVE YOU HERE TO DO THIS AND DIE ALONE.
THOUGH I CAN'T DIE WITH YOU...
...I WILL BE BY YOUR SIDE TO THE END.
SEEING ME OFF TO THE NETHER-WORLD...
YOU WOULD DEEPEN YOUR SENSE OF GUILT, STRAUSS?
I WILL NOT ABANDON YOU, ADELHEID.

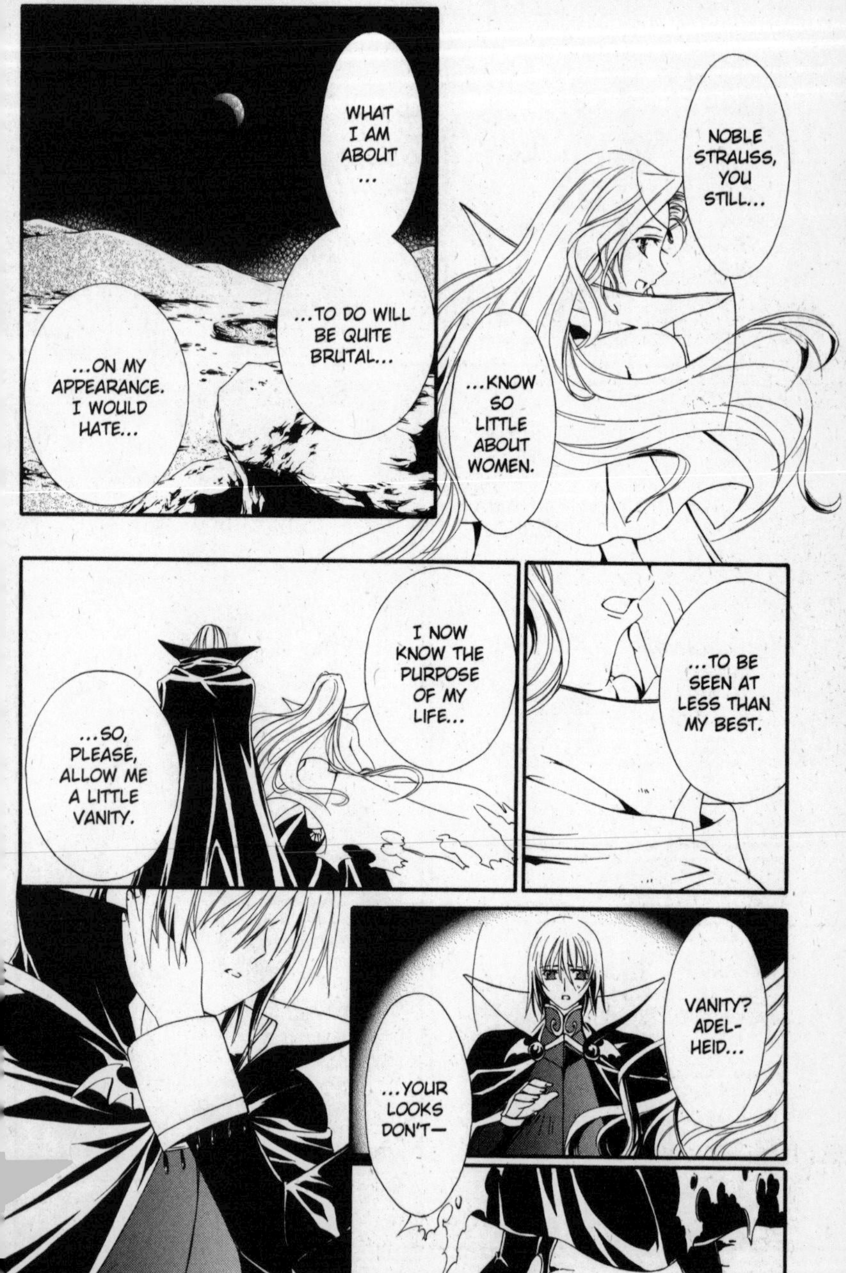
NOBLE STRAUSS, YOU STILL...
...KNOW SO LITTLE ABOUT WOMEN.
WHAT I AM ABOUT ...
...TO DO WILL BE QUITE BRUTAL...
...ON MY APPEARANCE. I WOULD HATE...
...TO BE SEEN AT LESS THAN MY BEST.
I NOW KNOW THE PURPOSE OF MY LIFE...
...SO, PLEASE, ALLOW ME A LITTLE VANITY.
VANITY? ADEL-HEID...
...YOUR LOOKS DON'T—

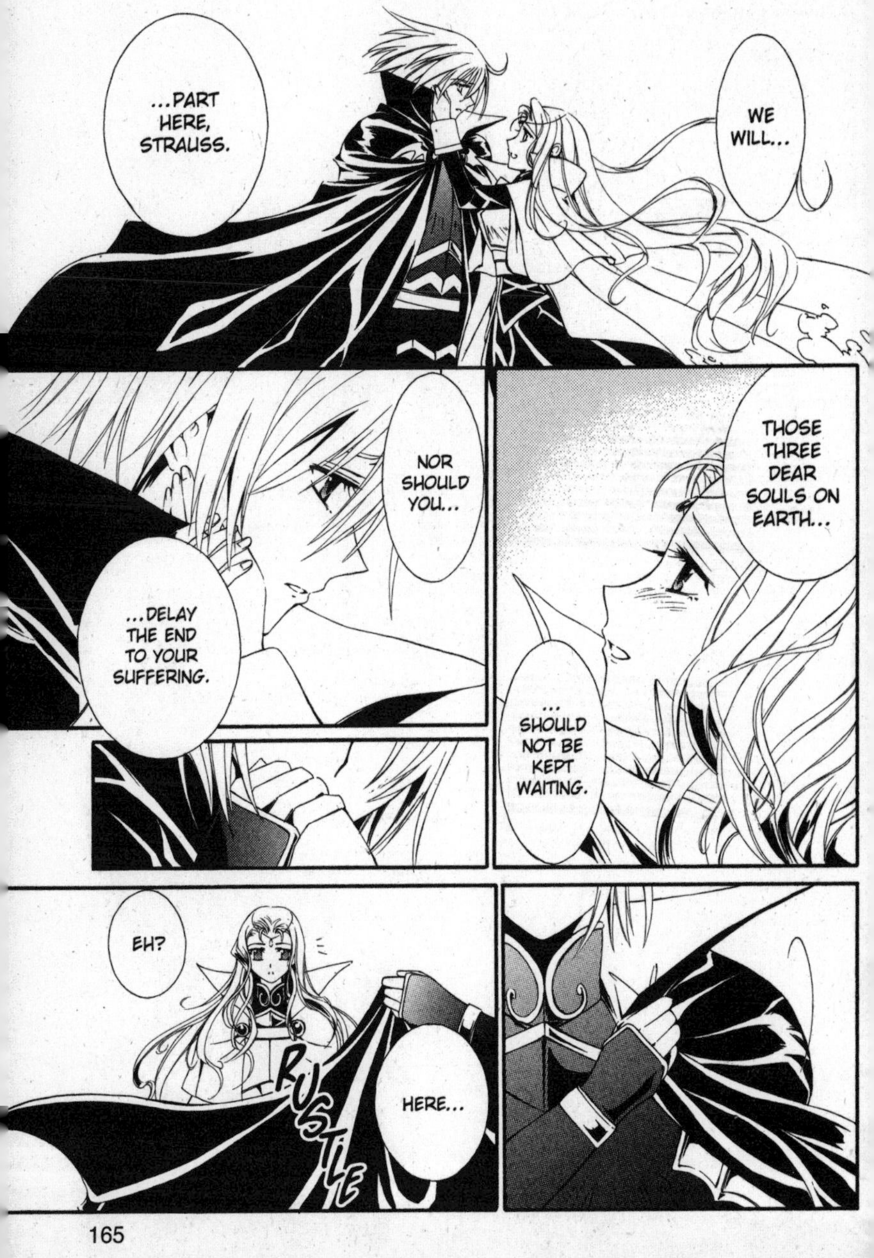
WE WILL...
...PART HERE, STRAUSS.
THOSE THREE DEAR SOULS ON EARTH...
...SHOULD NOT BE KEPT WAITING.
NOR SHOULD YOU...
...DELAY THE END TO YOUR SUFFERING.
EH?
RUSTLE
HERE...

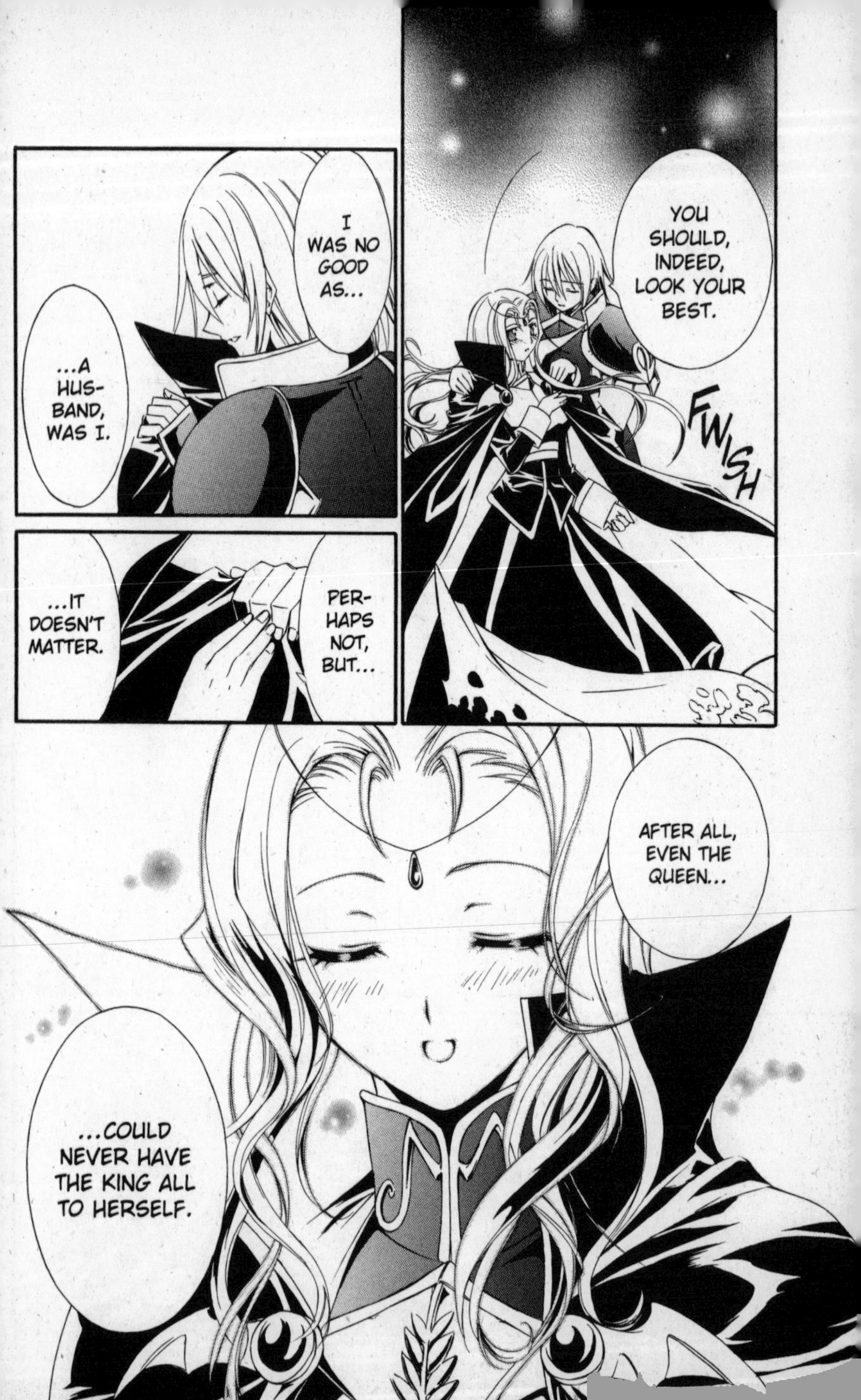
YOU SHOULD, INDEED, LOOK YOUR BEST.
FWISH
I WAS NO GOOD AS...
...A HUS-BAND, WAS I.
PER-HAPS NOT, BUT...
...IT DOESN'T MATTER.
AFTER ALL, EVEN THE QUEEN...
...COULD NEVER HAVE THE KING ALL TO HERSELF.

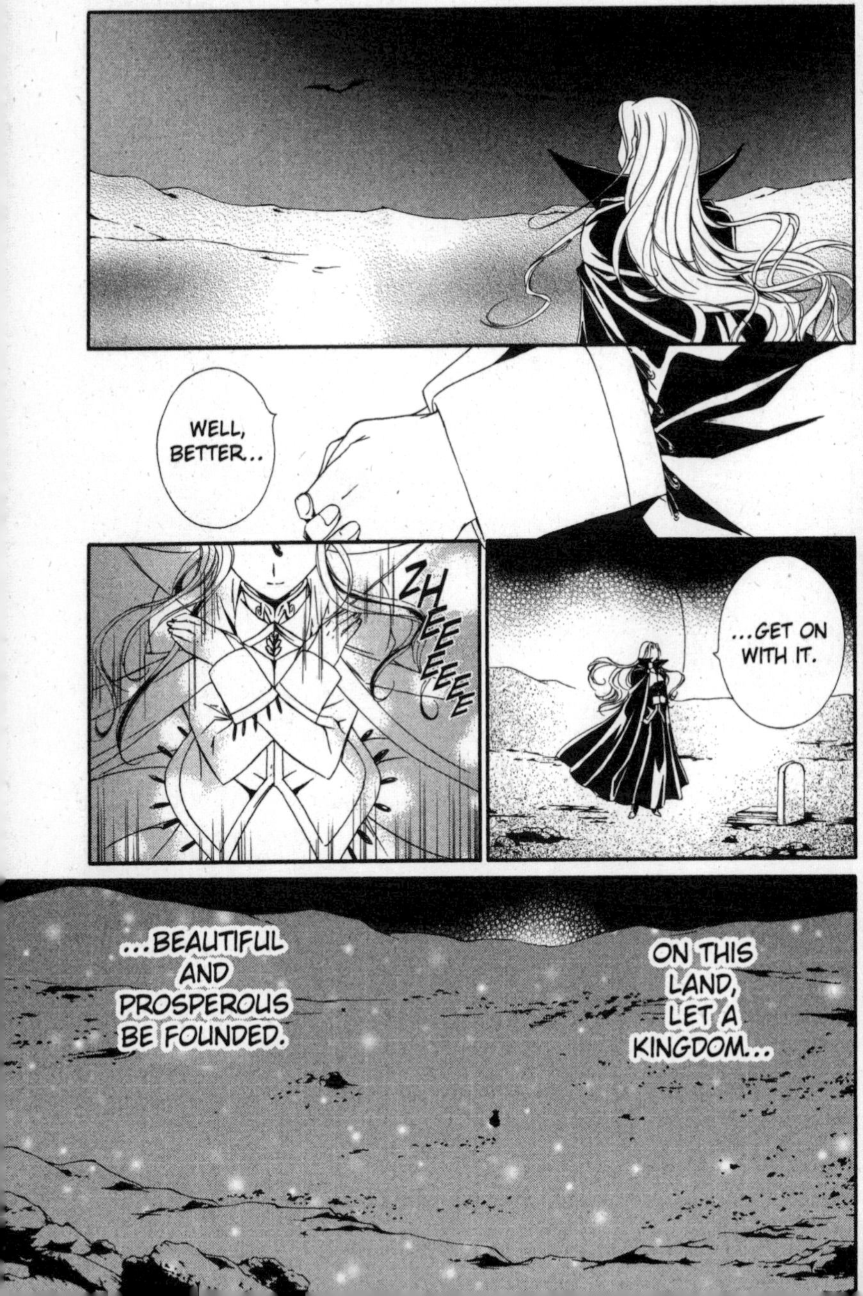
WELL, BETTER...
...GET ON WITH IT.
ZHEEEEEE
ON THIS LAND, LET A KINGDOM...
...BEAUTIFUL AND PROSPEROUS BE FOUNDED.

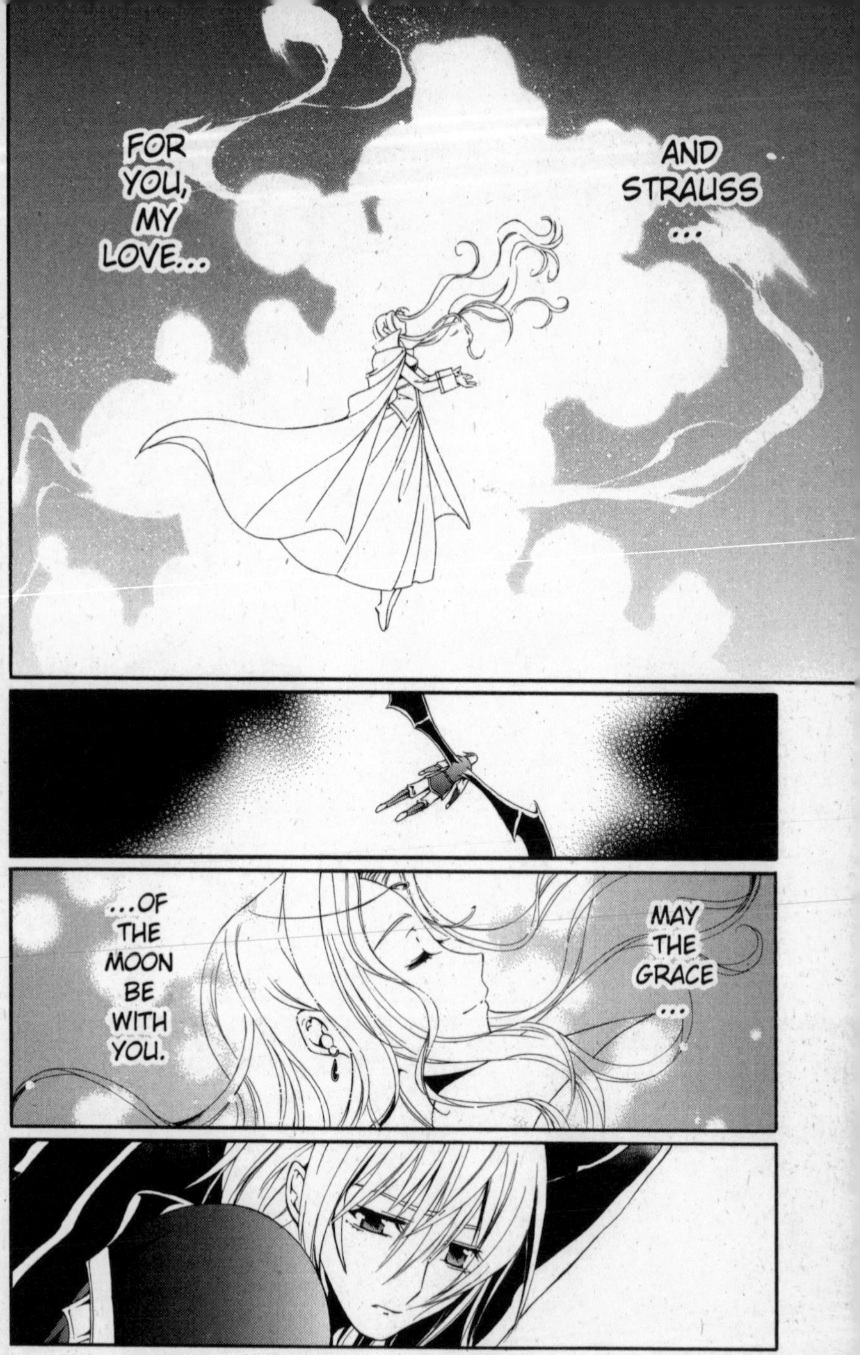
AND STRAUSS ...
FOR YOU, MY LOVE...
MAY THE GRACE ...
...OF THE MOON BE WITH YOU.

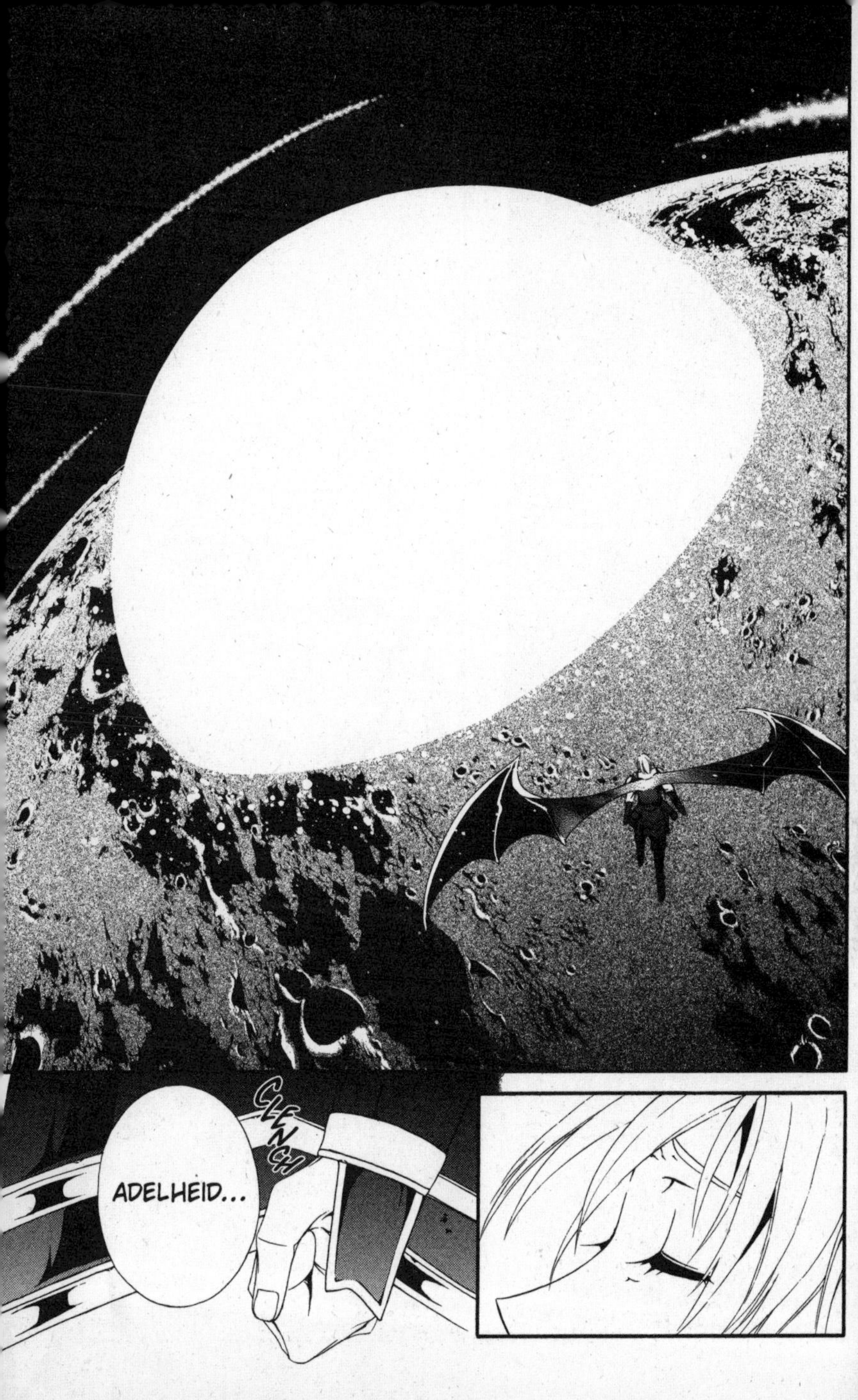
CLENCH
ADELHEID...

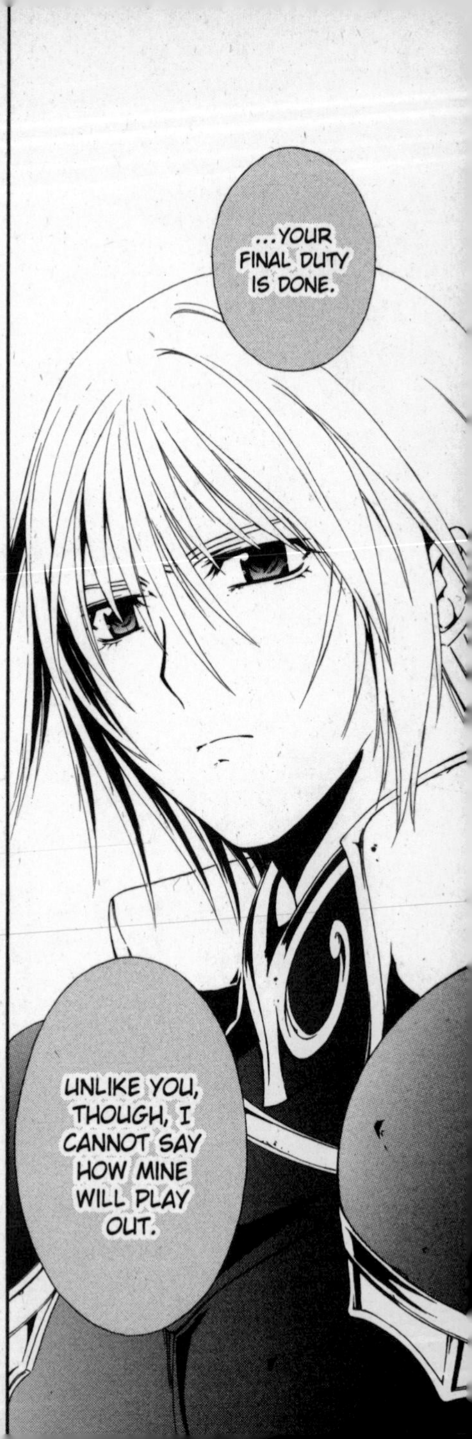
...YOUR FINAL DUTY IS DONE.
UNLIKE YOU, THOUGH, I CANNOT SAY HOW MINE WILL PLAY OUT.
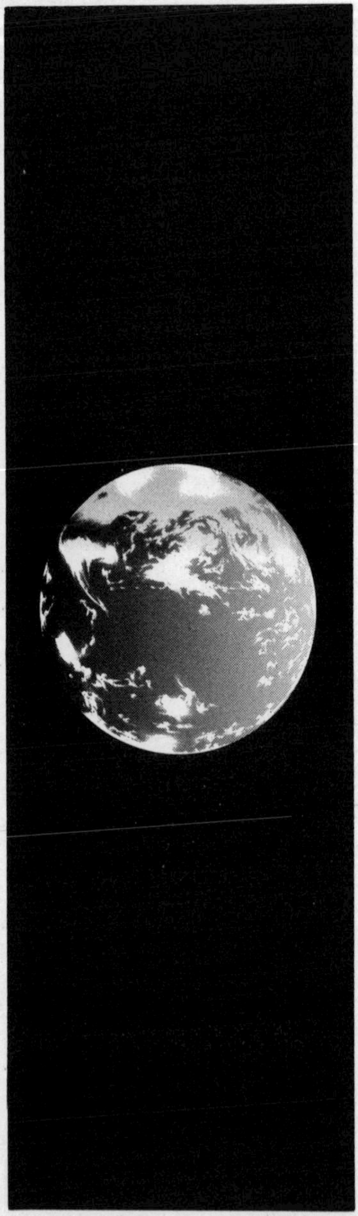

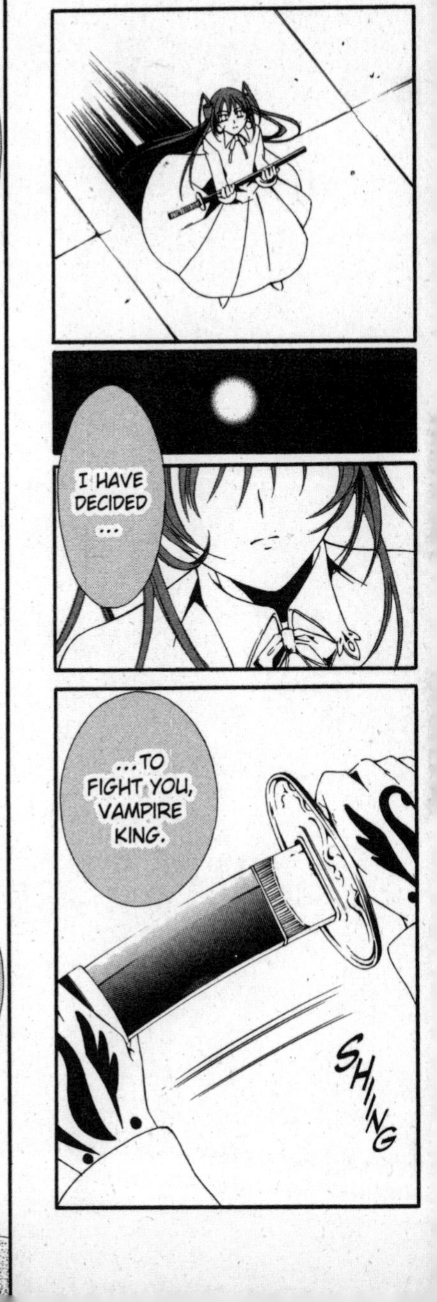
I HAVE DECIDED ...
...TO FIGHT YOU, VAMPIRE KING.
SHIING

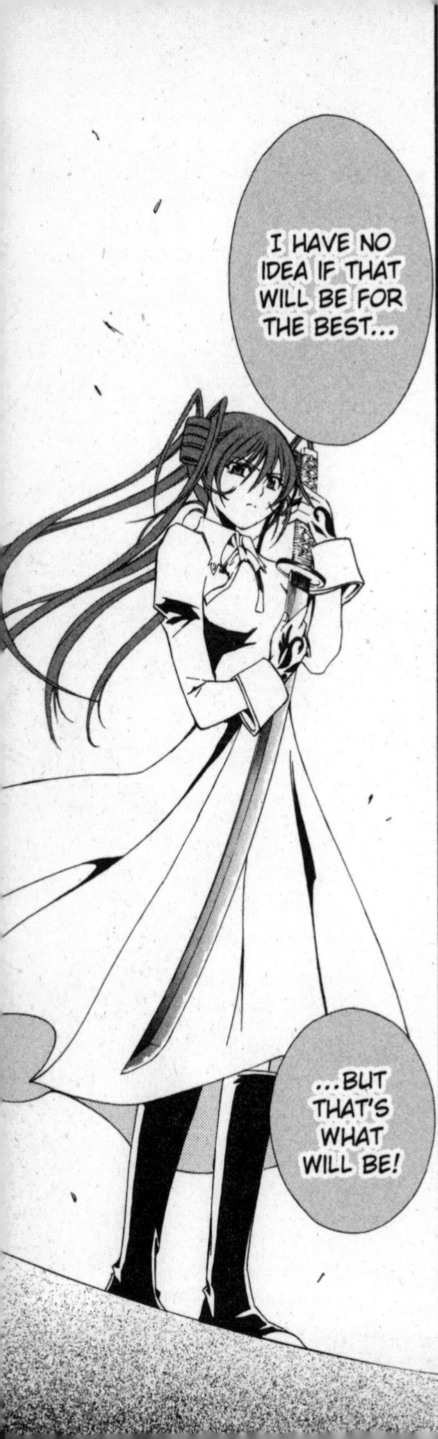
I HAVE NO IDEA IF THAT WILL BE FOR THE BEST...
...BUT THAT'S WHAT WILL BE!

THE RECORD OF A

FALLEN VAMPIRE

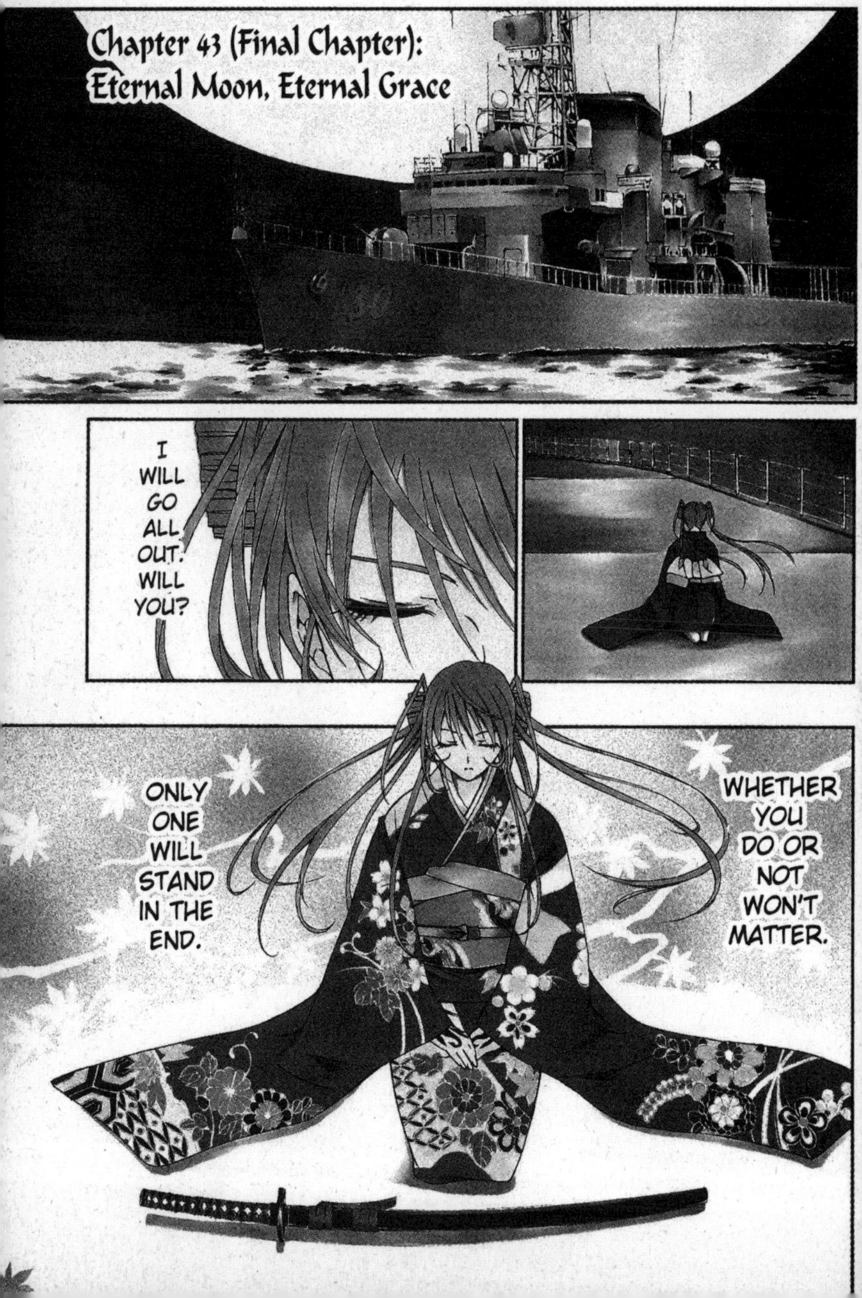
Chapter 43 (Final Chapter):
Eternal Moon, Eternal Grace
I WILL GO ALL OUT. WILL YOU?
WHETHER YOU DO OR NOT WON'T MATTER.
ONLY ONE WILL STAND IN THE END.

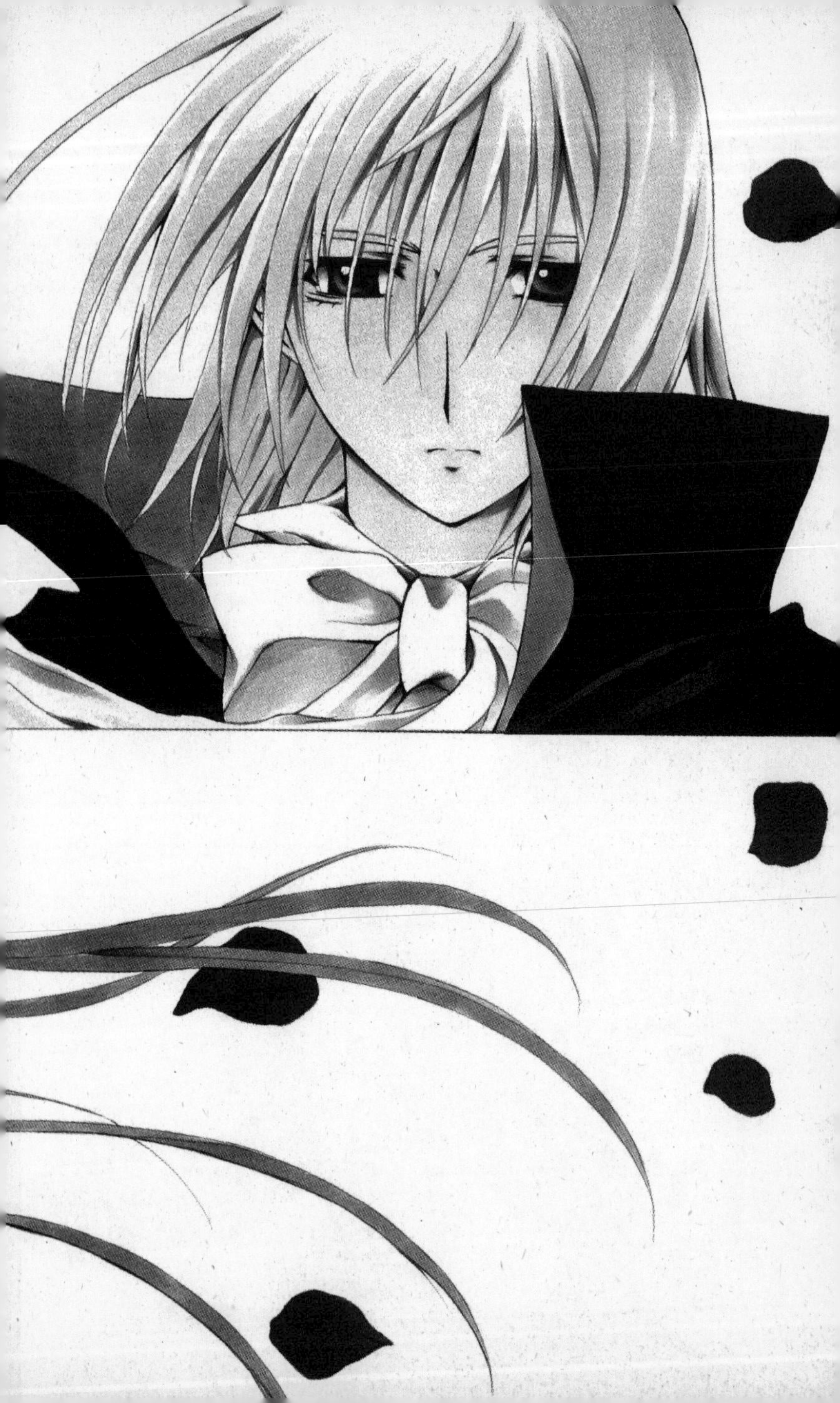

Chapter 43 (Final Chapter): Eternal Moon, Eternal Grace

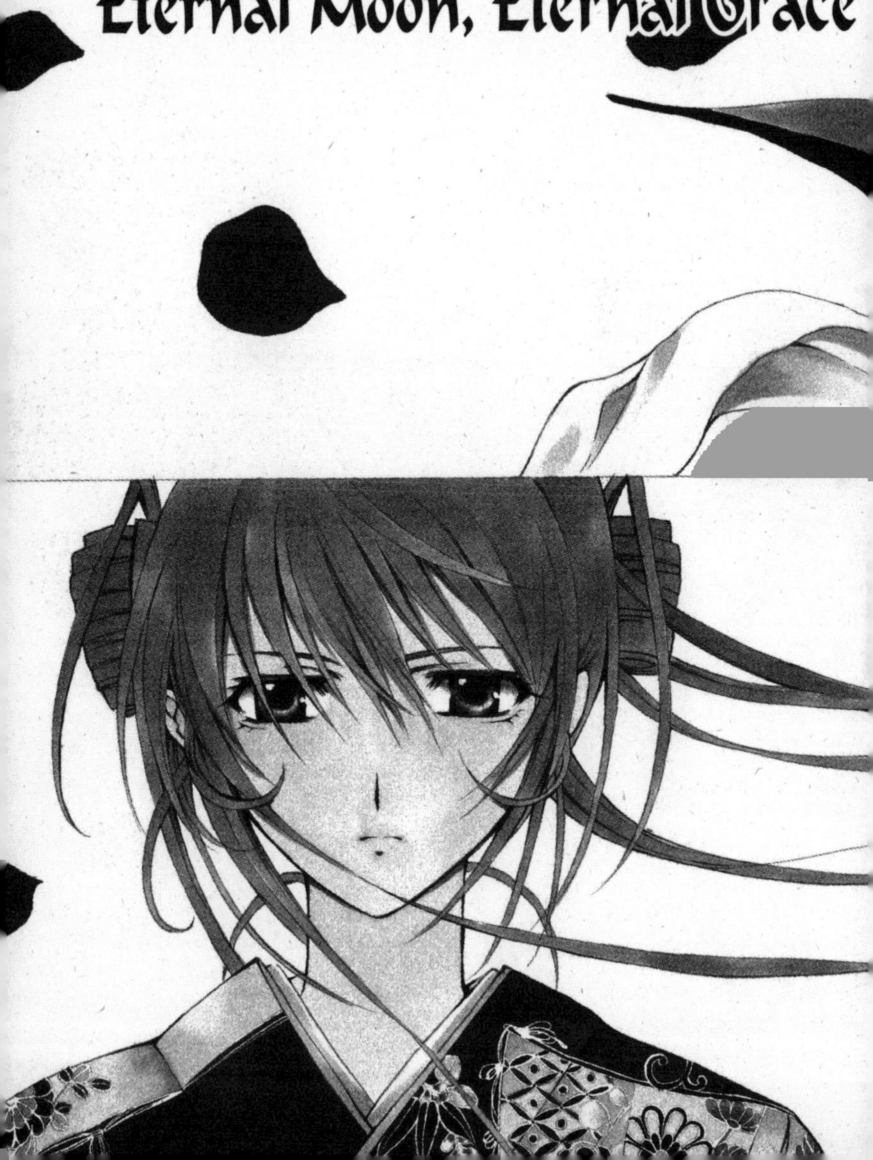

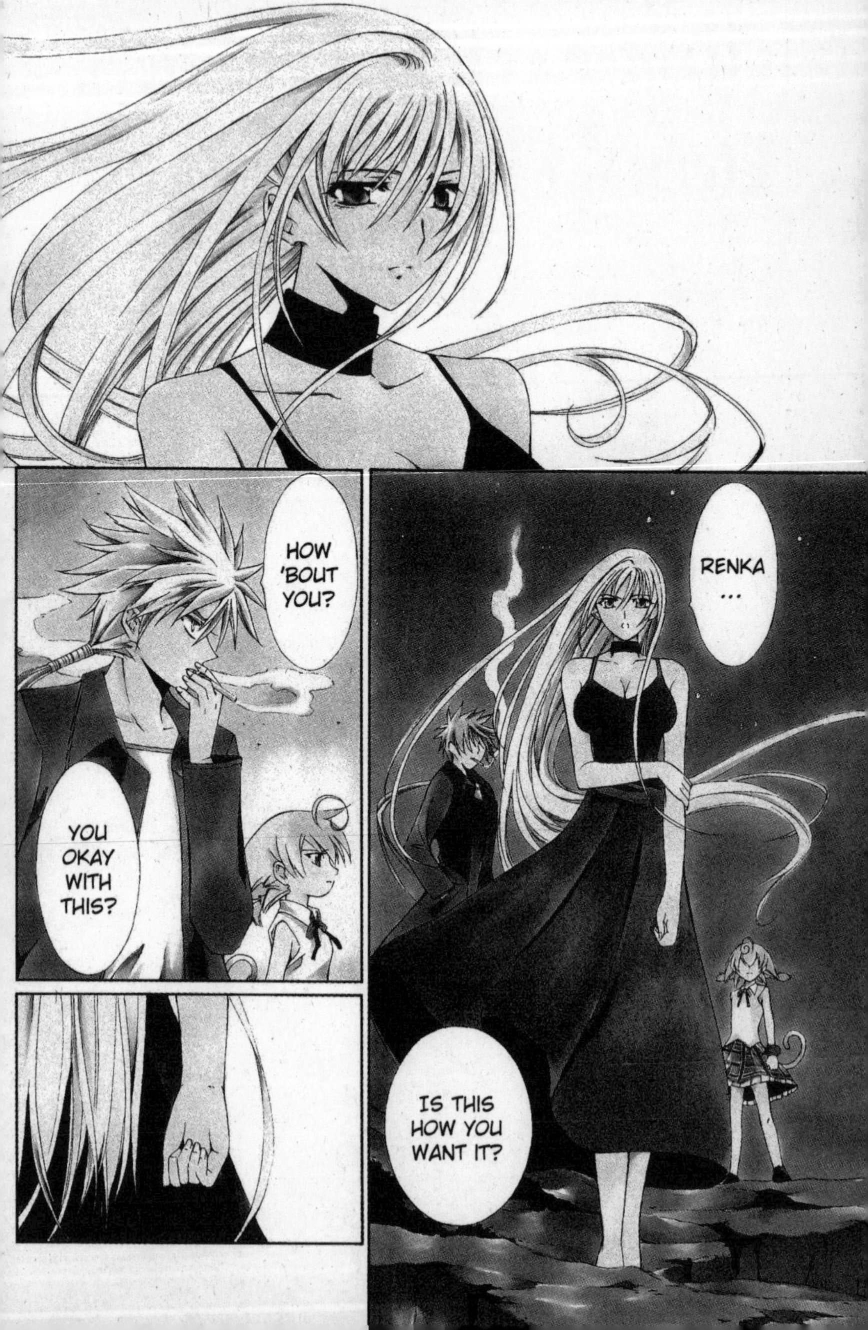
RENKA...
IS THIS HOW YOU WANT IT?
HOW 'BOUT YOU?
YOU OKAY WITH THIS?

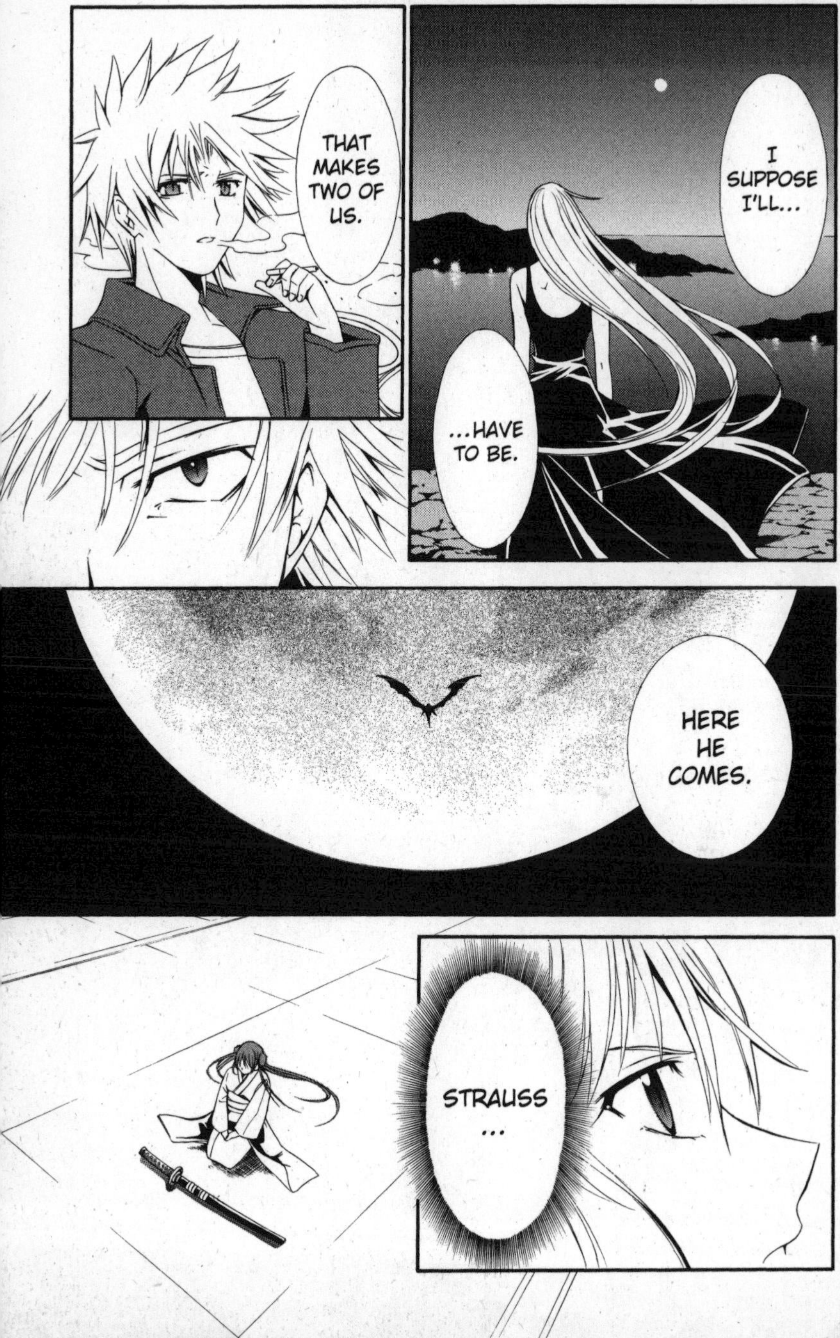
I SUPPOSE I'LL...
...HAVE TO BE.
THAT MAKES TWO OF US.
HERE HE COMES.
STRAUSS ...

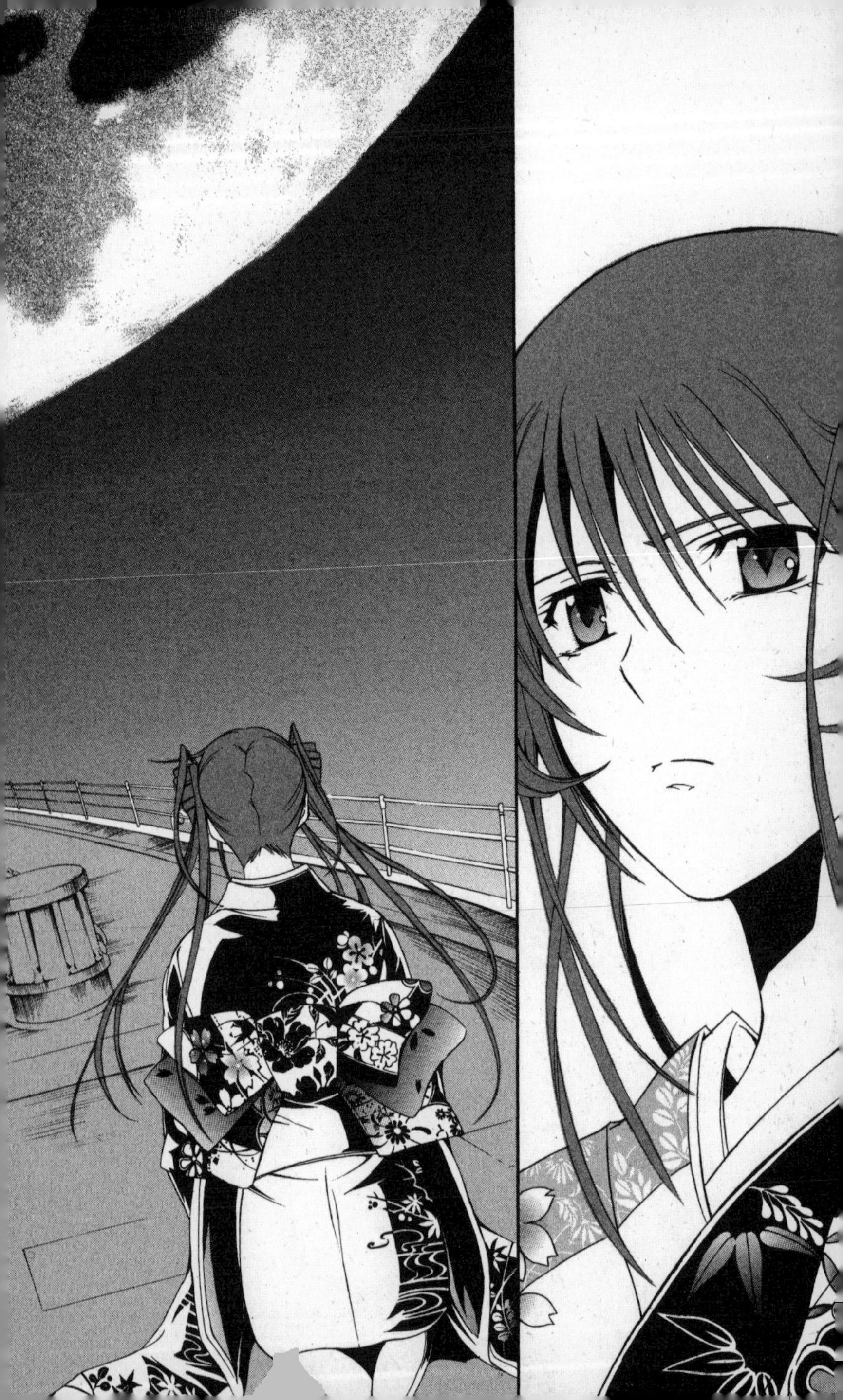

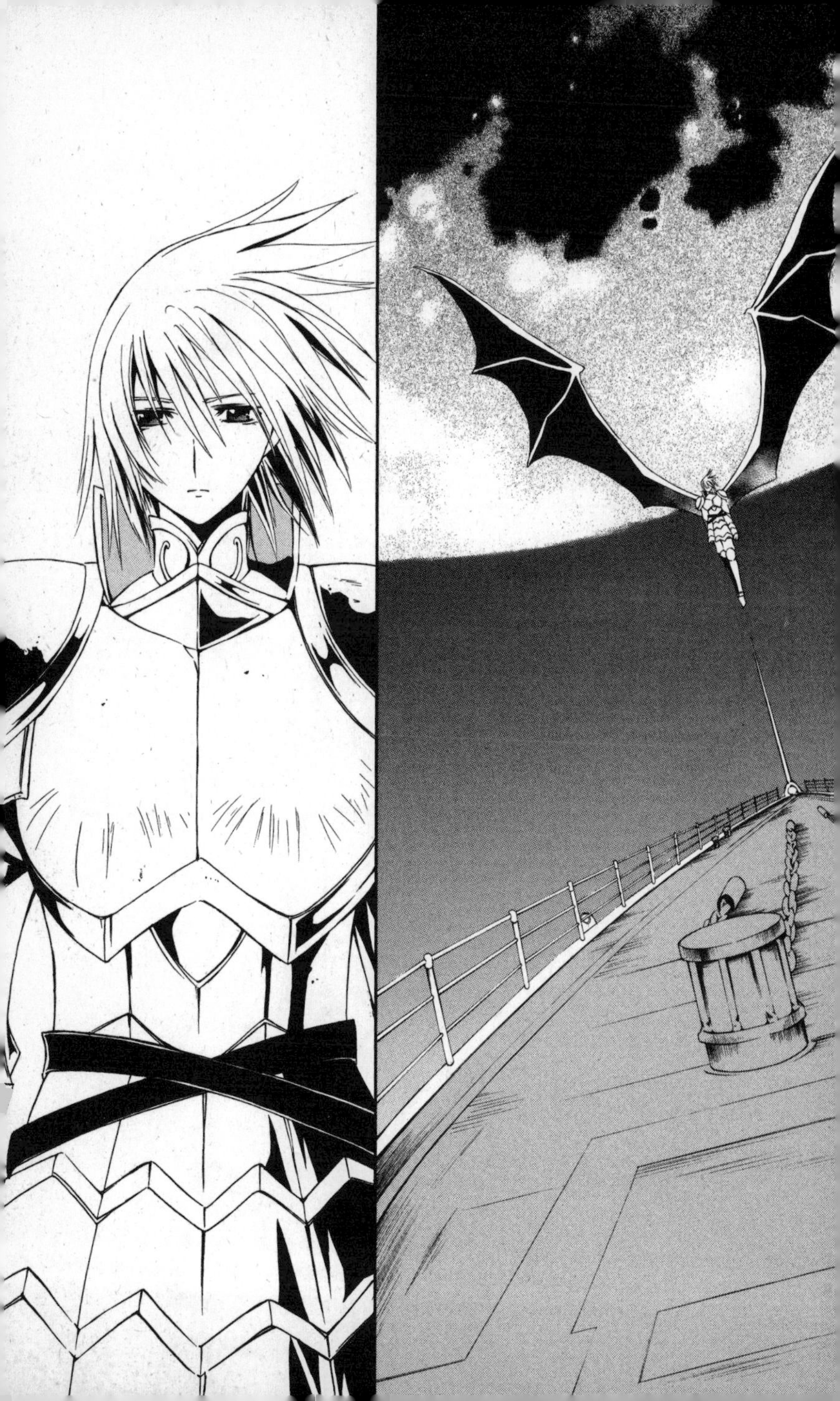

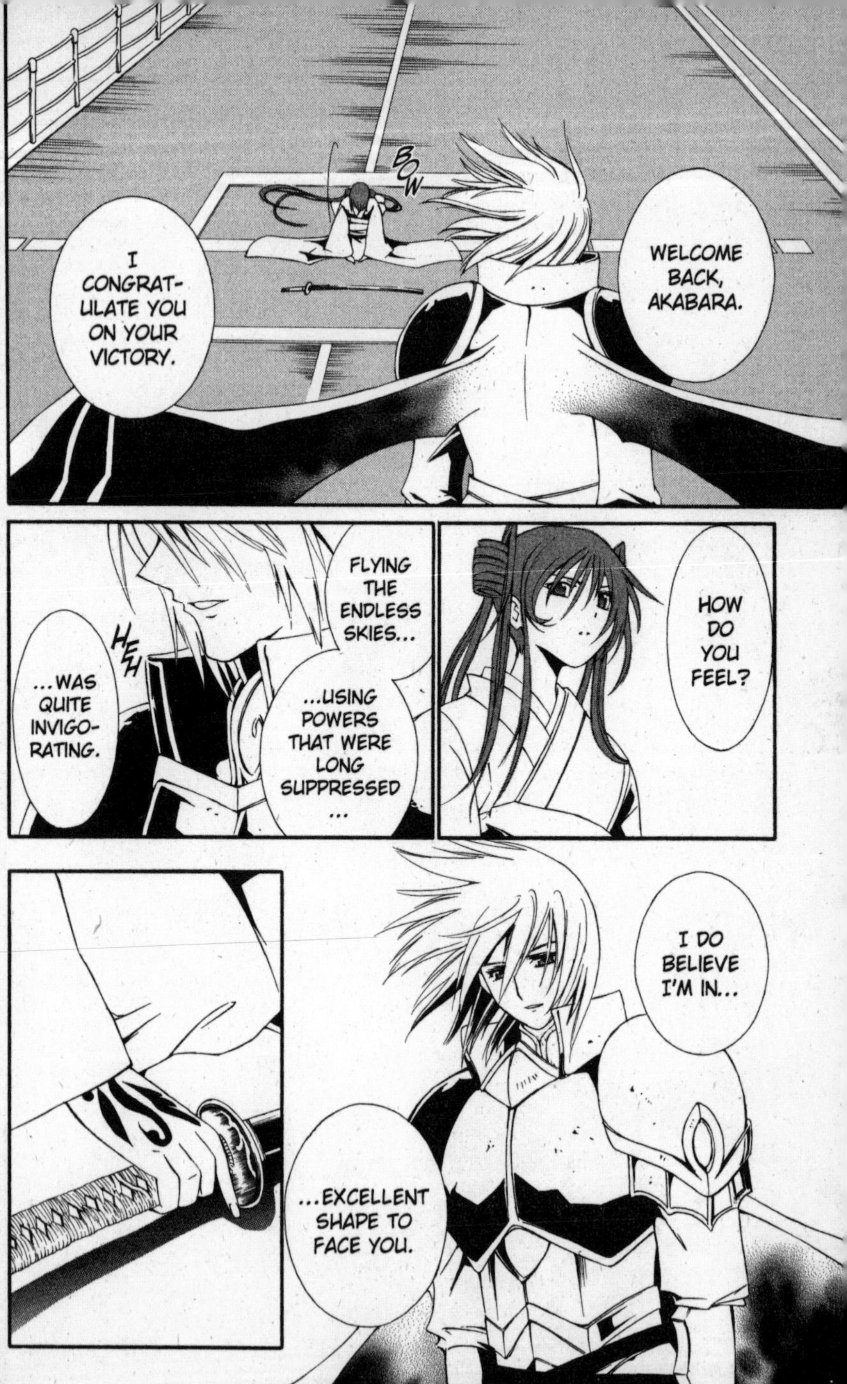
WELCOME BACK, AKABARA.
BOW
I CONGRAT-ULATE YOU ON YOUR VICTORY.
HOW DO YOU FEEL?
FLYING THE ENDLESS SKIES...
...USING POWERS THAT WERE LONG SUPPRESSED...
HEH
...WAS QUITE INVIGO-RATING.
I DO BELIEVE I'M IN...
...EXCELLENT SHAPE TO FACE YOU.

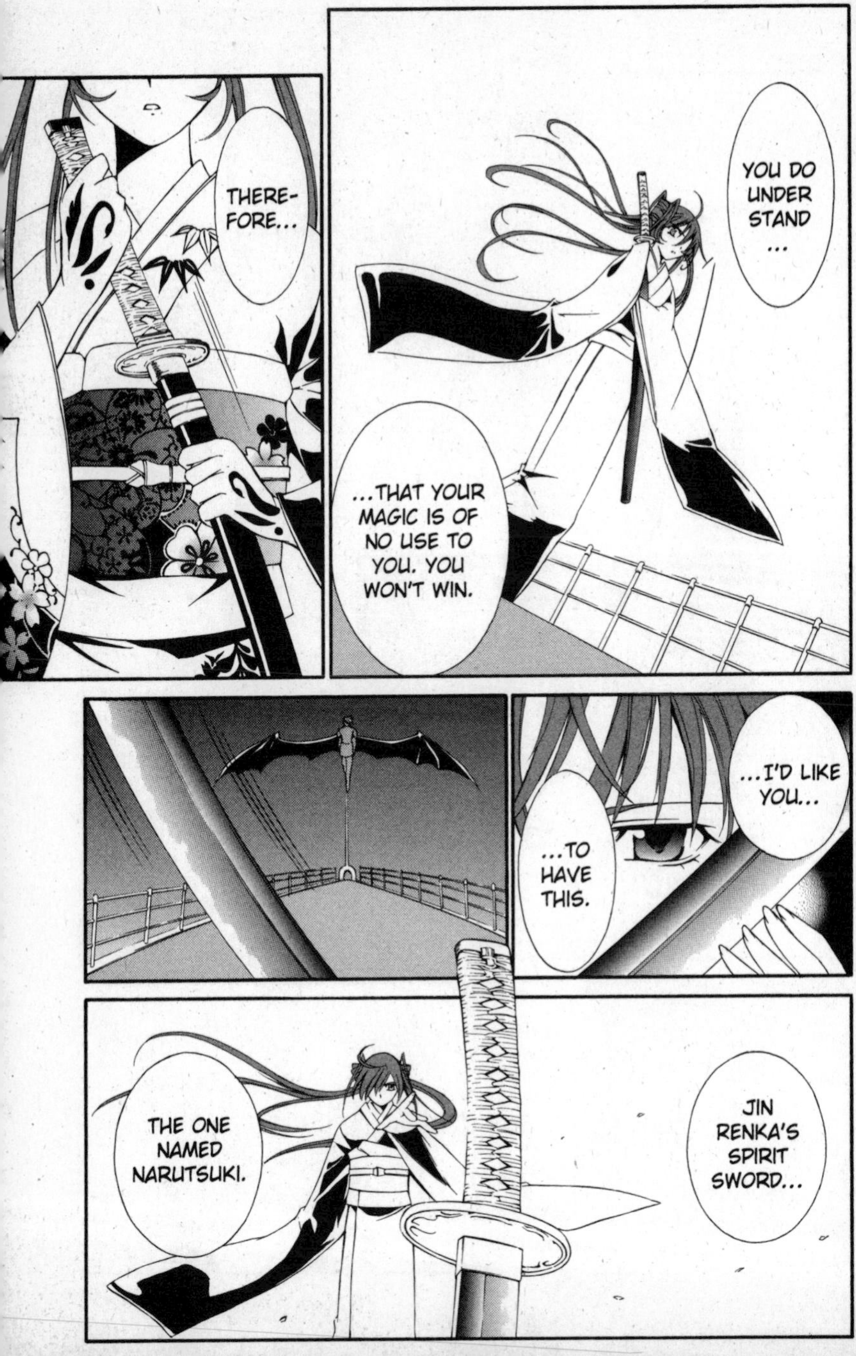
YOU DO UNDER STAND ...
...THAT YOUR MAGIC IS OF NO USE TO YOU. YOU WON'T WIN.
THERE-FORE...
...I'D LIKE YOU...
...TO HAVE THIS.
JIN RENKA'S SPIRIT SWORD...
THE ONE NAMED NARUTSUKI.

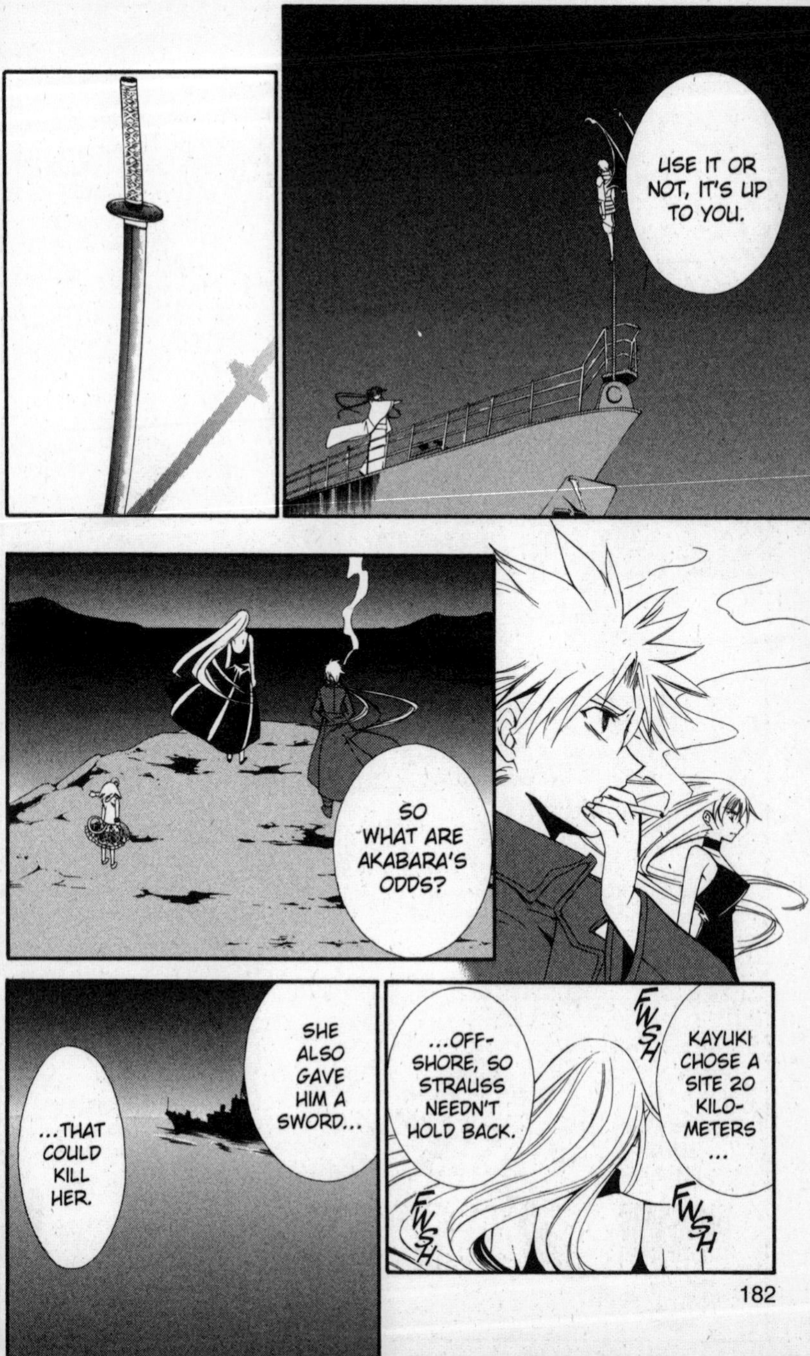
USE IT OR NOT, IT'S UP TO YOU.
SO WHAT ARE AKABARA'S ODDS?
KAYUKI CHOSE A SITE 20 KILO-METERS...
FWSH
...OFF-SHORE, SO STRAUSS NEEDN'T HOLD BACK.
FWSH
FWSH
SHE ALSO GAVE HIM A SWORD...
...THAT COULD KILL HER.

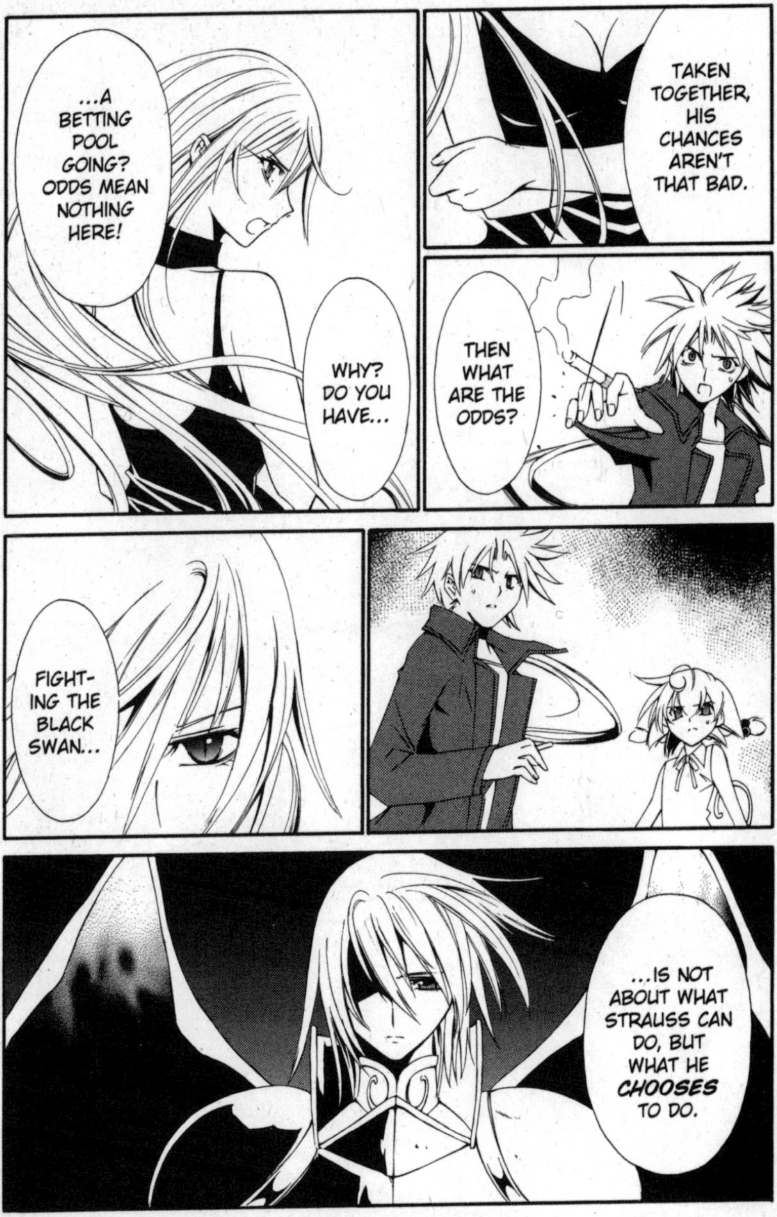
TAKEN TOGETHER, HIS CHANCES AREN'T THAT BAD.
THEN WHAT ARE THE ODDS?
WHY? DO YOU HAVE...
...A BETTING POOL GOING? ODDS MEAN NOTHING HERE!
FIGHTING THE BLACK SWAN...
...IS NOT ABOUT WHAT STRAUSS CAN DO, BUT WHAT HE *CHOOSES* TO DO.

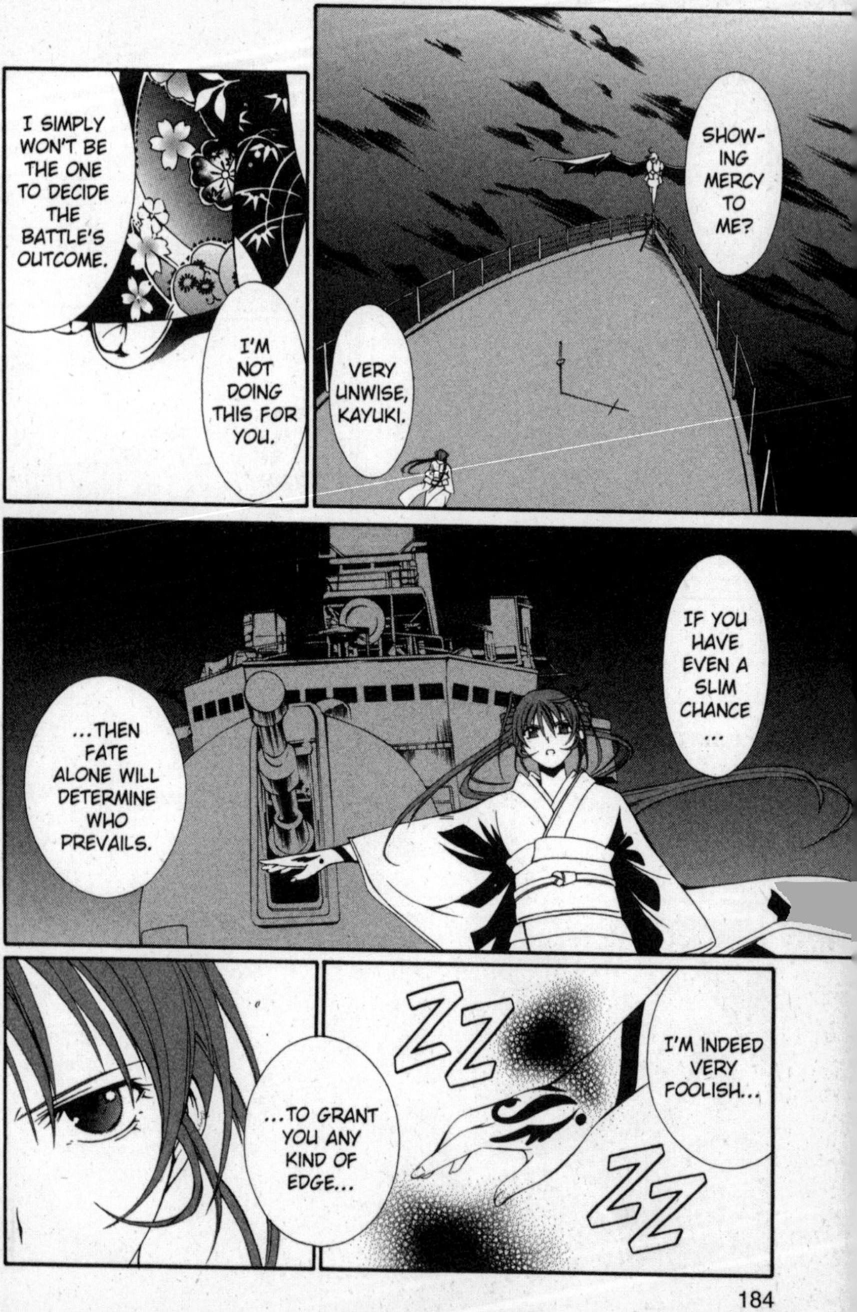
SHOWING MERCY TO ME?
VERY UNWISE, KAYUKI.
I'M NOT DOING THIS FOR YOU.
I SIMPLY WON'T BE THE ONE TO DECIDE THE BATTLE'S OUTCOME.
IF YOU HAVE EVEN A SLIM CHANCE...
...THEN FATE ALONE WILL DETERMINE WHO PREVAILS.
I'M INDEED VERY FOOLISH...
ZZ
ZZ
...TO GRANT YOU ANY KIND OF EDGE...

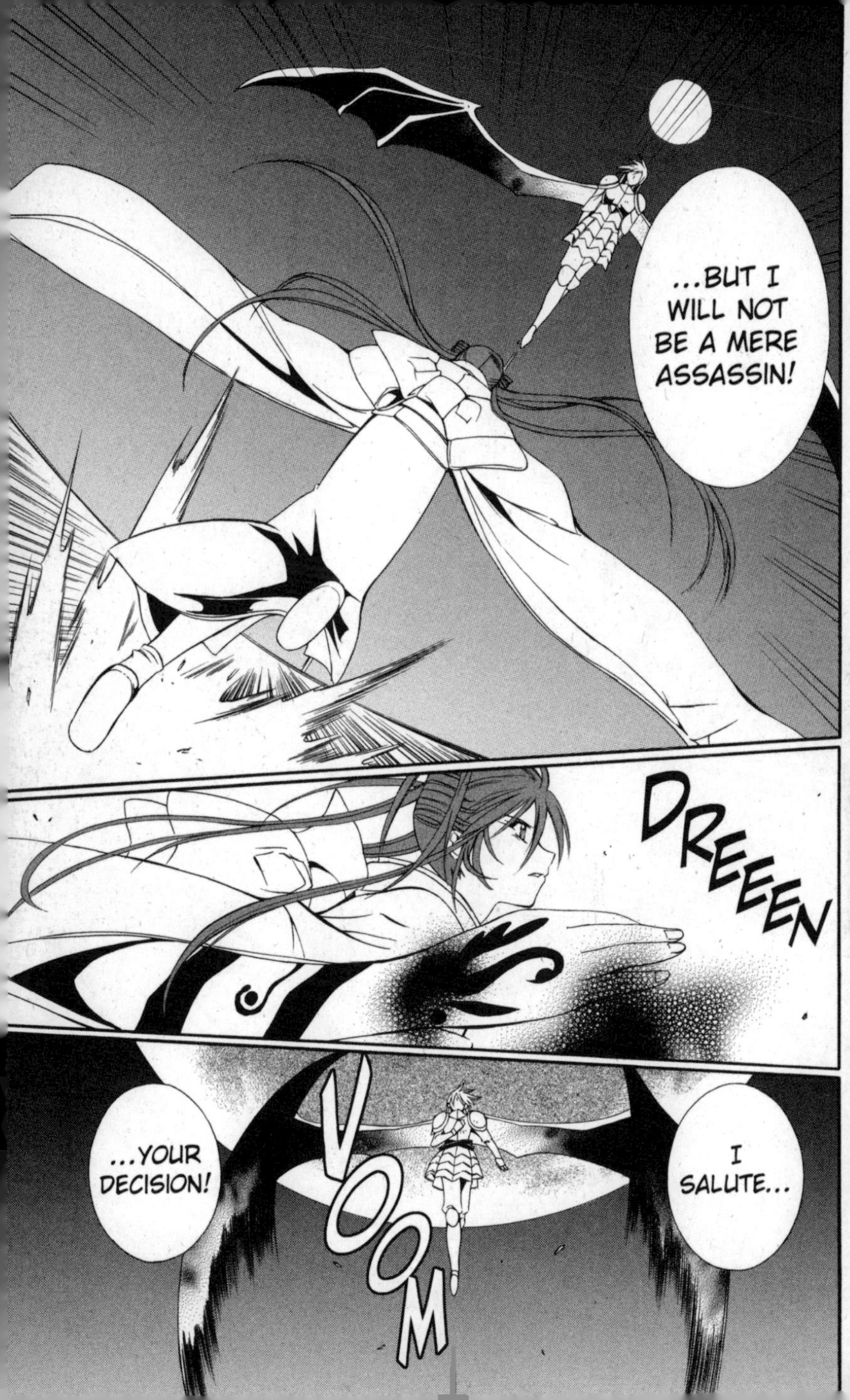
...BUT I WILL NOT BE A MERE ASSASSIN!
DREEEEN
I SALUTE...
VOOOM
...YOUR DECISION!

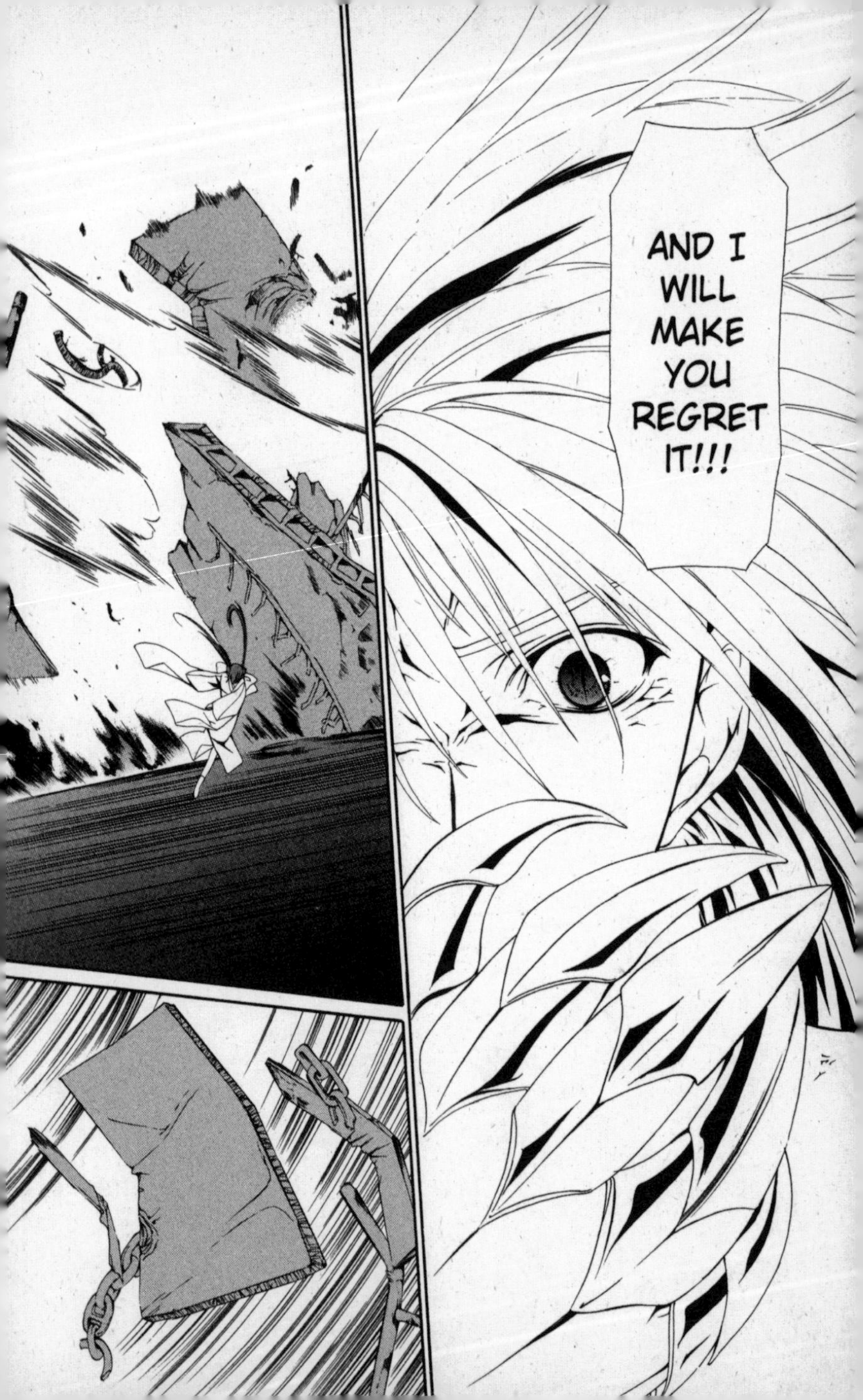
AND I WILL MAKE YOU REGRET IT!!!

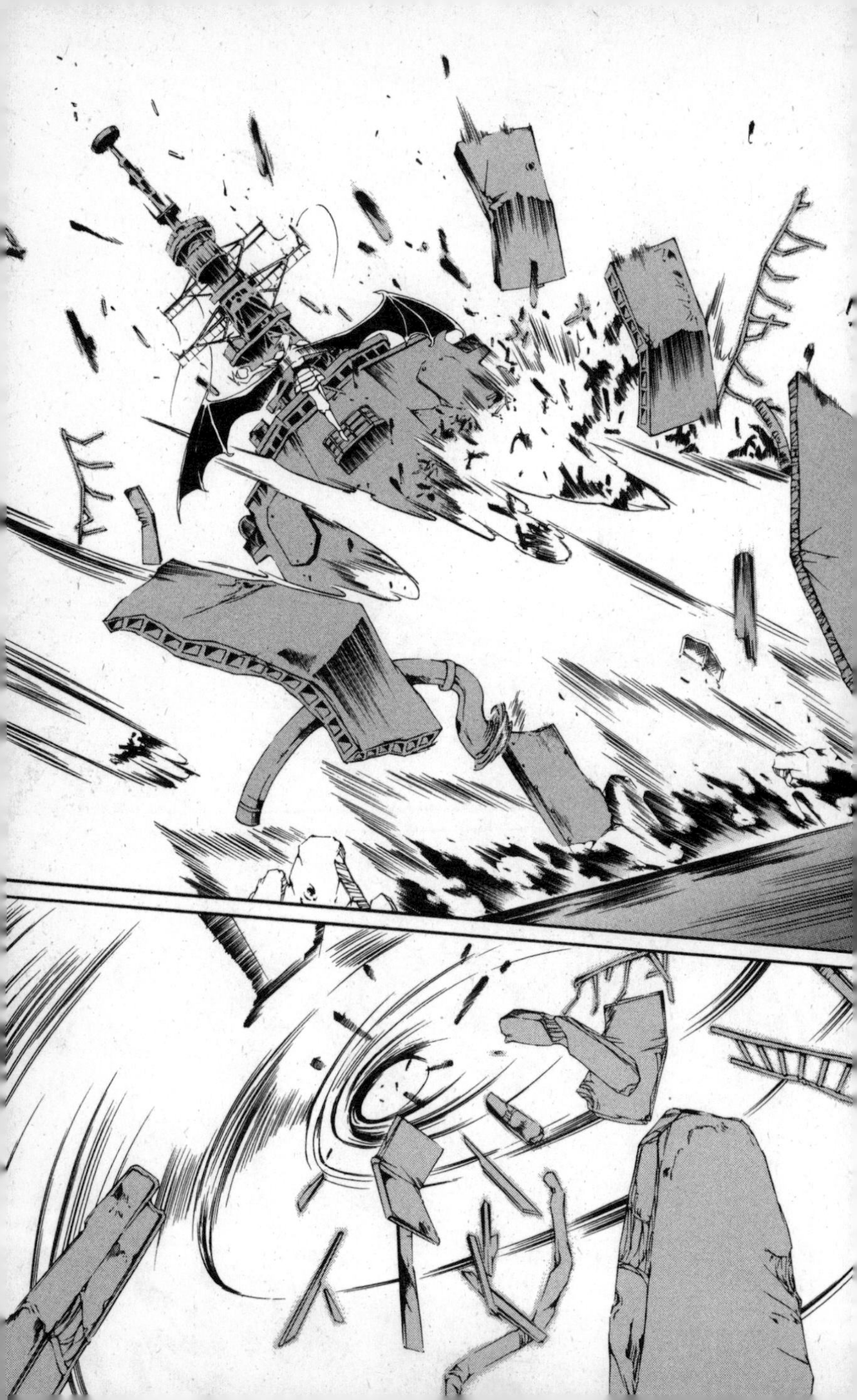

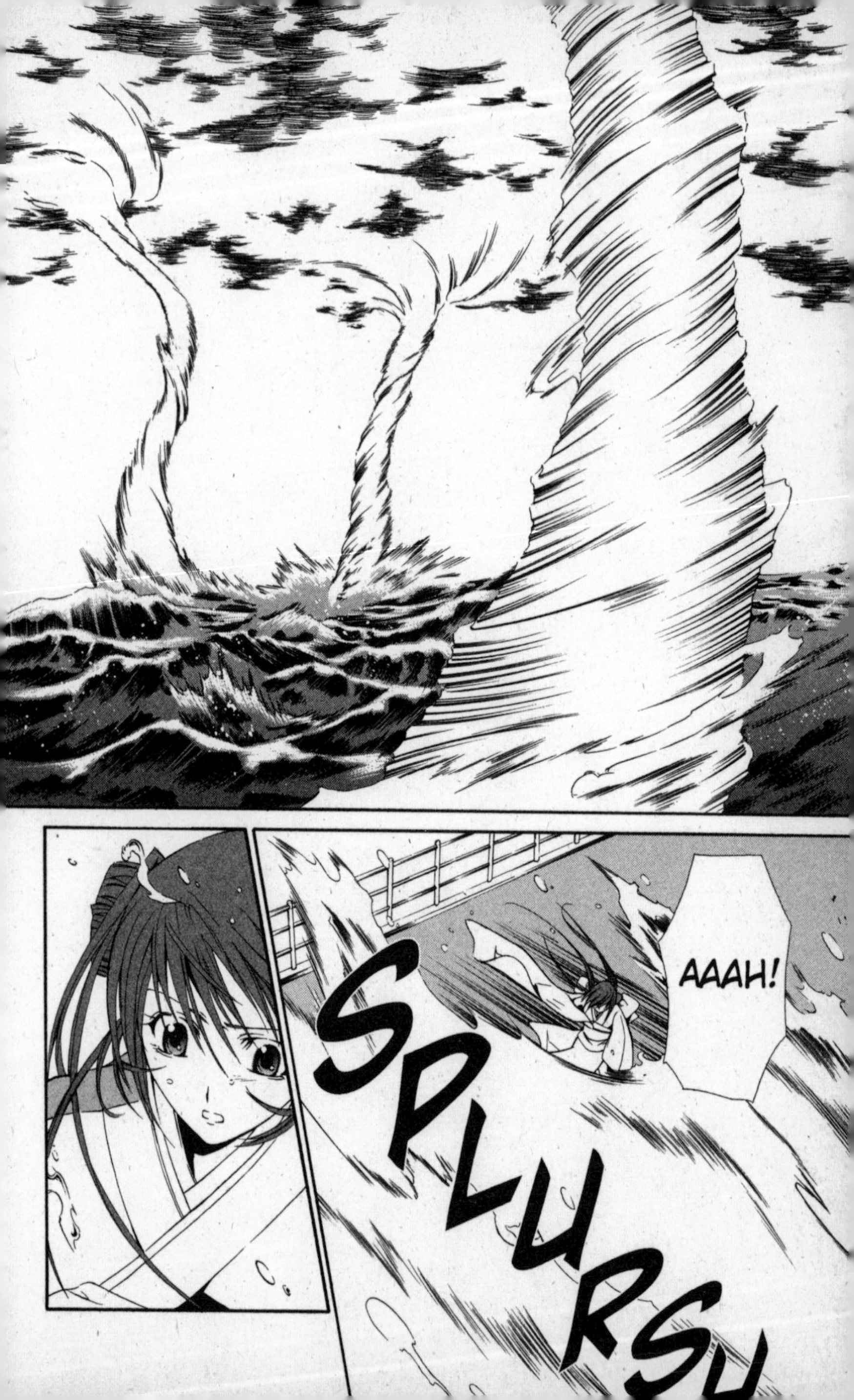
AAAH!
SPLURS

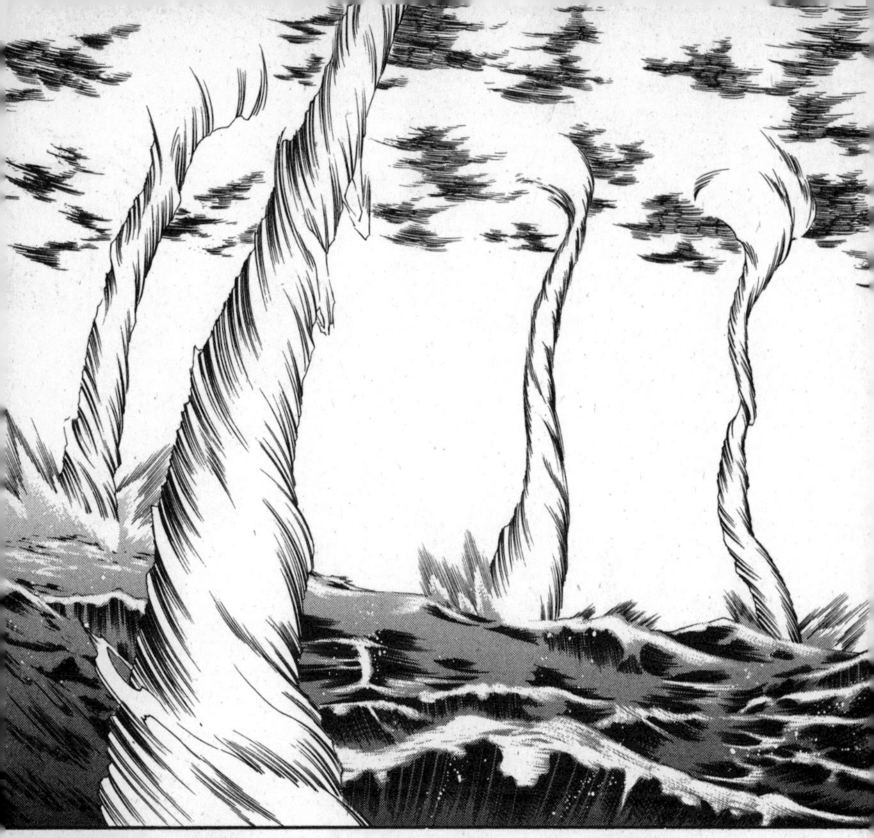

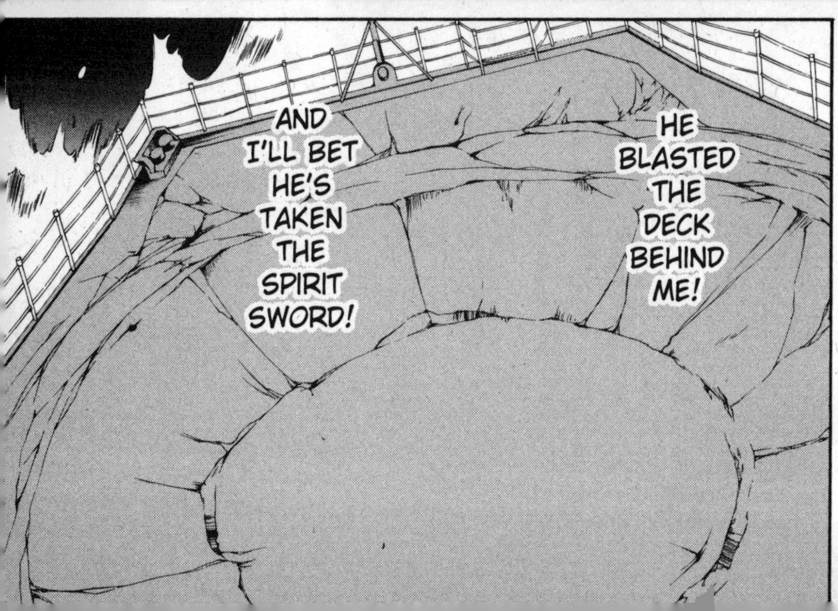
HE BLASTED THE DECK BEHIND ME!
AND I'LL BET HE'S TAKEN THE SPIRIT SWORD!

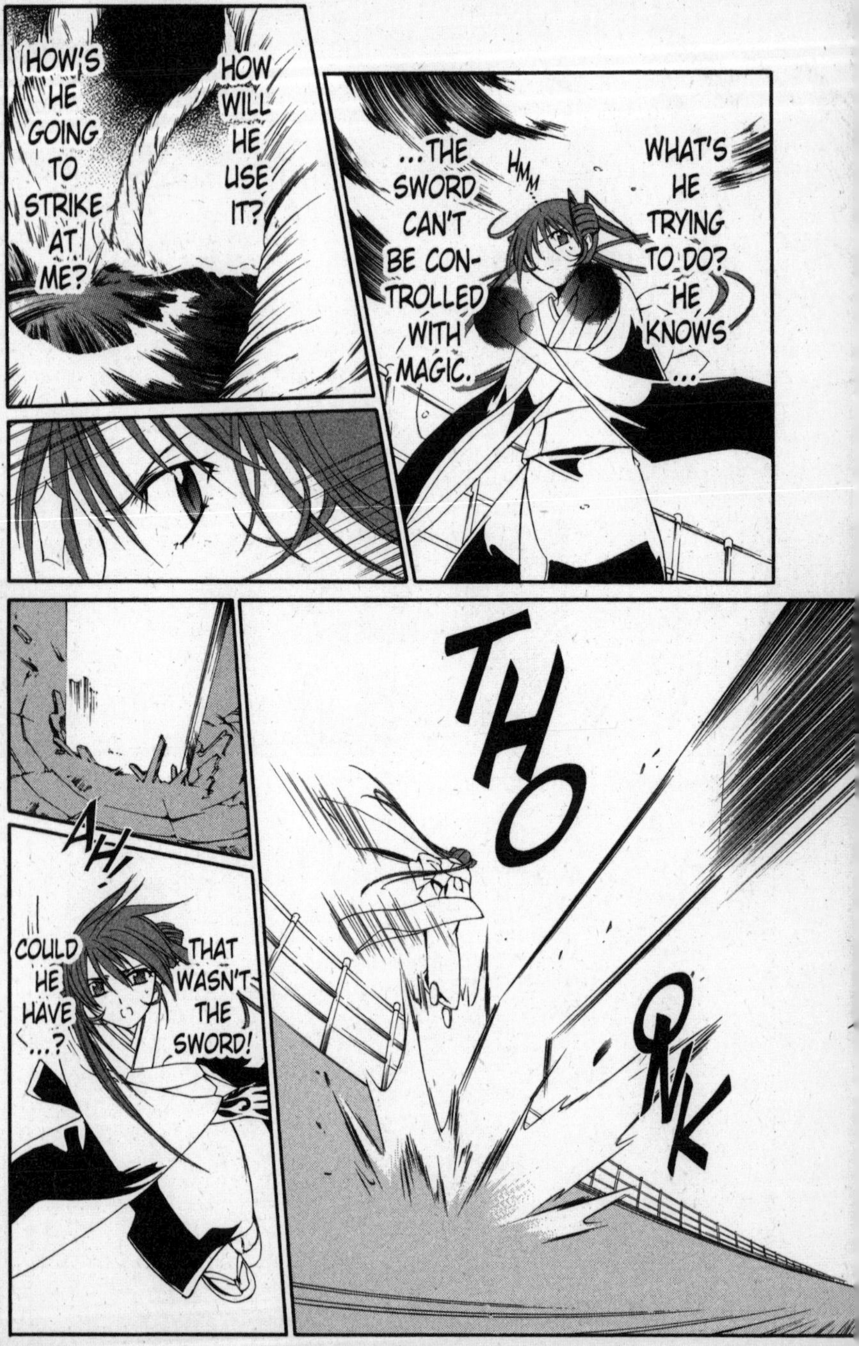
WHAT'S HE TRYING TO DO? HE KNOWS...
HMM
...THE SWORD CAN'T BE CON-TROLLED WITH MAGIC.
HOW WILL HE USE IT?
HOW'S HE GOING TO STRIKE AT ME?
THOONK
AH!
THAT WASN'T THE SWORD!
COULD HE HAVE...?

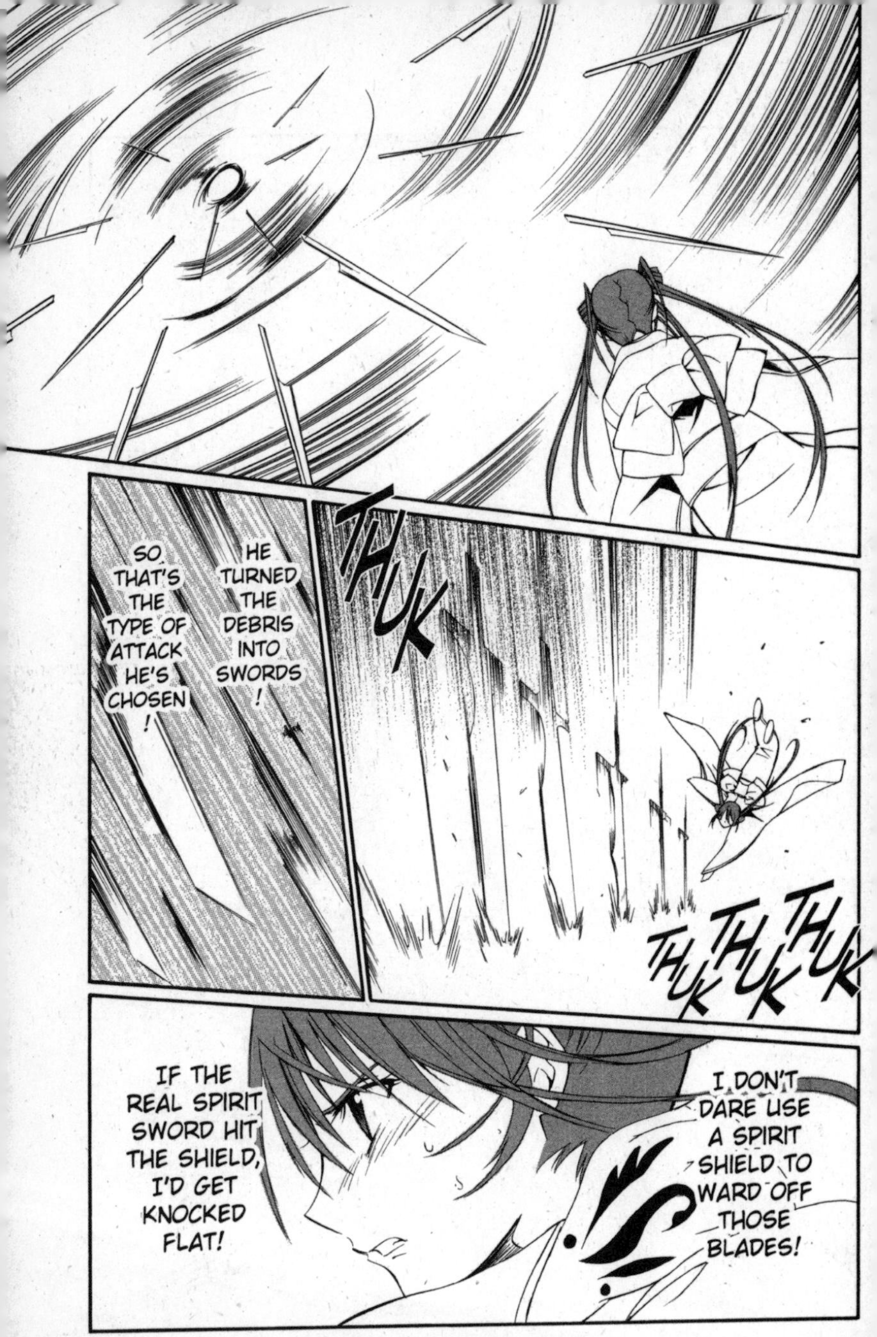
THUK
THUK THUK THUK
HE TURNED THE DEBRIS INTO SWORDS!
SO THAT'S THE TYPE OF ATTACK HE'S CHOSEN!
I DON'T DARE USE A SPIRIT SHIELD TO WARD OFF THOSE BLADES!
IF THE REAL SPIRIT SWORD HIT THE SHIELD, I'D GET KNOCKED FLAT!

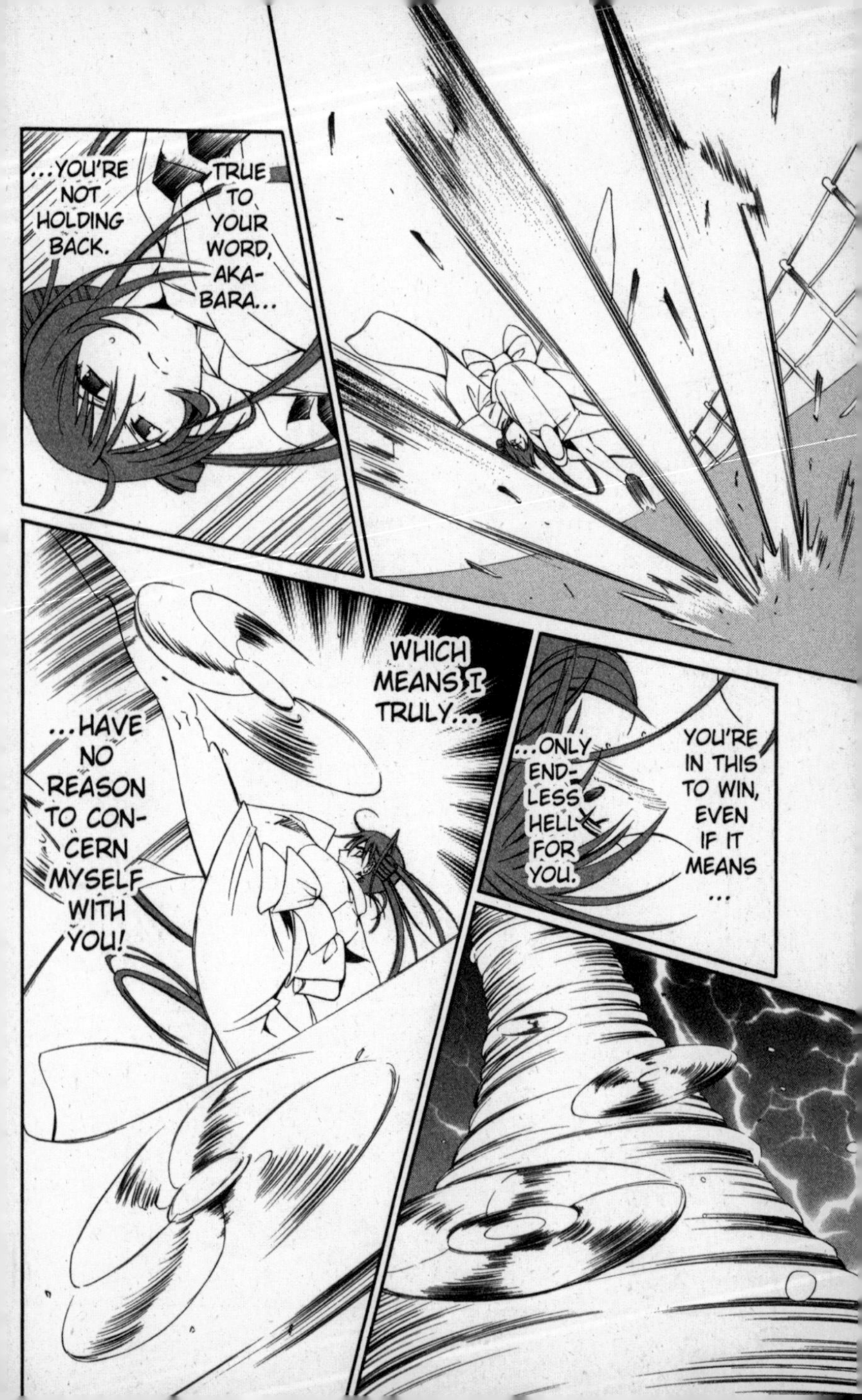
TRUE TO YOUR WORD, AKA-BARA...
...YOU'RE NOT HOLDING BACK.
YOU'RE IN THIS TO WIN, EVEN IF IT MEANS...
...ONLY END-LESS HELL FOR YOU.
WHICH MEANS I TRULY...
...HAVE NO REASON TO CON-CERN MYSELF WITH YOU!

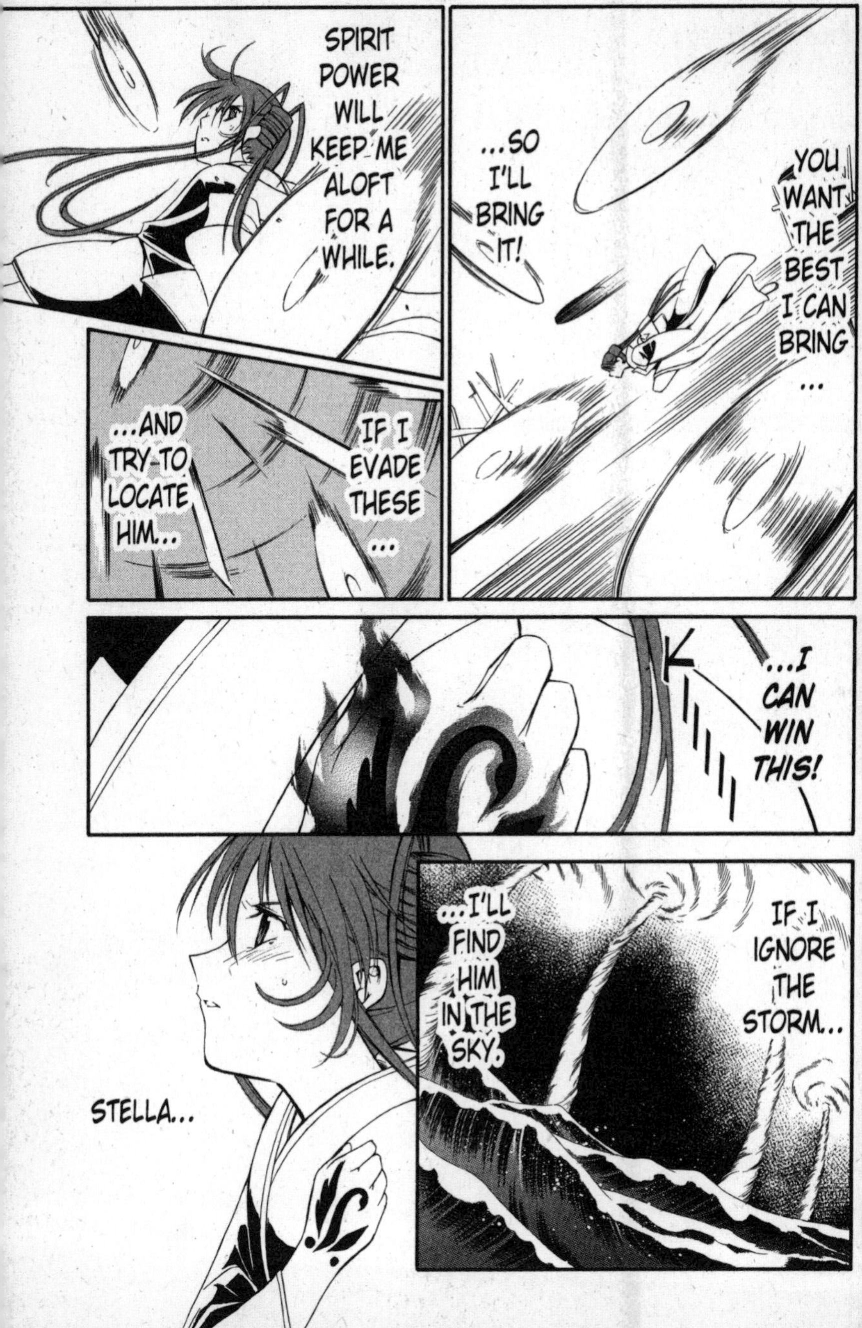
YOU WANT THE BEST I CAN BRING...
...SO I'LL BRING IT!
SPIRIT POWER WILL KEEP ME ALOFT FOR A WHILE.
IF I EVADE THESE...
...AND TRY TO LOCATE HIM...
...I CAN WIN THIS!
IF I IGNORE THE STORM...
...I'LL FIND HIM IN THE SKY.
STELLA...

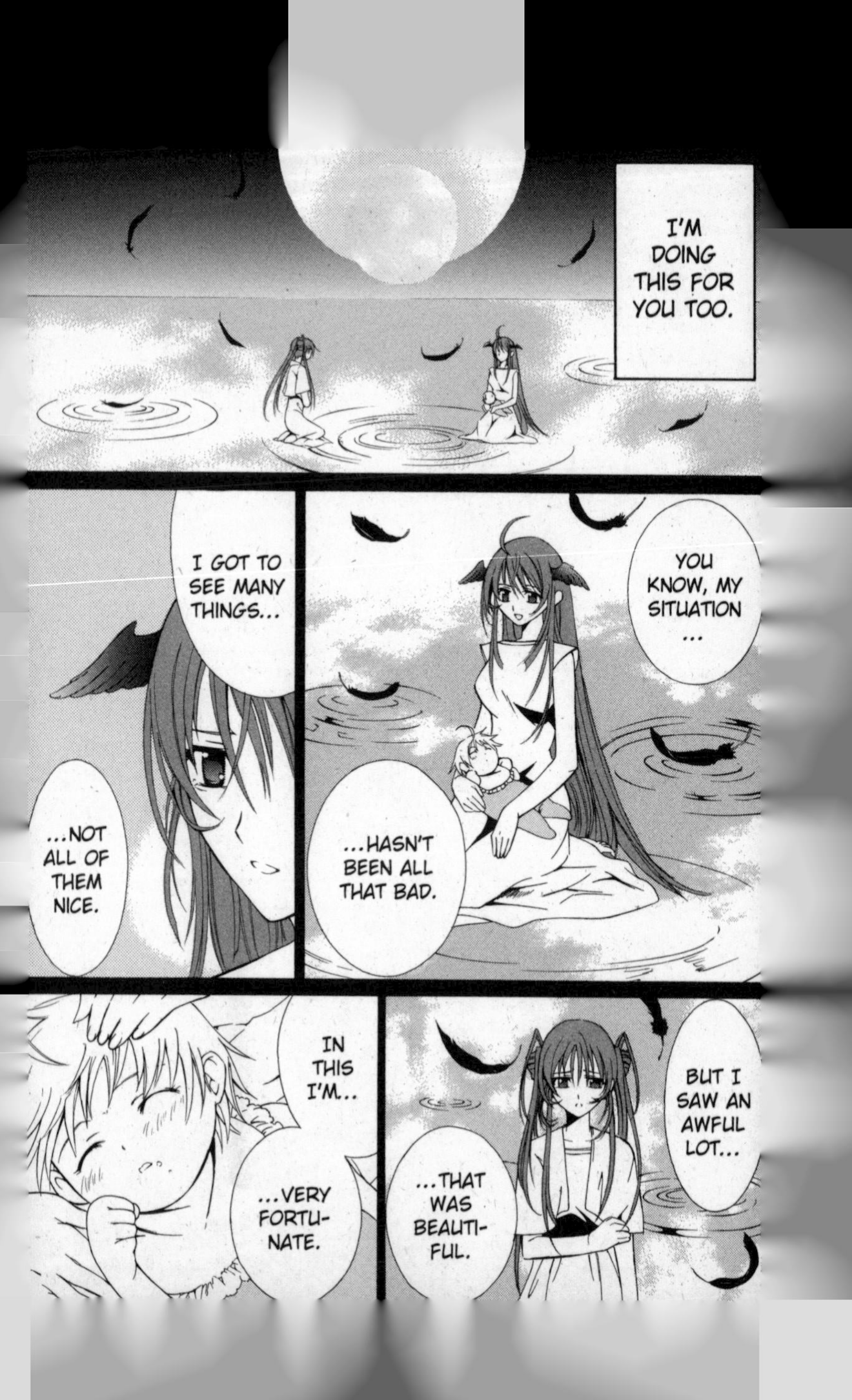
I'M DOING THIS FOR YOU TOO.
YOU KNOW, MY SITUATION ...
...HASN'T BEEN ALL THAT BAD.
I GOT TO SEE MANY THINGS...
...NOT ALL OF THEM NICE.
BUT I SAW AN AWFUL LOT...
...THAT WAS BEAUTIFUL.
IN THIS I'M...
...VERY FORTUNATE.

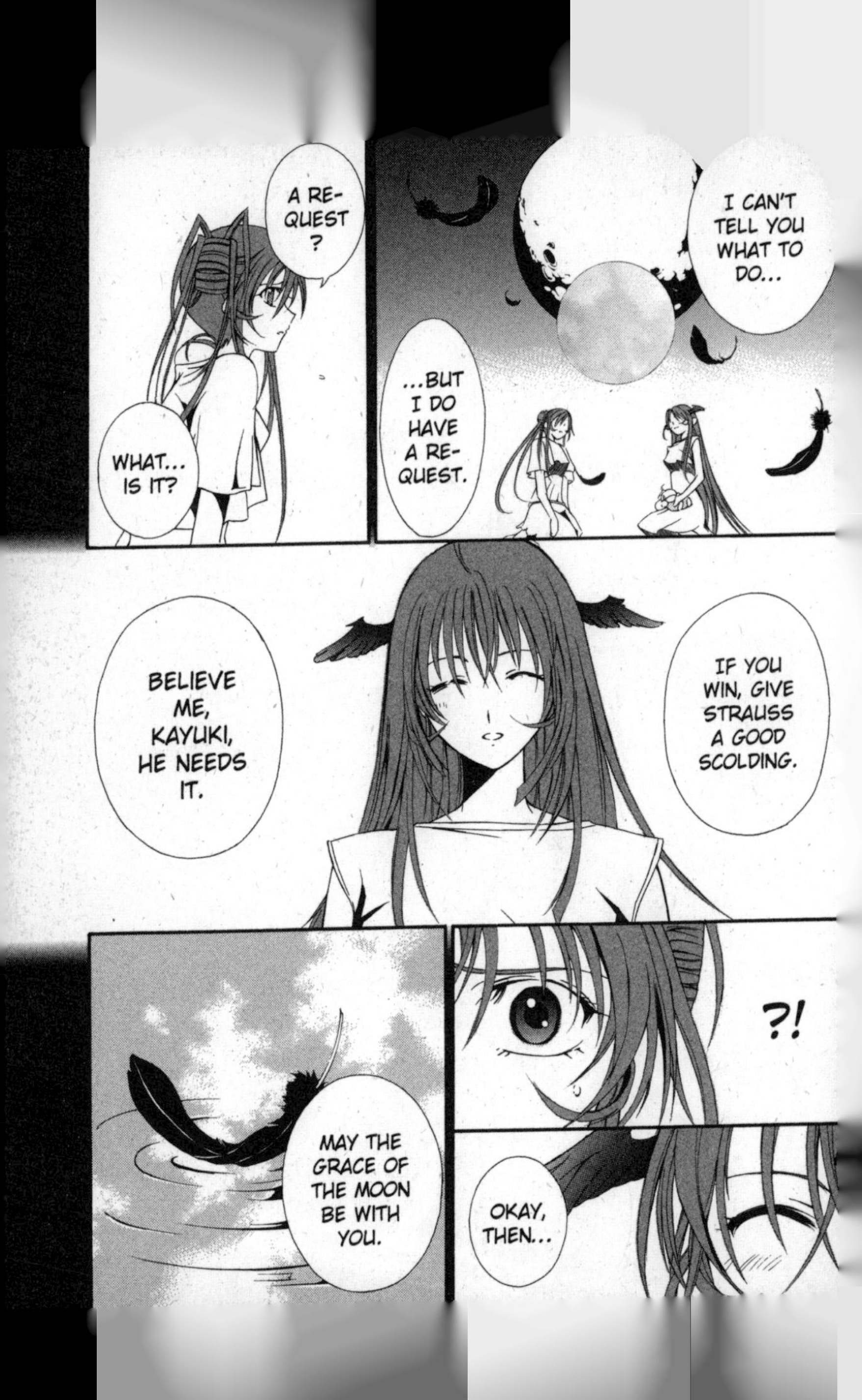
I CAN'T TELL YOU WHAT TO DO...
...BUT I DO HAVE A REQUEST.
A REQUEST?
WHAT... IS IT?
IF YOU WIN, GIVE STRAUSS A GOOD SCOLDING.
BELIEVE ME, KAYUKI, HE NEEDS IT.
?!
OKAY, THEN...
MAY THE GRACE OF THE MOON BE WITH YOU.

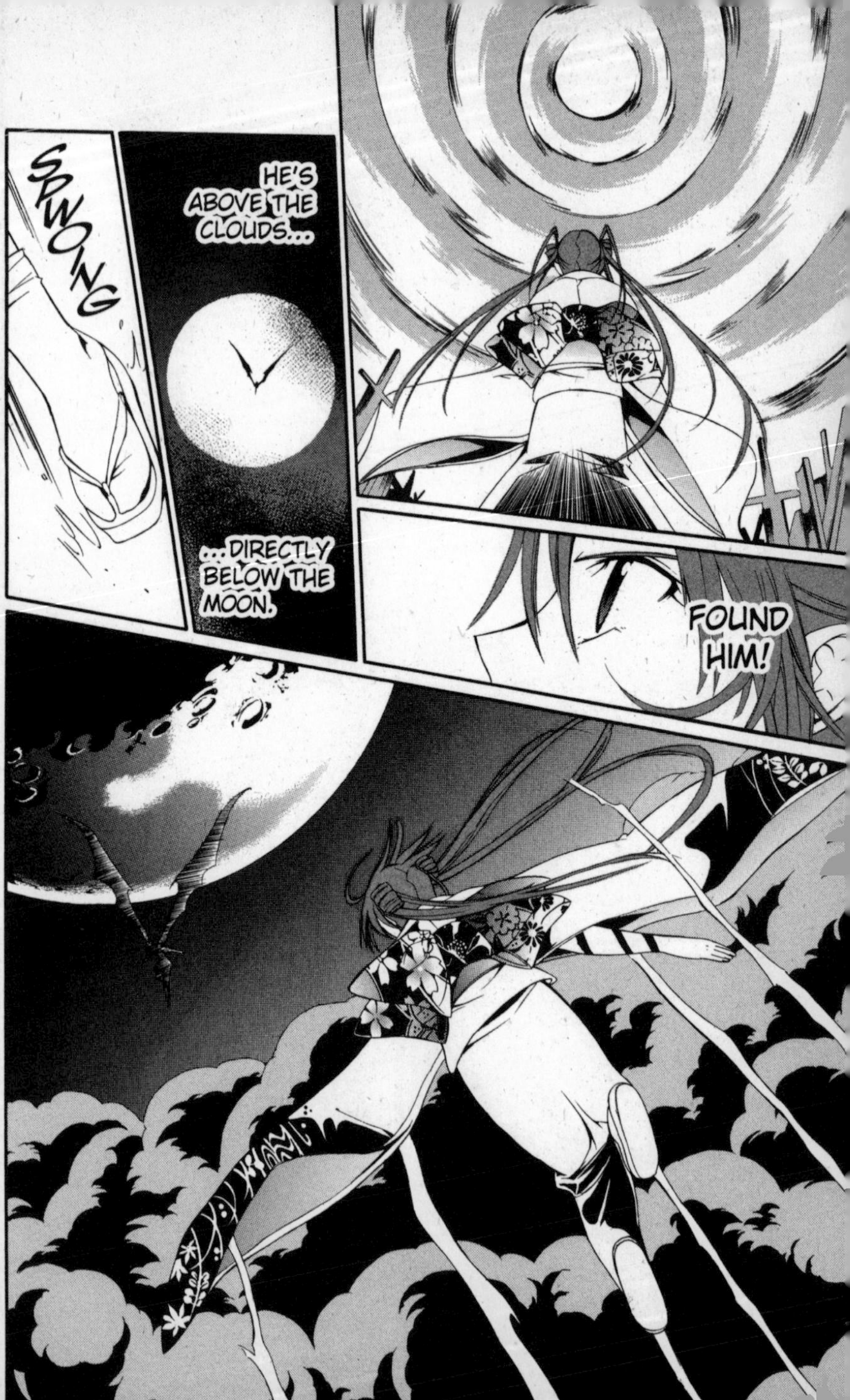
FOUND HIM!
HE'S ABOVE THE CLOUDS...
...DIRECTLY BELOW THE MOON.
SPWOING

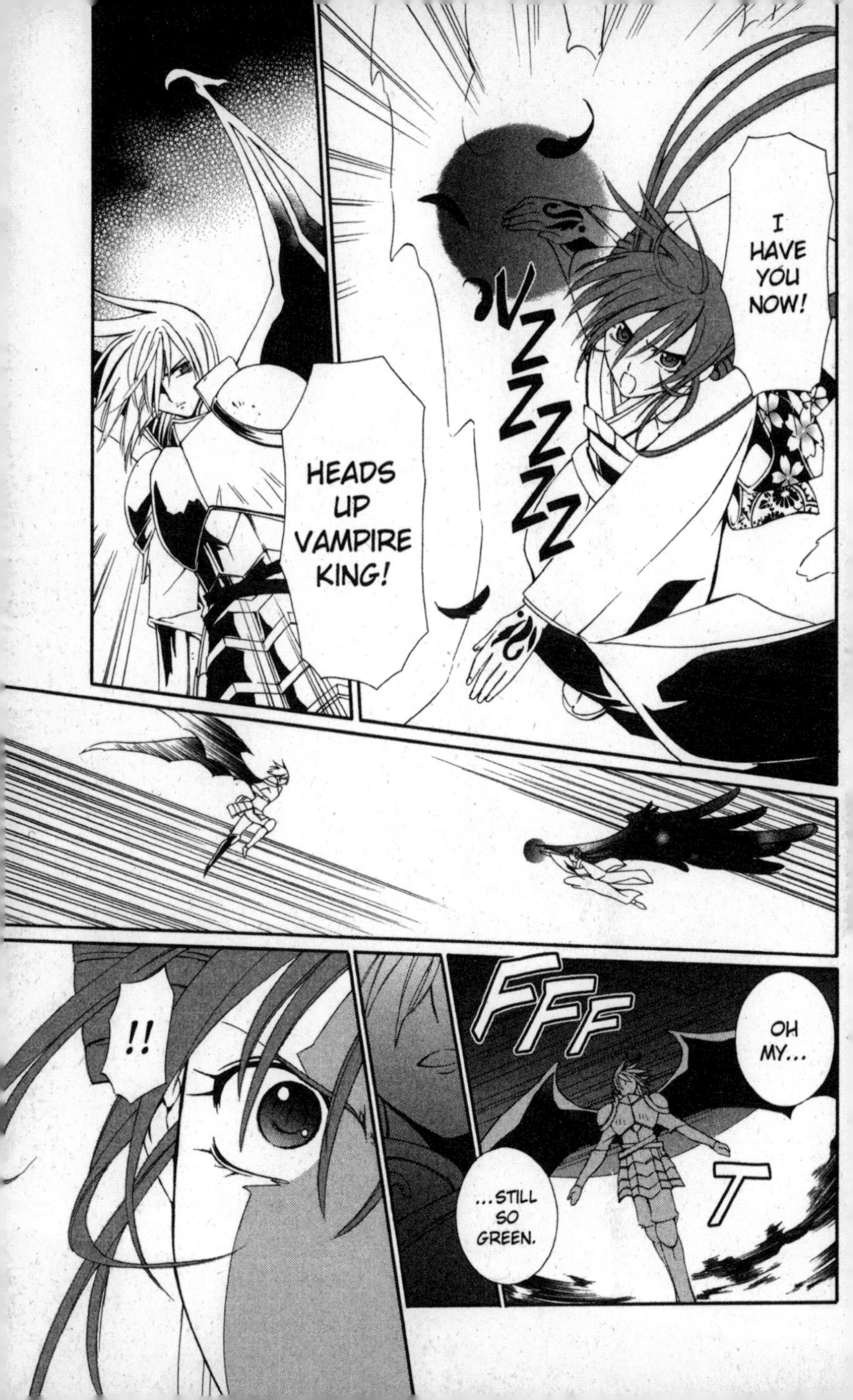
I HAVE YOU NOW!
VZZZZZ
HEADS UP VAMPIRE KING!
FFF
OH MY...
...STILL SO GREEN.
T
!!

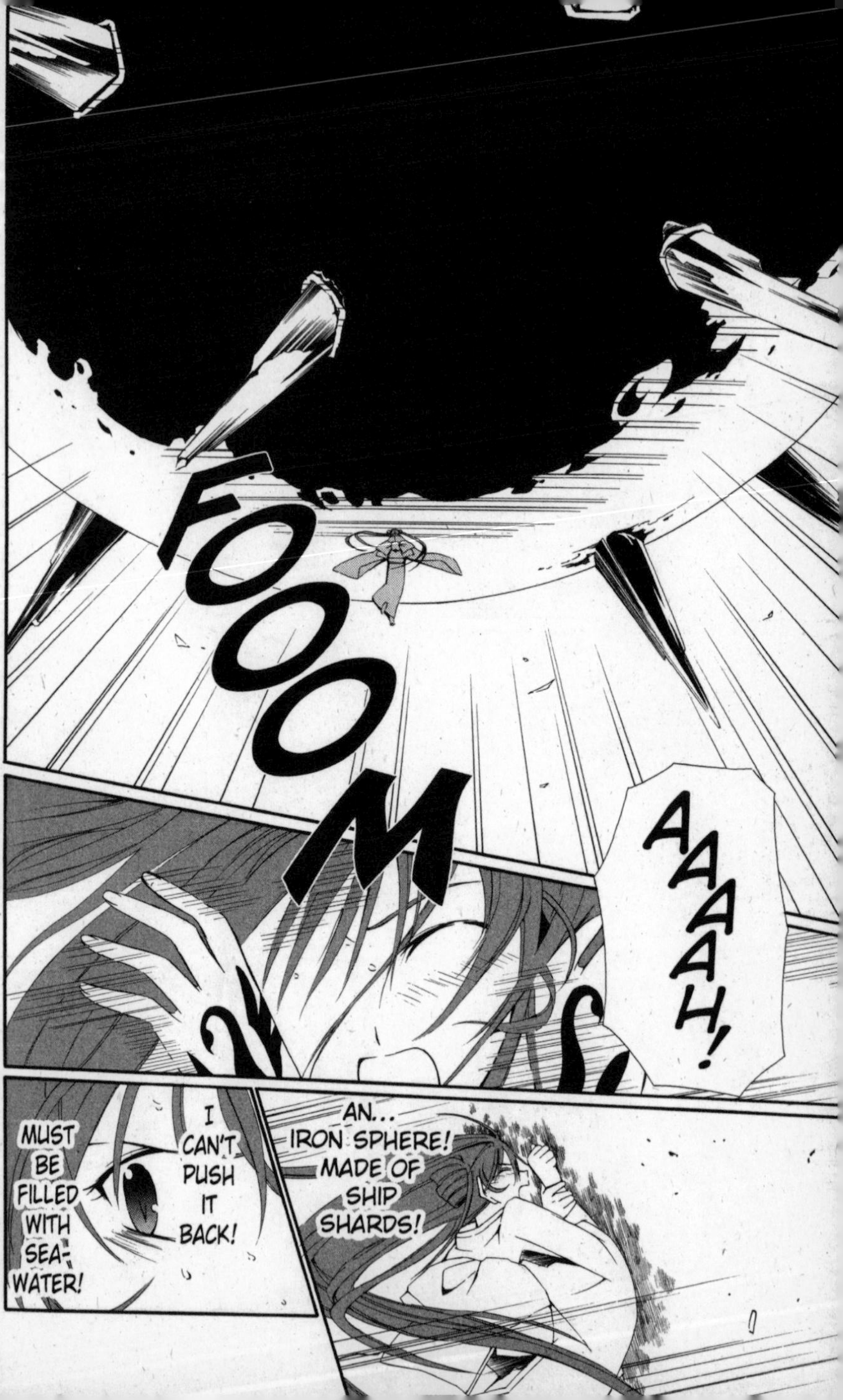
FOOOM
AAAAH!
AN... IRON SPHERE! MADE OF SHIP SHARDS!
I CAN'T PUSH IT BACK!
MUST BE FILLED WITH SEA-WATER!

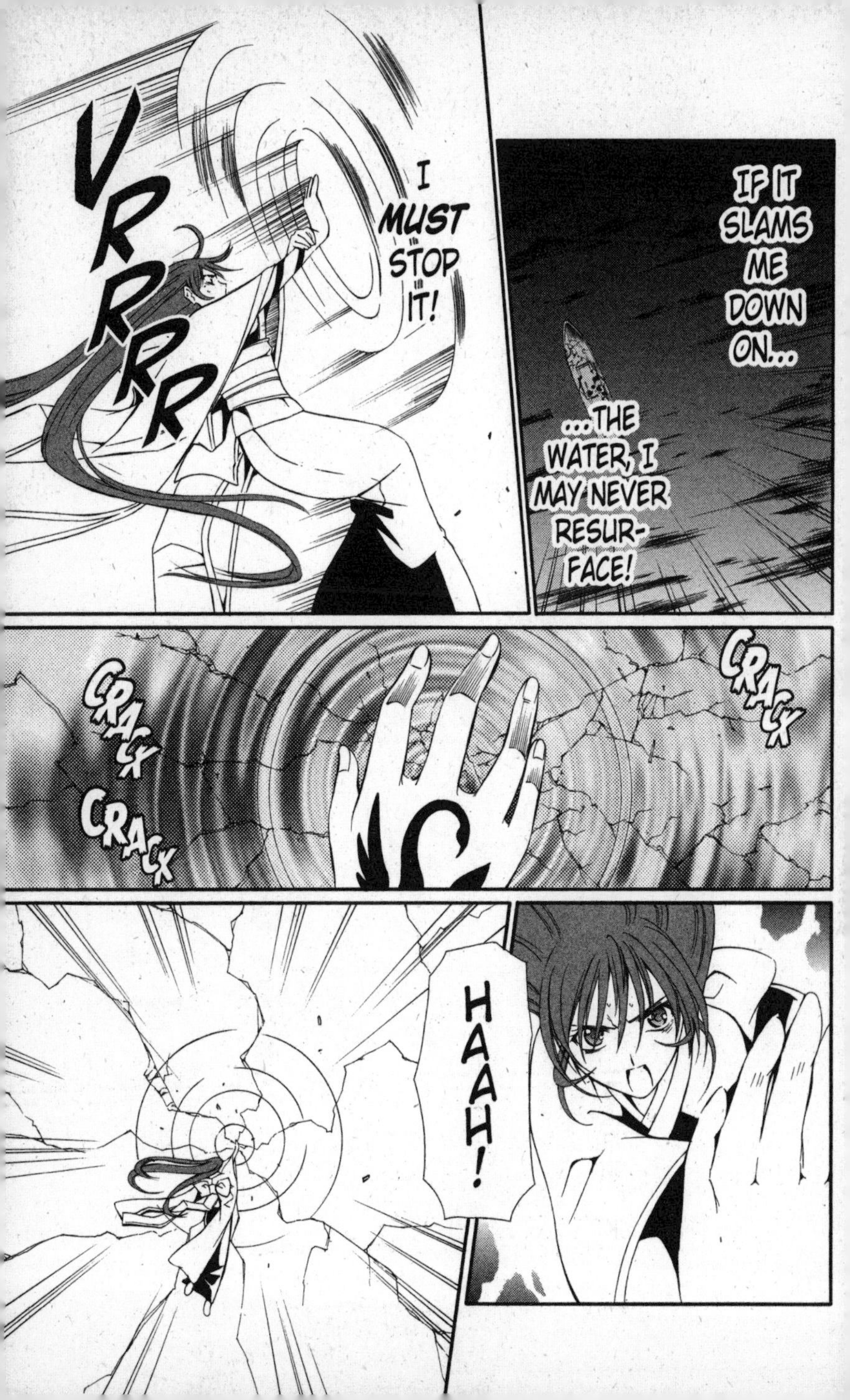
IF IT SLAMS ME DOWN ON...
...THE WATER, I MAY NEVER RESUR-FACE!
I MUST STOP IT!
VRRRRR
CRACK
CRACK
CRACK
HAAH!

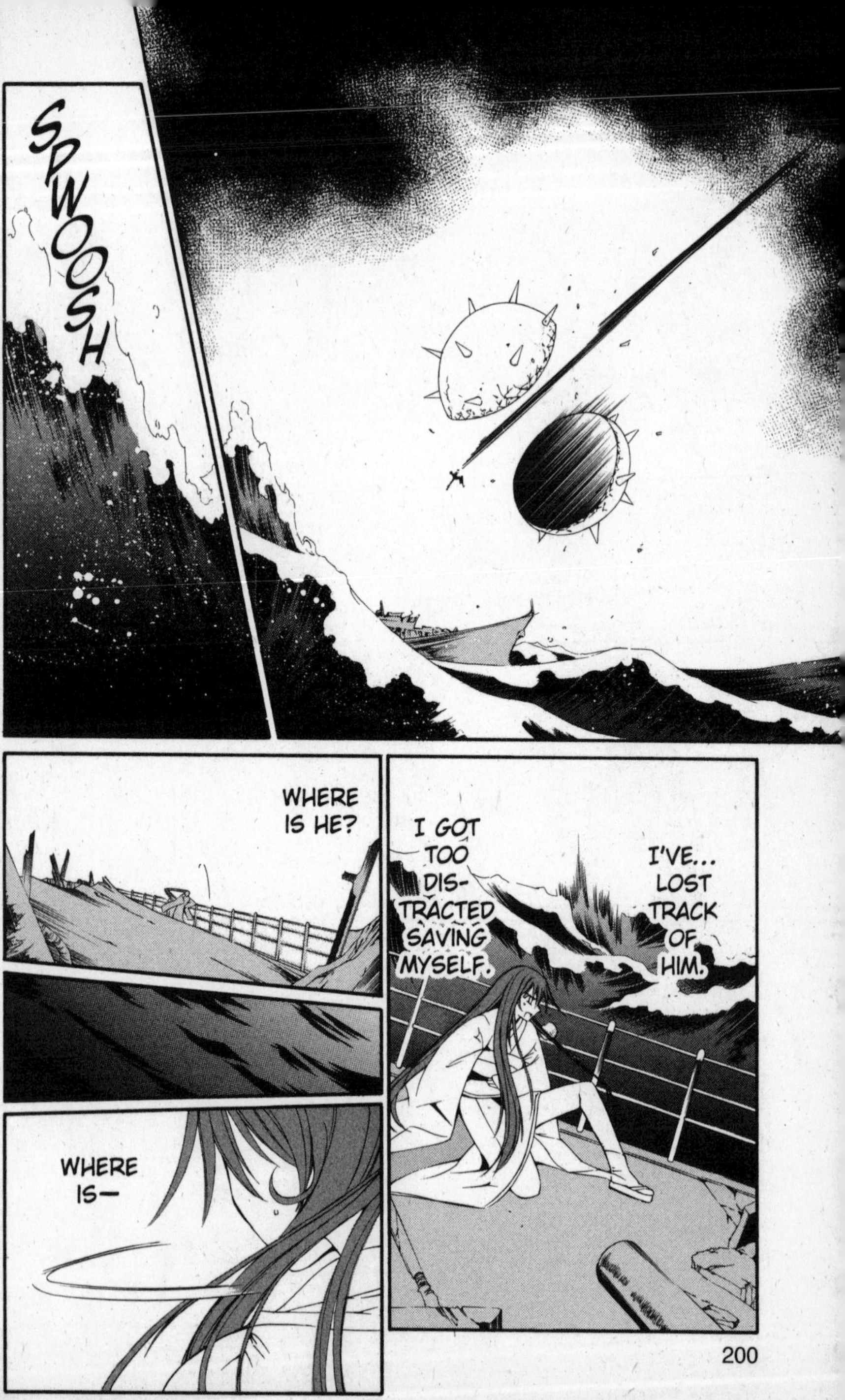
SPWOOSH
I'VE... LOST TRACK OF HIM.
I GOT TOO DIS-TRACTED SAVING MYSELF.
WHERE IS HE?
WHERE IS—

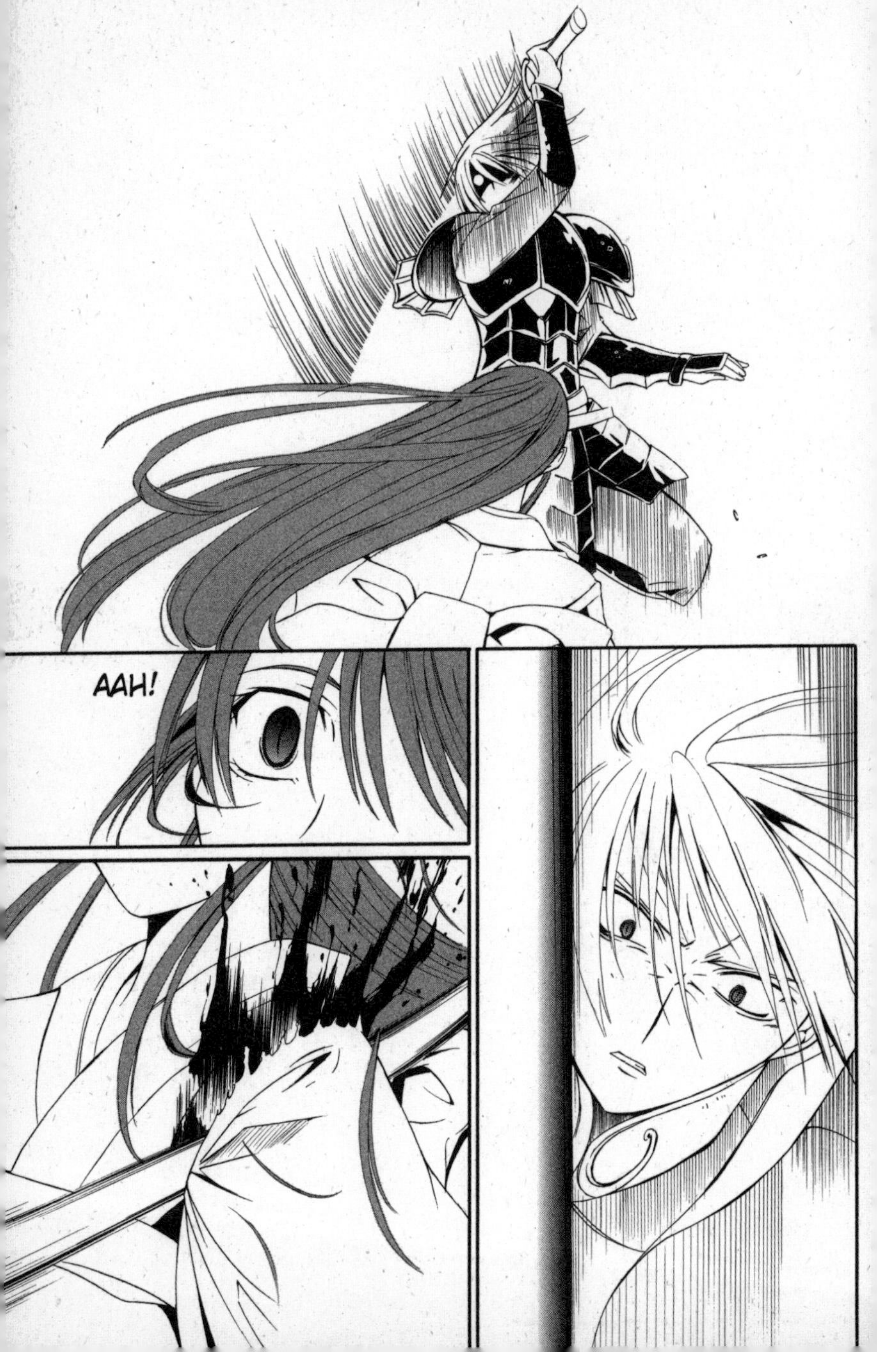
AAH!

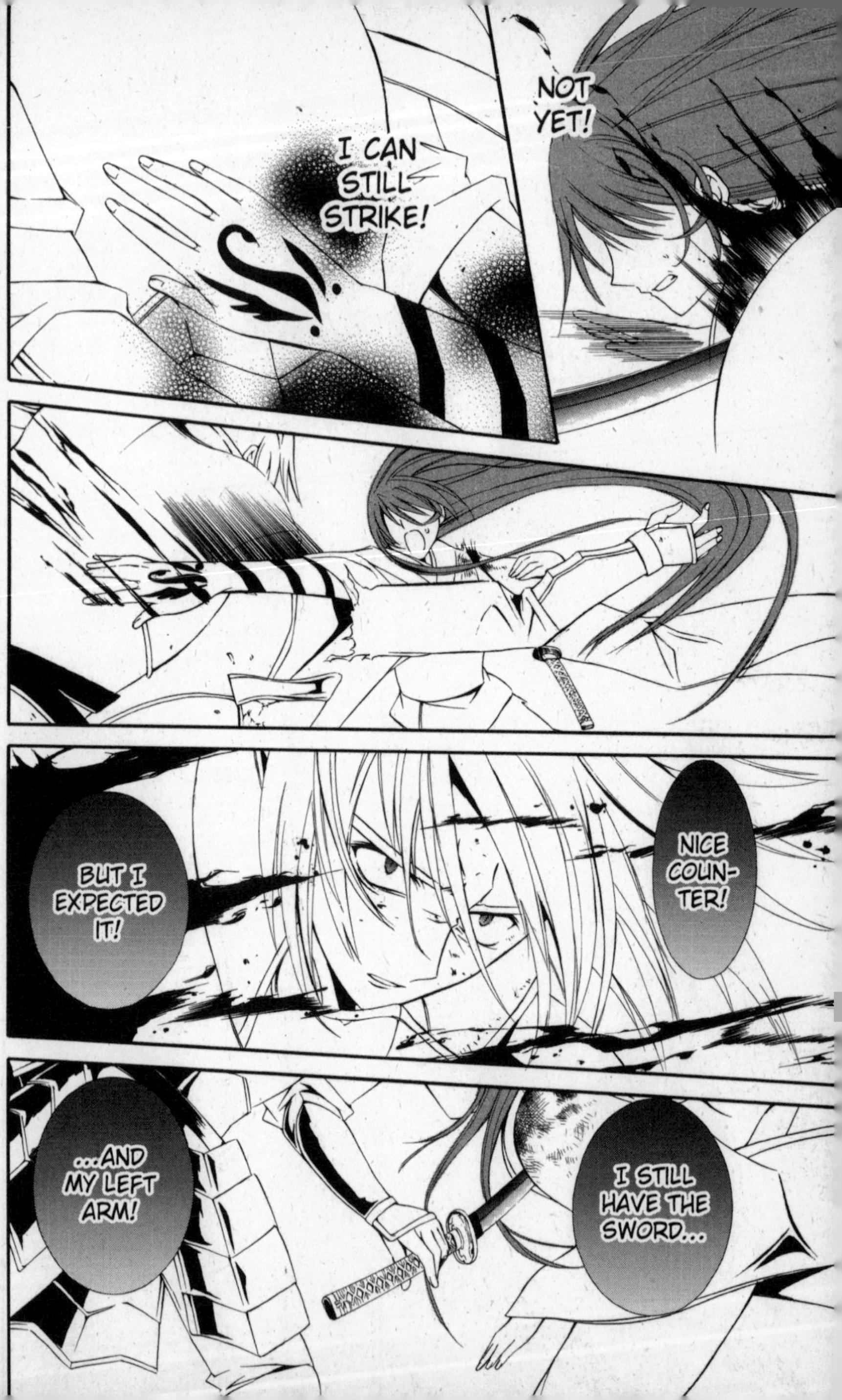
NOT YET!
I CAN STILL STRIKE!
NICE COUNTER!
BUT I EXPECTED IT!
I STILL HAVE THE SWORD...
...AND MY LEFT ARM!

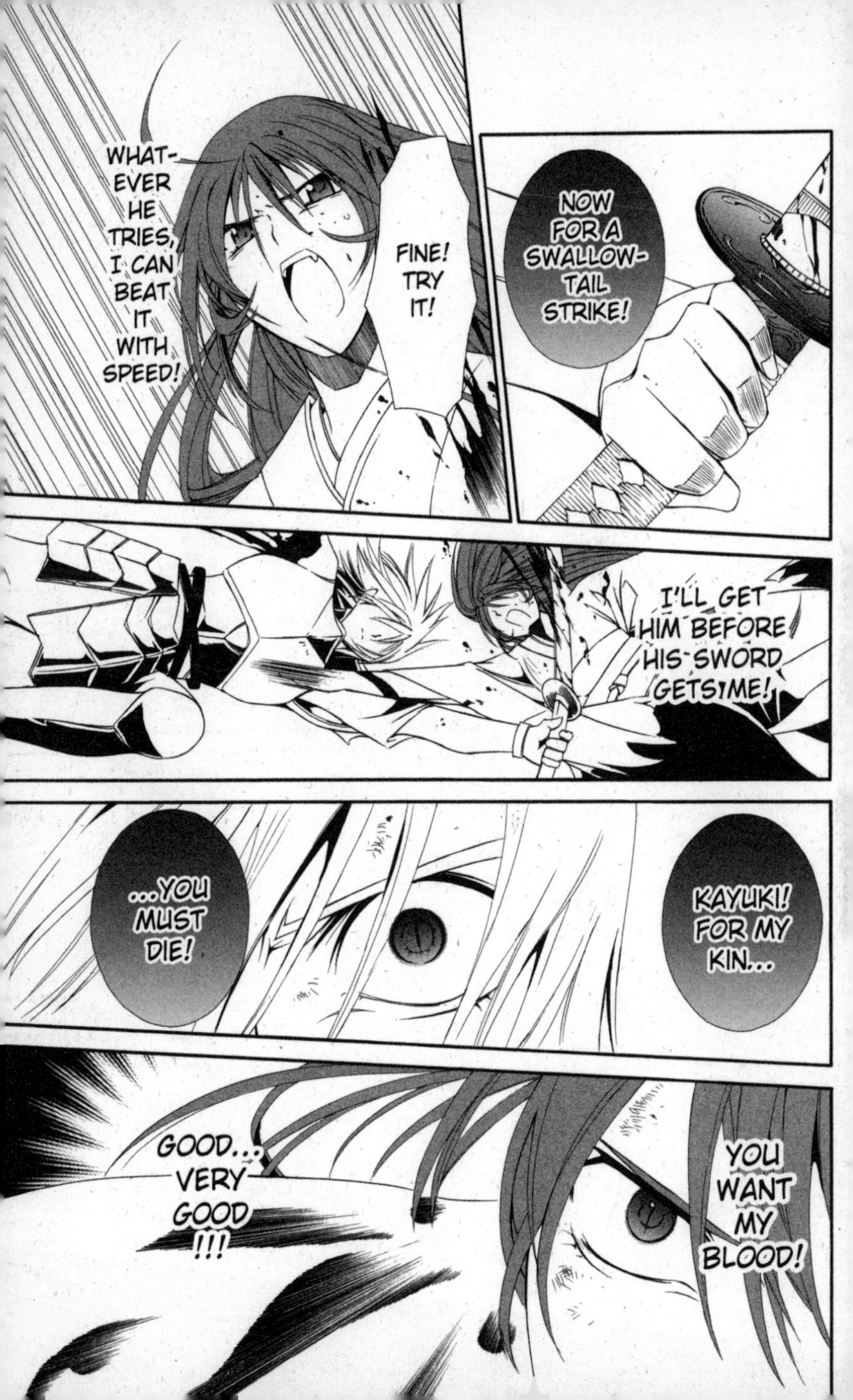
NOW FOR A SWALLOW-TAIL STRIKE!
FINE! TRY IT!
WHAT-EVER HE TRIES, I CAN BEAT IT WITH SPEED!
I'LL GET HIM BEFORE HIS SWORD GETS ME!
KAYUKI! FOR MY KIN...
...YOU MUST DIE!
YOU WANT MY BLOOD!
GOOD... VERY GOOD!!!

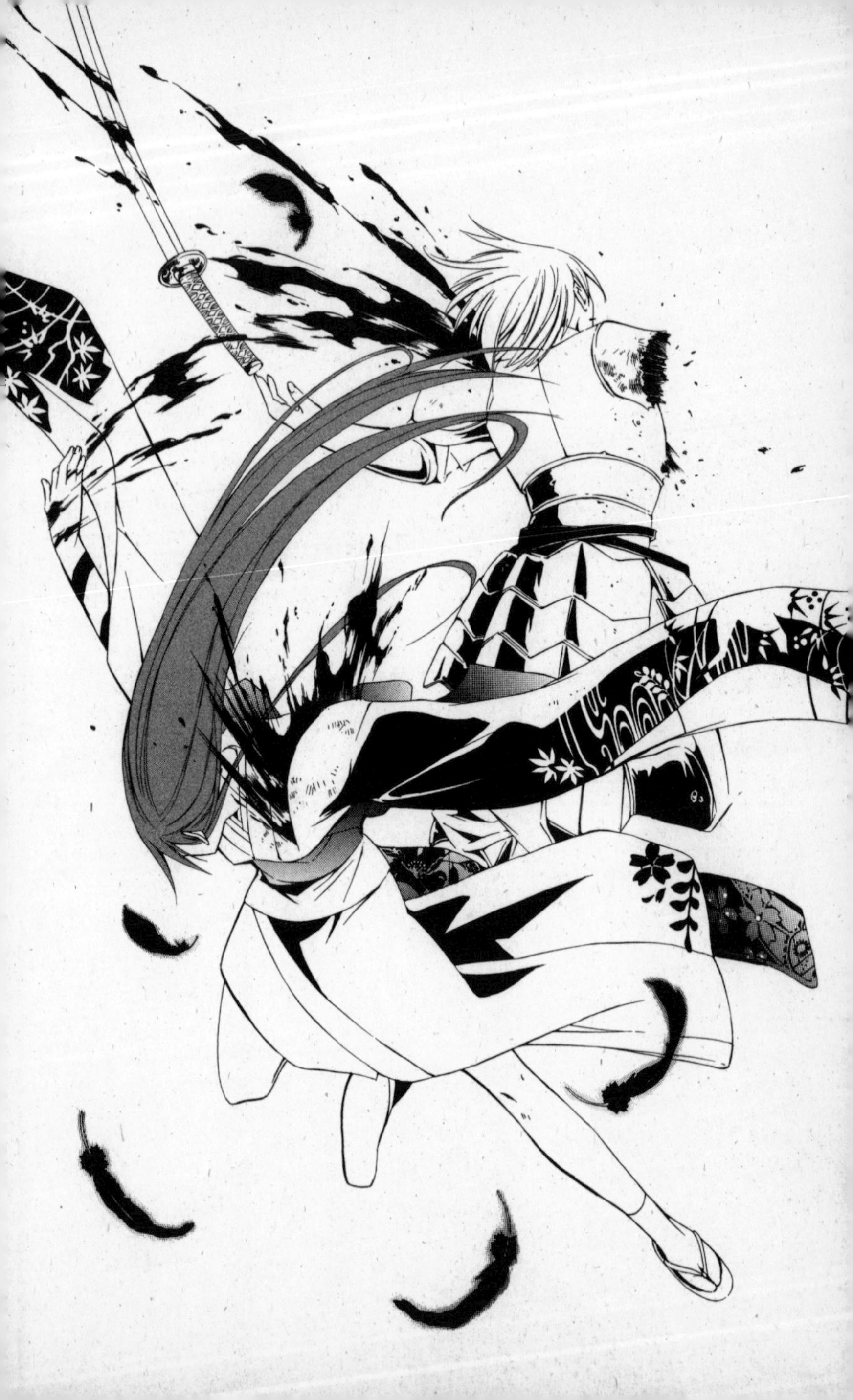

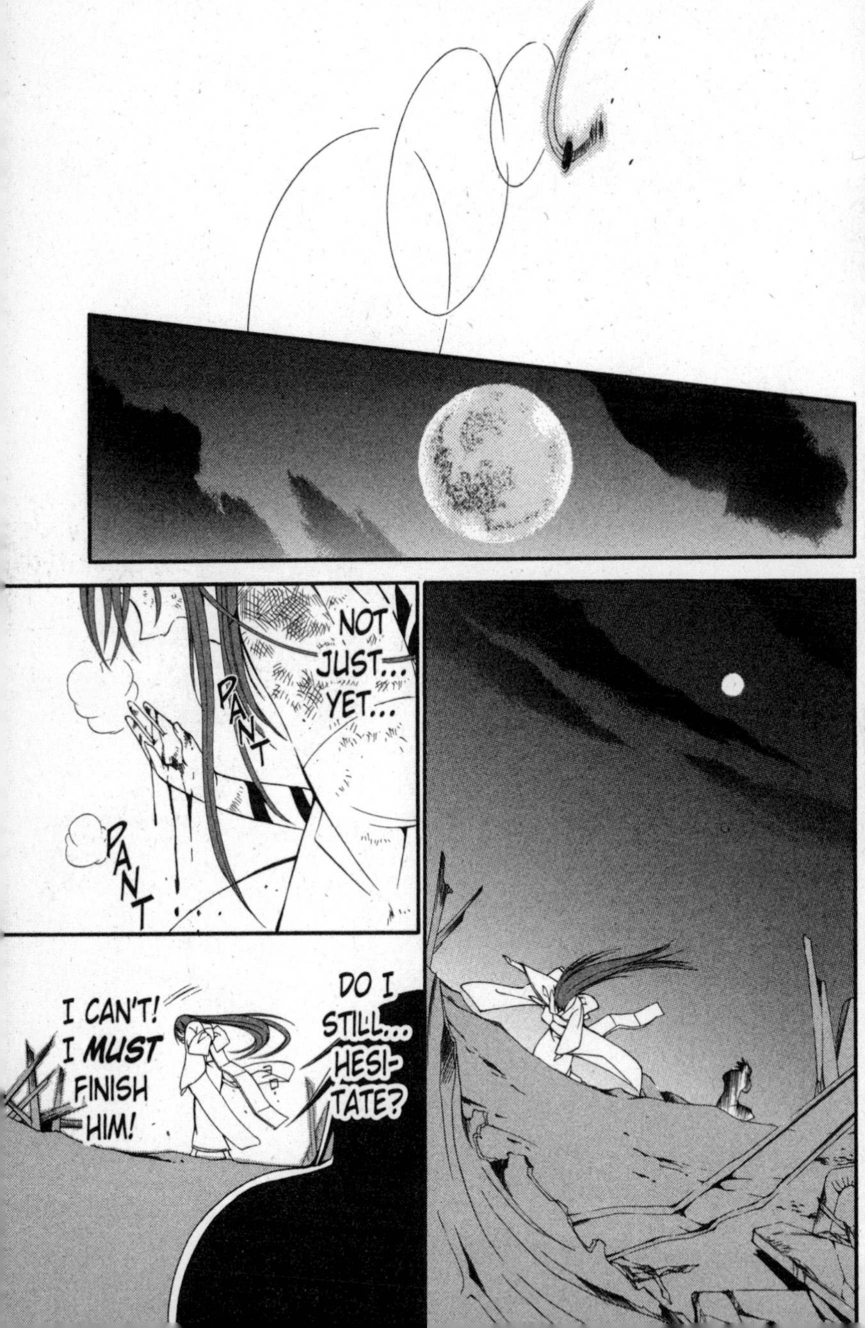
NOT JUST... YET...
PANT
PANT
DO I STILL... HESI-TATE?
I CAN'T! I MUST FINISH HIM!

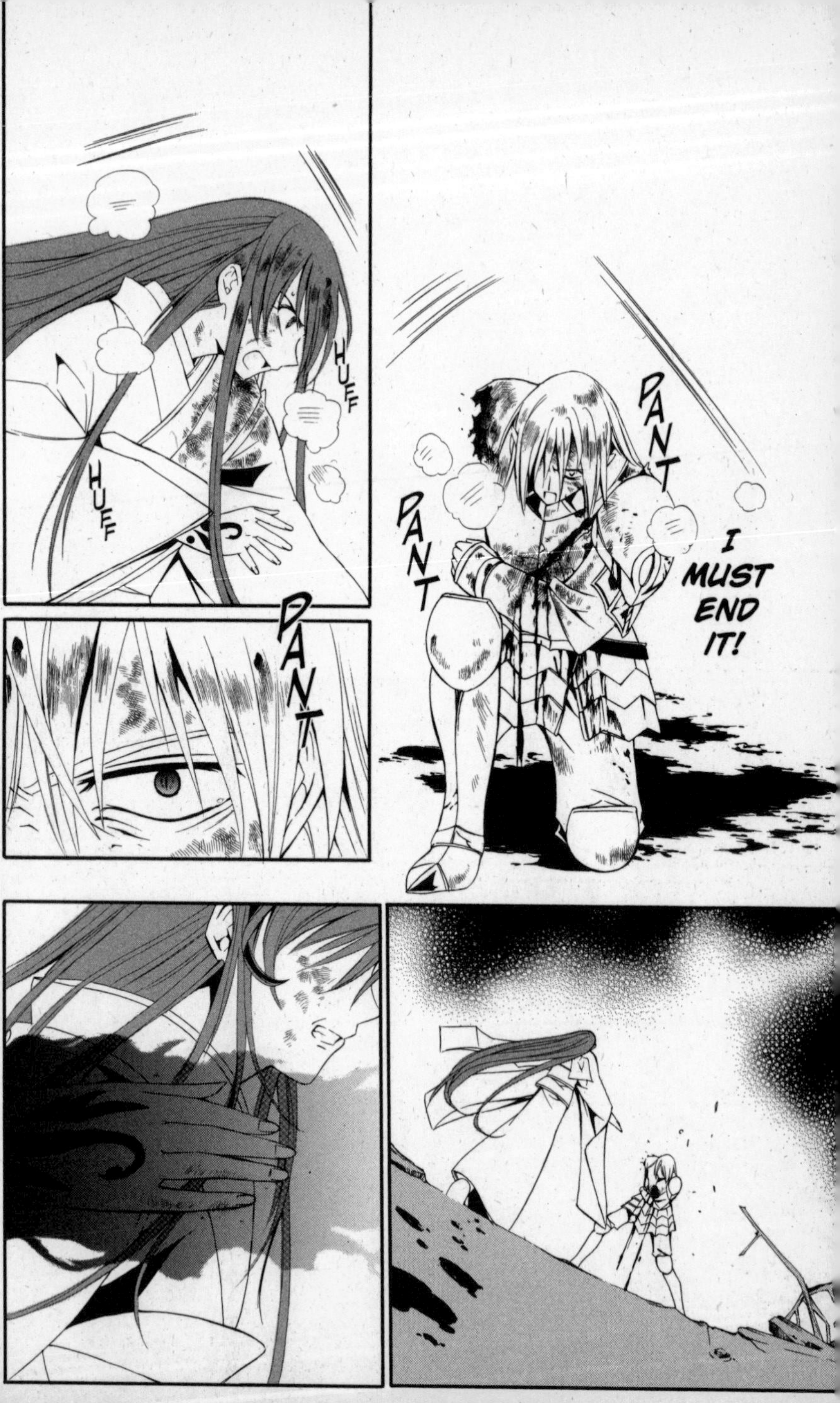
PANT
I MUST END IT!
PANT
HUFF
HUFF
PANT

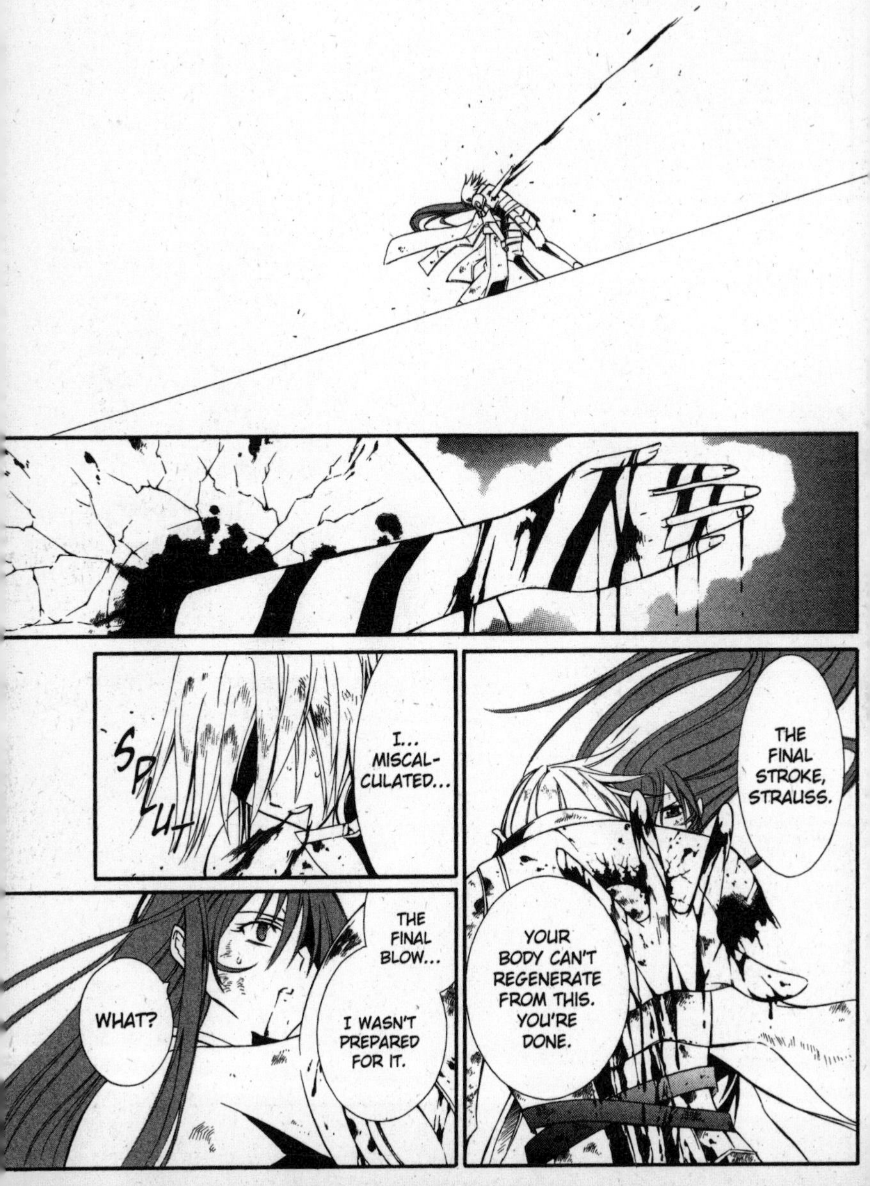
THE FINAL STROKE, STRAUSS.
YOUR BODY CAN'T REGENERATE FROM THIS. YOU'RE DONE.
SPLUT
I... MISCAL-CULATED...
THE FINAL BLOW...
I WASN'T PREPARED FOR IT.
WHAT?

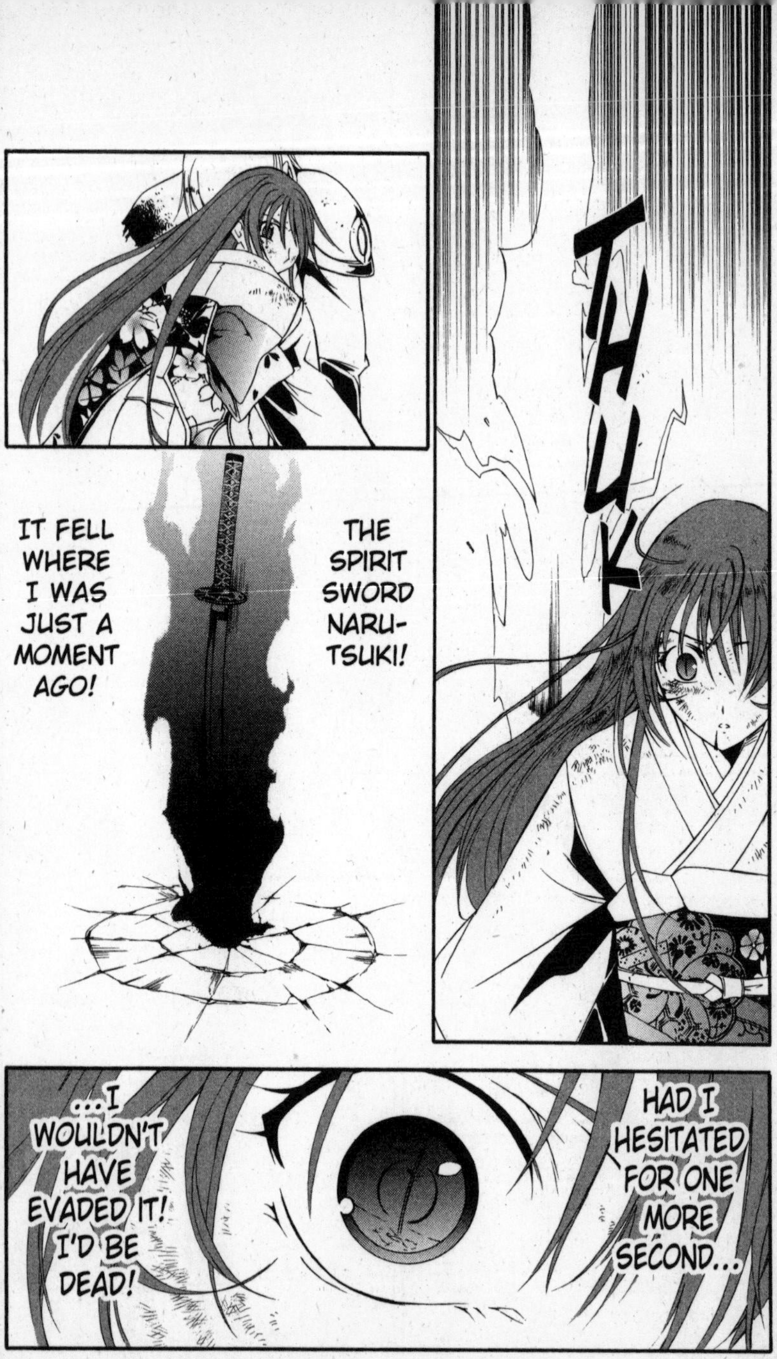
THUK
THE SPIRIT SWORD NARU-TSUKI!
IT FELL WHERE I WAS JUST A MOMENT AGO!
HAD I HESITATED FOR ONE MORE SECOND...
...I WOULDN'T HAVE EVADED IT! I'D BE DEAD!

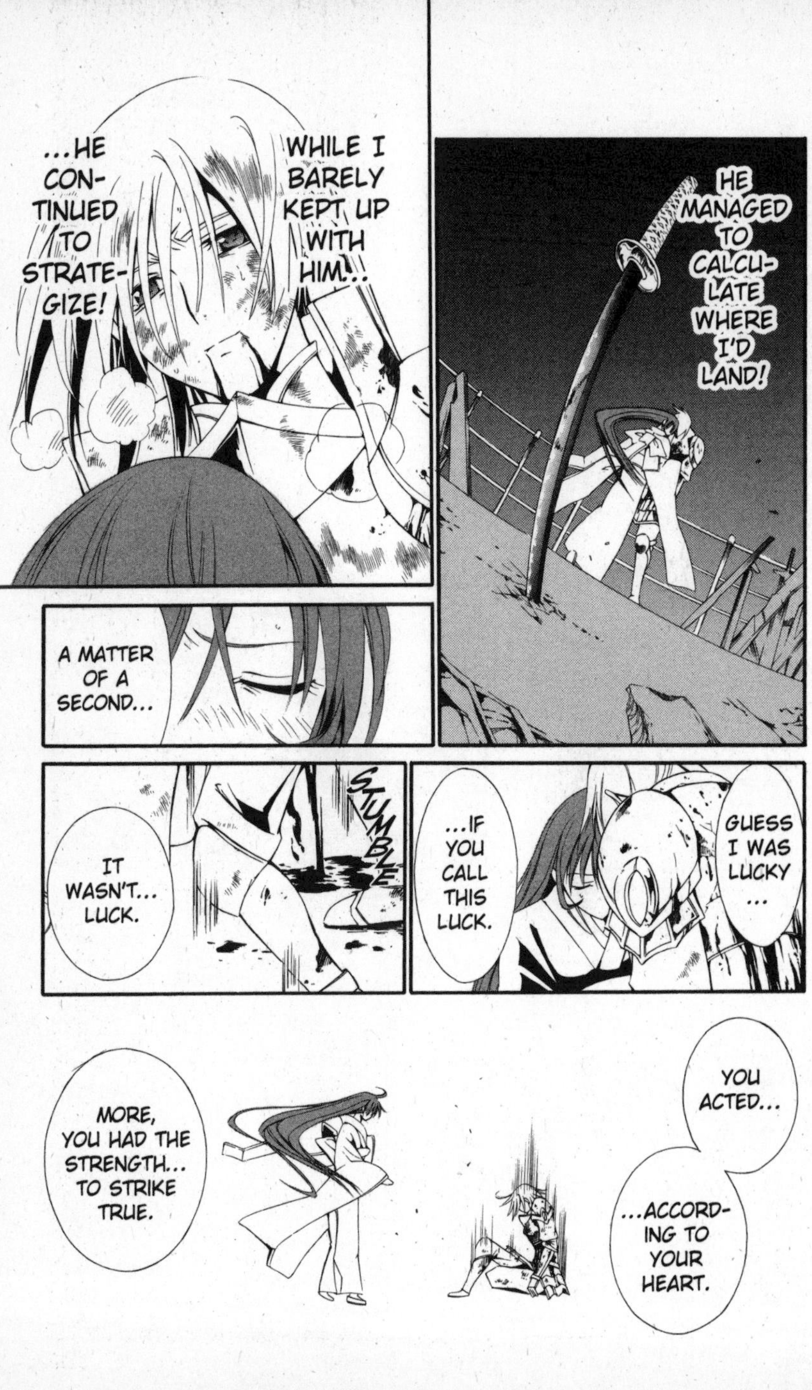
HE MANAGED TO CALCULATE WHERE I'D LAND!
WHILE I BARELY KEPT UP WITH HIM...
...HE CONTINUED TO STRATEGIZE!
A MATTER OF A SECOND...
GUESS I WAS LUCKY...
...IF YOU CALL THIS LUCK.
STUMBLE
IT WASN'T... LUCK.
YOU ACTED...
...ACCORDING TO YOUR HEART.
MORE, YOU HAD THE STRENGTH... TO STRIKE TRUE.

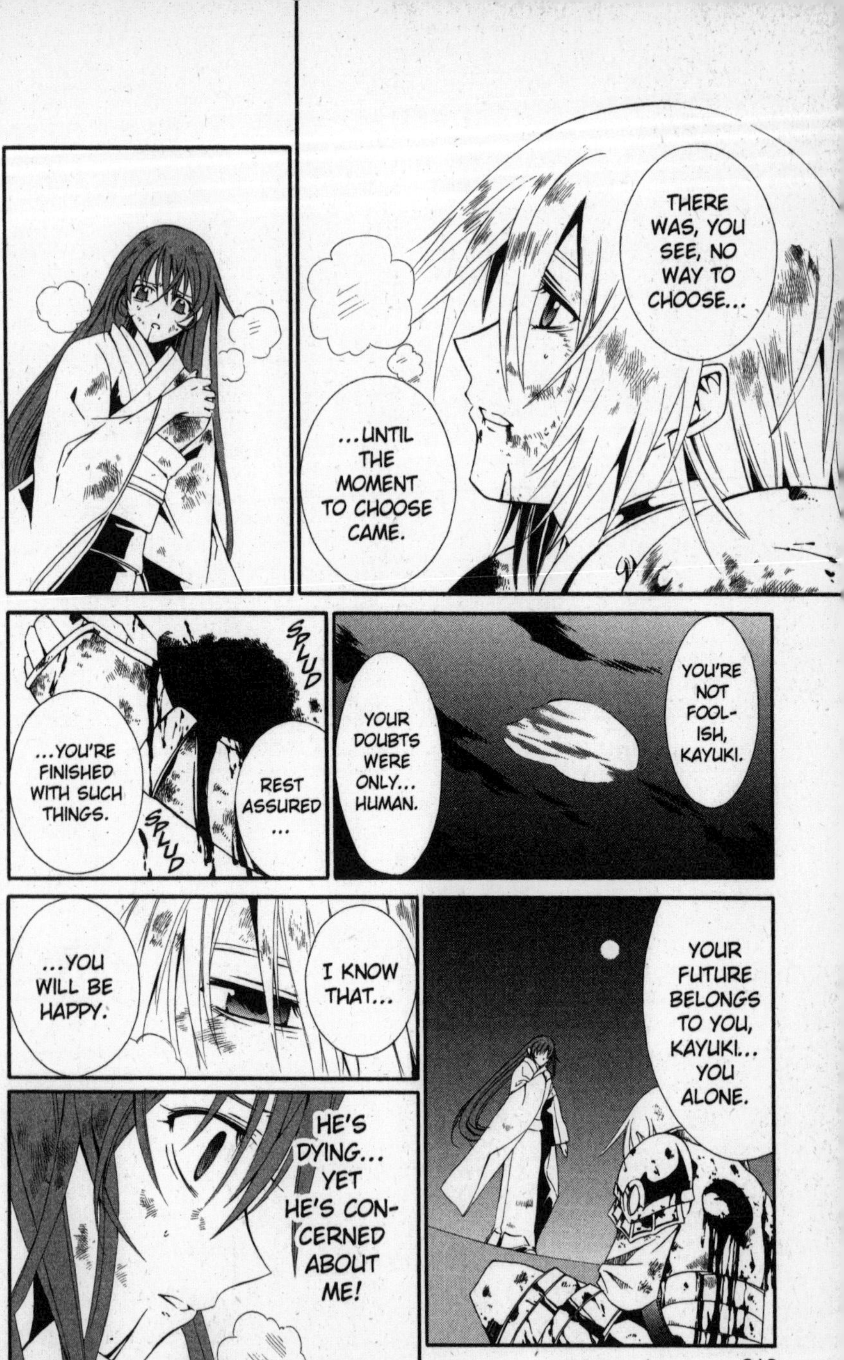
THERE WAS, YOU SEE, NO WAY TO CHOOSE...
...UNTIL THE MOMENT TO CHOOSE CAME.
YOU'RE NOT FOOL-ISH, KAYUKI.
YOUR DOUBTS WERE ONLY... HUMAN.
SPLUD
REST ASSURED ...
...YOU'RE FINISHED WITH SUCH THINGS.
SPLUD
YOUR FUTURE BELONGS TO YOU, KAYUKI... YOU ALONE.
I KNOW THAT...
...YOU WILL BE HAPPY.
HE'S DYING... YET HE'S CON-CERNED ABOUT ME!

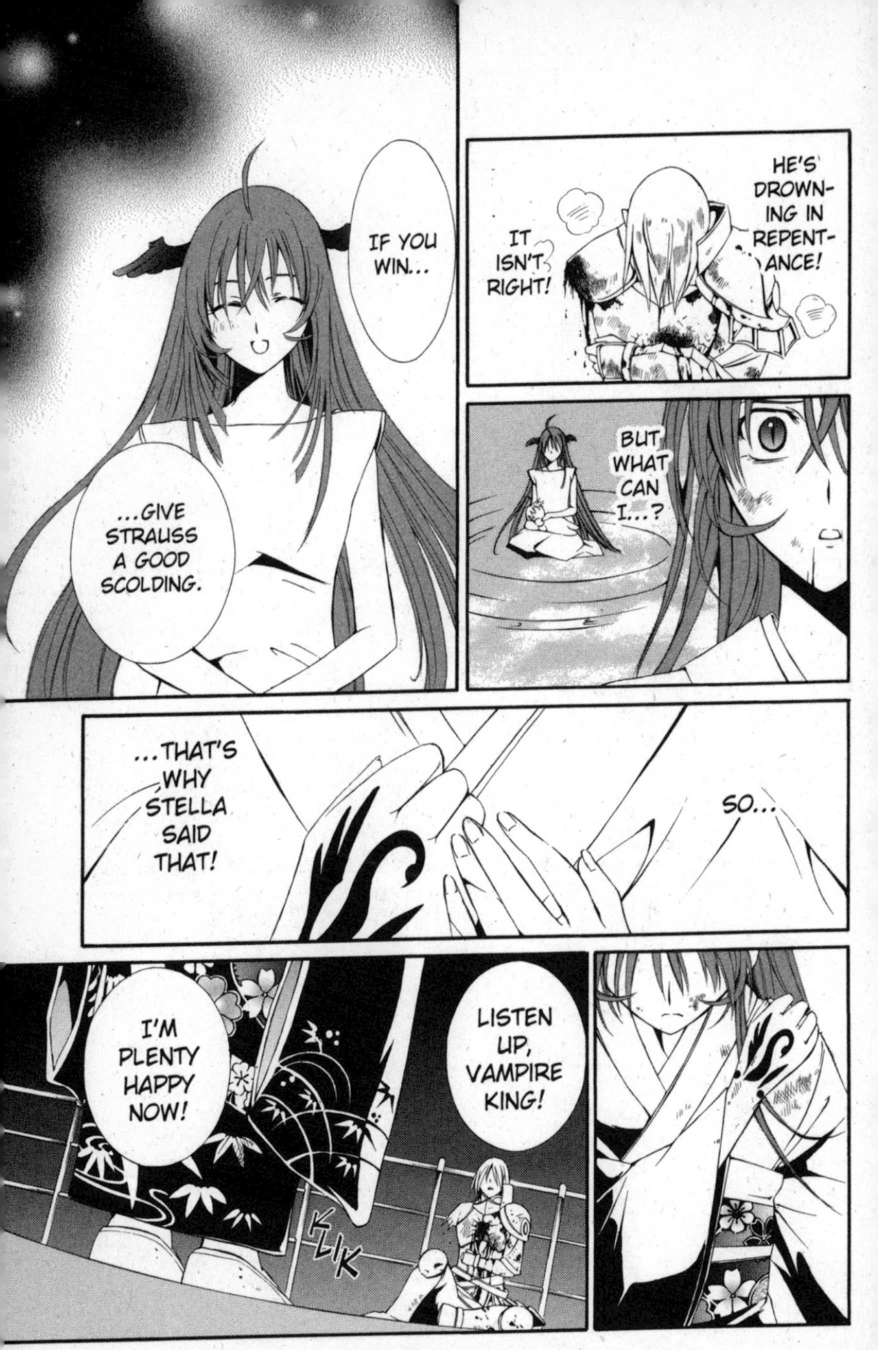
HE'S DROWNING IN REPENTANCE!
IT ISN'T RIGHT!
BUT WHAT CAN I...?
IF YOU WIN...
...GIVE STRAUSS A GOOD SCOLDING.
SO...
...THAT'S WHY STELLA SAID THAT!
LISTEN UP, VAMPIRE KING!
I'M PLENTY HAPPY NOW!
KLIK

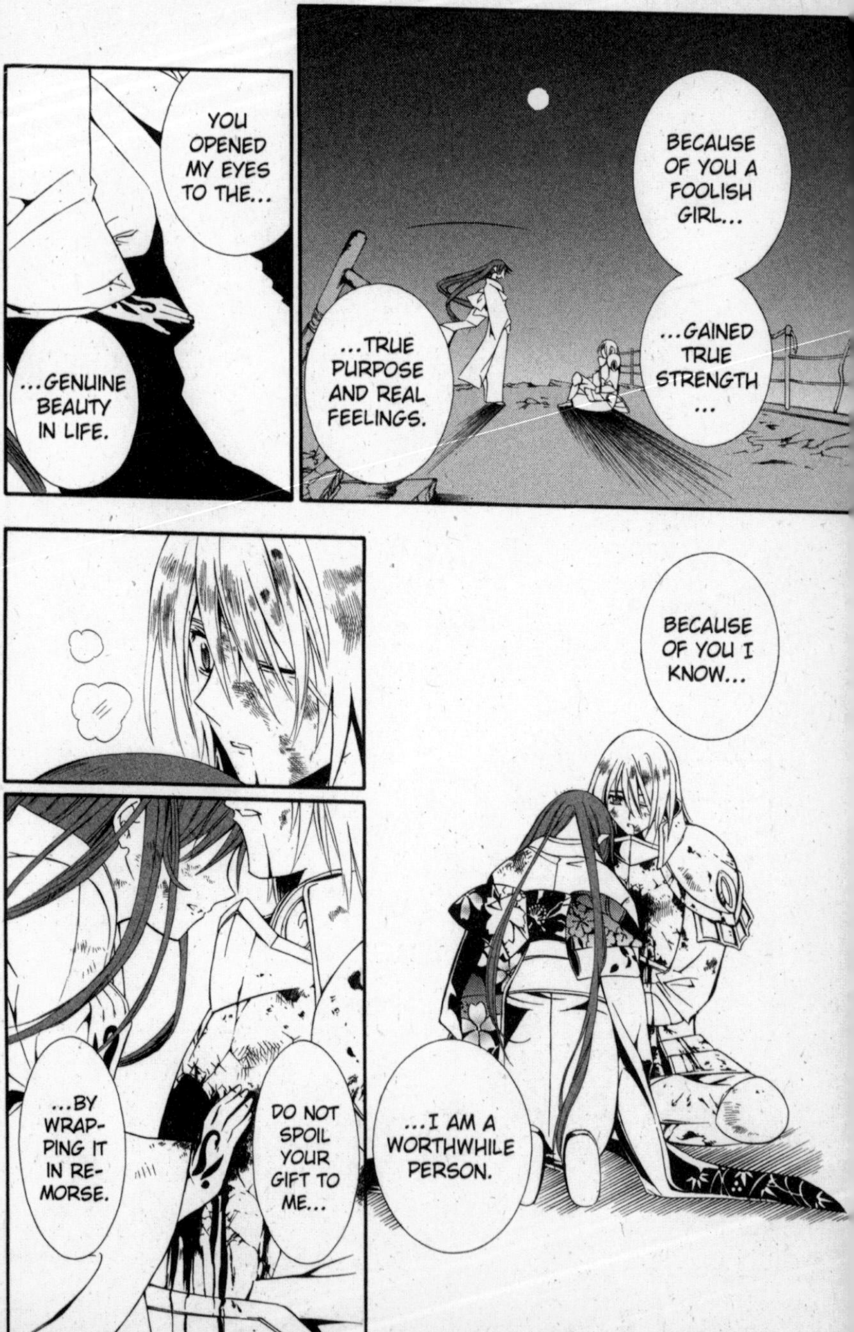
BECAUSE OF YOU A FOOLISH GIRL...
...GAINED TRUE STRENGTH ...
...TRUE PURPOSE AND REAL FEELINGS.
YOU OPENED MY EYES TO THE...
...GENUINE BEAUTY IN LIFE.
BECAUSE OF YOU I KNOW...
...I AM A WORTHWHILE PERSON.
DO NOT SPOIL YOUR GIFT TO ME...
...BY WRAP-PING IT IN RE-MORSE.

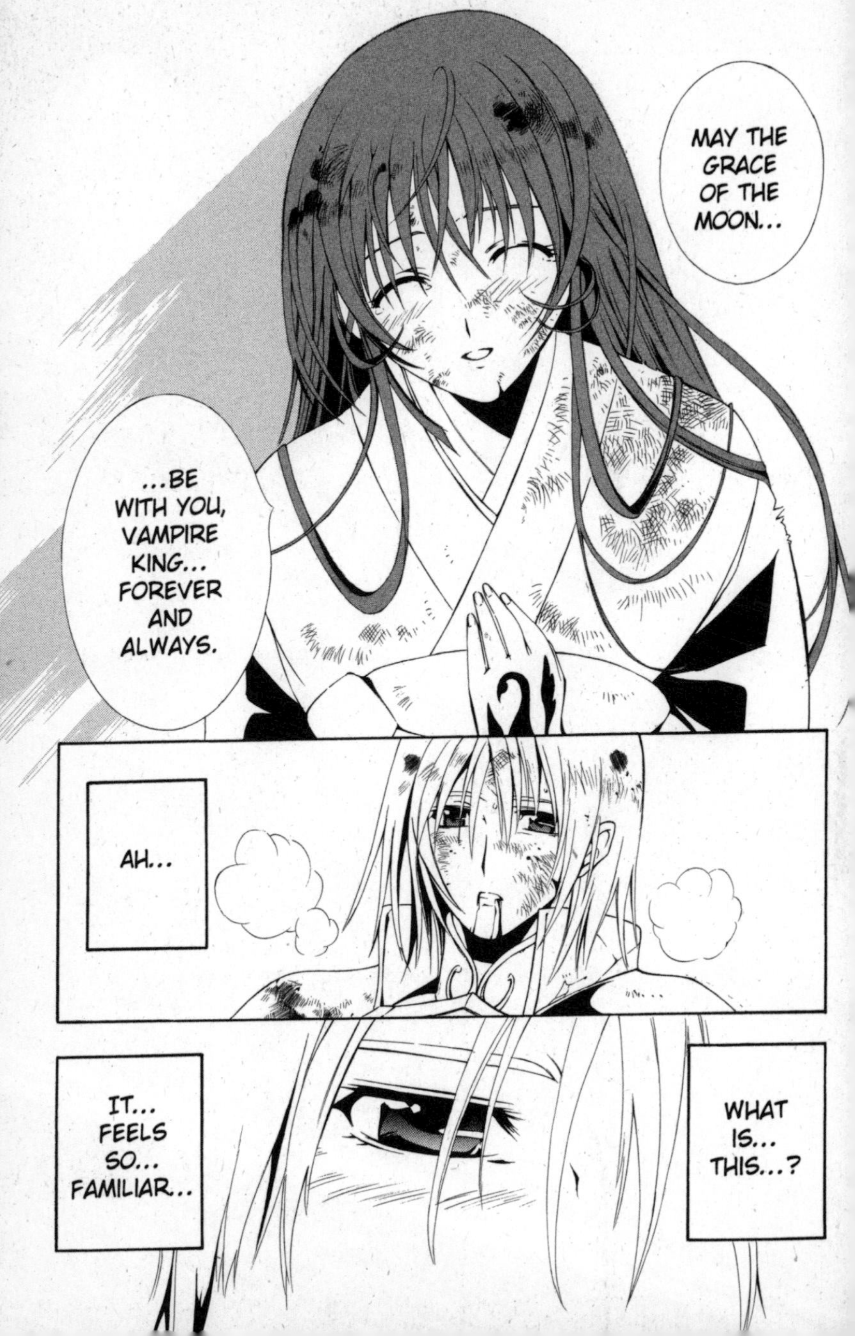
MAY THE GRACE OF THE MOON...
...BE WITH YOU, VAMPIRE KING... FOREVER AND ALWAYS.
AH...
WHAT IS... THIS...?
IT... FEELS SO... FAMILIAR...

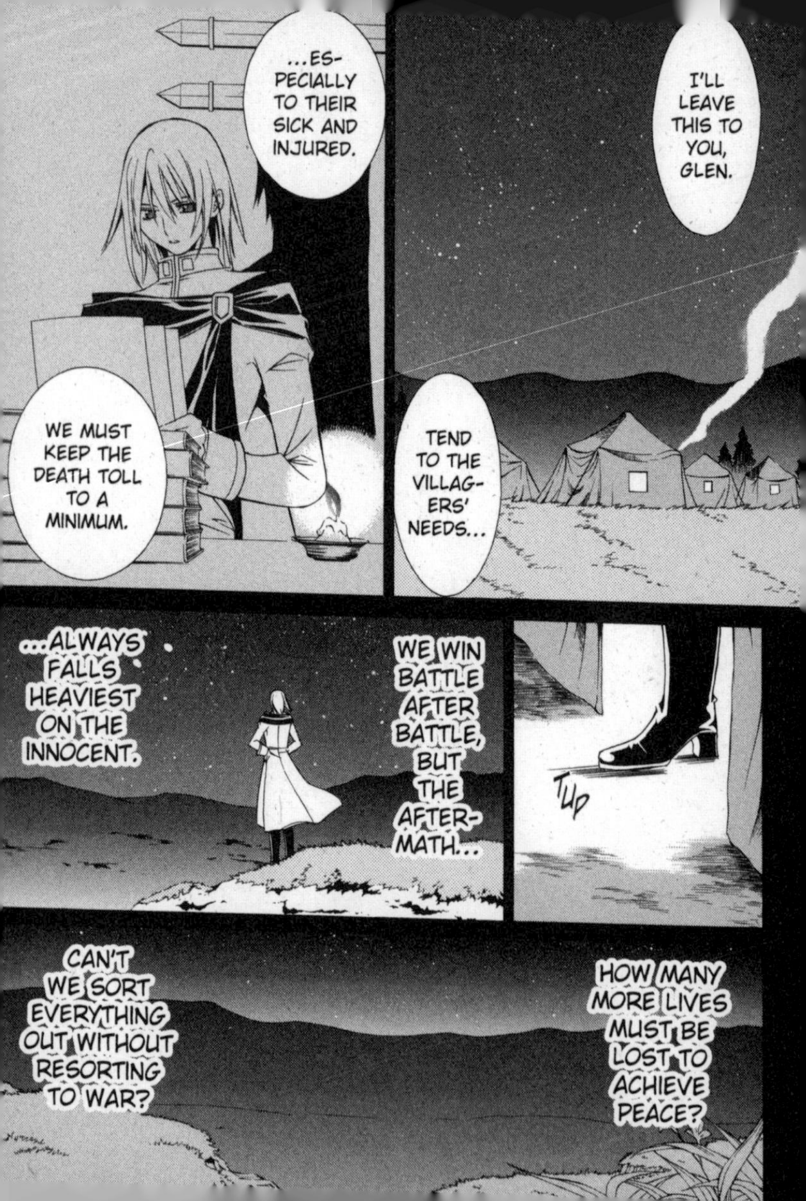
I'LL LEAVE THIS TO YOU, GLEN.
TEND TO THE VILLAGERS' NEEDS...
...ESPECIALLY TO THEIR SICK AND INJURED.
WE MUST KEEP THE DEATH TOLL TO A MINIMUM.
TUP
WE WIN BATTLE AFTER BATTLE, BUT THE AFTERMATH...
...ALWAYS FALLS HEAVIEST ON THE INNOCENT.
HOW MANY MORE LIVES MUST BE LOST TO ACHIEVE PEACE?
CAN'T WE SORT EVERYTHING OUT WITHOUT RESORTING TO WAR?

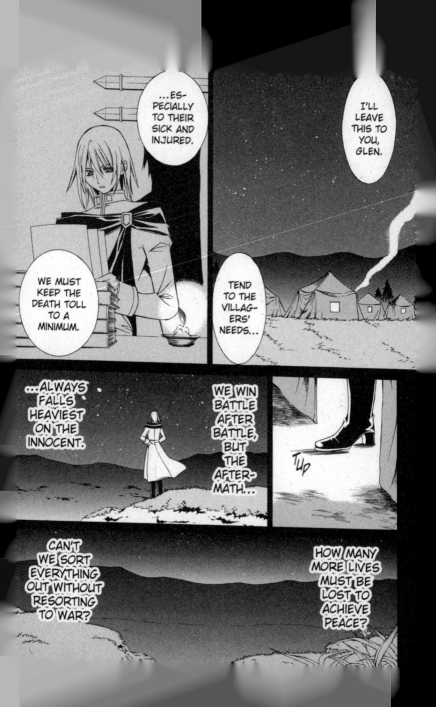

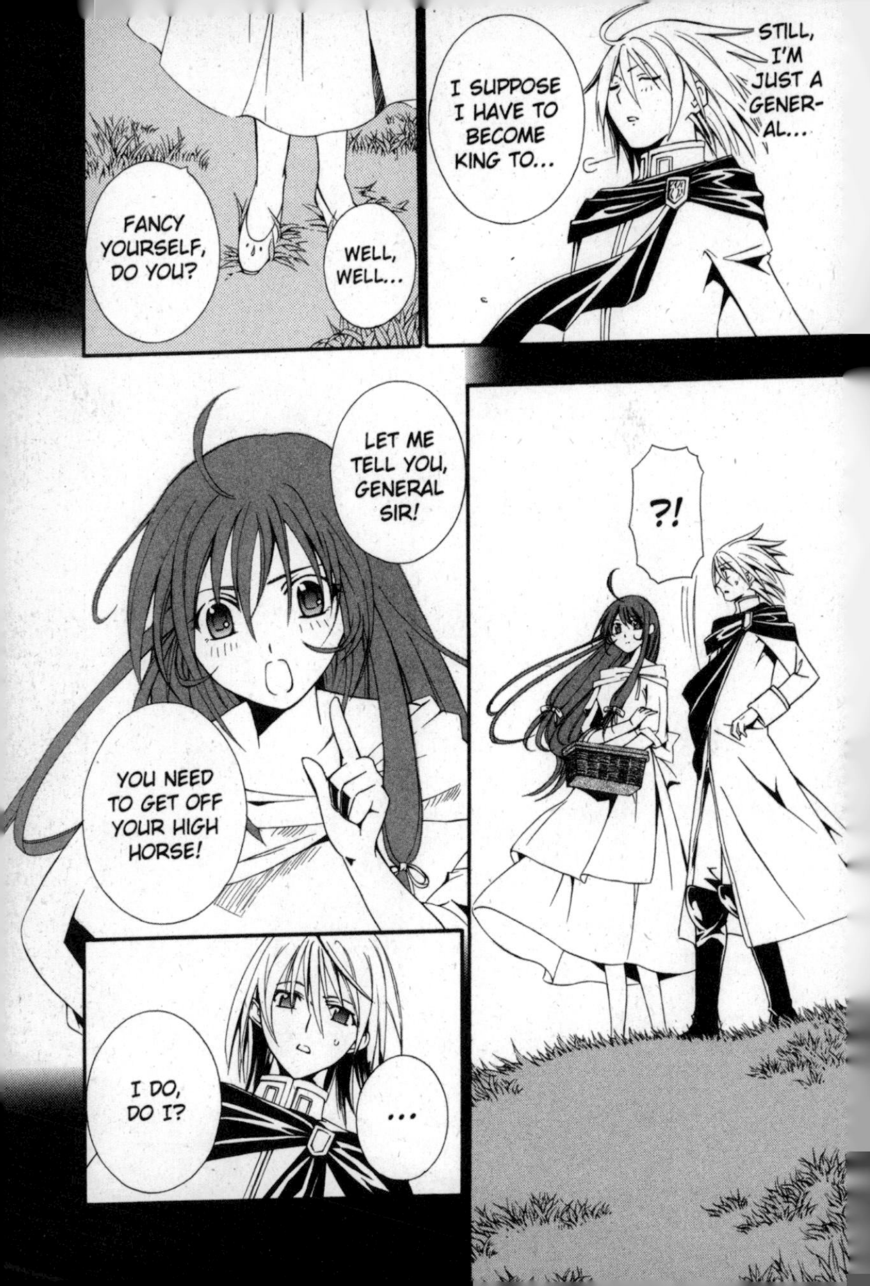
STILL, I'M JUST A GENERAL...
I SUPPOSE I HAVE TO BECOME KING TO...
WELL, WELL...
FANCY YOURSELF, DO YOU?
?!
LET ME TELL YOU, GENERAL SIR!
YOU NEED TO GET OFF YOUR HIGH HORSE!
...
I DO, DO I?

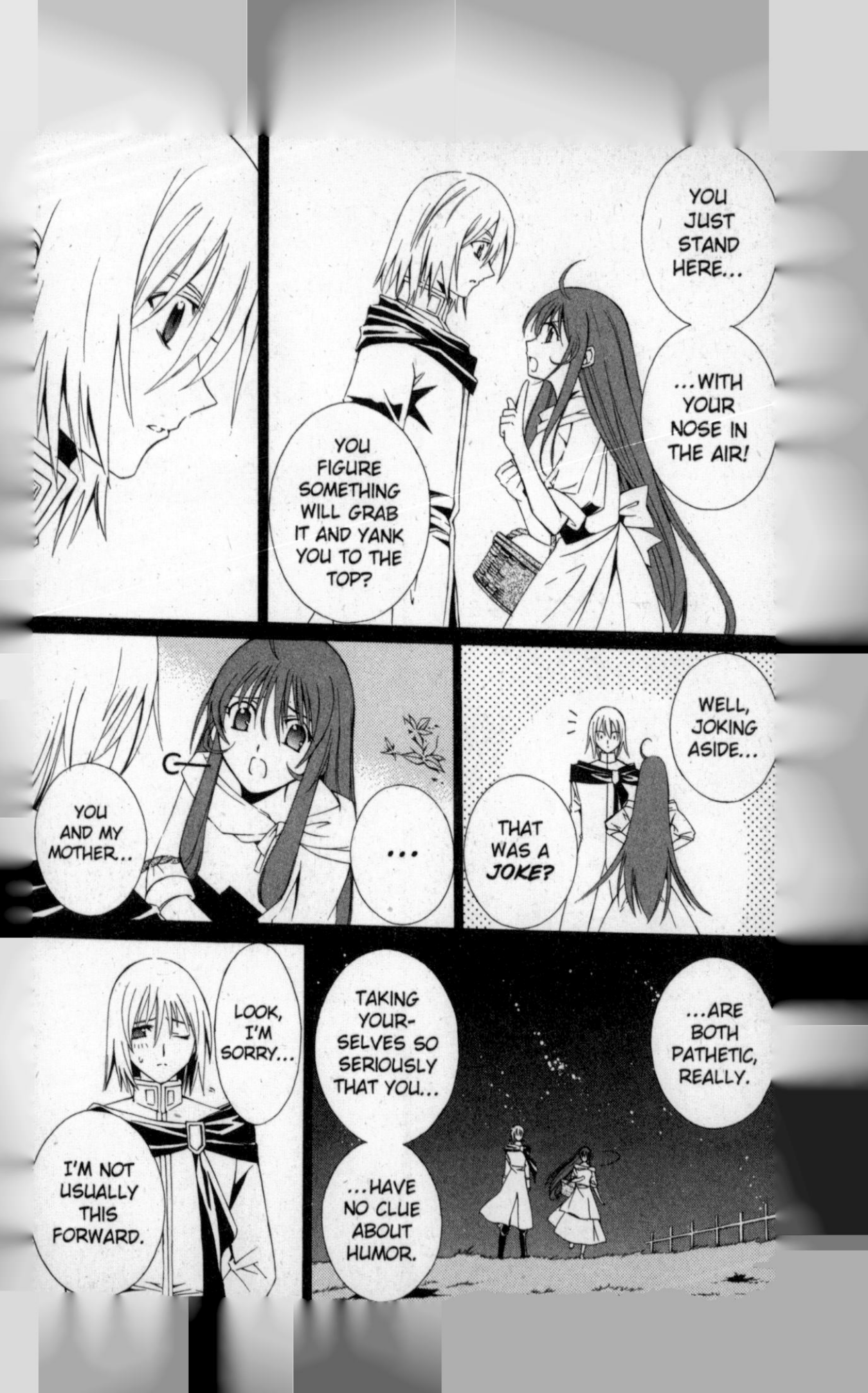
YOU JUST STAND HERE...
...WITH YOUR NOSE IN THE AIR!
YOU FIGURE SOMETHING WILL GRAB IT AND YANK YOU TO THE TOP?
WELL, JOKING ASIDE...
THAT WAS A *JOKE*?
...
YOU AND MY MOTHER...
...ARE BOTH PATHETIC, REALLY.
TAKING YOURSELVES SO SERIOUSLY THAT YOU...
...HAVE NO CLUE ABOUT HUMOR.
LOOK, I'M SORRY...
I'M NOT USUALLY THIS FORWARD.

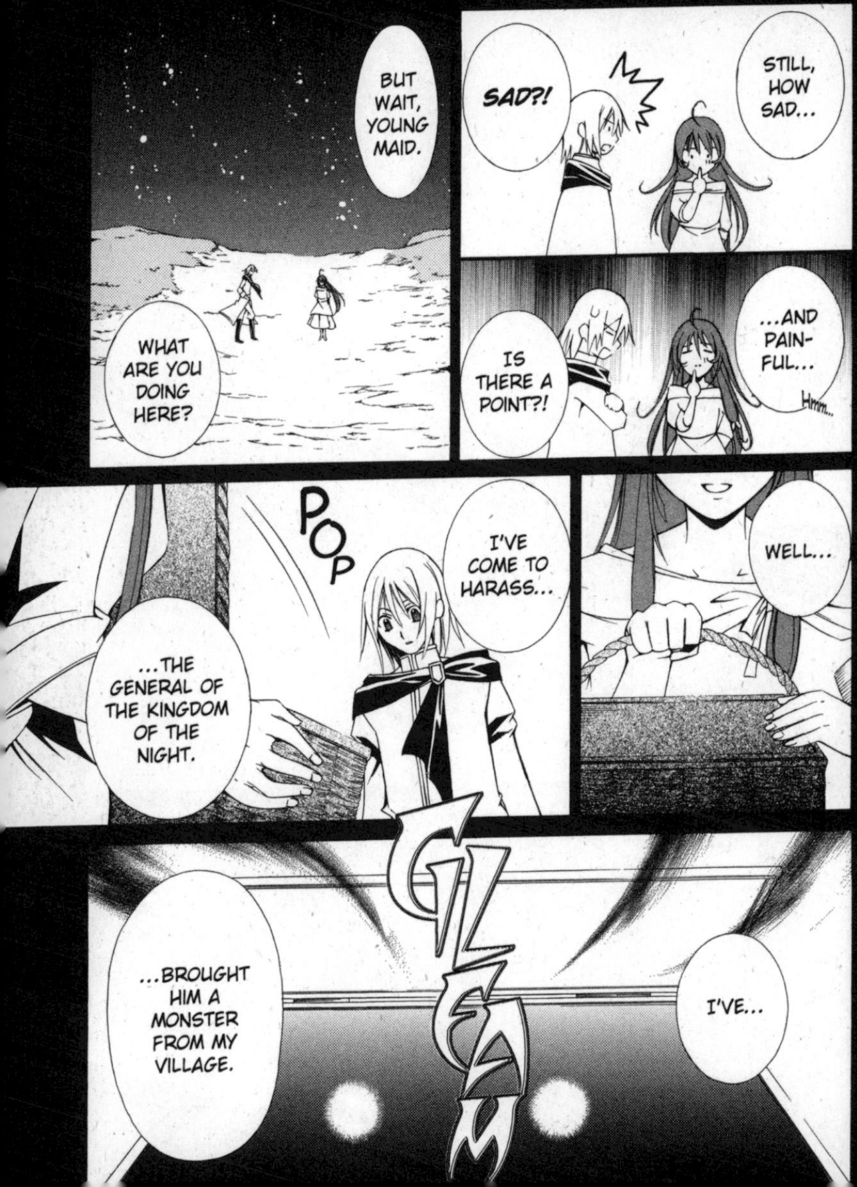
STILL, HOW SAD...
SAD?!
...AND PAIN-FUL...
Hmm...
IS THERE A POINT?!
BUT WAIT, YOUNG MAID.
WHAT ARE YOU DOING HERE?
WELL...
I'VE COME TO HARASS...
POP
...THE GENERAL OF THE KINGDOM OF THE NIGHT.
I'VE...
GLEAM
...BROUGHT HIM A MONSTER FROM MY VILLAGE.

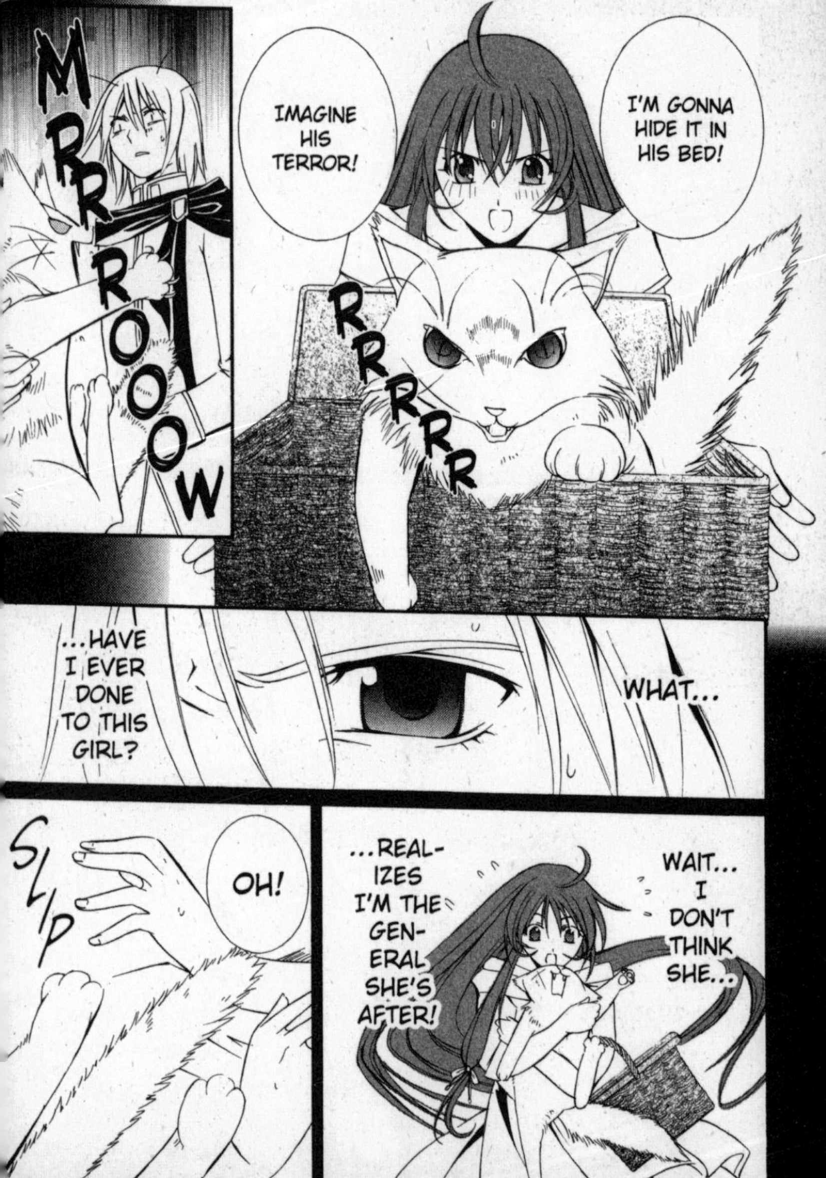
I'M GONNA HIDE IT IN HIS BED!
IMAGINE HIS TERROR!
RRRRRR
MRRRROOOW
WHAT...
...HAVE I EVER DONE TO THIS GIRL?
WAIT... I DON'T THINK SHE...
...REAL-IZES I'M THE GEN-ERAL SHE'S AFTER!
SLIP
OH!

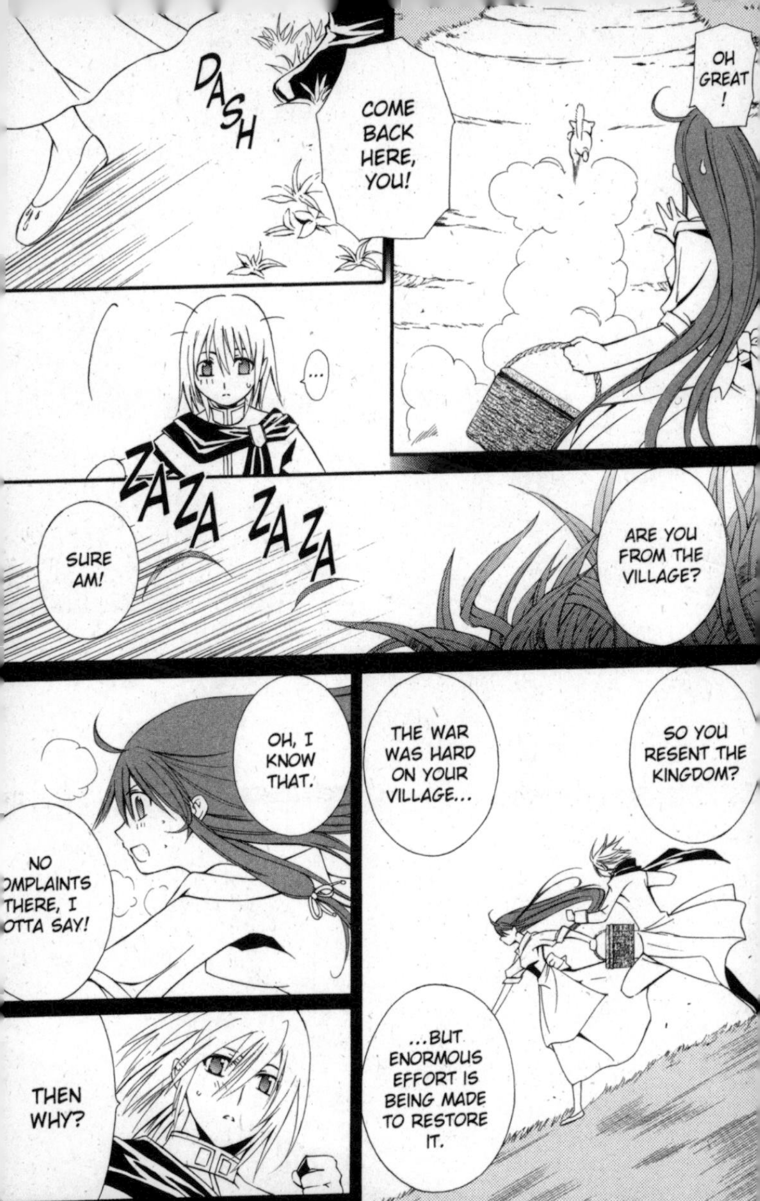
OH GREAT!
DASH
COME BACK HERE, YOU!
...
ZAZA ZAZA
ARE YOU FROM THE VILLAGE?
SURE AM!
SO YOU RESENT THE KINGDOM?
THE WAR WAS HARD ON YOUR VILLAGE...
...BUT ENORMOUS EFFORT IS BEING MADE TO RESTORE IT.
OH, I KNOW THAT.
NO OMPLAINTS THERE, I OTTA SAY!
THEN WHY?

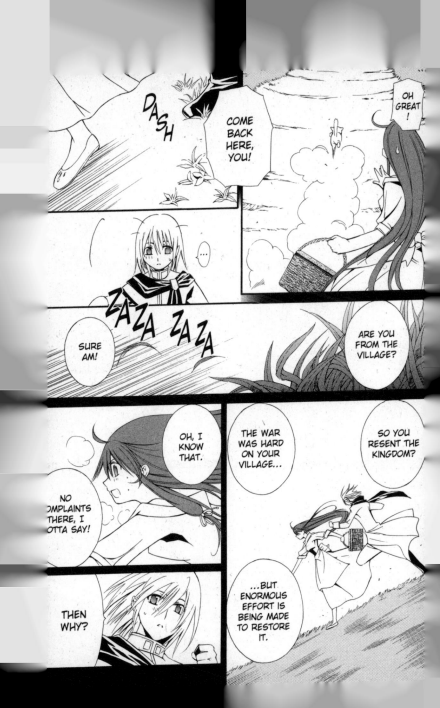

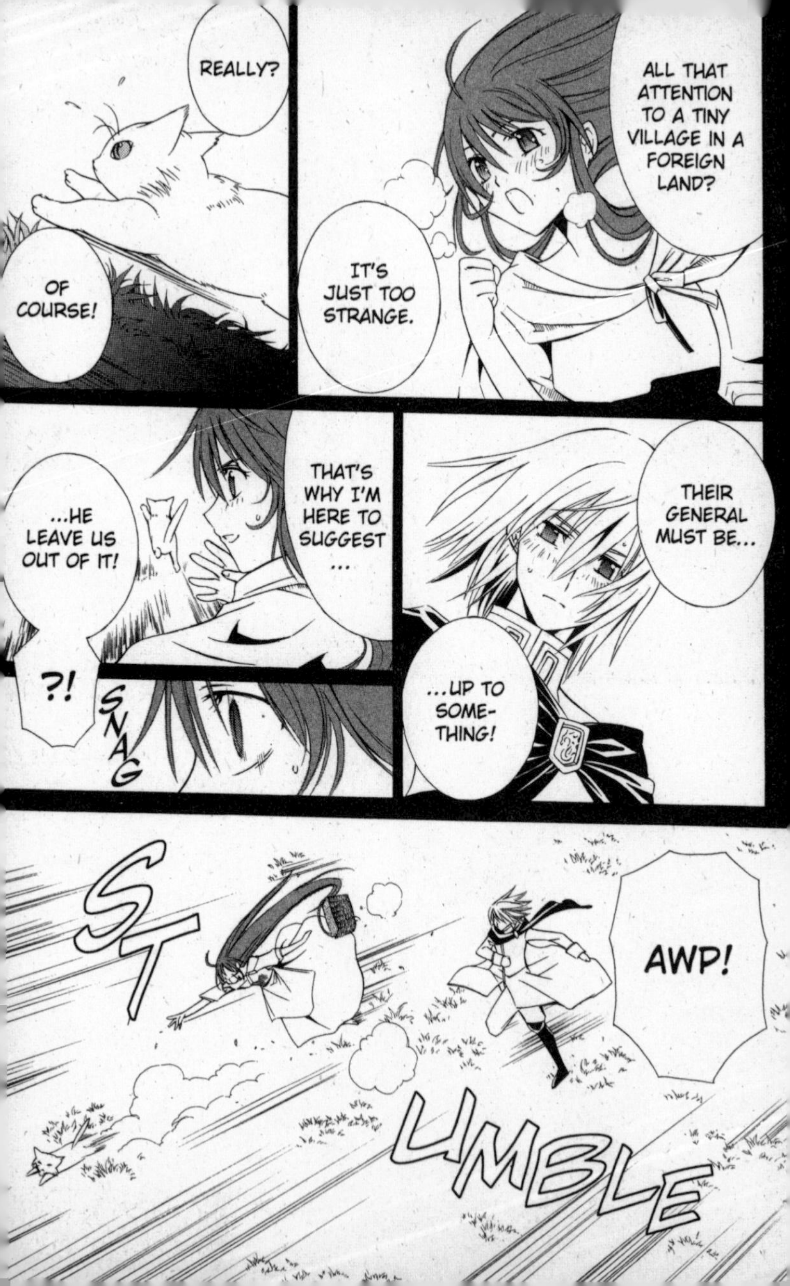
ALL THAT ATTENTION TO A TINY VILLAGE IN A FOREIGN LAND?
IT'S JUST TOO STRANGE.
REALLY?
OF COURSE!
THEIR GENERAL MUST BE...
...UP TO SOMETHING!
THAT'S WHY I'M HERE TO SUGGEST...
...HE LEAVE US OUT OF IT!
?!
SNAG
AWP!
ST
UMBLE

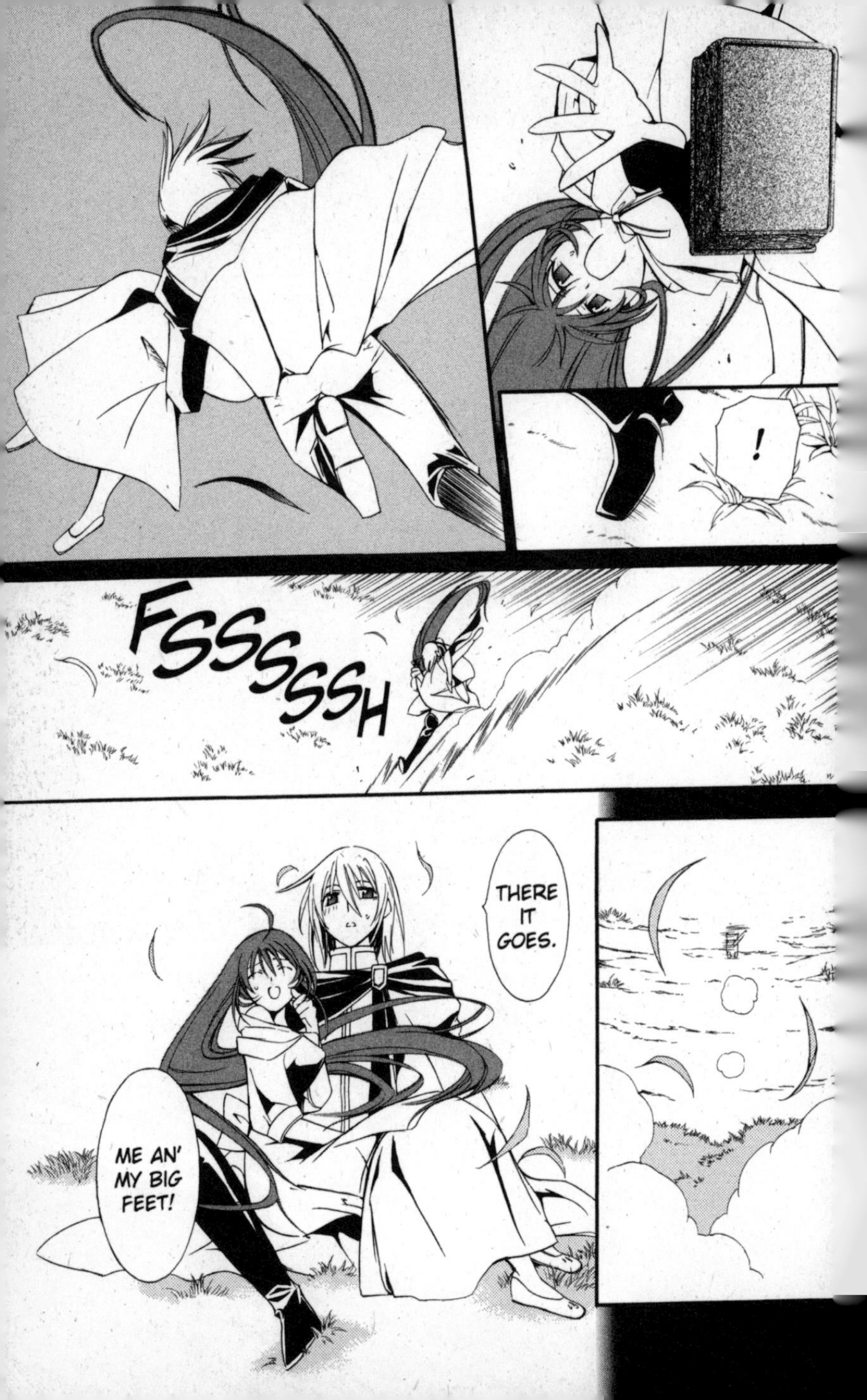
!
FSSSSSSH
THERE IT GOES.
ME AN' MY BIG FEET!

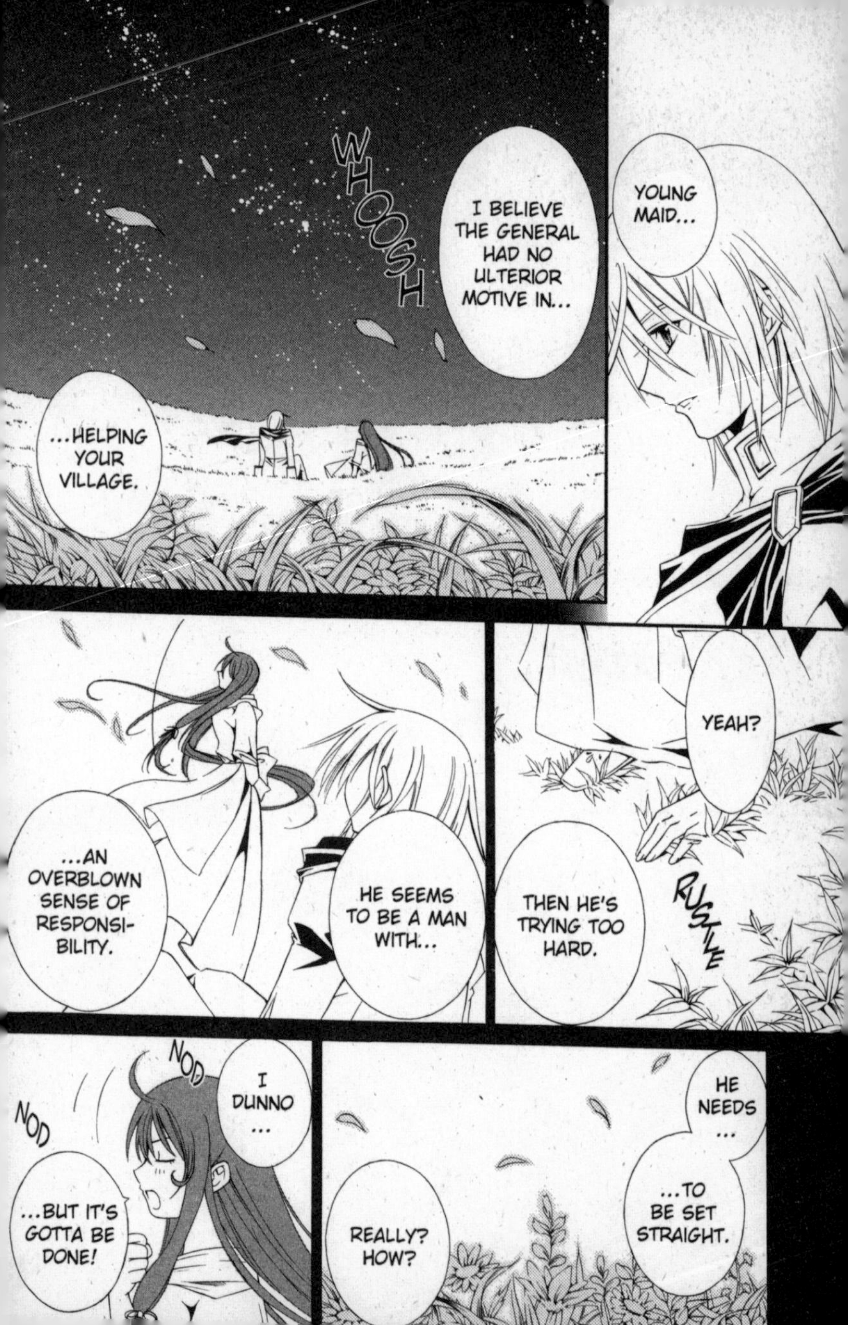
YOUNG MAID...
WHOOSH
I BELIEVE THE GENERAL HAD NO ULTERIOR MOTIVE IN...
...HELPING YOUR VILLAGE.
YEAH?
THEN HE'S TRYING TOO HARD.
RUSTLE
HE SEEMS TO BE A MAN WITH...
...AN OVERBLOWN SENSE OF RESPONSI-BILITY.
HE NEEDS...
...TO BE SET STRAIGHT.
REALLY? HOW?
I DUNNO...
NOD
NOD
...BUT IT'S GOTTA BE DONE!

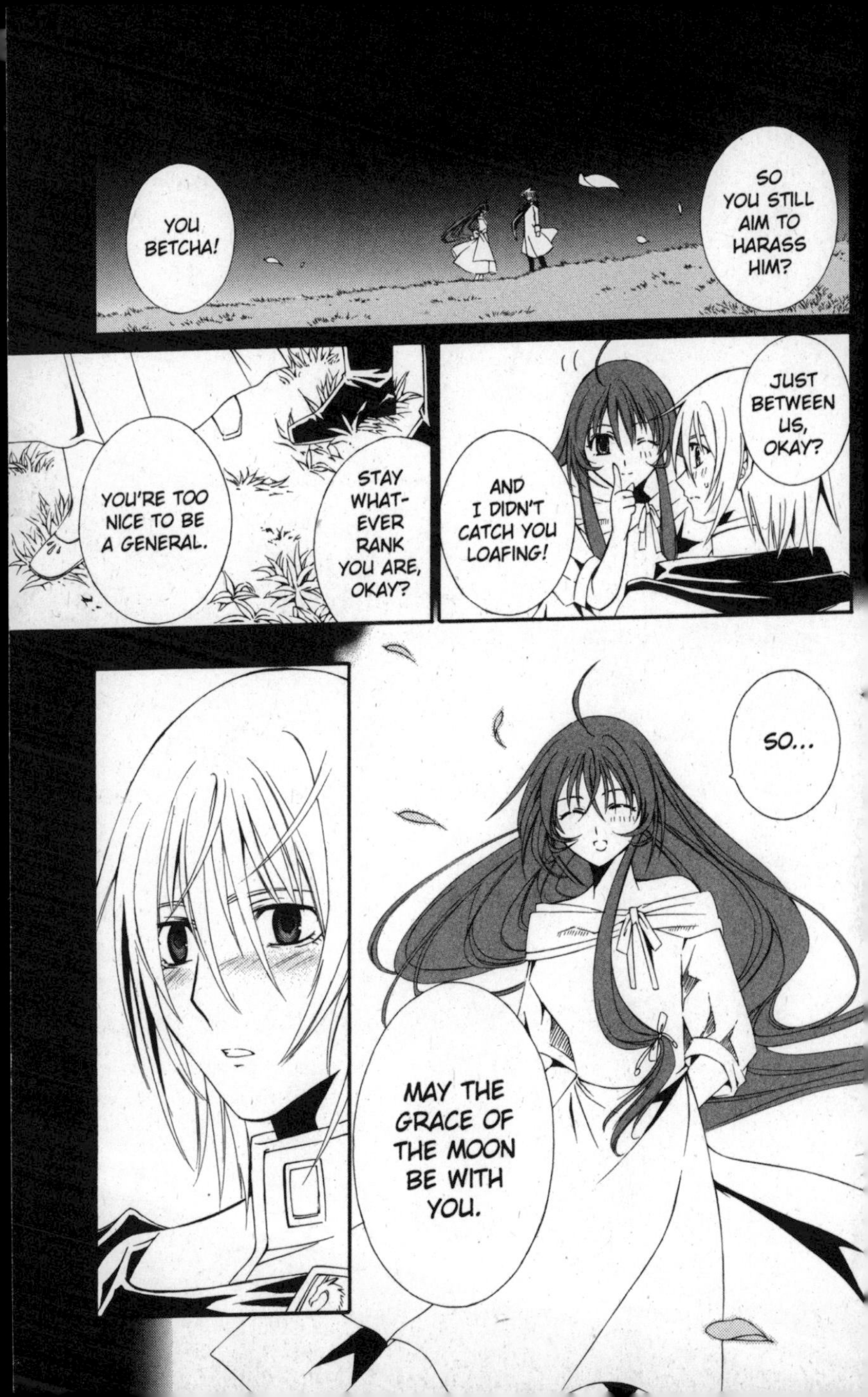
SO YOU STILL AIM TO HARASS HIM?
YOU BETCHA!
JUST BETWEEN US, OKAY?
AND I DIDN'T CATCH YOU LOAFING!
STAY WHAT-EVER RANK YOU ARE, OKAY?
YOU'RE TOO NICE TO BE A GENERAL.
SO...
MAY THE GRACE OF THE MOON BE WITH YOU.

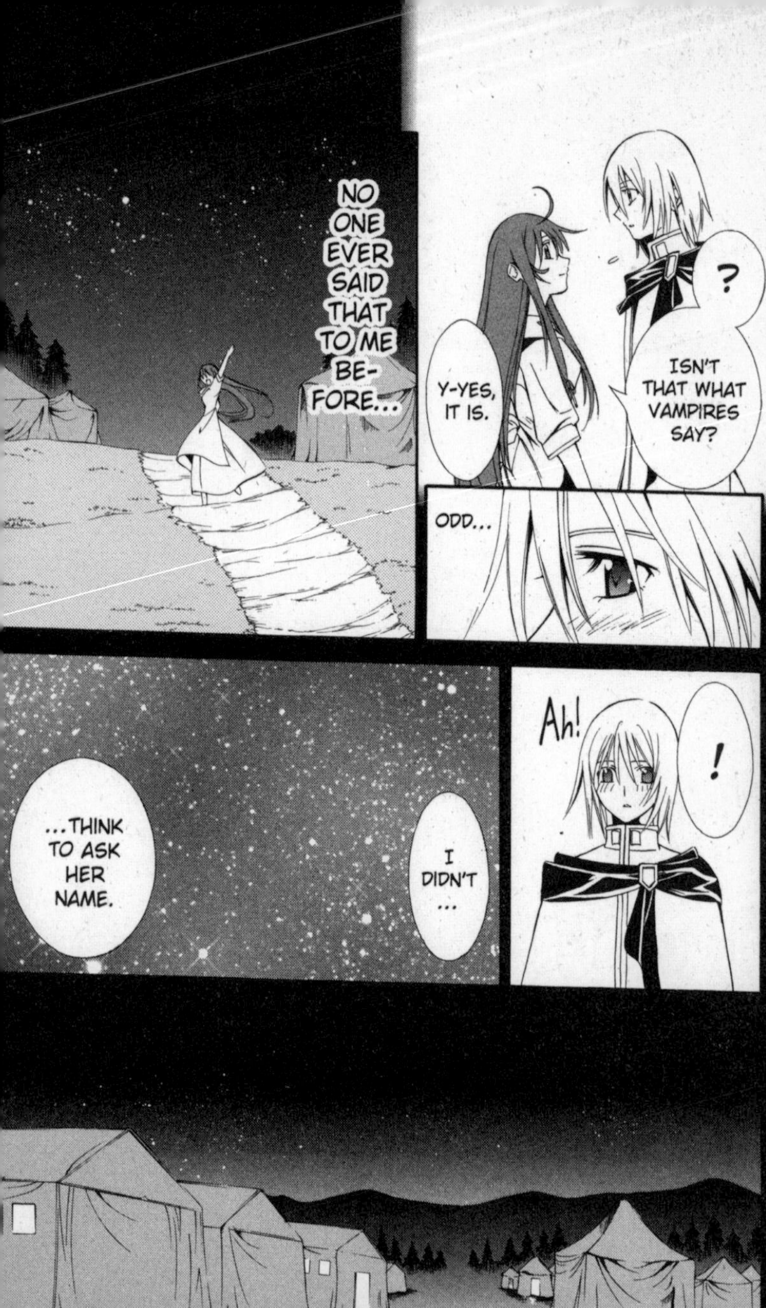
?
ISN'T THAT WHAT VAMPIRES SAY?
Y-YES, IT IS.
ODD...
NO ONE EVER SAID THAT TO ME BE-FORE...
!
Ah!
I DIDN'T ...
...THINK TO ASK HER NAME.

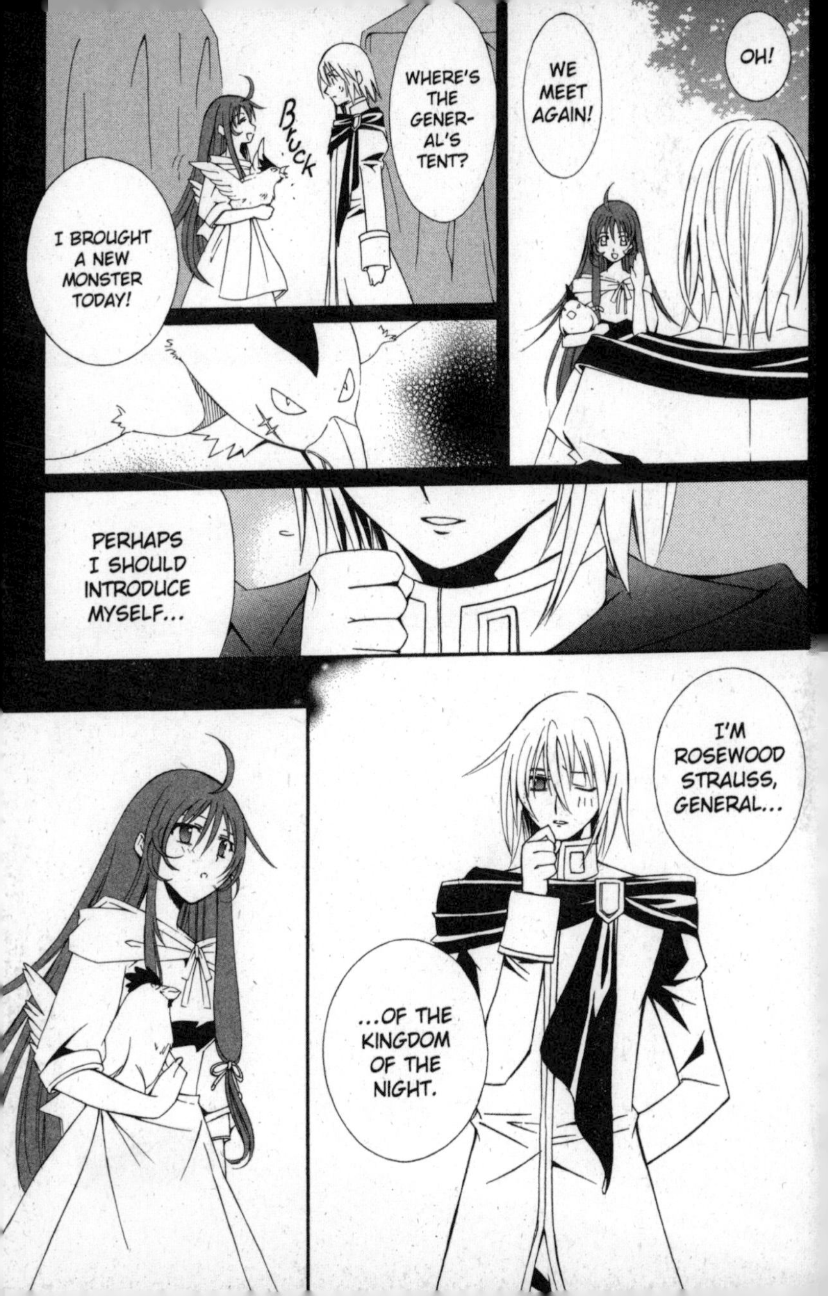
OH!
WE MEET AGAIN!
WHERE'S THE GENER-AL'S TENT?
BRUCK
I BROUGHT A NEW MONSTER TODAY!
PERHAPS I SHOULD INTRODUCE MYSELF...
I'M ROSEWOOD STRAUSS, GENERAL...
...OF THE KINGDOM OF THE NIGHT.

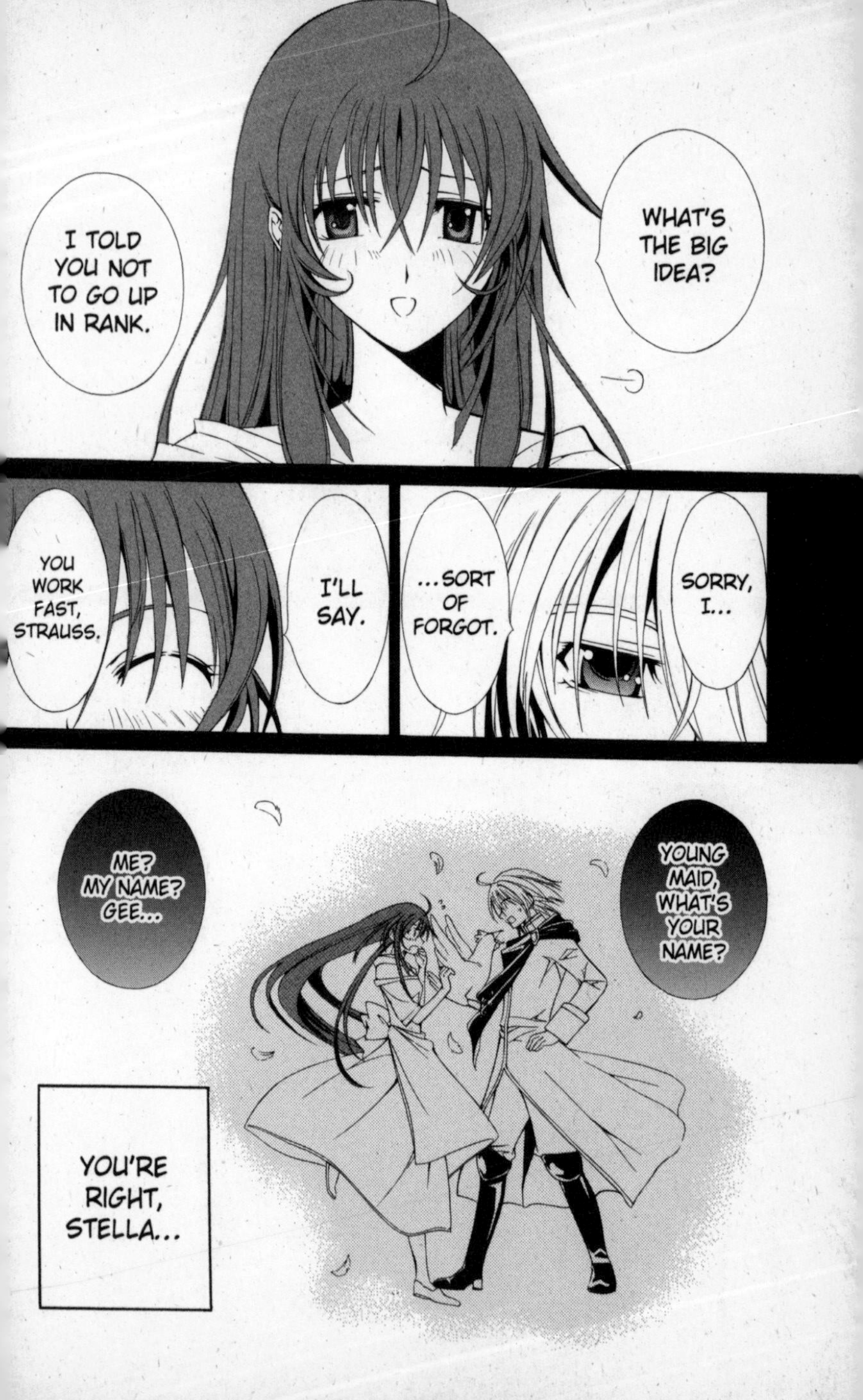
WHAT'S THE BIG IDEA?
I TOLD YOU NOT TO GO UP IN RANK.
SORRY, I...
...SORT OF FORGOT.
I'LL SAY.
YOU WORK FAST, STRAUSS.
YOUNG MAID, WHAT'S YOUR NAME?
ME? MY NAME? GEE...
YOU'RE RIGHT, STELLA...

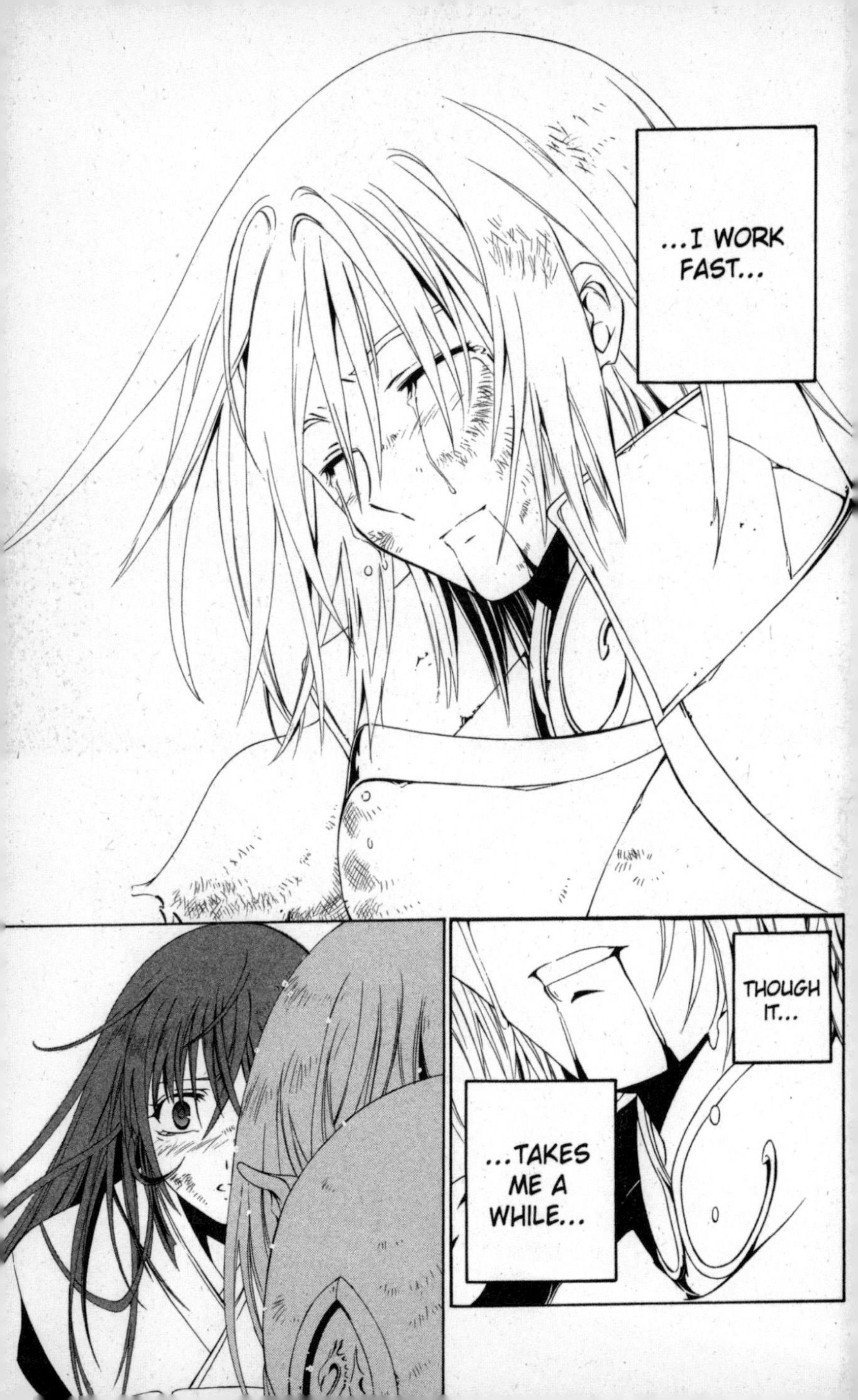
...I WORK FAST...
THOUGH IT...
...TAKES ME A WHILE...

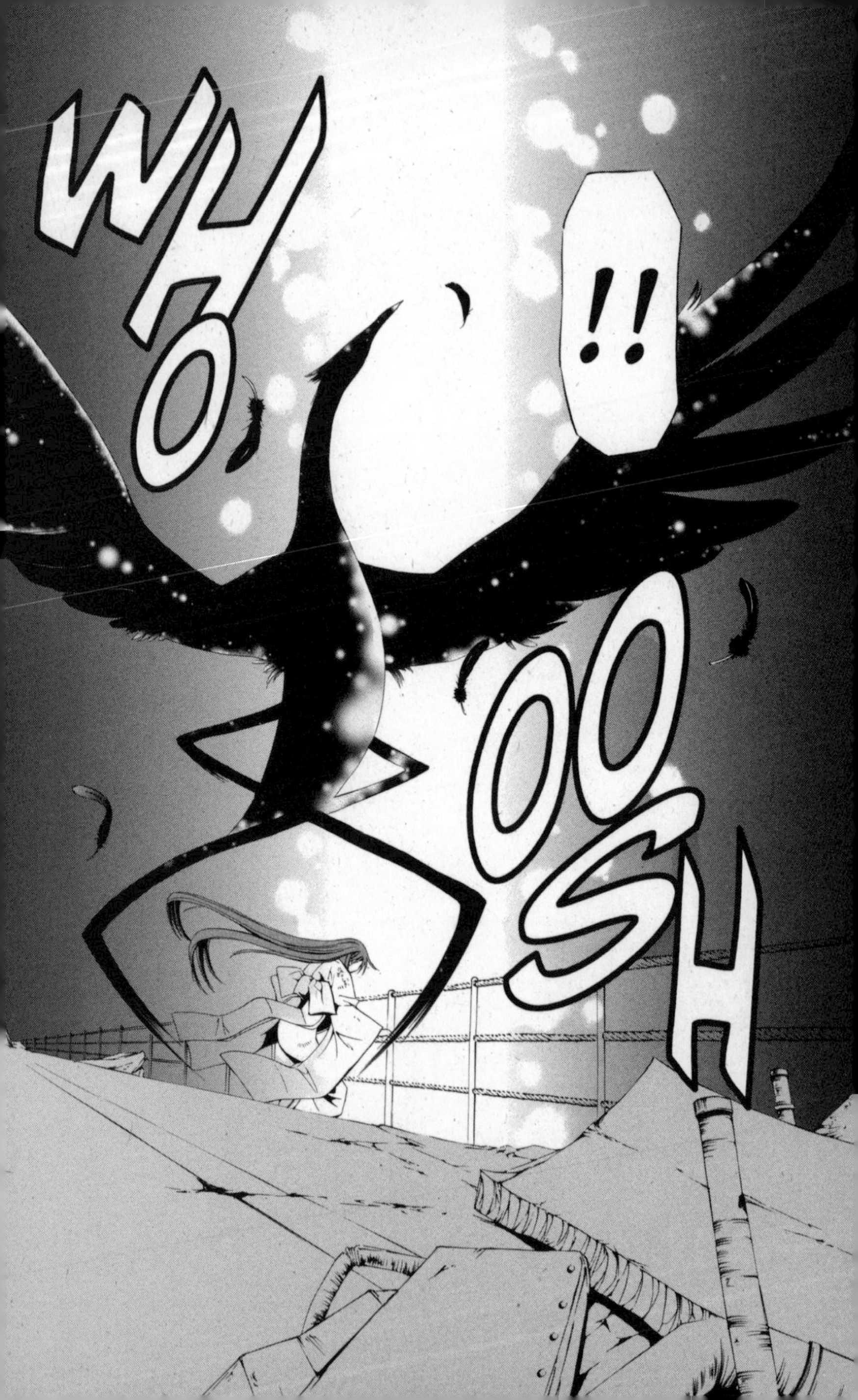

!!
WHOOOSH

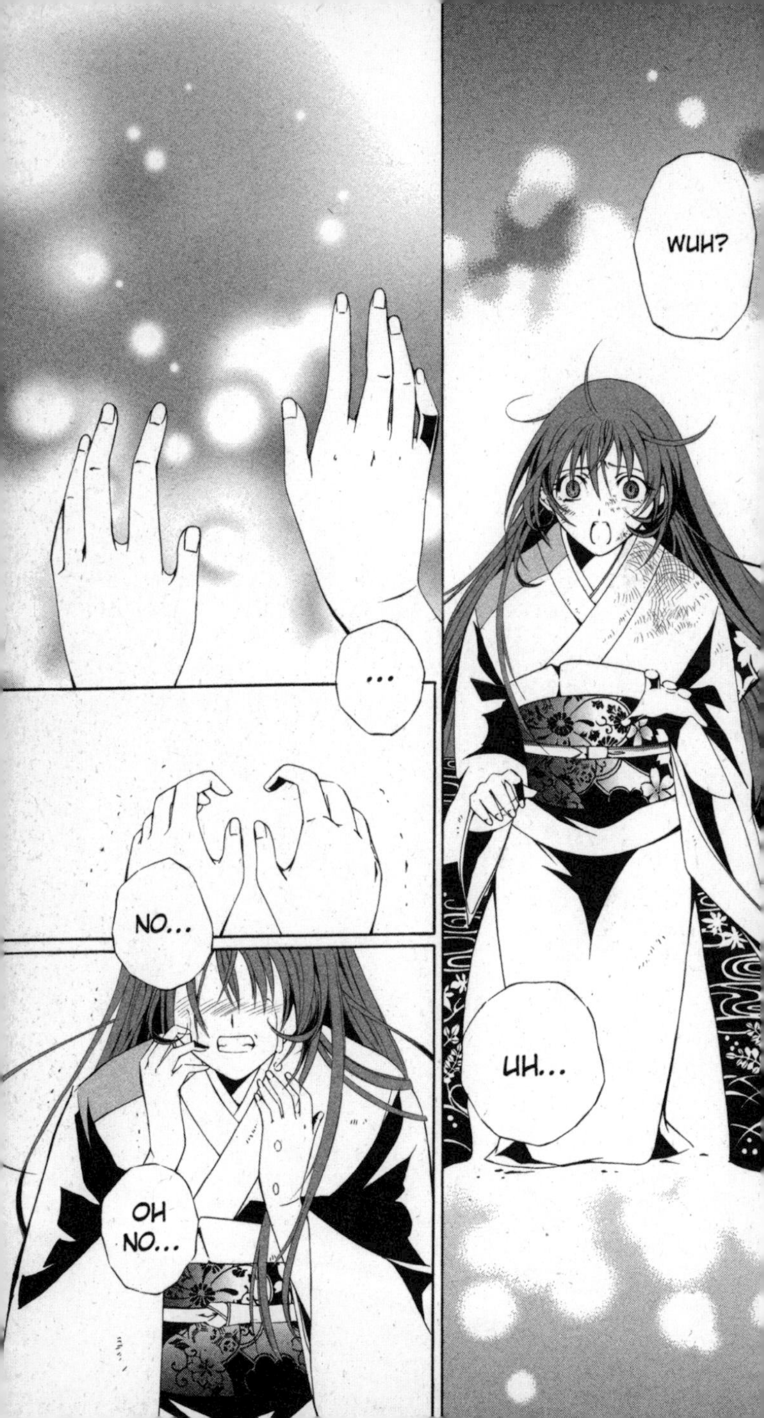
WUH?
UH...
...
NO...
OH NO...

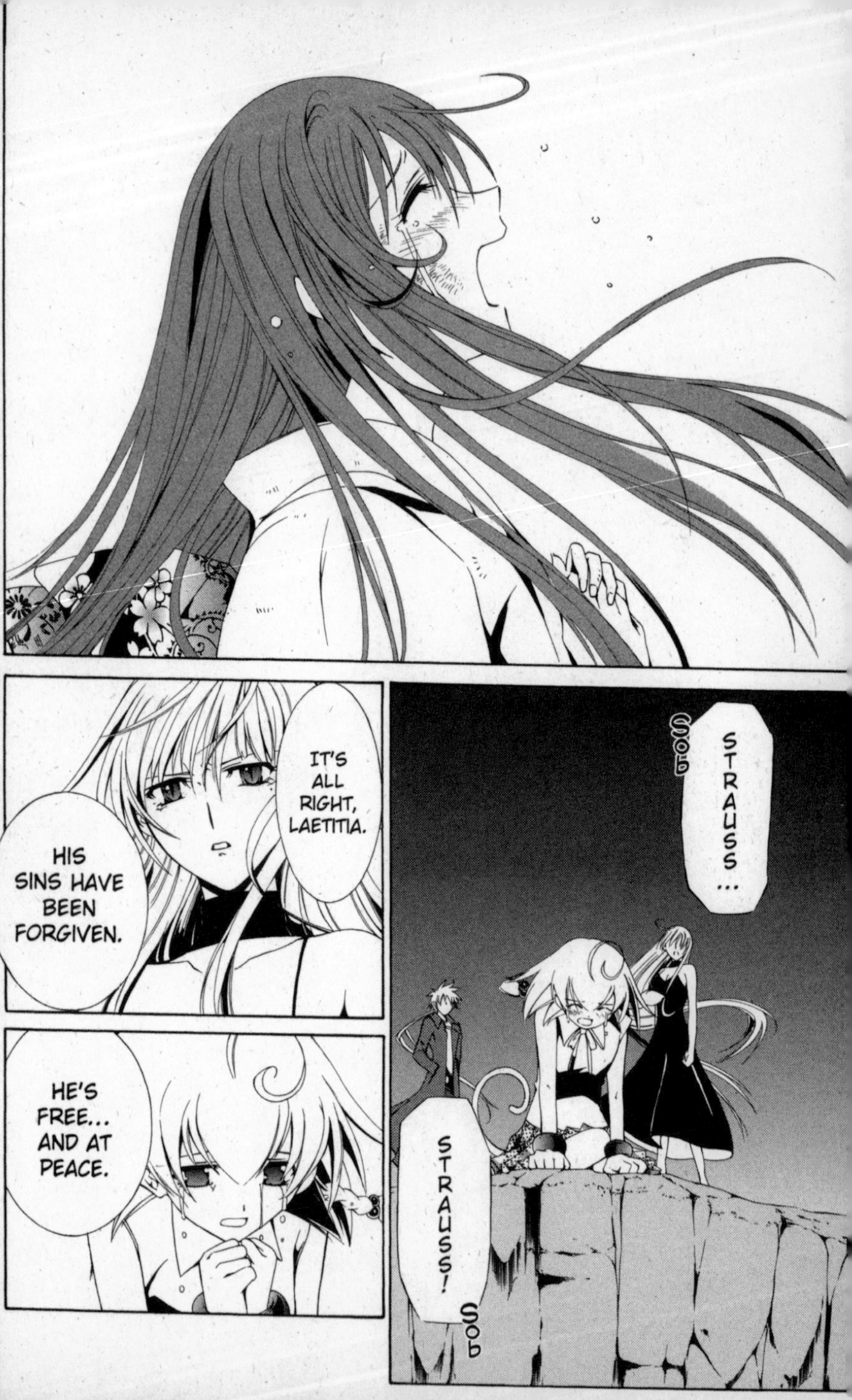
STRAUSS...
Sob
STRAUSS!
Sob
IT'S ALL RIGHT, LAETITIA.
HIS SINS HAVE BEEN FORGIVEN.
HE'S FREE... AND AT PEACE.

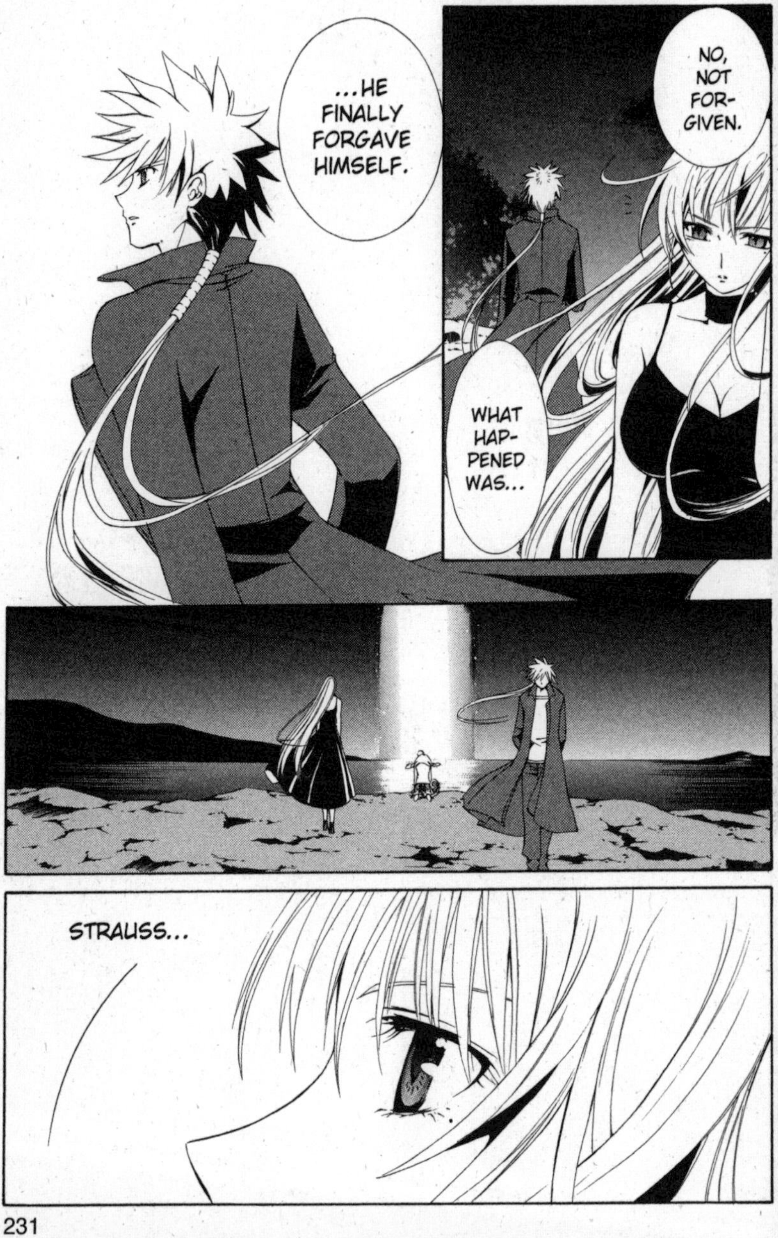
NO, NOT FOR-GIVEN.
WHAT HAP-PENED WAS...
...HE FINALLY FORGAVE HIMSELF.
STRAUSS...

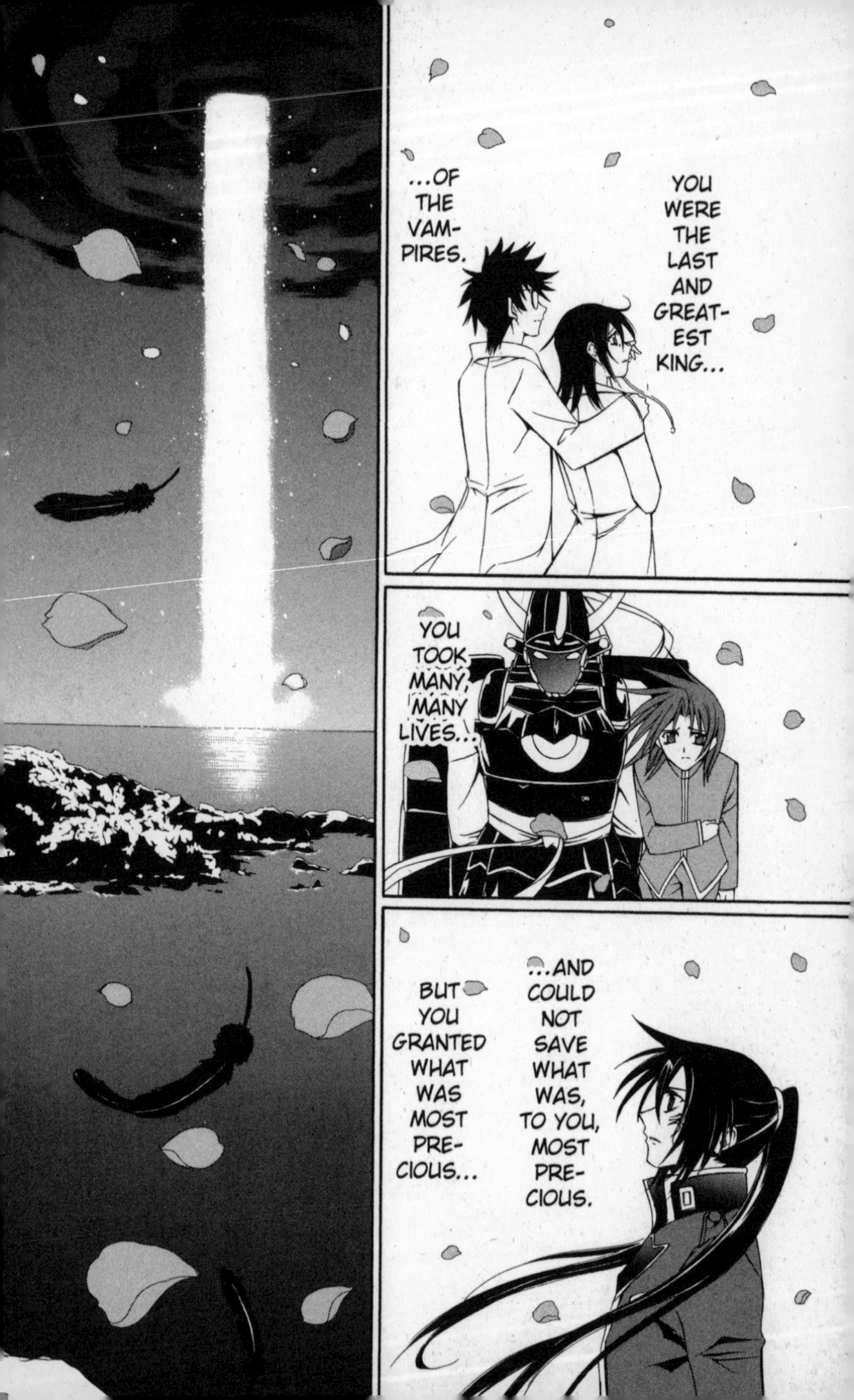
YOU WERE THE LAST AND GREAT-EST KING...
...OF THE VAM-PIRES.
YOU TOOK MANY, MANY LIVES...
...AND COULD NOT SAVE WHAT WAS, TO YOU, MOST PRE-CIOUS.
BUT YOU GRANTED WHAT WAS MOST PRE-CIOUS...

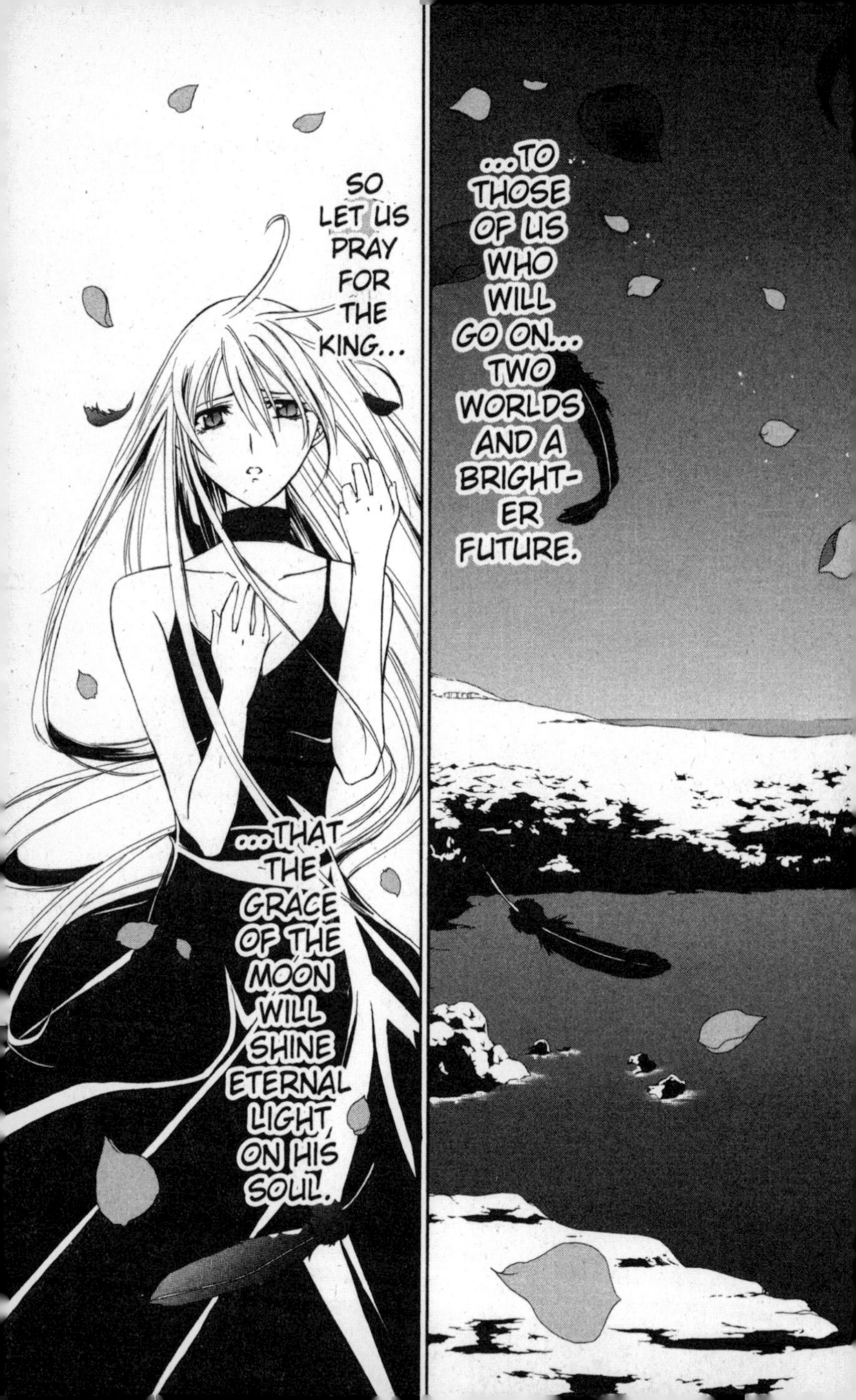
SO LET US PRAY FOR THE KING...
...THAT THE GRACE OF THE MOON WILL SHINE ETERNAL LIGHT ON HIS SOUL.
...TO THOSE OF US WHO WILL GO ON... TWO WORLDS AND A BRIGHTER-ER FUTURE.

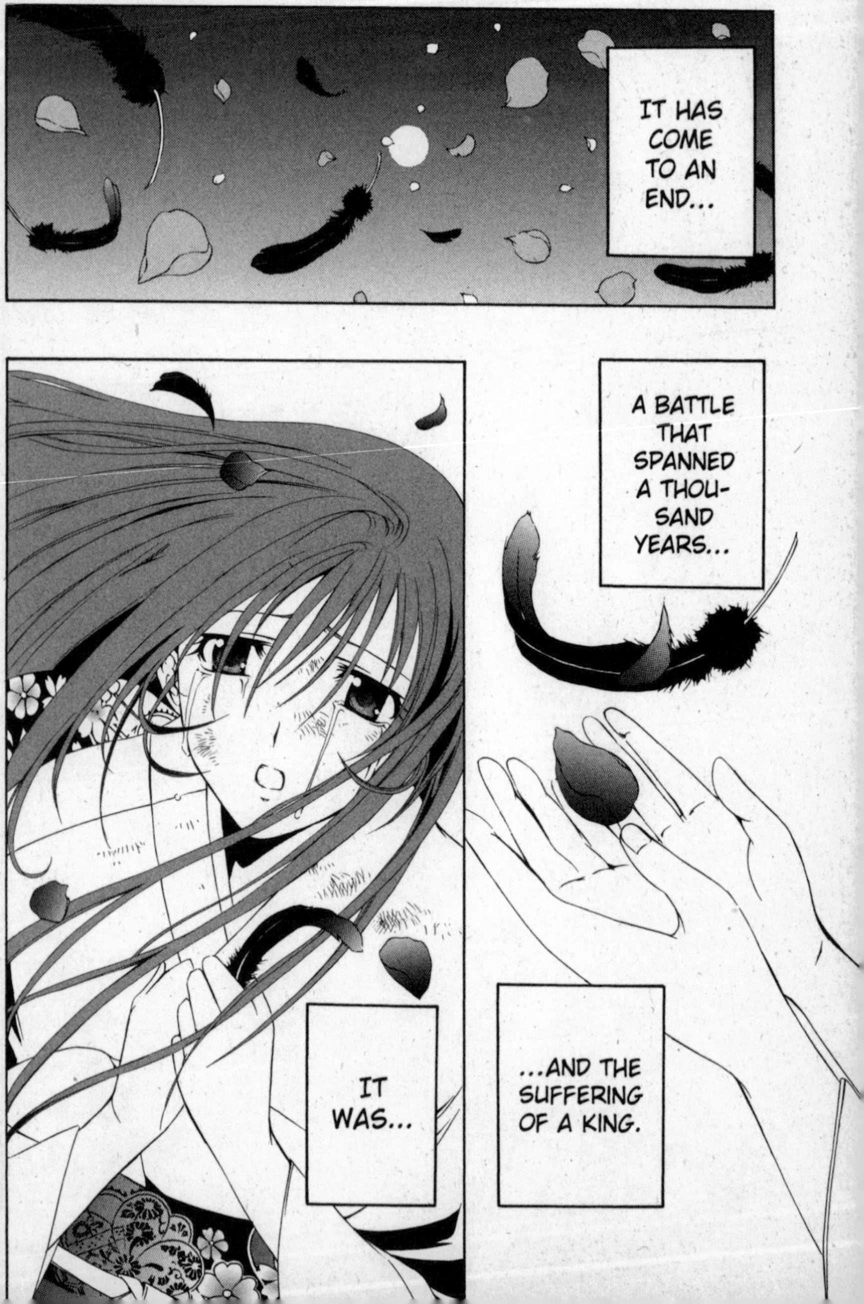
IT HAS COME TO AN END...
A BATTLE THAT SPANNED A THOUSAND YEARS...
...AND THE SUFFERING OF A KING.
IT WAS...

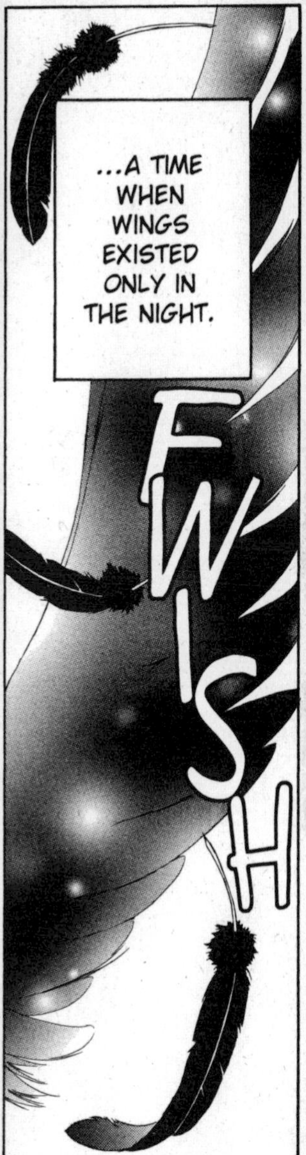
...A TIME WHEN WINGS EXISTED ONLY IN THE NIGHT.
FWISH
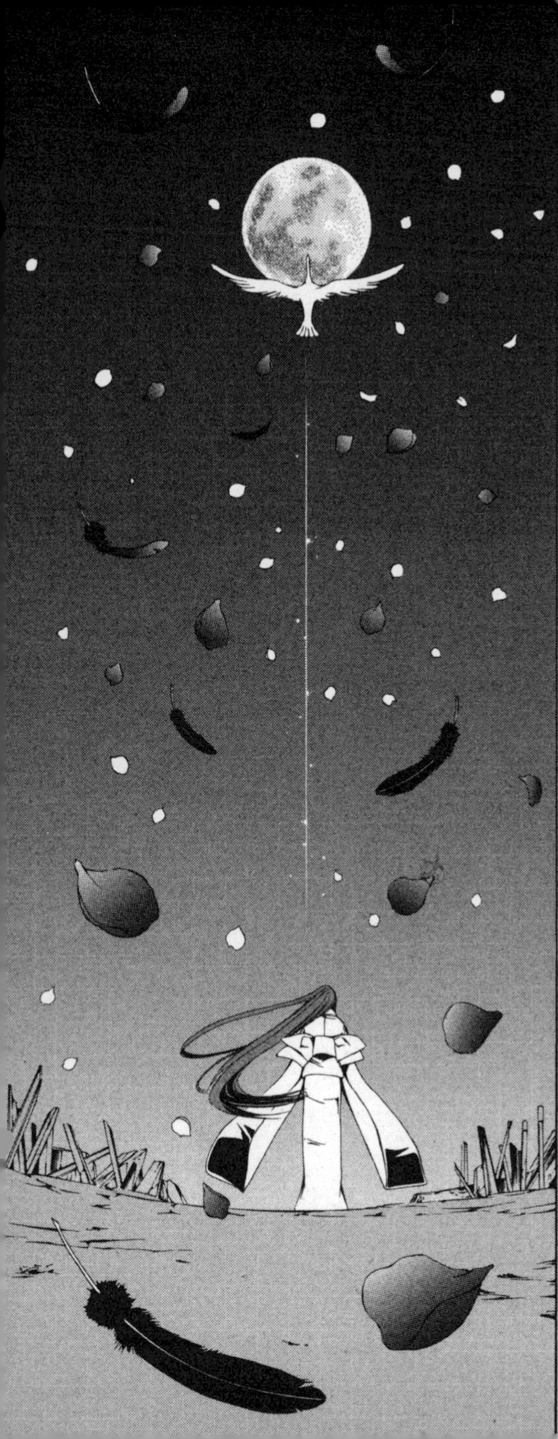

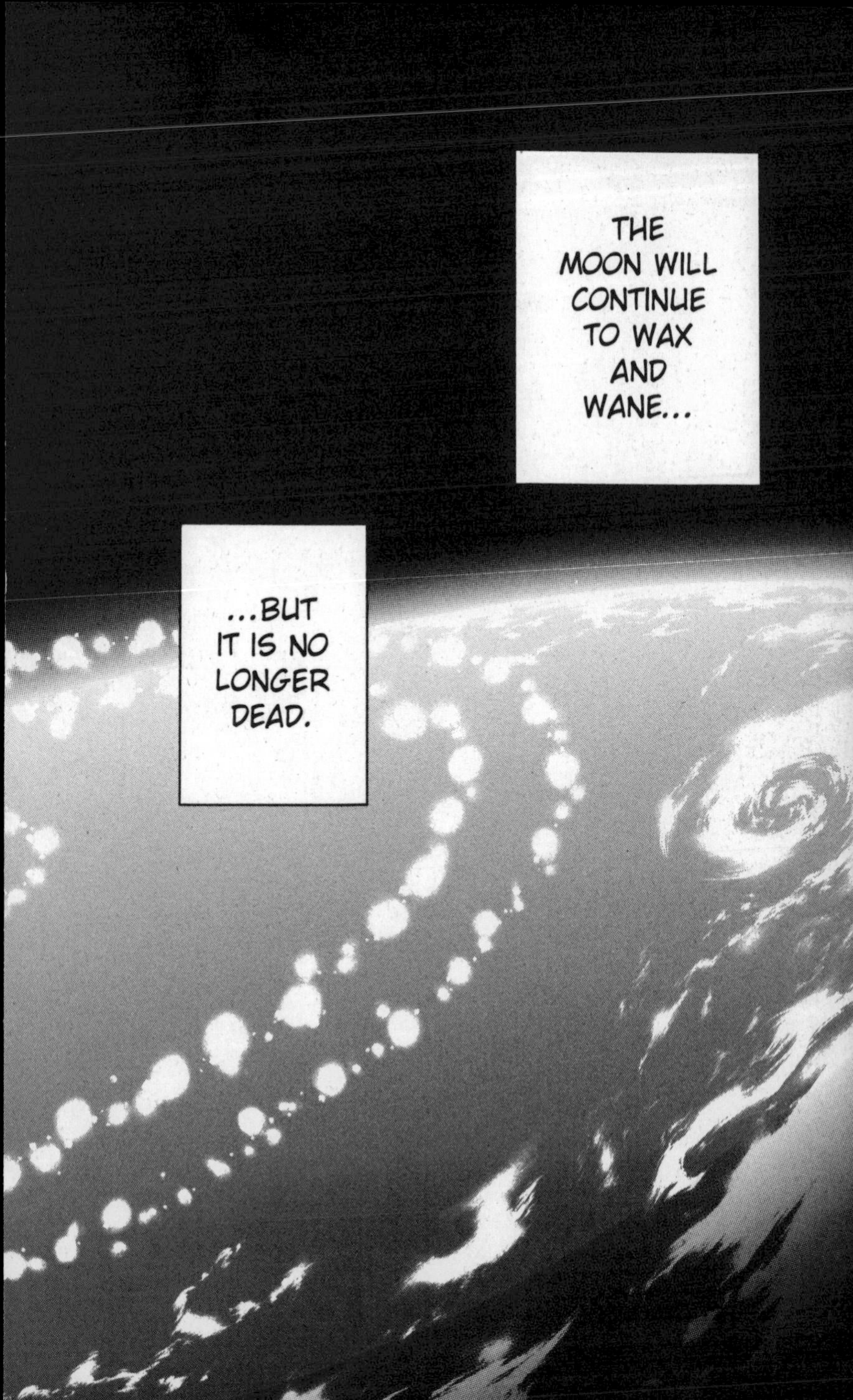
THE MOON WILL CONTINUE TO WAX AND WANE...
...BUT IT IS NO LONGER DEAD.

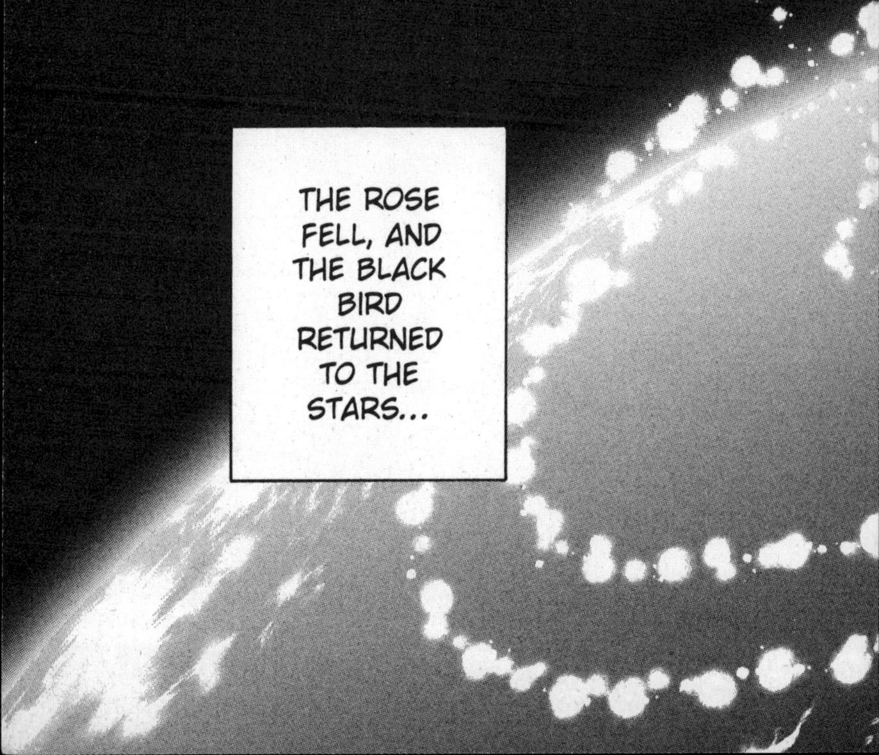
THE ROSE FELL, AND THE BLACK BIRD RETURNED TO THE STARS...

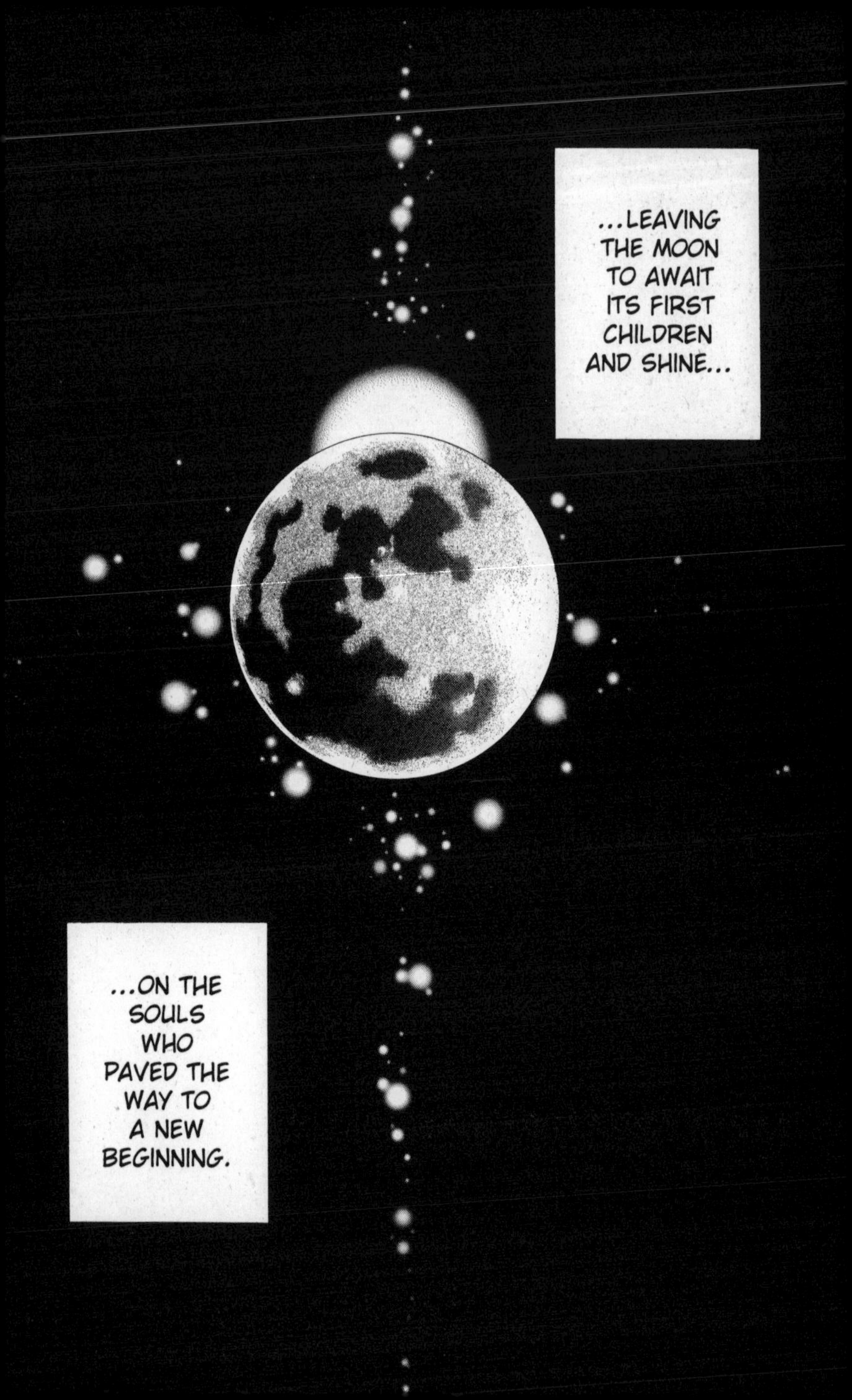
...LEAVING THE MOON TO AWAIT ITS FIRST CHILDREN AND SHINE...
...ON THE SOULS WHO PAVED THE WAY TO A NEW BEGINNING.

THE RECORD OF A

FALLEN VAMPIRE

THE RECORD OF A FALLEN VAMPIRE 9!

THE SITUATION WHILE WORKING ON THE FINAL EPISODE WAS SO CHAOTIC I ENDED UP REDOING JUST ABOUT EVERYTHING THAT WENT INTO THIS VOLUME. THIS ADDED TO AN ALREADY HIGH PAGE COUNT, BUT I HAVE TO SAY IT GAVE ME A SENSE OF ACHIEVEMENT. I DID MY BEST TO SHOW THE RESPECT I HAVE FOR THE STORY.

THAT WAS SUPPOSED TO BE THE END OF IT, BUT...
WHAT'S THIS? I HAVE TO DO SOME EXTRAS?
ELEVEN PAGES?! *ACK! KOFF KOFF!*

SPLAT

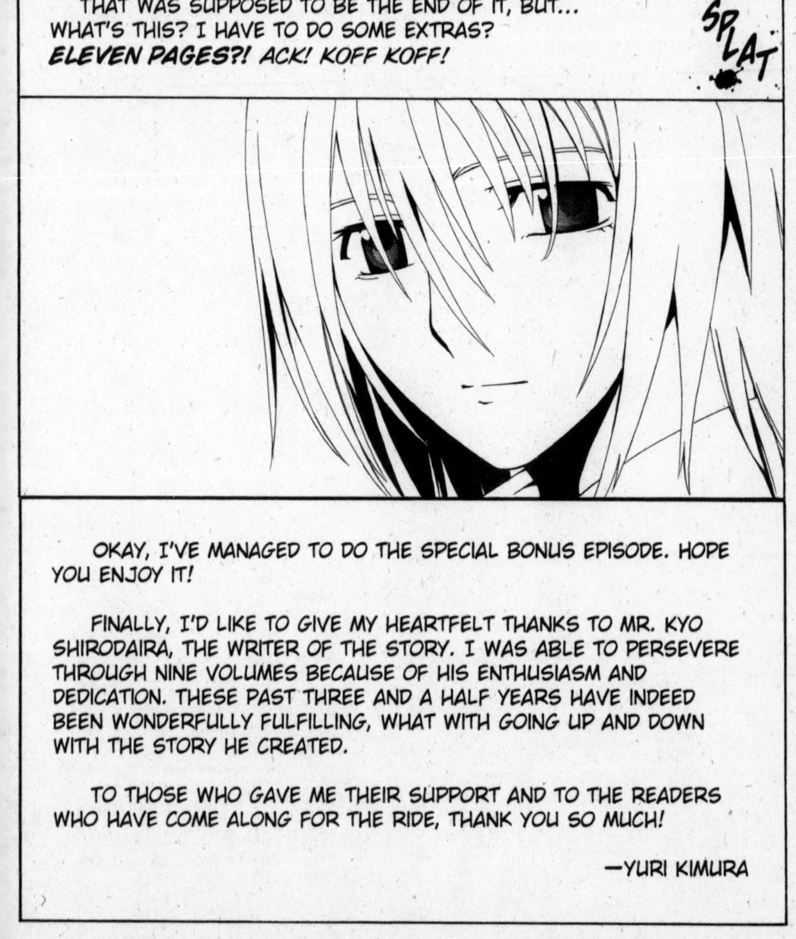

OKAY, I'VE MANAGED TO DO THE SPECIAL BONUS EPISODE. HOPE YOU ENJOY IT!

FINALLY, I'D LIKE TO GIVE MY HEARTFELT THANKS TO MR. KYO SHIRODAIRA, THE WRITER OF THE STORY. I WAS ABLE TO PERSEVERE THROUGH NINE VOLUMES BECAUSE OF HIS ENTHUSIASM AND DEDICATION. THESE PAST THREE AND A HALF YEARS HAVE INDEED BEEN WONDERFULLY FULFILLING, WHAT WITH GOING UP AND DOWN WITH THE STORY HE CREATED.

TO THOSE WHO GAVE ME THEIR SUPPORT AND TO THE READERS WHO HAVE COME ALONG FOR THE RIDE, THANK YOU SO MUCH!

—YURI KIMURA

THE RECORD OF A FALLEN VAMPIRE 9

SPECIAL THANKS
MARUKO ASAGAYA
TEPPEI TAKUMI
(THANKS A MILLION FOR YOUR
ASSISTANCE TO THE END!)

•

SAYAKA KIMURA
(I COULDN'T HAVE DONE THE
ARTWORK WITHOUT YOU.
ENDLESS THANKS! $\times \infty$)

•

K & Y
(THANK YOU FOR YOUR HELP
WITH THE MISSILES AND
WARSHIPS, ETC.)

•

DR. TAKAHASHI
(BECAUSE OF YOU, I NEVER
GOT SERIOUSLY ILL THESE LAST
THREE AND A HALF YEARS!)

•

EDITOR
NOBUAKI YUNOMURA
(MY APOLOGIES FOR HAVING
CAUSED SO MUCH TROUBLE!)

•

KYO SHIRODAIRA
(THANK YOU FOR THE FUN
BONUS EPISODE!
WE'VE DONE IT!)

AUTHOR'S AFTERWORD

I AM KYO SHIRODAIRA. THIS IS VOLUME 9, THE FINAL VOLUME. I WOULD LIKE TO THANK ALL THE READERS WHO HAVE READ THROUGH THE SERIES THUS FAR.

CREATING A STORY FOR A MONTHLY PUBLICATION IS OFTEN DIFFICULT, WITH TECHNICAL, PHYSICAL AND TIME LIMITATIONS AS WELL AS MANY UNEXPECTED EVENTS. I WAS ABLE TO MANAGE TO WORK OUT THE FORESHADOWING AND LAND ON THE INTENDED SPOT BECAUSE OF ALL THE ENCOURAGEMENT THE READERS HAVE GIVEN ME.

JUST ONE REGRET: I WANTED TO GET INTO DETAILS OF SUCH THINGS AS THE *RAISON D'ÊTRE* OF THE VAMPIRES AS STAR TRAVELERS AND THE HISTORY OF THE FIO CIVILIZATION AND INTEGRATE THEM INTO THE STORY, BUT I COULDN'T. SOME OF THEM COME FROM A MORE SCI-FI BACKGROUND, AND WORKING TOO MUCH WITH THESE WOULD'VE SENT THE STORY IN A DIFFERENT DIRECTION. (THERE'S ALSO THE FACT THAT THE IDEA WASN'T REALLY SUITABLE FOR A MANGA AS WELL AS NOT REALLY BEING NECESSARY.)

SOME READERS MAY FEEL THAT THE ASPECTS OF THIS THAT WERE LEFT IN THE STORY WERE RATHER JARRING. THAT IS ENTIRELY MY FAULT.

I WOULD SUPPOSE, HOWEVER, THAT MANY OF YOU WILL BE MORE INTERESTED IN THE REASON FOR WHY THE STORY ENDED IN SUCH A WAY. PERHAPS MANY WILL CRITICIZE ME FOR NOT BRINGING IT TO A HAPPIER CONCLUSION OR FOR MAKING IT TOO SENTIMENTAL.

THE PROTAGONIST'S DEATH IS ALSO A COMMON PATTERN, WHICH MAY BE ANOTHER SOURCE OF CRITICISM.

THERE WERE SEVERAL STORIES I HAD IN MIND WHEN WORKING ON THIS STORY, AND *CYRANO DE BERGERAC* WAS ONE OF THEM. IT'S A FAMOUS DRAMA WRITTEN IN THE 19TH CENTURY BY EDMOND ROSTAND. IT DEALS WITH A REAL PERSON AND WAS LATER ADAPTED INTO STAGE PLAYS AND MOVIES. THE JAPANESE TRANSLATION (BY YUTAKA NAGANO AND SHINTARO SUZUKI) IS AVAILABLE FROM IWANAMI SHOTEN. *CYRANO* HAD MUCH INFLUENCE ON HOW *THE RECORD OF A FALLEN VAMPIRE* ENDED.

SO HOW EXACTLY DID IT AFFECT THIS STORY? TO NAME JUST ONE THING, THE FINAL CONVERSATION BETWEEN KAYUKI AND STRAUSS IS INFLUENCED BY THAT BETWEEN THEIR *CYRANO* COUNTERPARTS, CYRANO AND ROXANNE. IF YOU GET A CHANCE, PLEASE READ/WATCH *CYRANO DE BERGERAC*. IT IS ONE OF THE GREAT CLASSICS.

FINALLY, I WOULD LIKE TO THANK YURI KIMURA FOR HAVING DEALT WITH THE HARDSHIP OF VISUALIZING FICTIONAL SCENES AND CHARACTERS WITH HER PEN FOR FOUR LONG YEARS. WITHOUT HER, THIS STORY WOULD NEVER HAVE MADE IT OUT TO THE WORLD. I WOULD ALSO LIKE TO GIVE THANKS TO THE EDITOR FOR GIVING ME THE CHANCE TO WRITE THIS STORY AND, ONCE AGAIN, TO ALL THE READERS WHO HAVE JOURNEYED WITH US FROM START TO FINISH.

AND SO, WE CONCLUDE THIS TALE OF VAMPIRES. I HOPE TO SEE YOU ALL AGAIN IN A NEW STORY IN THE FUTURE.

THE RECORD OF A

FALLEN VAMPIRE

ROSERED STRAUSS, VAMPIRE KING.
THE VERY EPITOME OF VERSATILITY.

A MASTER OF SPORTS AND MARTIAL ARTS,
POSSESSING BOUNDLESS KNOWLEDGE...
HE EMBODIES THE CONTENTS OF ALL
THE GREAT LIBRARIES OF THE WORLD.

THERE IS ABSOLUTELY NOTHING THAT
THIS MAN... THIS VAMPIRE... CAN'T DO.

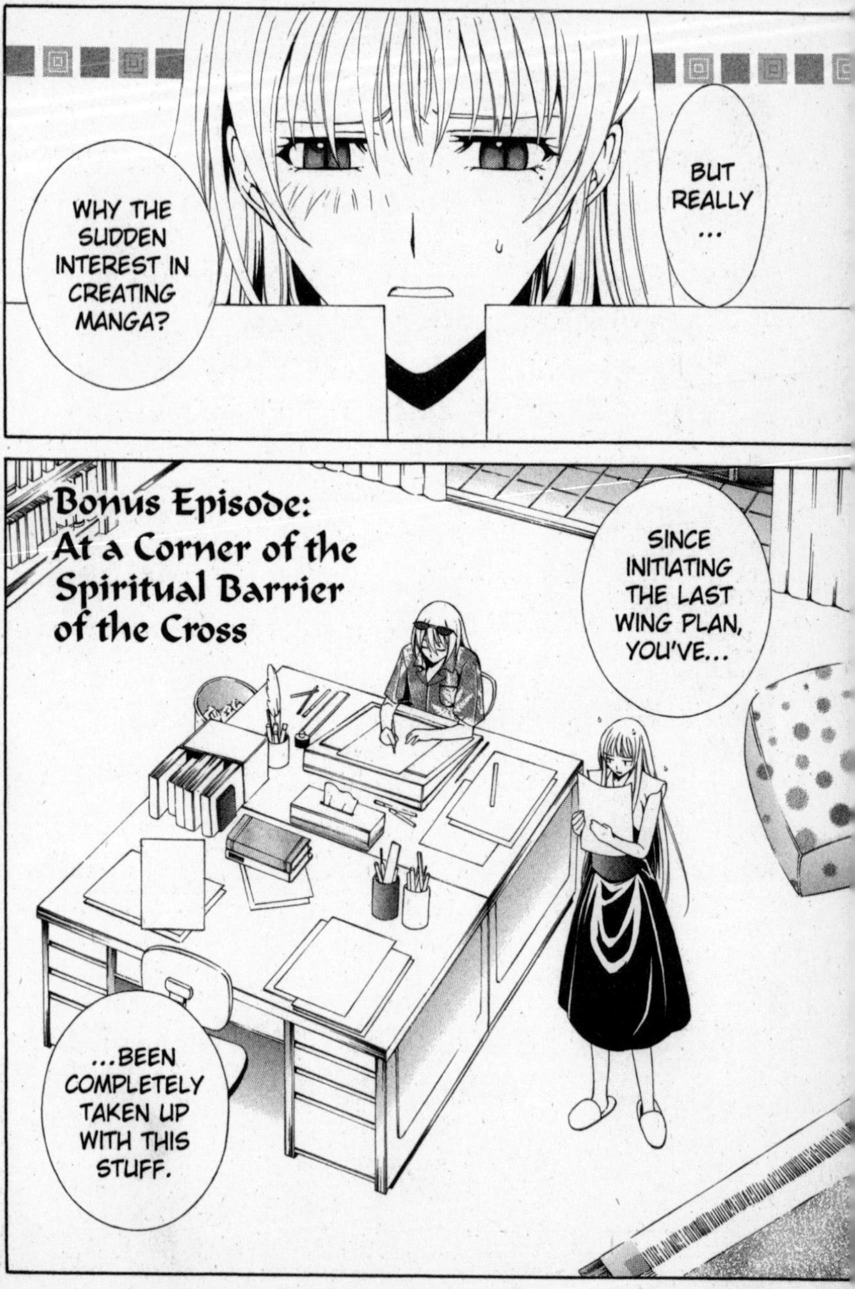
BUT REALLY...
WHY THE SUDDEN INTEREST IN CREATING MANGA?
Bonus Episode: At a Corner of the Spiritual Barrier of the Cross
SINCE INITIATING THE LAST WING PLAN, YOU'VE...
...BEEN COMPLETELY TAKEN UP WITH THIS STUFF.

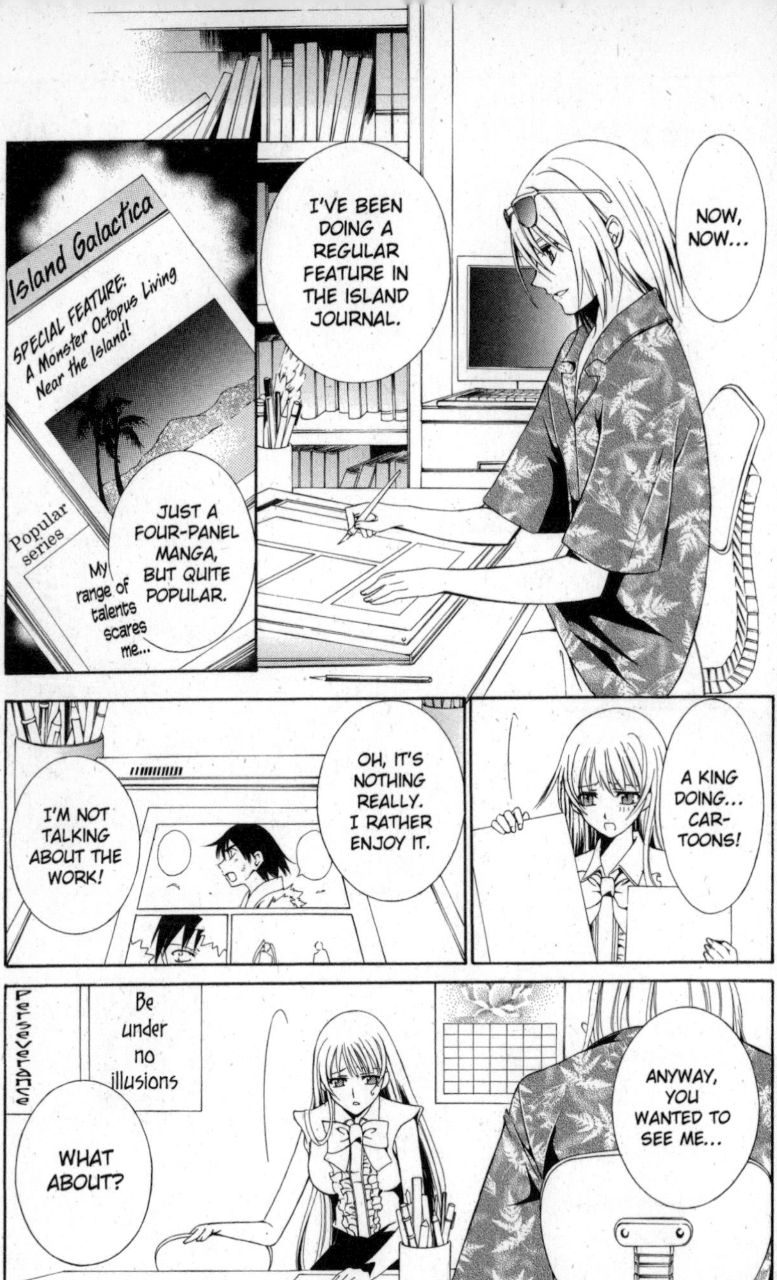
NOW, NOW...
I'VE BEEN DOING A REGULAR FEATURE IN THE ISLAND JOURNAL.
Island Galactica
SPECIAL FEATURE: A Monster Octopus Living Near the Island!
Popular series
JUST A FOUR-PANEL MANGA, BUT QUITE POPULAR.
My range of talents scares me...
A KING DOING... CAR-TOONS!
OH, IT'S NOTHING REALLY. I RATHER ENJOY IT.
I'M NOT TALKING ABOUT THE WORK!
ANYWAY, YOU WANTED TO SEE ME...
Be under no illusions
Perseverance
WHAT ABOUT?

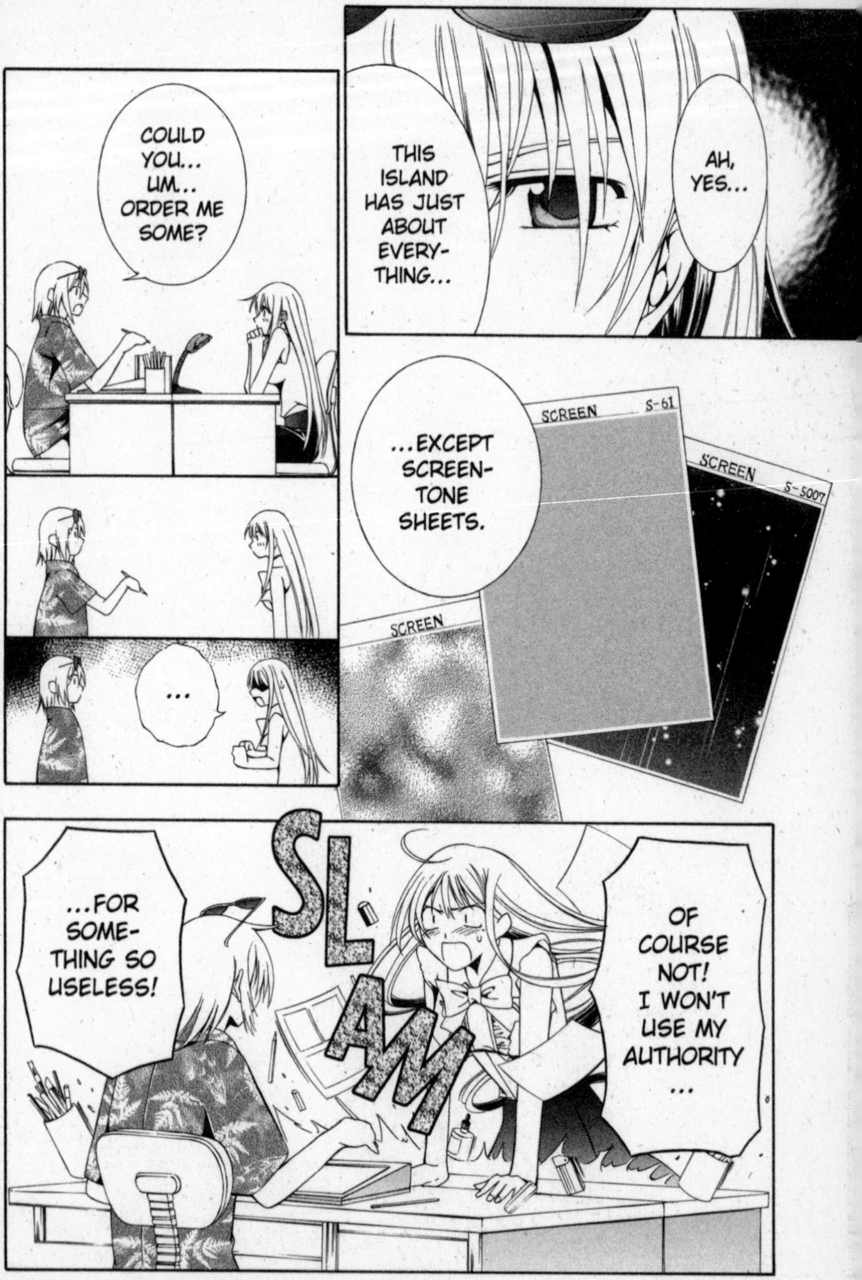
AH, YES...
THIS ISLAND HAS JUST ABOUT EVERY-THING...
...EXCEPT SCREEN-TONE SHEETS.
SCREEN S-61
SCREEN S-5007
SCREEN
COULD YOU... UM... ORDER ME SOME?
...
OF COURSE NOT! I WON'T USE MY AUTHORITY ...
SLAM
...FOR SOME-THING SO USELESS!

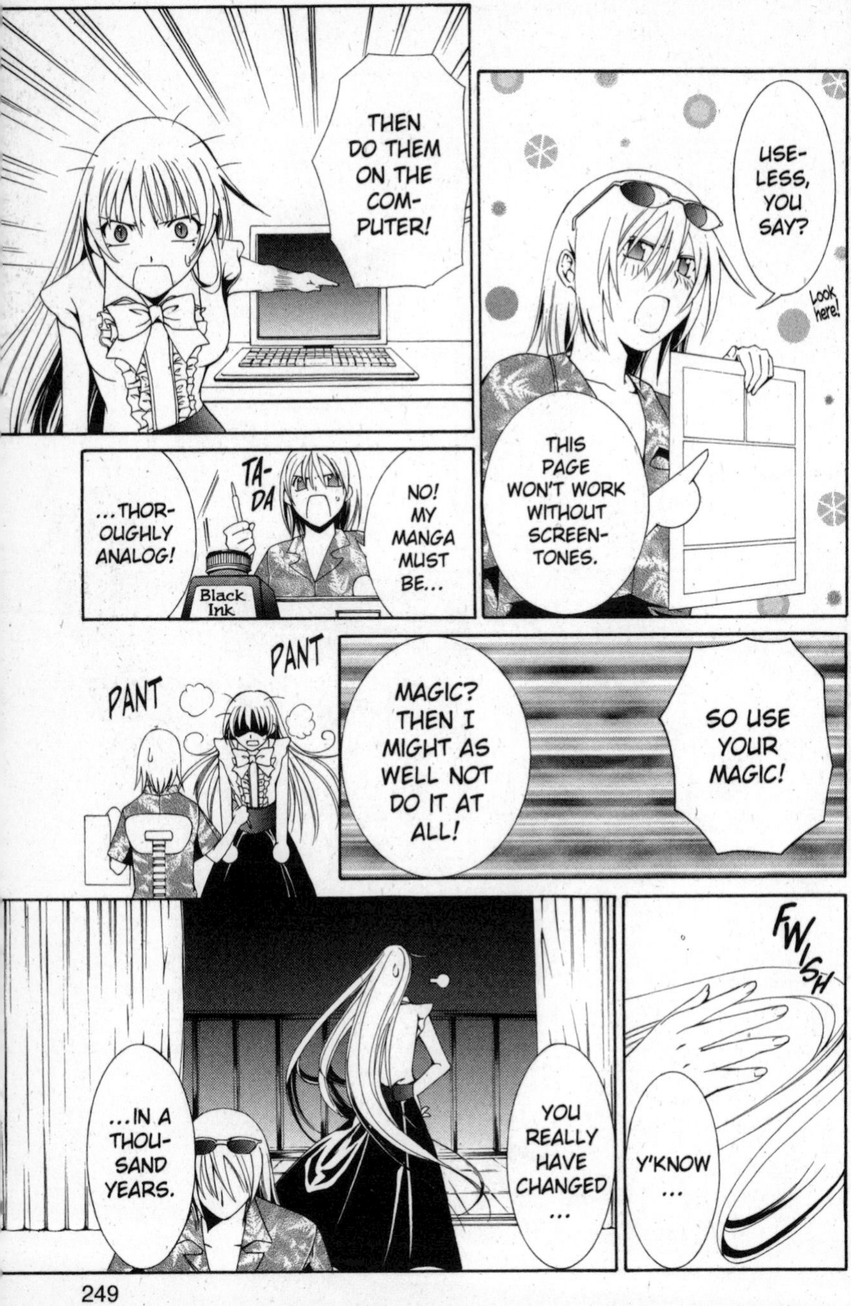
USE-LESS, YOU SAY?
Look here!
THIS PAGE WON'T WORK WITHOUT SCREEN-TONES.
THEN DO THEM ON THE COM-PUTER!
NO! MY MANGA MUST BE...
TA-DA
...THOR-OUGHLY ANALOG!
Black Ink
SO USE YOUR MAGIC!
MAGIC? THEN I MIGHT AS WELL NOT DO IT AT ALL!
PANT
PANT
FWISH
Y'KNOW...
YOU REALLY HAVE CHANGED...
...IN A THOU-SAND YEARS.

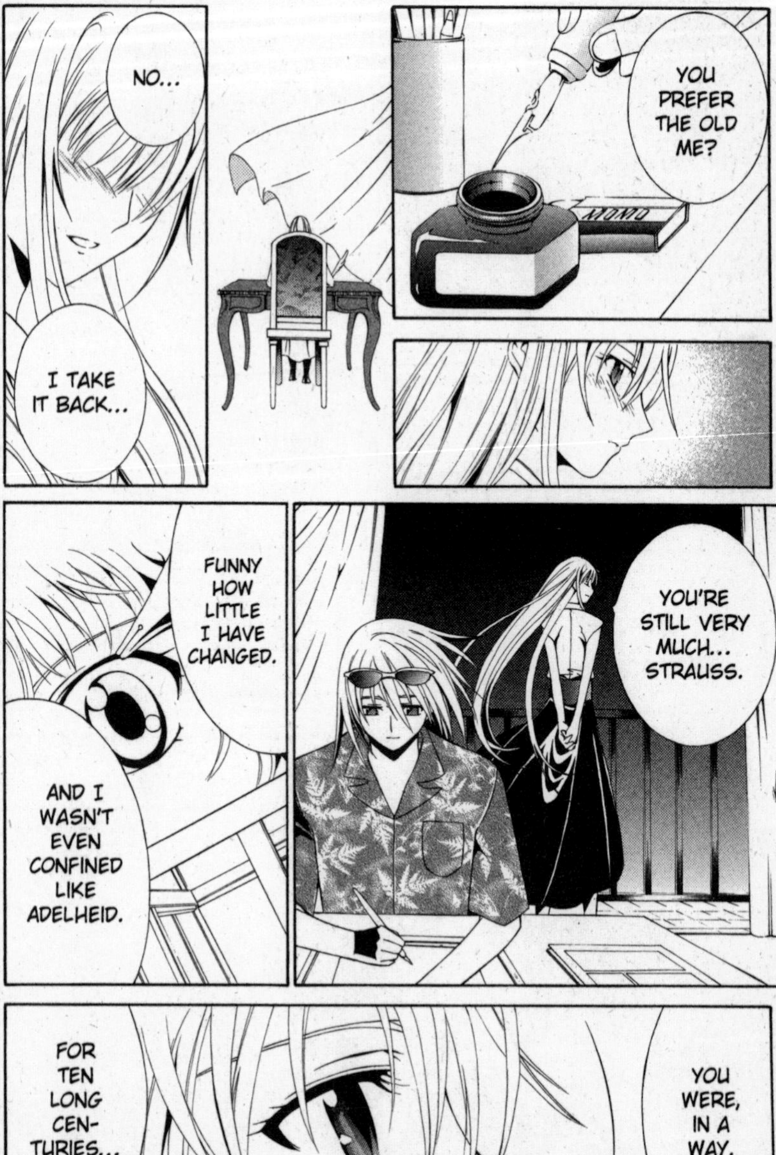
YOU PREFER THE OLD ME?
NO...
I TAKE IT BACK...
YOU'RE STILL VERY MUCH... STRAUSS.
FUNNY HOW LITTLE I HAVE CHANGED.
AND I WASN'T EVEN CONFINED LIKE ADELHEID.
YOU WERE, IN A WAY.
FOR TEN LONG CEN- TURIES...

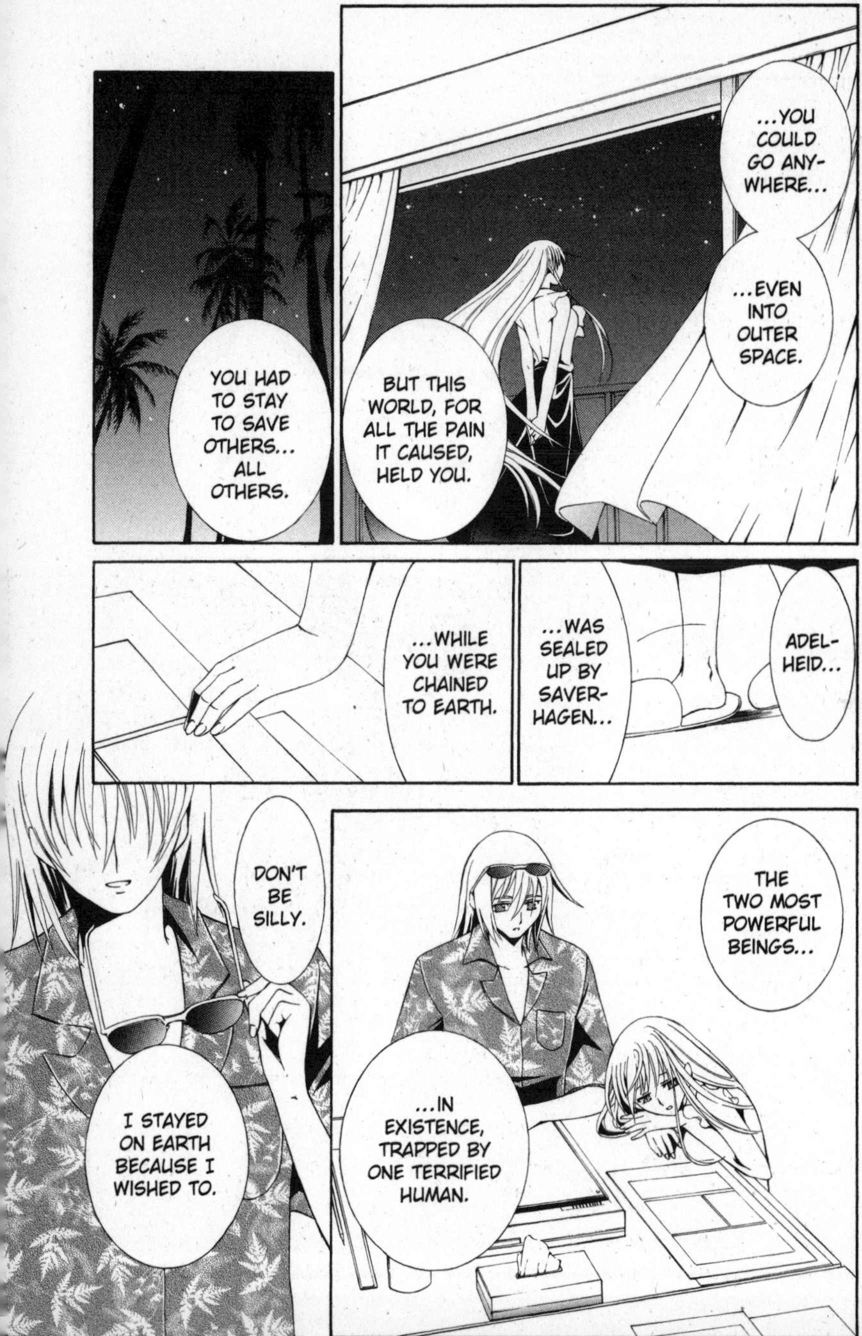
...YOU COULD GO ANY-WHERE...
...EVEN INTO OUTER SPACE.
BUT THIS WORLD, FOR ALL THE PAIN IT CAUSED, HELD YOU.
YOU HAD TO STAY TO SAVE OTHERS... ALL OTHERS.
ADEL-HEID...
...WAS SEALED UP BY SAVER-HAGEN...
...WHILE YOU WERE CHAINED TO EARTH.
THE TWO MOST POWERFUL BEINGS...
...IN EXISTENCE, TRAPPED BY ONE TERRIFIED HUMAN.
DON'T BE SILLY.
I STAYED ON EARTH BECAUSE I WISHED TO.

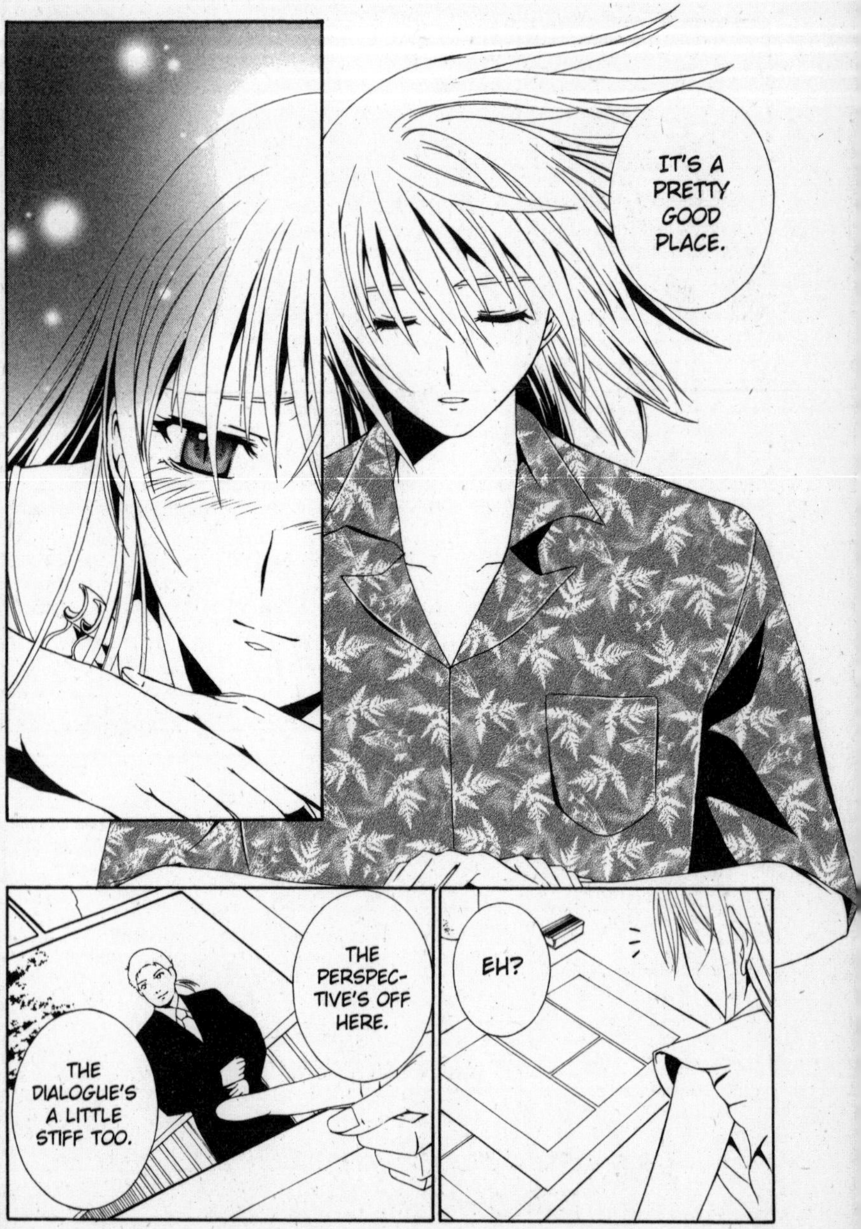
IT'S A PRETTY GOOD PLACE.
EH?
THE PERSPEC-TIVE'S OFF HERE.
THE DIALOGUE'S A LITTLE STIFF TOO.

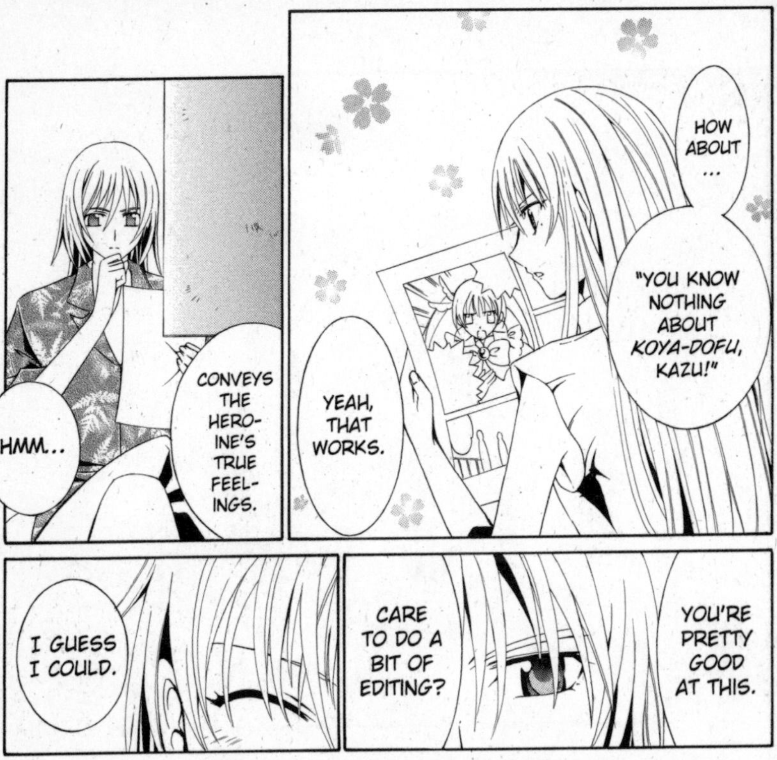
HOW ABOUT ...
"YOU KNOW NOTHING ABOUT KOYA-DOFU, KAZU!"
YEAH, THAT WORKS.
CONVEYS THE HERO-INE'S TRUE FEEL-INGS.
HMM...
YOU'RE PRETTY GOOD AT THIS.
CARE TO DO A BIT OF EDITING?
I GUESS I COULD.

"AKABARA" ROSEWOOD STRAUSS IS QUITE VERSATILE.
SO IS HIS ADOPTED DAUGHTER,
BRIDGET IRVING FLOSSHART.

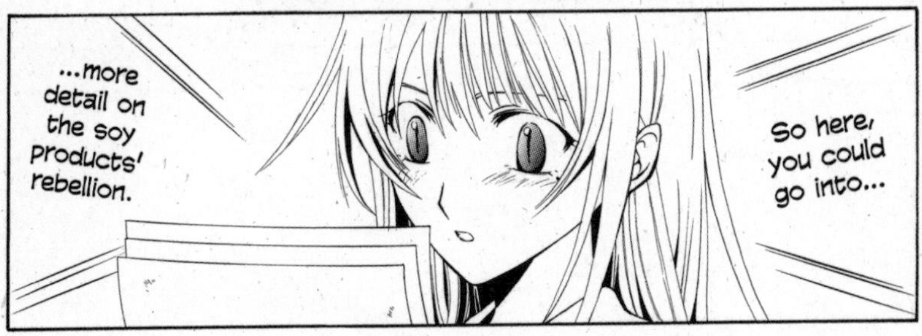
So here, you could go into...
...more detail on the soy products' rebellion.

LIKE HER FATHER, SHE HAS A TALENT
FOR GRAPHIC NARRATIVE.

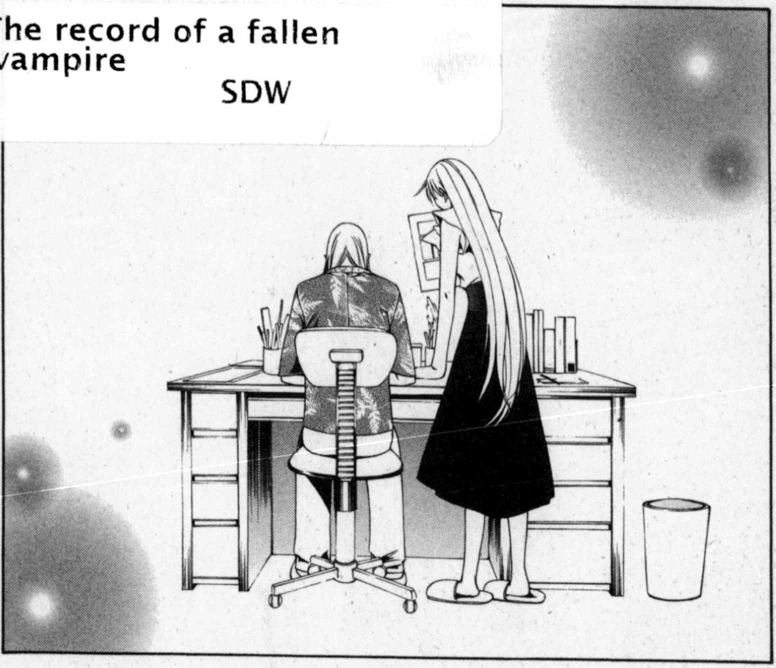

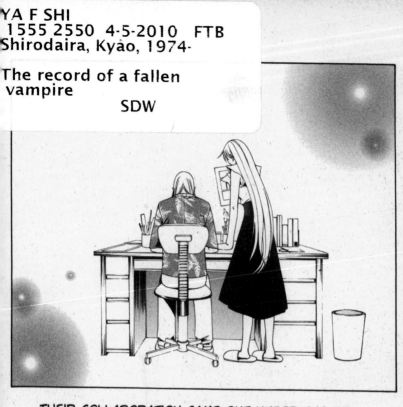

THEIR COLLABORATION CAME OUT UNDER THE TITLE
MAGIC TOFU LOVE HURRICANE!
IT LATER BECAME A LEGENDARY MANGA
OF UNKNOWN AUTHORSHIP.

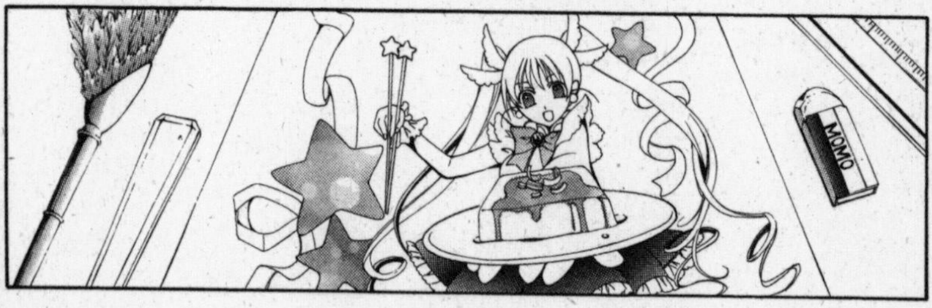
MOMO

BUT THAT'S ANOTHER STORY.

THE RECORD OF A FALLEN VAMPIRE 9 (THE END)

THE RECORD OF A
FALLEN VAMPIRE

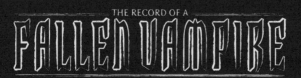

THE RECORD O A FALLEN VAMPIRE

VOL. 9
VIZ MEDIA EDITION

STORY BY: **KYO SHIRODAIRA**   ART BY: **YURI KIMURA**

Translation & Adaptation...**Andrew Cunningham**
Touch-up Art & Lettering...**Susan Daigle-Leach**
Design...**Ronnie Casson**
Editor...**Gary Leach**

VP, Production...**Alvin Lu**
VP, Sales & Product Marketing...**Gonzalo Ferreyra**
VP, Creative...**Linda Espinosa**
Publisher...**Hyoe Narita**

VAMPIRE JYUJIKAI vol.9 © 2007 Kyo Shirodaira, Yuri Kimura/
SQUARE ENIX. All rights reserved. First published in Japan in 2007
by SQUARE ENIX CO., LTD. English translation rights arranged with
SQUARE ENIX CO., LTD. and VIZ Media, LLC.

Printed in the U.S.A.

Published by VIZ Media, LLC
P.O. Box 77010
San Francisco, CA 94107

10 9 8 7 6 5 4 3 2 1
First printing, May 2010

www.viz.com